The Quimby Manuscripts

Containing Messages of New Thought, Mesmerism and Spiritual Healing from the Author

By Phineas Parkhurst Quimby

Edited by Horatio W. Dresser

Including all of the original illustrations

PANTIANOS
CLASSICS

Published by Pantianos Classics

ISBN-13: 978-1545520321

First published in 1921

Contents

Editor's Preface to the Second Edition

FOR many years a mass of documents of interest to Christian Scientists and to their critics as well, has been withheld from publication, although earnestly sought. These documents were written by Dr. P. P. Quimby, of Portland, Maine, and contain his views regarding mental and spiritual healing. They became familiar to Mrs. Mary Baker Eddy when she visited Dr. Quimby as a patient, and it has been charged by her critics that many of the ideas later promulgated in her teachings were born of the Quimby theories.

In order to set this controversy at rest, many attempts have been made to gain access to the Quimby manuscripts, but heretofore without success except in piecemeal or disjointed form. The present editor, however, has been fortunate in securing from Mrs. George A. Quimby, owner of the manu-scripts, permission to print the documents in full. Many of them now see the light of the printed page for the first time. Others give a full and authentic version of material from which only short extracts have previously appeared.

The editor's point of view is that of the expositor, never critical save as the author of the manuscripts might have criticized his own work. All subject-matter in brackets is by the editor, also all footnotes. Italics and quotation-marks have been introduced to a slight extent. Scriptural quotations have not been corrected, because Dr. Quimby was in the habit of paraphrasing in order to show how he interpreted the Bible. Some of the articles have been condensed to avoid repetition, but no material changes have been made. The terms Science, Truth, Wisdom, have been capitalized throughout in conformity with the usage in some of the articles in which these words are synonyms for Christ, or God. The same is true of the general terms for Quimby's theory, the Science of Health, the Science of Life and Happiness. The term Christian Science is used with reference to the growth of the original teaching of Jesus. In this edition several errors have been corrected and Chapter twelve has been re-written.

Publishers' Note

This book is without question the most important contribution to the subject of mental healing ever published. It gives the history of the discoveries and practice of P. P. Quimby, whose researches began in 1840, and tells in his own words how he came to develop the silent method of healing and to acquire his theory known as the "Science of Health."

The book as a whole contains an adequate statement of Quimby's original theory as found in his manuscripts, 1846-65. The volume also contains the writings, hitherto inaccessible, which Mrs. Eddy borrowed during her stay in Portland as Quimby's patient. The editor is a son of Mr. Julius A. Dresser, who was the most active of Quimby's followers at the time Mrs. Eddy was under treatment and who loaned Mrs. Eddy the copy-books which made her acquainted with the Quimby manuscripts.

Chapter One - Biographical Sketch

WHEN a man of ability and influence in the world has been misrepresented, a golden opportunity is put before us. Once in touch with his spirit, we may have the good fortune to catch his vision, see the marvels he might have achieved had he lived until our day, his genius recognized, his truth made our own. It will not then be necessary to devote much time to the controversies which have grown up around his name.

Such an opportunity is put before the truth-loving world in the case of Phineas Parkhurst Quimby, gone from among us since January 16, 1866. He was not great as some account greatness. We need not praise him to do him justice. But he loved his fellowmen, lived and labored, and laid down his life for them. He was a very genuine lover of truth, and faithfully stood for a great truth of surpassing value for humanity. Whoever does this is worthy of our endeavors to put his work in its real light. Because he was persistently misrepresented, the world demands to know the full truth about him, and in knowing it may come into surer possession of his gift to humanity.

Because Dr. Quimby, as he was called by his patients and friends, has been put in a false light for many years, he is given opportunity to speak for himself, in his own words, from his letters, manuscripts and other documents, preserved precisely as he left them. Time has kept for our purposes everything needed to make the record complete.

Quimby's writings were not meant for publication, although their author hoped to revise them for a book, and he had already written experimental introductions. The lapse of time has brought many changes of thought, hence notes and explanations are necessary. The therapeutic movement which grew out of Quimby's pioneer work has also undergone changes. Time has shown that the original teachings have come to possess a value which might not have been theirs had they been published fifty years ago. Now that the teachings are given to the world, many new estimates will be made. The majority of us are little accustomed to thinking in terms of inner experience without the embellishments of literary art or the interpretations of sects and schools; and some effort will be required to take up the point of view of a writer who wrote precisely as he thought.

There is little to add to the biographical sketch published by his son George A. Quimby, in the New England Magazine, March, 1888, so far as external details are concerned. Quimby was born in Lebanon, New Hampshire, February 16, 1802. When two years of age his home was moved to Belfast, Maine, where he spent his boyhood days without noteworthy incident. The family home remained in Belfast. There Quimby began his first investigations in mental phe-nomena. Thither he went for rest and change in the years of his greatest activities as spiritual healer in Portland, and there his earthly life came to an end, after more than twenty years devoted to the type of work which gives him title to fame among original minds.

His education in the schools was so meagre that he did not learn to spell and punctuate as most writers do. But when he misspelled he did so uniformly, and his phonetic spellings are convenient means of identification in his manuscripts. The same is true of his peculiar use of words. In one of his papers he says, with reference to his education, that if he has learning enough to convey his ideas to the world that will suffice. Had he been granted the opportunity as a young man, he would naturally have sought the best training in the special sciences, as that was the tendency of his mind. But there are other sorts of education which some of us value more. If to be educated is to have power to quicken in men and women knowledge of themselves, love for spiritual truth and love for God, then indeed he was educated in high degree. The significant fact is that with only a common-school education, and with but slight acquaintance with the ages of human thought, Quimby made the best use of his powers and grappled with the greatest problems with clear insight. To see why he came to believe as he did is to pass far beyond the external facts of his biography, and turn to his inner life with its out-reachings.

Quimby early manifested ability as an inventor, but his mechanical interests do not explain him. So, too, in his occupation as watch and clockmaker there is no hint of his peculiar ability in discerning the human heart. His power as inventor was limited by his interest in mechanics. Before the period of his experiments in mental phenomena there is only one incident of any significance recorded, the recovery of his health in part without the aid of medicine; but even in this case his meagre account fails to tell us whether the change was in any sense permanent. It was not until his investigations were well begun that he wholly regained his health and began to see that health is a spiritual possession. But in reviewing this introductory period of his life everything once more depends on what we call education. Inventive or creative ability, combined with love for facts, the facts and laws of the special sciences, is a splendid beginning if one is to devote maturer years to establishing a spiritual science. Perhaps it was Quimby's love for natural facts which kept him from ignoring the existence and reality of the natural world, when he became absorbed in the study of the mind.

Quimby's mind was scientific in the good sense of the term. He did not stop many years in the domain of mechanics. He was not content with letters patent as signs of his ability. Nor was he satisfied with studies in mesmerism, spiritism and kindred phenomena. The impressive fact is that he continued his researches until he laid the basis for a new structure in the world of thought. During the period of his preliminary investigations he read books on the sciences to some extent. But with the beginning of his life-work he branched out in a new direction, working entirely alone, amidst opposition and with no books to help him. His more productive years should therefore be judged by his high ideal of a spiritual science.

His great love for truth, his desire to prove all things for himself, is then the most prominent characteristic of his early manhood. Apparently, those who knew him well in the early years of his life in Belfast saw nothing peculiar or exceptional in him. Hence there is nothing recorded that gives us any clue until, putting aside conventional standards of thought, we seek the man's inner type, the sources of his insight in the Divine purpose. Yet there is an advantage in being known by one's fellow townsmen as honest, upright, dedicated to practical pursuits, and by no means peculiar. For when Quimby took up a study that was unpopular, he was a prophet with honor in his own country. From his home town he went forth to engage in public experiments, well recom-mended. And in his own town he began the practice of spiritual healing, winning there the reputation which led him to move to Portland, in 1859, and enlarge his work.

Was he a religious man? In one of his articles he says, "I have been trying all my life, ever since I was old enough to listen, to understand the religious opinions of the world, and see if people understand what they profess to believe." Not finding spiritual wisdom, he was inclined to be sceptical, and later spent much time setting his patients free from religious beliefs. George Quimby tells us emphatically that his father was not religious in the sense in which one might understand the term religion as applied to organizations, churches and authorized text-books. We shall see reasons for this distinction as we proceed. But if to believe profoundly in the indwelling presence of God as love and wisdom, if to live by this Presence so as to realize its reality vividly in the practice of spiritual healing, is to be religious, then indeed few men have been more truly religious than he. Those of us who have known his chief followers have felt from them a spiritual impetus coming from his work which surpasses what we have elsewhere met in actual practice.

After he ceased to experiment with mesmerism, and began to study the sick intuitively, he took his starting-point in religious matters from the state in which he found his pa-tients. He found many of them victims of what we now call the old theology. The priests and ministers of that theology were to him blind guides. Hence, as he tells us, he made war on all religious opinions and on all priestcraft. Jesus was to him a reformer who had overcome all his religion before beginning to establish "the Truth or Christ." Quimby was very radical in opposing doctrinal conceptions of Christ. He uniformly called Jesus "a man like ourselves," that he might win for the Master new recognition as the founder of spiritual science. To him "the Science of the Christ" was greater than a religion.

Did he allow his own personality to become a centre of interest and admiration? Not at all. He realized of course that his patients would look up to him as to any physician who had restored them to health when there was apparently no hope. So he sometimes freely spoke of his "power or influence." But this was to divert attention from doctors and medicines. He then disclosed the way to his great truth, and kept his "science" steadily before his patient's mind. His manuscripts contain scarcely a reference to himself save to show what be learned from early investigations, why he is not a spiritualist, humbug or quack, and why he believed man possesses "spiritual senses" in touch with Divine wisdom. Thus he often speaks of himself in the third person as "P. P. Q." not "the natural man," but the one who has seen a great truth which all might understand.

In his constructive period in Portland, Quimby had around him, not ardent disciples who compared him with the great philosophers or with Jesus, but a small group who defended him against misrepresentation, and regarded him as he wished to be regarded, as a lover of truth. His patients became his special friends, and it was to those most interested that he gave forth his ideas most freely. The Misses Ware, who did most of the copying of the manuscripts and made changes in them according to his suggestions when he heard them read, were especially fitted for this service, since they brought forward no opinions of their own and were devoted to this part of the work. So, too, Mr. Julius A. Dresser, who spent his time after his own recovery, in June, 1860, conversing with new patients and inquirers, explaining Quimby's theory and methods, was particularly adapted to aid the great cause to which his life was dedicated. A few followers wrote brief articles for the press, but none had the confidence to undertake any elaborate exposition, hoping as they did that the manuscripts would soon be given to the world and that these would disclose the new truth in its fulness.

It has been supposed that Quimby did no teaching, and this is true so far as organized instruction is concerned. But he did the same kind of teaching that all original men engage in, he conversed with his followers, speaking out of the fulness of experience and with the force of native insight. Thus he began the educational part of his treatment as soon as his patients were in a state of mind to listen responsively. Then he explained his "Truth" more at length as responsive-ness grew and interest was awakened. Coming out of his office filled with insights from his latest sitting, he would share his views with interested groups. Sometimes, too, his essays would be read and the contents discussed. His writings were loaned to patients and followers who were especially interested, and after February, 1862, copies of his "Questions and Answers" were kept in circulation among patients. The Misses Ware and Mr. Dresser had freer access to the writings and were in a position to make supplementary explanations. In a way, this is the best sort of instruction in the world, this teaching by the conversational method when the works and evidences in question are immediately accessible to those in-terested to follow the implied principles and learn all they can.

This was the way in which the author of "Science and Health" received her instruction. Mrs. Eddy, then Mrs. Patterson, had the full benefit of these exceptional oppor-tunities. Soon after she had sufficiently recovered from her invalidism to give attention to the principles of which she had witnessed such an impressive demonstration in her own case, she manifested great interest in the new truths. Mr. Dresser, who understood Quimby's ideas and methods par-ticularly well, talked at length with her, and later loaned her Vol. I of the manuscripts, printed in Chap. XIV. We learn from George Quimby who, as his father's secretary, was always present, that she talked at length with Dr. Quimby, in his office, at the close of the silent sittings. She was present in the groups of interested listeners above referred to. She heard essays read and discussed. Submitting some of her first attempts at expressing the new ideas in her own way, she also had the benefit of Dr. Quimby's criticism. Then too she had opportunity to copy "Questions and Answers," on which she was later to base her teachings. We have direct testimony on all these points from those in regular association with Dr. Quimby, and from those who knew Mrs. Eddy when she was noting down remembered sayings and modifying manuscripts preparatory to teaching. Here, in brief, was the origin of Mrs. Eddy's type of Christian Science as she later gave it forth in successive editions of "Science and Health." Her indebtedness was that of the student to the teacher with an original mind. Our interest is to note Quimby's power of quickening such responsiveness by sharing his insights, con-tributing his peculiar terms, and explaining his methods.

The only member of the little group not formerly a patient was Quimby's son, George. Dr. Quimby hoped that his son would devote himself to "the Truth," for George had exceptional opportunites as his father's secretary during the Portland period to see the fruits of the new Science. Fortunately for us, George had an exceptional memory for all important details, he was conscientious to the limit in pre-serving the manuscripts until the time should come to fulfil all conditions and publish them, and his keen sense of humor was oftentimes the saving grace of the long-drawn-out controversy which began in 1883. He had as intimate knowledge of his father's teachings and methods as one could have who had not himself demonstrated them by healing or being healed, or by teaching. His correspondence with inquirers discloses little interest in the spiritual side of his father's teachings, and so he dwells rather on the mental theory of the origin of disease and its cure. But he well knew that what he calls the "religious" part of Mrs. Eddy's book and church were her own, not his father's, as greatly indebted as she was for the ideas and methods without which her work could never have come to be.

Quimby's followers were remarkably free from hero-worship. Hence they did not put down wise sayings to any extent, did not make note of impressive incidents, and have not handed down material for the elaborate biography which some have hoped the editor of this book would write. All this is in perfect keeping with the truth which Quimby taught. It is disappointing to those who care little except for human anecdotes. It is taken as a matter of course by those who love truth above its prophets.

His patients tell us that Quimby had remarkable insight into the character of the sick. He judged character, not by ex-ternal signs, not through reasoning from facts to conclusions, but by silent impressions gained as he rendered his mind open to discern the real life and "see it whole." The quest for facts and the inventive ability of his earlier years became the love for truth regarding his patients and the creative insight of his constructive period. He was in the habit of telling the truth as he saw it, even if it aroused momentary resentment in the mind of his patients. If a patient was in bondage to medical or priestly opinion, he disclosed this servitude with startling directness. He addressed himself to the real or "scientific" man, summoning the true self into power.

One of his patients has said, "P. P. Quimby's perceptive powers were remarkable. He always told his patient at the first sitting what the latter thought was his disease; and, as he was able to do this, he never allowed the patient to tell him anything about his case. Quimby would also continue and tell the patient what the circumstances were which first caused the trouble, and then explain to him how he fell into his error, and then from this basis he would prove . . . that his state of suffering was purely an error of mind, and not what he thought it was. Thus his system of treating diseases was really and truly a science, which proved itself. . . . He taught his patients to understand . . . and [they were] in-structed in the truth as well as restored to health." (1).

(1). J. A. Dresser, in "The True History of Mental Science," revised edition, p. 23.

That is to say, Quimby's work, emulating that of Jesus, was fundamental and central. It began with bodily and mental healing, when this was called for first, as it was in nearly every instance. It became spiritual and regenerative if a person desired. For he could not compel a person to be born anew. He could but disclose the way persuasively. That his way was indeed persuasive was seen in the case of followers who came to him as a last resort, deeming him some sort of irregular practitioner, his method a "humbug," and went away deeply touched by his spirit and the power of the great truths he had to give.

Some effort will be required to discern his inner type, on the part of those who have heard adverse opinions circulated about him during the long controversial years. It is by no means a mere question of doing him justice at last. He desired no credit, and there is no reason for underestimating what others have done in order to win recognition for him. His work and teachings were both like and unlike the teachings and work of his later followers. He undoubtedly possessed greater intuition and greater healing power than the therapeutists who have come after him. He did not stop with nervous or functional diseases, but more often healed organic disorders. A closet full of canes and crutches left by patients in his office in Portland in the last years of his practice testified to his remarkable power. His followers lacked the requisite confidence to try to heal as he did, while he was still with them. Later, when his ideas and methods began to become known outside of Maine and New Hampshire, the therapeutists who took up the work had to depend upon questioning their patients, and some of the early writers restated the Quimby philosophy in a much more abstract way. The reader will see why the Christian Science of Mrs. Eddy's type could not have come into being without Quimby's work as healer and teacher, but will as surely see that what Quimby meant by "Science" was something greater and nobler. What was most original with Quimby was his method of silent spiritual healing, with its dependence on the Divine presence. Without this method neither Mrs. Eddy nor any other follower could have developed the special variations of the theory known as Divine or mental science. The present-day disciple of mental healing will recognize much that is familiar in Quimby's writings and will be deeply interested to learn how it all came to be; but will also notice that the language is different, and that far-reaching consequences will follow if this theory is taken seriously.

No ideas of value spring into fulness of being from the human brain. If we realize that in all discoveries there are periods of groping, followed by times of readjustment or assimilation, and then a constructive period, we shall expect the same in the case of Dr. Quimby. He needed his mechanical interests and his love of invention as incentives to progress of sufficient power to carry him beyond allegiance to medical science. Then his interest in mesmerism, awaking with the beginnings of that subject in 1838, becoming more active in 1840, and leading to his public exhibitions, 1843-47, afforded opportunity for a yet greater reaction against prevailing points of view and yielded problems enough for many a year. Next came his intermediate period, 1847-59, with its gradual assimilation of new truths, the development of a new method of treating the sick, and the first expressions of his "Science of Health." Finally, came the constructive period, concident with the years of his greater work among the sick, in Portland, 1859-65, and continuing to the time of his death, in Belfast, January 16, 1866. He was a public experimenter for four years only. He was a mental and spiritual healer from 1847 through the long period when he was acquir-ing his original views about life and health. Thus we have before us an inner history from small beginnings, in place of an alleged "revelation."

It will be necessary to give some attention to the mesmeric period, 1843-47, for two reasons. First, because it put Mr. Quimby in possession of those clues which he was to follow until he rejected the hypotheses of mesmerism and animal magnetism, and developed a theory and method of his own; second, because the assertion has been made that he never passed out of this period, but remained until his death a mere mesmerist and magnetic healer (whatever that may be). The fact that there was a long intermediate period, 1847-59, will be a surprise to those who have supposed that one could suddenly acquire ideas and methods of greatest value. The fact of a gradual mental and spiritual development will be to some the conclusive 'evidence that they are learning the full "true history" of the discovery of Christian Science. The "Quimby writings" are now published because they are unquestionably the most important contributions to the subject, because they show how the modern theory and practice of spiritual healing came into being. From the point of mere arguments in the light of history these writings were surpassed by the works of Rev. W. F. Evans, who acquired Quimby's ideas when a patient under his care in Portland, in 1863. The underlying theory has been greatly elaborated since his time. The same ideas and methods have been applied in fields which he did not enter. Quimby was, if you please, a pioneer and specialist, devoted to truth as his own insight led to it, without regard to prior teachings save those of the New Testament. But it still remains impressively significant that entirely alone in an unfriendly age, he acquired ideas and discovered methods which gave him title to fame. His writings therefore have a special value of their own.

We have incorporated some of Quimby's letters in the volume because they prepare the way for the articles and essays by showing Quimby's great love for facts. In these letters Quimby shows himself a friend of the sick. He tells his patients precisely where they stand in such a way as to encourage true faith and well-grounded hope. He writes about symptoms in some detail because his patients must first know that they are getting well physically, because they need tangible evidence, and do not yet understand how he can diagnose their cases intuitively and heal them at a distance. He shows that he wishes those only as patients who will take him in entire good faith, responding willingly to his efforts. Hence he returns money when patients seem to be purchasing his skill as healer. He aims above all to point the way to his Truth or Science.

Disciples of mental healing who have taken their clues from Divine Science or Mrs. Eddy's version will think they are hearing about an inferior theory, because matters of fact are made prominent in Quimby's writings instead of the anticipated idealism and the affirmations or denials to which they are accustomed. But they are likely to be unmindful of the unfriendly age in which Quimby worked, if not neglectful of a larger truth. 'Quimby, with far-reaching insight, grasped the whole situation, and looked through existing conditions to the ideal. This is a much more courageous venture than the denial of actuality in fondness for the abstract. Quimby's standard calls for a Science that can be demonstrated, can prove itself thoroughly Christian in thought, life, interpretation of Scripture, and all. It will send us back to the Gospel anew to ask why the process of coming to judgment is essential to spiritual rebirth, why we must adopt life as given in its fulness in order to enter-tain as ideal "the Christ." We will then see why Quimby never denied the existence of the natural world, although sometimes referring to it as a mere shadow, and contending that matter contains no intelligence. We will also note that he assigns "mind" to a very subordinate position in contrast with spirit, since his investigations had shown him that the average mind is subject to opinions, it is indeed a "mind of opinions," later called by Mrs. Eddy "mortal mind." Then we shall find him turning to that Wisdom: which sees through all opinions or errors, dissipating them in favor of Science. The truth he sought to establish was a concretely verifiable truth, written in the human heart and in the Word which Jesus taught. Consequently, what was needed was not mere affirmation but real understanding, like workable knowledge of mathematics.

To read deeply in these writings is to see that the best use one can make of them is to cultivate the mode of life they call for, a life which looks forward to health and freedom, productivity and an old age that is never old. Quimby laid down his life in over-sacrifice to those needing to be led into this life of the Spirit. His work quickened a deeply spiritual impetus in those followers who spread his ideas in the world. It is primarily a question of this spiritual impetus, if we would understand the discovery of spiritual healing. His teachings are true if they do indeed contain a Science which inculcates creative humility.

Those who have supposed that Quimby borrowed from Berkeley or Swedenborg will see why this could not have been the case. Quimby was not a reader of philosophy or theology. He was not in any sense a borrower, after he took up the theory of mesmerism and found how meagre was the supposed science, and branched out into the field of his own investigations. His experience in practising the silent method of spiritual healing, after 1847, led the way to his idea of God as indwelling Wisdom, as we find it expressed in his best essays.

This same practice led to his view of matter and the natural world in general as a subordinate expression of Spirit, in contrast with the eternal inner life of man. His conversations with patients tended to awaken faith in the same great Wisdom which to him was the source of all guidance and all true knowledge. The prime result, he believed, would be a "Science of Life and Happiness" which could be taught even to children, and which will banish all error from the world.

Chapter Two - History of the Manuscripts

To many it seems strange indeed that the publication of the Quimby manuscripts has been so long delayed. As far back as 1882, Mr. Julius Dresser began to make it publicly known in Boston that the writings existed, and that when published they would disclose the real history of the discovery of spiritual healing. Naturally, there was a strong desire to have them published. In his pamphlet, "The True History of Mental Science," issued in 1887, Mr. Dresser expressed the opinion that "no such depth of understanding has yet seen the light in print as those manuscripts contain," that is, on the subject of spiritual healing. It was not Mr. Dresser's privilege at that time to publish more than one of the articles, and the best he could do was to give a good reason why Dr. Quimby had no opportunity to revise the writings before publication prior to his death.

"I think I see a wisdom in nearly everything," said Mr. Dresser. "If those writings had been published, as Dr. Quimby intended, or even at any time since, previous to now, they would have found a public unprepared for them. Therefore they are in the hands of a person whose sympathies are not stirred by a work in the truth, as some of ours are, to issue them before their time. But those manuscripts will be published at a future day"

We had a copy of the manuscripts in the household until 1893, when by arrangement with Mr. George Quimby, the owner, this copy was sent to Belfast to be kept with the other copies. The household copy was used in connection with instruction in classes, and from time to time portions of the articles were read in the classes on spiritual healing. But we were not permitted to give the writings further publicity. We frequently urged their owner to publish them, but Mr. Quimby did not believe the right time had come. When we compiled "The Philosophy of P. P. Quimby," in 1895, we were still unable to secure the right to print more than brief excerpts from two of the manuscript volumes, since Mr. Quimby did not wish any essay printed in full till all the chief writings should be published. Many efforts were made as the years passed to secure further privileges. Mr. Quimby was frequently besought by interested people, clergymen, writers, healers and editors, some of whom traveled to Belfast to argue the point. Mr. Quimby answered all letters courteously, sometimes giving his reasons at length, and explaining his father's ideas; but he stoutly refused to publish the writings. Many rumors could have been denied had he relented. For example, it could have been conclusively shown that nothing whatever was settled by a suit in court in 1883 concerning these writings, for the simple reason that the owner declined to have them taken into court. Ever since that suit took place rumors have been persistently started to the effect that the writings were proved not to exist. Again, it would have been shown once for all in what respects Mrs. Eddy was indebted to Dr. Quimby for ideas and methods. Many misunderstandings have arisen because the writings were not published, and all these must now gradually be cleared away, as matters are put in their true light by the publication of the present volume.

Mr. Quimby gave abundant evidence to honest inquirers to show that he actually possessed the writings, and that they were genuine. But it was still necessary for those of us who knew the facts at first hand to explain the matter to those who came to inquire. With one exception we had not seen any of the manuscript books between 1893 and 1921, and inquirers had to take our word for it that the writings existed.

Although there was a tacit understanding between us with regard to the publication of the writings when certain conditions should be fulfilled, Mr. Quimby died several years ago without making provision for the disposition of them. When "A History of the New Thought Movement" was published, in 1919, I could do no more than express the hope that I might print the manuscripts at some future time. At last the way opened in December, 1920, for the publishing of those portions of the writings which have historical or permanent value. Mr. Quimby wished his father's Mss. to be published when their truth could be established without furthur controversies or misstatements. He knew that I was acquainted with their history from the beginning, knew those who copied the writings, knew that they were authentic, and that they were not the "first scribblings" of any other person. It was the wish of the family that I should do the editing and annotat-ing.

As the statement has been made that some one else served as Dr. Quimby's secretary, revising and copying his manuscripts for him, or giving him her own writings, it is necessary to state once more that his son George was the secretary during the period in question, in Portland, 1859-60, while the copying was done either by him or by the Misses Ware, of Portland. George Quimby explained how this came about in his article in the New England Magazine, March, 1888. His statement is as follows:

"Among his earlier patients in Portland were the Misses Ware, daughters of the late Judge Ashur Ware, of the United States Supreme Court; and they became much interested in 'the Truth,' as he called it. But the ideas were so new, and his reasoning so divergent from the popular conceptions, that they found it difficult to follow him or remember all he said; and they suggested to him the propriety of putting into writing the body of his thoughts.

"From that time on he began to write out his ideas, which practice he continued until his death, the articles now being in the possession of the writer of this sketch. The original copy he would give to the Misses Ware; and it would be read to him by them, and, if he suggested any alteration, it would be made, after which it would be copied by the Misses Ware or the writer of this; and then reread to him, that he might see that all was just as he intended it. Not even the most trivial word or the construction of a sentence would be changed without consulting him. He was given to repetition; and it was with difficulty that he could be induced to have a repeated sentence or phrase striken out, as he would say, 'If that idea is a good one, and true, it will do no harm to have it in two or three times.'"

It will be seen then with what care the exact wishes of Dr. Quimby were carried out. The manuscript books were loaned to some extent by the Misses Ware, Mrs. Sabine and Mr. Dresser, but only when they deemed it wise and under conditions. The copies were kept in security after Dr. Quimby's death so that their teachings should be given to people who appreciated them, and so that they should not be published before the right time. Thus the few came to know that they existed. From the Misses Ware we had abundant opportunity to learn the method of producing and copying the writings as above described.

Mr. A. J. Swarts, one of the pioneers of the movement now known as New Thought, took pains to investigate the facts in order to clear away misapprehensions which prevailed concerning the discovery of Christian Science. Mr. Swarts had nothing against Mrs. Eddy nor any reason for defending Dr. Quimby except to bring out the truth. After visiting Belfast, where he had opportunity to read excerpts from the press concerning Quimby's work and to hear portions of the manuscripts read by George Quimby, Mr. Swarts published his findings in the Mental Science Magazine, Chicago, April, 1888. (1) Learning that the facts of her indebtness to Quimby were becoming known through the endeavors of Mr. Swarts, Mrs. Eddy sent from Boston over her own signature to the Portland Daily Press, while Mr. Swarts was in Portland, a paid article called an "Important Offer." Among other things, Mrs. Eddy offered to pay the cost of printing the Quimby manuscripts, the qualification being, in Mrs. Eddy's own words, "provided that I am allowed first to examine said manuscripts, and that I find they were P. P. Quimby's own compositions, and not mine that were left with him many years ago, or that they have not since his death, in 1865, been stolen from my published works." Inasmuch as everything depended on her own decision, of course no attention was paid to this offer. Readers interested to follow this controversy in detail will be able to do so by means of the summary in the Appendix. They will then see that with the publication of this volume the matter has become one of "internal evidence," since the writings show plainly that they were produced by a mind of Dr. Quimby's type as that mind has been characterized by those who knew him intimately, hence that the manuscripts could not have been the products of the one who claimed to have written them.

Most of the writings were produced prior to October 1862, the later articles being mostly repetitions of earlier statements and on the whole not so clear. All the significant terms and expressions such as Science, Science or Christ, Science of Health, the Science of Life and Happiness, were in regular use by 1861. No patient of Quimby's could have explained to him in 1862 that there was a "deeper principle" than magnetism or mesmerism underlying his cures, for he had come to that conclusion himself in 1847, when he gave up his former practice. Nor would this patient have undertaken to explain away his "manipulations," because she knew that the occasional rubbing of the head was no essential part of the treatment. In The Evening Courier and the Portland Advertiser, Mrs. Eddy committed herself publicly to the view that Quimby's works were wrought by the Christ-principle, in contrast with the idea that he healed as did spiritists, mesmerisers and magnetic healers. After Quimby's death she made good this view of his work by writing her "Lines on the Death of Dr. P. P. Quimby, who healed with the Truth that Christ taught, in contradistinction to all isms." The internal evidences show that this estimate was the true one, and that every adverse opinion since circulated has been created since 1872.

The most important date in the whole history might be called January 7, 1921, when there came into the editor's hands the entire collection of letters, original writings, copies, and the other material so carefully preserved since the death of Dr. Quimby. I went through the entire collection in the spirit of fresh investigation. Some of the material I had never seen, and the collection proved richer in valuable data than I had thought. The rest I had not seen for twenty-seven years, with the exception referred to above. I give the facts concerning all this material as thus found.

The material consisted of the following: (1) Original manuscripts of articles and letters in P. P. Quimby's handwriting, with his own spelling,*(See the facsimile of George Quimby's writing on the wrapper at the end of this volume.)* and no changes made by any other hand; (2) 6 manuscript books containing revised articles copied by the Misses Ware and George Quimby, with emendations made here and there by these writers under the direction of Dr. Quimby; (3) 3 sets of manuscript books containing the copies formerly belonging to Miss Sarah Ware, Mrs. Sabine (formerly Miss S. M. Deering, Dr. Quimby's patient), and Julius A. Dresser; (4) a manuscript book of pieces by Dr. Quimby prior to 1856, Dr. Quimby's letters to patients, 1860, and Miss Emma Ware's catalogue of all the articles, 1859-65; (5) the private journal of Lucius Burkmar, 1843, Quimby's "subject" in his mesmeric period; (6) miscellaneous notes, letters and articles in separated sheets, copied from the originals on these sheets before being copied into books; (7) letters of patients to Dr. Quimby, including 14 by Mrs Eddy, then Mrs. Patterson, and letters by Dr. Patterson; (8) Quimby's letters to patients after 1860; (9) 3 copies for circulation of Quimby's "Answers to Questions," 1862, with George Quimby's note on one of them that these were writ-ten before Mrs. Eddy visited Mr. Quimby as patient; and (10) newspaper scrapbook of articles about Dr. Quimby, 1840-65. There was also placed at my disposal the entire correspondence between George Quimby and inquirers and critics, as well as all newspaper and magazine articles on the Christian Science controversy to date. And the material put into my hands was all that had existed, save that it was customary to destroy articles in their first form after they had been revised in consultation with the Misses Ware and copied as before indicated. P. P. Quimby's handwriting is distinctive, unmistakable, as the facsimiles show. So too is that of
Miss Emma Ware, Miss Sarah Ware and George Quimby.

Having all the material at hand, every page or line of it whatsoever, I am able not only to corroborate all statements made by George Quimby concerning the manuscripts, but to state facts which he did not mention in print. I have read carefully through all the original manuscripts, which were copied by George Quimby and the Misses Ware, and have taken note in conscientious detail to see if any revisions or changes were in the handwriting of Mrs. Eddy, then Mrs. Patterson: there is not a page, a sentence or word that bears evi-dence of any such thing, all revisions or changes having been made by the Misses Ware as already described. There is not anywhere a page or even a line of her own by Mrs. Patterson-Eddy, no "first scribblings." Her name is not written on the back of any page. Nor is there any evidence of any idea that might have been suggested by her, had she been in a state to make any suggestions of value. Instead, there is an assemblage of writings that would have filled her mind with chagrin had she realized how fully Quimby's ideas were developed, long before she ever saw him. (2) There is all the material any one could desire to make the argument irrefragable.

The writings were plainly the work of one mind, with continuity of thought from first to last. Even the unfinished fragments are of interest, for they indicate the state of mind of their author. Dr. Quimby tells us that he frequently wrote when "excited" by learning how greatly his patients had suffered from bondage to priestcraft. Consequently at times he did not even capitalize the first personal pronoun, but started in at once with the main idea. Quimby wrote as he thought. If his thought comprised several subjects at once, he wrote so, seldom pausing to indicate paragraphs. The copyists would then suggest changes here and there to bring out his meaning, not to interpose any view of their own; for they knew his thought exceedingly well, his peculiar use of words, and whatever was part of his style. The titles were suggested in conference with the author, although some of the articles remained unnamed till after Quimby's death, and a few bear more than one title in different stages of revision. The dates were entered in the book when the articles were copied.

With his characteristic humor, George Quimby sometimes wrote at the close of an article copied on detached pages, "Finished, thank the Lord; G. Q., scribe." If there were miscellaneous pages of notes or any other statement by herself or her sister, Miss Emma Ware was careful to write on the margin, "Not Dr. Quimby's." All these little matters are significant, for they show the fidelity of those who did their part to transmit these writings intact.   A few of the articles were copied after Quimby's death, by Miss Emma Ware. In some of the copy-books a few alterations had been made, under Dr. Quimby's direction, with a view to preparing the articles for a book. Two pages from Vol. I as thus revised are reproduced in facsimile at the end of this volume.

The originals and first copies were kept in his safe by George Quimby, and the other copies referred to above were returned to Mr. Quimby after the death of their sometime owners. Visitors and correspondents would labor to persuade him that he was keeping the truth from the world. But he believed he was faithful to the greater good in withholding the writings until the last echo of the controversy had died away. After his death the writings were kept in storage in a bank, and there they remained secure until January 1921.(3)

Notes

(1) Reprinted in "The True History of Mental Science," revised edition, 1899.
(2) See, for example, Chap. XIV, containing Vol. I.
(3) For a complete list of the pieces and articles, see Appendix. The package of articles and pieces on separate sheets mentioned above bears this inscription on the outside, "First copies from Father's original manuscripts, afterwards copied into blank books by Emma G. Ware, Sarah Ware, George A. Quimby." This is written in George Quimby's hand. The complete list of the articles is in the handwriting of Miss Emma Ware.

Chapter Three - Quimby's Restoration To Health

IDEALLY speaking it is of secondary consequence where an original mind begins to investigate human life. What signifies is the searching thought which discloses real conditions, laws, the causes of our misery and the way to freedom. Such thinking is likely to be productive in high degree if it be concrete, adapted to the actual state of the world, without too much theorizing, with a view to direct benefits.

In Mr. Quimby's preliminary researches we find a capital instance. He began with a purely conventional point of view, defending in thought and attitude the prevailing medical practice of the day, and so he took the world as he found it. Moreover, he had a personal need. This is the way he states the situation be was in in an article already published in part in "The True History of Mental Science." (1)

"Can a theory be found, capable of practice, which can separate truth from error? I undertake to say there is a method of reasoning which, being understood, can separate one from the other. Men never dispute about a fact that can be demonstrated by scientific reasoning. Controversies arise from some idea that has been turned into a false direction, leading to a false position. The basis of my reasoning is this point: that whatever is true to a person, if he cannot prove it, is not necessarily true to another. Therefore, because a person says a thing is no reason that he says true. The greatest evil that follows taking an opinion for a truth is disease. Let medical and religious opinions, which produce so vast an amount of misery, be tested by the rule I have laid down, and it will be seen how much they are founded in truth. For twenty years I have been testing them, and I have failed to find one single principle of truth in either. This is not from any prejudice against the medical faculty, for, when I began to investigate the mind, I was entirely on that side. I was prejudiced in favor of the medical faculty; for I never employed any one outside of the regular faculty, nor took the least particle of quack medicine.

"Some thirty years ago I was very sick, and was considered fast wasting away with consumption.(2) At that time I became so low that it was with difficulty I could walk about. I was all the while under the allopathic practice, and I bad taken so much calomel that my system was said to be poisoned with it; and I lost many of my teeth from that effect. My symptoms were those of any consumptive; and I had been told that my liver was affected and my kidneys were diseased, and that my lungs were nearly consumed. I believed all this, from the fact that I had all the symptoms, and could not resist the opinions of the physician while having the proof with me. In this state I was compelled to abandon my business; and, losing all hope, I gave up to die,-not that I thought the medical faculty had no wisdom, but that my case was one that could not be cured.

"Having an acquaintance who cured himself by riding horseback, I thought-I would try riding in a carriage, as I was too weak to ride horseback. My horse was contrary; and once, when about two miles from home, be stopped at the foot of a long hill, and would not start except as I went by his side. So I was obliged to run nearly the whole distance. Having reached the top of the hill I got into the carriage; and, as I was very much exhausted, I concluded to sit there the balance of the day, if the horse did not start. Like all sickly and nervous people, I could not re-main easy in that place; and, seeing a man ploughing, I waited till he had ploughed around a three-acre lot, and got within sound of my voice, when I asked him to start my horse. He did so, and at the time I was so weak I could scarcely lift my whip. But excitement took possession of my senses, and I drove the horse as fast as he could go, up hill and down, till I reached home; and, when I got into the stable, I felt as strong as I ever did."

Here, then, was a significant fact, this reaction produced by excitement, suggesting that medical diagnosis was wrong. No other experience seems to have followed this one, and when Quimby began to experiment with mesmerism he still accepted the prevailing medical theories. So, too, he began by taking devotees of mesmerism at their own word, since that appeared to be the best way to learn the truth concerning their phenomena.

There are two reasons for bearing these facts in mind, first that we may note how far he travelled to the point where he lost all faith in the medical faculty and proposed a theory of disease of his own; second, because we can hardly understand the interests of his intermediate period unless we realize that he was still in process and had not at first wholly rejected the physical theory of disease. Some other investigation might have been as profitable to him. The point is that he learned so much from his mesmeric experi-ments that he gave them up forever, and in giving them up came to himself and found a new truth of incalculable benefit to humanity.

There is no reason for apologizing as if it were discreditable that Quimby was once a mesmerist and was known through his ability to "magnetize" a patient or hypnotic subject. There was nothing to be ashamed of in this procedure. The only unpardonable thing that has been said about him is that he was "an ignorant mesmerist" and that he remained so. Ignorant he was not by any means, and he ceased to be a mesmerist because he was exceptionally skilful, so acute in exercising his powers that he learned the limit-ations of all such experiments.

We have his own statement to the effect that when he began to investigate mesmerism he was still an entire believer in the medical science and practice of the day. We also have his own exposition of the experiences which led to his change in point of view. We have contemporary testimony to his exceptional powers and the impression produced by his public experiments. Then too we have the testimony of his son, George, associated with his father as secretary when the mes-meric experiments were things of the past. Finally, we have the direct information coming to us from those who were most intimately acquainted with Quimby's practice in his later years, from 1859 to 1866 in Portland.

In the account of his father's life published in the New England Magazine, George Quimby says,

"He had a very inventive mind, and was always interested in mechanics, philosophy and scientific subjects. During his middle life, he invented several devices on which he obtained letters patent. He was very argumentative, and always wanted proof of anything, rather than an accepted opinion. Anything which could be demonstrated be was ready to accept; but he would combat what could not be proved with all his energy, rather than admit it as a truth.

"With a mind of this combination, it is not strange that, when a gentleman visited Belfast, about the year 1838, and gave lectures and experiments in mesmerism, Mr. Quimby should feel deeply interested in the subject. Here was a new, to him at least, phenomenon; and he at once began to investigate the subject; and on every occasion when he could find a person who would allow him to try, he would endeavor to put him into a mesmeric sleep. He met with many failures, but occasionally would find a person whom he could influence.

"At that time Mr. Quimby was of medium height, small in stature, his weight about one hundred and twenty-five pounds, quick motioned and nervous, with piercing black eyes, black hair and whiskers; a well-shaped, well-balanced head; high, broad forehead, and a rather prominent nose, and a mouth indicating strength and firmness of will; persistent in what he undertook, and yet not easily defeated or discouraged.

"In the course of his trials with subjects, he met with a young man named Lucius Burkmar, over whom he had the most wonderful influence; and it is not stating it too strongly to assert that with him he made some of the most astonishing exhibitions of mesmerism and clairvoyance that have been given in modern times.

"At the beginning of these experiments, Mr. Quimby firmly believed that the phenomenon was the result of animal magnetism, and that electricity had more or less to do with it. Holding to this, he was never able to perform his experi-ments with satisfactory results when the 'conditions' were not right, as he believed they should be.

"For instance, during a thunder-storm his trials would prove failures. If he pointed the sharp end of a steel instrument at Lucius, he would start as if pricked with a pin; but when the blunt end was pointed toward him, he would remain unmoved.

"One evening, after making some experiments with excellent results, Mr. Quimby found that during the time of the tests there had been a severe thunder-storm, but, so interested was he in his experiments, he had not noticed it.

"This led him to further investigate the subject; and the results reached were that, instead of the subject being influenced by any atmospheric disturbance, the effects produced were brought about by the influence of one mind on another. From that time he could produce as good results during a storm as in pleasant weather, and could make his subject start by simply pointing a finger at him as well as by using a steel instrument.

"Mr. Quimby's manner of operating with his subject was to sit opposite to him, holding both his hands in his, and looking him intently in the eye for a short time, when the subject would go into the state known as the mesmeric sleep, which was more properly a peculiar condition of mind and body, in which the natural senses would, or would not, operate at the will of Mr. Quimby. When conducting his experi-ments, all communications of Mr. Quimby with Lucius were mentally given, the subject replying as if spoken to aloud.

"For several years, Mr. Quimby traveled with young Burkmar through Maine and New Brunswick, giving exhibitions, which at that time attracted much attention and secured notices through the columns of the newspapers.

"It should be remembered that at the time Mr. Quimby was giving these exhibitions ... the phenomenon was looked upon in a far different light from that of the present day. At that time it was a deception, a fraud, a humbug; and Mr. Quimby was vilified and frequently threatened with mob violence, as the exhibitions smacked too strongly of witch-craft to suit the people.

"As the subject gained more prominence, thoughtful men began to investigate the matter, and Mr. Quimby was often called upon to have his subject examine the sick. He would put Lucius into the mesmeric state, and prescribe remedies for its cure.(3)

"After a time Mr. Quimby became convinced that whenever the subject examined a patient his diagnosis of the case would be identical with what either the patient himself or some one present believed, instead of Lucius really looking into the patient, and giving the true condition of the organs; in fact, that he was reading the opinion of some one, rather than stating truth acquired by himself.

"Becoming firmly satisfied that this was the case, and having seen how one mind could influence another, and how much there was that had always been considered as true, but was merely some one's opinion, Mr. Quimby gave up his subject, Lucius, and began the developing of what is now known as mental healing, or curing disease through the mind ...

"While engaged in his mesmeric experiments, Mr. Quimby became more and more convinced that disease was an error of the mind, and not a real thing. As the truths of his discovery began to develop, and grow in him, just in the same proportion did he begin to lose faith in the efficacy of mesmerism as a remedial agent in the cure of the sick; and after a few years he discarded it altogether.

"Instead of putting the patient into a mesmeric sleep, Mr. Quimby would sit by him; and, having given him a detailed account of what his troubles were, he would simply converse with him and explain the causes of the troubles, and thus change the mind of the patient . . ."

Despite the fact, however, that Lucius when in the mesmeric sleep would often read what was in the mind of the patient and diagnose the case according to opinions expressed by physicans, Lucius also discerned at other times the actual state of the body. That he possessed remarkable clairvoyant power in such cases is shown by experiments in which Lucius described events and things at a distance, when en rapport with the mind of some one in the audience who thought of some distant place which he wanted Lucius to visit. There is also documentary evidence to show that Lucius could accurately describe the condition of the body after death.

There was much to learn from these experiments, therefore, besides the significant fact that a patient would often feel in regard to his own body as medical diagnosis suggested that he feel. Lucius would sometimes prescribe a remedy so simple or so absurd that Mr. Quimby saw there could be no virtue in the medicine. Plainly, both the disease and its cure must be explained on another basis. This we see clearly when we realize that Mr. Quimby himself experienced the benefits of the clairvoyant descriptions, thereby over-coming what had appeared to be threatening diseases, although the true explanation was not the one offered by Lucius.

In the article quoted from above, written when Mr. Quimby had developed and proved his theory of disease so that he could look back and understand the whole phenomenon, so new and at first so baffling in his mesmeric period, he says, "When I commenced to mesmerise, I was not well, according to the medical science; but in my researches I found a remedy for my disease. Here was where I first discovered that mind was capable of being changed.

"Also that, disease being a deranged state of mind, the cause I found to exist in our belief. The evidence of this theory I found in myself; for, like all others, I had believed in medicine. Disease and its power over life, and its curability, are all embraced in our belief. Some believe in various remedies, and others believe that the spirits of the 'dead prescribe. I have no confidence in the virtue of either. I know that cures have been made in these ways. I do not deny them. But the principle on which they are done is the question to solve; for disease can be cured, with or without medicine, on but one principle. I have said I believed in the old practice and its medicines, the effects of which I had within myself; for, knowing no other way to account for the phenomena, I took it for granted that they were the result of medicine.

"With this mass of evidence staring me in the face, how could I doubt the old practice? Yet, in spite of all my prejudices, I had to yield to a stronger evidence than man's opinion, and discard the whole theory of medicine, practised by a class of men, some honest, some ignorant, some selfish, and all thinking that the world must be ruled by their opinions.

"Now for my particular experience. I had pains in the back, which, they said, were caused by my kidneys, .which were partially consumed. I also was told that I had ulcers on my lungs. Under this belief, I was miserable enough to be of no account in the world. This was the state I was in when I commenced to mesmerise. On one occasion, when I had my subject [Lucius] asleep, he described the pains I felt in my back (I had never dared to ask him to examine me, for I felt sure that my kidneys were nearly gone) and he placed his hand on the spot where I felt the pain. He then told me that my kidneys were in a very bad state,-that one was half-consumed, and a piece three inches long had separated from it, and was only connected by a slender thread. This was what I believed to be true, for it agreed with what the doctors told me, and with what I had suffered; for I had not been free from pain for years. My common sense told me that no medicine would ever cure this trouble, and therefore I must suffer till death relieved me. But I asked him if there was any remedy. He replied, 'Yes, I can put the piece on so it will grow, and you will get well.' At this I was completely

15

astonished, and knew not what to think. He immediately placed his hands upon me, and said he united the pieces so they would grow. The next day he said they had grown together, and from that day I never have experienced the least pain from them.

"Now what is the secret of the cure? I had not the least doubt but that I was as he had described; and, if he had said, as I expected that he would, that nothing could be done, I should have died in a year or so. But, when he said he could cure me in the way he proposed, I began to think: and I discovered that I had been deceived into a belief that made me sick. The absurdity of his remedies made me doubt the fact that my kidneys were diseased, for he said in two days they were as well as ever. If he saw the first condition, he also saw the last; for in both cases he said he could see. I Concluded in the first instance that he read my thoughts, and when he said he could cure me he drew on his own mind; and his ideas were so absurd that the disease vanished by the absurdity of the cure. This was the first stumbling-block I found in the medical science. I soon ventured to let him examine me furthur, and in every case he would describe my feelings, but would vary the amount of disease; and his explanation and remedies always convinced me that I had no such disease, and that my troubles were of my own make.

"At this time I frequently visited the sick with Lucius, by invitation of the attending physician; and the boy examined the patient and told facts that would astonish everybody, and yet every one of them was believed. For instance, he told a person affected as I had been, only worse, that his lungs looked like a honeycomb, and his liver was covered with ulcers. He then prescribed some simple herb tea, and the patient recovered; and the doctor believed the medicine cured him. But I believed that the doctor made the disease; and his faith in the boy made a change in the mind, and the cure followed. Instead of gaining confidence in the doctors, I was forced to the conclusion that their science is false. Man is made up of truth and belief; and, if he is deceived into a belief that he has, or is liable to have, a disease, the belief is catching, and the effect follows it. I have given the experience of my emancipation from this belief and from confidence in the doctors, so that it may open the eyes of those who stand where I was. I have risen from this belief; and I return to warn my brethren, lest, when they are disturbed, they shall get into this place of torment prepared by the medical faculty. Having suffered myself, I cannot take advantage of my fellow-men by introducing a new mode of curing disease and prescribing medicine. My theory exposes the hypocrisy of those who undertake to cure in that way. They make ten diseases to one cure, thus bringing a surplus of misery into the world, and shutting out a healthy state of society. They have a monopoly, and no theory that lessens disease can compete with them. When I cure, there is one disease the less; but not so when others cure, for the supply of sickness shows that there is more disease on hand than there ever was. Therefore, the labor for health is slow, and the manufacture of disease is greater. The newspapers teem with advertisements of remedies, showing that the supply of disease increases. My theory teaches man to manufacture health; and, when people go into this occupation, disease will dimin-ish, and those who furnish disease and death will be few and scarce".

Note

(1) This statement was written in 1863.
(2) By Julius A. Dresser, 1887.
(3) These descriptions and the remedies prescribed were in accord with the medical practice of the day, as Mr. Quimby was not yet enlightened in regard to the mental factors of disease. The discovery on Mr. Quimby's part that mind was the chief consideration marked a turning-point in his thought. - Ed.

Chapter Four - The Mesmeric Period

Turning for the time being from the direct line of development of Mr. Quimby's views, we find interesting confirmations of his experiments in newspaper clippings and letters of the period, 1840-47. The first of these are from Quimby' s home town, Belfast. One of these writers says, in part
"Before we proceed to describe the experiments, we will say that Mr. Quimby is a gentleman, in size rather smaller than the medium of men, with a well-proportioned and well-balanced phrenological head, and with the power of concentration surpassing anything we have ever witnessed. His eyes are black and very piercing, with rather a pleasant expression, and he possesses the power of looking at one object even without winking, for a length of time."
Newspaper writers were fair on the whole in what they said of him, while there were public-spirited citizens who were ready to write testimonials to physicians and other citizens of prominence in neighboring towns, that Mr. Quimby might be well received. In these testimonials and letters one finds the terms "mesmerism," "magnetism" and "animal magnetism" used interchangeably without much idea of what they stood for. Plainly such words equalled "x," as symbols for a power little short of a mystery, although Quimby was credited with entire honesty in performing his experiments.

Apparently, it was still assumed that by making passes over a man's head he could be put to sleep by means of some "fluid." Hence interest centered about material facts, and there was no recognition of the fact, now a'commonplace, that the human mind is amenable to suggestion, and that supposed magnetic effects are mere products of one mind on another. The mesmeric sleep was not understood, and so it was an easy matter to speak of the subject as "magnetised." The chief value, therefore, of these contemporary references is found in their testimony to the facts, the authenticity of the public exhibitions and the results coming from examinations made by Lucius. Letters of recommendation were still necessary in those days.

Writing from Belfast, Nov. 18, 1843, and addressing himself to Hon. David Sears, Mr. James W. Webster makes the following statement:

"The bearer, Mr. Phineas P. Quimby, visits your city for the purpose of exhibiting the astonishing mesmeric powers of his subject, Master Lucius Burkmar. Mr. Quimby, as also the young man, are native citizens of this place, and sustain in the community unblemished moral characters.

"Mr. Quimby is not an educated man, nor is he pretending or obtrusive; but I think if you should take occasion to converse with him you will discern many traces of deep thought and reflection, particularly upon the subject above mentioned.

"His boy will I think demonstrate in an extraordinary manner the phenomena of magnetic influence, more especially in that department usually termed clairvoyance; and should you take an opportunity to be put in communication with him, I doubt not you will be gratified with the results. Time and distance with him are annihilated, and he travels with the rapidity of thought. I think he will describe to you the appearance of any edifice, tower or temple, and even that of any person either, in Europe or America, upon which or upon whom your imagination may rest. I say this much from the fact that I have been in communication with him [mentally] myself and do know that he describes remote places and even the appearance of persons at great distances which he never before could have heard or thought of. . . ."

Writing to Dr. Jacob Bigelow, apparently a physician of prominence, Dr. Albert T Wheelock writes from Belfast under date of Nov. 10, 1843, and describes an experiment in "animal magnetism" under mesmeric conditions in the case of an operation for the removal of a polypus from the nose. With a physician's care in describing symptoms, the writer gives an account of the patient's general condition and mentions her desire to be "magnetised." Dr. Wheelock then goes on as follows:

"As she was entirely unacquainted in the town, at her request I procured the attendance of a gentleman who had the reputation of being a good magnetiser (Mr. P. P. Quimby), although entirely faithless on my own part, as I told her at that time . . . I am quite confident that the lady and Mr. Quimby had never met before and that there was nothing previously concerted. I am also confident that she took no drug to induce stupor. In ten minutes after com-mencing, she was put into a state of apparent natural sleep, breathing and pulse natural, color of countenance unchanged. Mr. Q. asked her if she felt well. 'Yes.' I immediately, in the presence of several noted citizens who were called in at their request, began to remove the polypus, and did it thor-oughly. . . . I was operating perhaps 4 or 5 minutes at least. During the whole time she evinced not the slightest symptom of pain, either by any groaning, sighing or motion whatever, but was in all these respects like a dead body. I felt convinced that I [could] have amputated her arm. In about ten minutes after she was waked up, but said she was unconscious that anything had been done, complained of no pain, and found that she could now breathe freely through her nose, that previously had been entirely closed up, for several months. . . . Mr. Quimby . . . is an intelligent gentleman and worthy of the utmost confidence."

Another communication, addressed to Nathan Hale, Dr. Jacob Bigelow, and Dr. John Ware, of Boston, dated Belfast, Nov. 6, 1843, has been deprived of its signature through much handling. It is intended to show the authenticity of the experiments performed by Quimby and his subject. The writer, who is careful in stating facts, says that the subject told him even his own thoughts which the writer kept to himself, also words that he simply visualized. Lucius when blindfolded told minute facts concerning things at a distance of half a mile which no one in the room knew, facts which he could not know by "any means within the limit of common experience." The writer says:

"I have good reason to believe that he can discern the internal structure of an animal body, and if there be anything morbid or defective therein detect and explain it. The important advantage of this to surgery and medicine is obvious enough. He, that is, his intellect, can be in two places at the same time. He can go from one point to another, no matter how remote, without passing through the intermediate space. I have ascertained from irrefragable experiments that he takes ideas first directly from the mind of the person in communication with him, and, second, without reference to such mind, directly from the object or thing to which his attention is directed; and in both instances without any aid from his five bodily senses. He can perceive without using either of the common organs of perception. His mind when he is mesmerised seems to have no relation to body, distance, place, time or motion. He passes from Belfast to Washington, or from the earth to the moon, not as horses, steam engines or light, but swifter than light, by a single act of volition.

"In a word, he strides far beyond the reach of philosophy. He demonstrates, as I think, better than all physical, meta-physical or moral science, the immateriality of the human soul, and that its severance from the body involves not its own destruction. At least he proves this of himself. And I suppose other souls are like his. . . . Mesmerism as manifested by this boy lets in more light than any other window that has been opened for 1800 years. This may look like gross extravagance, but if you have the same luck I have you will find it is not so."

Another observer who was greatly impressed by Quimby's public lectures, accompanied by experiments performed through the aid of Lucius, writes from East Machias, Feb. 1845, concerning experiments in private which he thinks more remarkable still. He says, in part:

"The power of perceiving the seat of the disease, and of describing the most minute symptoms which I do not guess but know, his subject possesses when in the mesmeric sleep is astonishing beyond words to express. He has examined my wife twice and . . . I venture to say that all have been perfectly satisfied that there is not the least deception in regard to the matter, but the most satisfactory proof of an extraordinary, I may almost say miraculous, insight. . .

Lucius [sees] every particular in regard to the internal struc-ture and state of the body, especially describing the causes of disease. . . . I write this without the knowledge or suggestion of Mr. Quimby, but hoping that hereby some who may receive inestimable benefit may not lose this opportunity. . . . Mr. Johnson has been put in communication with Lucius in public, and Mrs. Johnson this morning at our home, and he described with astonishing accuracy precisely the object which she had in her mind, which Mr. Quimby calls thought-reading, and which I am just as certain is real as that I am here and the sun shines to-day, and also things which she did not have in her mind in regard to the persons and places which she took him to visit in spirit. This if true, as has often happened to Mr. Quimby, will place the power of clairvoyance beyond the shadow of a doubt. [Lucius] has it beyond a shadow of a doubt as far as perceiving disease and every internal organ of the body is concerned . . . and we shall write immediately to discover [the facts of the things discerned through] clairvoyance."

The following excerpt from the Bangor Democrat, April, 1843, gives us the date of Mr. Quimby's first experiment away from his home town, not his "native" town, of Belfast.

"Mr. Quimby of Belfast has visited here by invitation, and made exhibitions in public for the first time out of his native town. Some of our citizens are well acquainted with him, and others are acquainted with citizens of Belfast who have the most entire confidence in him: it is therefore preposterous that he attempts to practice imposition.

"He has with him two young men, brothers, one 23 and the other 17. They are clairvoyant subjects. The first evening the experiments were not successful, but one made in private we will relate as a sample of the rest. The young man was magnetised by Mr. Quimby, when one of our citizens was put in communication with him. In imagination he took the boy to St. John, New Brunswick, before the new Custom House, and asking him what he could see, he said a building with a stone front and the rest of it brick. He then began to read the letters on it. 'C-u-s-t-o-m. Oh, this is the Custom House.' He then took him inside of the building and asked what he could see there, when he described the stone steps leading into the second story, the iron railing, curiously formed, and when taken into one of the rooms, de-scribed a man employed in writing.

"The gentleman says no one knew where he proposed to take the boy: the boy had never seen the building, and yet he described it as accurately as any one who

has seen it. This gentleman's word is not to be questioned by any one.

"Such was the experiment, and others can tell as well as I whether it was humbuggery, witchcraft, a juggler's trick, magic, or the mysterious power that one person exerts over another. Real or unreal, it is extraordinary."

The next excerpt, from the Waldo Signal, Belfast, Jan. 25, 1844, is typical of those indicating that a general effort was made to avoid all collusion and if possible to explain the strange phenomena.

"We learn from the Norridgewock Workingman of the 18th inst. that our townsman, Mr. P. P. Quimby, has recently been in that place lecturing upon the science of animal magnetism, and illustrating the subject by numerous experiments. On the evening of the 12th a committee was appointed, con-sisting of several of the most intelligent men of N. to scrutinize the experiments for the ostensible purpose of satisfying themselves and the audience that there was no deception in the matter. The result was highly satisfactory, Mr. Quimby showing no disposition to avoid any scrutiny required by the committee"

Again, we have a letter confirming one of the experiments in clairvoyance. The letter is dated Eastport, Me., May 3d, 1845.

"Mr. Quimby,

"Sir: The lady you mesmerised at my house on Saturday last and then requested her to take you to her father's house, a distance of about four hundred miles, you recollect, gave a minute description of the family and what they were about at that time. You also remember, I presume, that she stated that Mr. G., a member of the family died on the 14th ult., and that a Mrs. B., a particular friend of hers, had been there on a visit, was taken sick there, but had so far recovered that her brother had carried her home.

"On the Tuesday following her making the above statement she received a letter from her father in which he wrote that Mr. G. died about 8 o'clock, A. M. on the 14th of April, also stating that Mrs. B. had been there on a visit, and that she was taken sick so as to be obliged to stay a week longer than she intended, and that she had got so well that her brother had carried her home.

"You are aware that I have been sceptical about most of your mesmeric experiments. I therefore feel bound to give you the above statement of facts, and am willing you should show this to your friends. But I am not willing to have my name appear in print."

Other letters express the conviction that the time for ridicule has passed: people should attend the public demonstra-tions, see for themselves, then bring the sick to be diagnosed by Lucius, that the real nature of their maladies may be learned. There is much testimony regarding Lucius' wonderful clairvoyance in the mesmeric state, and always the conviction that there is no collusion. One of the letters is from Mr. Quimby himself, in which he refers to the case of a patient put into a state of sleep during three hours while an operation upon the teeth was being performed. The patient felt no pain. Mr. Quimby states that while the patient was asleep he told her mother that he would show her how he could talk with the daughter mentally. He then stepped toward the patient but did not put his hand upon her, merely sent her a thought. The patient thereupon laughed out in response to this thought and satisfied all in the room that it was an instance of thought-transference. This experience is significant, for it points forward to the time, presently to come, when Quimby will be able to dispense with his subject, and communicate directly either through telep-athy or by the aid of his own clairvoyance, apart from mesmerism.

The last letter of this period is dated Lowell, Sept. 26, '47, and is an appeal addressed to Mr. Quimby to make an examination by the aid of Lucius of her husband's body, with the hope that the cause of his sudden death may be deter-mined. Mr. Quimby assented, the examination was made, and in this instance the description is appended to the letter in Lucius's own words. Lucius describes the condition of the heart, which was somewhat enlarged, the state of the lungs and stomach, liver, blood, and so on. He says, "This I write while I am in communication with Mr. Quimby in the magnetic state."

Later, when reading over what he has written, he realizes that his description as there given does not show why death came about suddenly, and so he returns to the description, still confining his statement to an account of symptoms, and the probable sensations experienced just before death. This is what we might expect from a clairvoyant whose power consisted for the most part in making wonderfully accurate descriptions of things, events, states and conditions, or in reading thoughts in a person's mind; never the interpretation of these states in terms of their real meaning. This remained for Quimby himself to discern when, having found the limitations under which Lucius made these descriptions, he saw the difference between mere symptoms and inner causes. Lucius might describe the actual state of an un-tenanted body, and throw a little light on the feelings its owner may have had just before he left the flesh; but he could not tell the whole story. His descriptions raised as many problems as they appeared to solve. His clairvoyance was remarkable. But it was the perception of an inferior mind in a passive condition. What was needed was intuition, showing the real state of the individual behind all these symptoms.

Fortunately, for our present interests, there still exists a personal journal in which, beginning December 26, 1843, Lucius noted down matters of interest during his travels with Mr. Quimby. Most of these details are with reference to the towns visited, the interest or credulity aroused by the experi-ments, or the people met along the way. Plainly Lucius has no theory concerning his own powers. He accepts and uses the term "magnetism" or "magnetised," as matter of con-venience, without manifesting any interest to inquire what is behind. He is aware that Mr. Quimby possesses power over him, but that fact neither troubles nor interests him. Apparently, he was glad when the public exhibitions were successful, and he notes that scepticism is overcome. But there he always leaves the matter.' One concludes that Lucius had exceptional receptive powers, so that under other auspices he might have been a spiritistic medium; but that he was almost entirely lacking in analytical power. Consequently, Lucius merely states facts and then leaves them. What he says concerning things discerned by him in the mesmeric state is probably what he could recall when he heard Mr. Quimby and others talking about his descriptions, when awakened into his normal condition.

For example, we find him referring to some of Mr. Quimby's cures in the early period when Quimby himself still believed that "magnetism" had something to do with them. "Quimby," he writes, "has been doing miracles. He has cured a man that couldn't walk nor speak. It has produced a great excitement here among the people. He [the patient] has been confined to his house about a year, and never has spoken or walked. In one hour [Mr. Quimby] made him walk about the room and speak so as to be heard in another room."

Referring to the prevalent scepticism, he writes on another occasion: "As a general thing we didn't find the people so bitter upon the subject of animal magnetism as we thought we should. We generally had the most influential men of the place upon our side of the question, and as a general thing satisfied all sceptics beyond a doubt."

Two years later we find Lucius still noticing this scepticism, and remarking that the people seem to be very bitter upon the subject of magnetism. "But," he continues, "we have satisfied a great many, some very hard cases. This afternoon I examined Mr. Hooper. Thought the kidney and uthera was diseased. Said there was a seated pain in the lower part of the abdomen, also a pain in the small of the back. Thought the pain in the small of the back was caused by sympathy with the kidneys. Recommended a plaster of Burgundy pitch to be worn upon the back. Told him not to drink cold water, for it did not agree with the kidneys. Also examined Mr. Pillsbury's wife. Examined head and pronounced the brain diseased, said there was a congestion of the brain and large clots of blood laid upon the brain, and it would produce convulsions and fits. While I was examining her head she had one of these fits, as I was told by Mr. Quimby."

It is interesting to note that Lucius frequently says merely what he "thought," and draws upon his own opinions. For example, he writes, "Examined Mrs. Barker. Said there was a difficulty in the blood, described one of the valves of the heart as being thicker than the other. Thought she didn't have exercise enough. Said the valve being deranged caused the blood to stop. Was asked what sensation it produced. Said it produced a faintness, said this was the great difficulty; thought there was no other functional or organic disease. At the same time examined Mrs. Bennett. This (as I understood from the Doctor) was a nameless disease."

In another case Lucius discerns what he takes to be spinal complaint and expresses the opinion that the patient "will never get well," although he once more recommends a "plaster of Burgundy pitch," to be put upon the small of the back for relief. These statements show how limited is the range of his own thought in the matter. He tells us nothing whatever concerning inner causes, and nothing about the general state of mind of those he examines. All this remained for Mr. Quimby to discover.

Plainly, Lucius's ability is more manifest when it is a question of describing material things, under the suggestion of some one in the audience who mentally tells him where to travel in spirit. Thus he speaks of being "put in communication with Mr. Buck, and being taken by him to his house." Lucius described the room, "and saw a map lying upon the floor, and told the audience that before he left his house he put a map upon the floor." These descriptions were con-vincing to the audience, because they proved that Lucius could actually see at a distance.

Lucius also had mind enough to follow Mr. Quimby's lectures to some extent, for he speaks of one occasion when the lecturer "spoke of mind, and how the mind was acted upon while in the mesmeric state." The most significant statement is that Quimby, in his remarks, "clearly demonstrated that there was no fluid, and he showed the relation between mind and matter." But, in confession of his own lack of interest in this striking demonstration, Lucius simply goes on to say, with only a comma between, I have been having a chit chat with a very pretty girl her name is Abey Redman but mum is the word." (1)

Rightly interpreted, this explanation leads beyond "animal magnetism" by showing that it is not a question of a supposed "fluid" or of electricity, but of mental influences which no mesmeric theory could account for. But Lucius has no inkling of this. He does note, however, that Mr. Quimby is himself beginning to cure in a remarkable way. He writes, "Mr. Quimby has performed a miracle here. He took a man that had a lame shoulder. It was partially out of joint. He worked upon it, and the man said there was no pain in it. This astonished them. This afternoon the man went about his work as well as ever. . . . [Mr. Quimby] took a man out of the audience (a perfect stranger to him) and effected a cure on his arm. The man bad not ben able to raise it up for two years and in a few minutes he was able to raise his arm up to his head, and moved it round free from pain " (2)

So far as Lucius is able to follow, such cases merely show Mr. Quimby's power to exert "magnetic influence," whatever that was supposed to be. He speaks, for example, of a patient to whom Quimby was taken by a Dr. Richardson. "The case was that of a woman who fell down and injured the elbow joint so that she couldn't move it without excruciating pain. He magnetised her and made her move her arm about just as he pleased without any pain."

Turning to Mr. Quimby's own account of his experiments, we find once more that what Quimby was interested in was not the alleged "magnetism," but the activities which resulted when a subject or patient accepted a certain idea and responded to it. For example, in an article dated 1863, Mr. Quimby states that he found his mesmeric subject possessing a psychical sense of smell such that Lucius could not only detect any odor at a distance, but "describe the flower or person that threw the odor." Noticing Lucius's responsiveness to what he had perceived, or at other times merely thought he perceived, Mr. Quimby resolved to try an experiment of another sort, namely, to prove that similar consequences would follow when there was no real object at all, but merely an idea.

"I said," writes Mr. Quimby, that "I could create objects that my subject could see. So, of course I could create things that would frighten him, and I could create all kinds of fruit which he would eat and be affected by. For instance, when awake he was very fond of lemons, and was always eat-ing them. I thought I would break him of it. So when I had him asleep I would create mentally a lemon, and he would see it. Then I would make him eat it till he would be so sick that he would vomit. Then he would beg me not to make him eat any more lemons. I never mentioned the conversation to him in his waking state. After trying the experiment two or three times, it destroyed his taste for lemons, and he had no desire for them and could not even bear the taste of them."

From this experiment Mr. Quimby infers that "ideas that cannot be seen are as as real as those which can be seen ... Then man can account for his troubles as easily as he can account for injuries caused by an accident. . . . Some ideas contain no intelligence because the author puts none in them." If a subject or a patient can be unpleasantly affected by a mere suggestion, one can utilize this power by directing the mind with intelligence, and so disabuse it of its errors. Since minds are reached directly in any event by mere "opin-ions," working mischief, we all have it in our power to reach minds wisely, and no "subject" is required. Thus it becomes a question of developing that "wisdom," as Quimby later called it, which should free people from adverse suggestions.

Mr. Quimby further saw that even when a subject is clairvoyant this state is of short duration, and the subject readily lapses into the mere mind-reading of those present. So the diagnosis of a disease, as well as the opinion that a certain remedy will be effective, may be in part mere mind-reading. In an article addressed to the editor of a Portland paper, Feb-ruary, 1862, protesting against being classed with spiritists, mesmerists, and clairvoyants, Mr. Quimby says, "I was one of the first mesmerisers in the state who gave public experiments, and I had a subject who was considered the best then known. He examined and prescribed for dis-eases just as this class do now... The capacity of thought-reading is the common extent of mesmerism. Clairvoyance is very rare...

"When I mesmerised my subject, he would prescribe some little simple herb that would do no harm or good of itself. In some cases this would cure the patient. I also found that any medicine would cure if he ordered it. This led me to investigate the matter, and arrive at the stand I now take that the cure is not in the medicine, but in the confidence of the doctor or medium. A clairvoyant never reasons nor alters his opinion; but, if in the first state of thought-reading he prescribes medicine, he must be posted by some mind interested in it, and must also derive his knowledge from the same source from which the doctors derive theirs.

"The subject I had left me, and was employed by _____, who employed him in examining diseases in the mesmeric sleep, and taught him to recommend such medicines as he got up himself in Latin; and, as the boy did not know Latin, it looked very mysterious. Soon afterwards he was at home again, and I put him to sleep to examine a lady, expecting that he would go on in his old way; but instead of that he wrote a long prescription in Latin. I awoke him, that he might read it; but he could not. So I took it to the apothecary who said he had the articles, and that they would cost twenty dollars. This was impossible for the lady to pay. So I returned and put him to sleep again; and he gave me his usual prescription of some little herb, and [the patient] got well"

This result convinced Mr. Quimby that if mediums and subjects had not acquired their alleged knowledge from the "common allopathic belief," and if it were not for "the superstition of the people," very few cures would be wrought. The fact that the medium's eyes are closed, for example, adds to the mystery. The people as readily responded to the suggestions of doctors who helped them create their diseases, in the first place, as to the supposed wisdom of the medium in the second. It is all a matter of suggestion any way. But real service to the sick would consist in showing them how they had been deceived. Mr. Quimby's experience with mesmerism had taught him the real secret of humbuggery in the case of both mediums and of mesmerists or supposed "magnetic healers." He had to pursue his investigations far enough to be thoroughly convinced, and to come into possession of the true principle. Moreover it was necessary for him to experiment with Lucius long enough to make the highly important discovery that he, Quimby, was clairvoyant, too, without the aid of mesmerism, and without any of the psychical manifestions through which the spiritists influenced people.

Notes

(1) This sentence, a characteristic one, is given exactly as found in the ,journal.
(2) These preliminary cases must have taught Mr. Quimby much in regard to the re-establishing of confidence, for later we find him begin-ning as soon as possible to encourage patients to make an effort to walk or raise their arms, in instances where this power had been lost.

Chapter Five - The Principles Discovered

To note how radical was the change through which Mr. Quimby passed as he turned from the mesmeric point of view, we need to revert for the moment to his first experiments. In one of his descriptive articles he tells us that the first time he sat down to try to mesmerise another man he took a chair by him and the two, joining hands with a young man as subject, tried to will the latter to sleep. Their hypothesis was that electricity would pass from their organisms into that of the subject. So by "puffing and willing," they tried to convey their electricity until at last the subject fell asleep. Having the young man in their power the two men then tried to determine which one had the greater influence.

"So we sat the subject in the chair, the gentleman stood in front of him and I behind him, and the gentleman tried to draw him out of the chair; but he could not start him. Then we reversed positions, and I drew the subject out of the chair This showed that I had the greater power or will. This ended the first experiment."

Later, Mr. Quimby, experimenting alone, put the subject asleep in five minutes. But as he was new at that sort of thing he did not know what to do next. So procuring books he learned what one is supposed to do. He did not then realize that the results obtained depended upon the theory one adopts and the phenomena one accordingly anticipates. But later he became convinced that acceptance of the theory of magnetism and the mesmeric sleep predisposed his mind to produce the results, and that if had never heard of a book on the subject the results would have been very different. Furthermore, he concluded that however absurd the ideas acquired by the operator, the operator will prove them "true" by his experiments, since, as he tells us, "beliefs make us act, and our acts are directed by our beliefs." Mr. Quimby had to be credulous in the beginning in order to find out that he had merely proved a belief and was far from truth.

At the outset, then, the hypothesis was that the subject responded merely because the operator contained more electricity and had the stronger will, and will-power itself seemed to be little more than magnetism, so-called. But as matter of fact the books simply told a person how to become an operator without explaining anything that he did: there was no science of the thing at all. Even the conditions to be complied with were hypothetical. Thus Mr. Quimby found that if he had any steel about him it affected the subject, and so he had to keep all steel away as long as he believed that steel had anything to do with his failures. Again, if a sceptic sat too near, he failed. Stumbling along at first, he found him-self as ignorant of the phenomena as when he began, so long as he held to the hypothesis of a magnetic current and the notion that precise material conditions were essential. The resource was to drop the prevailing views and set out in quest of another explanation.

In this early period of investigation, Mr. Quimby was entirely sceptical in regard to clairvoyance and kindred phenomena, also sceptical of any experiment where the subject had any foreknowledge of what was to be done. To avoid any possible error or ground for doubt, he therefore adopted the rule, and held steadily to it during the four years of his association with Lucius, never to let the subject know what was expected of him save mentally. Even if he merely wished Lucius to give him his hand, he would ask him mentally, never audibly. During the entire four years there was no evidence that Lucius knew in his waking state what he did when in the mesmeric sleep. There was a great advantage in favor of this rule, for Quimby could be absolutely sure of his results.

By depending solely upon his mental communications with Lucius, Mr. Quimby was able to attain a high degree of success, and to learn in due course that the whole process was mental, that neither the state of the weather, the presence of metals, nor the passing of an alleged current from one organism to the other had anything to do with the actual result.

That Lucius received no impression from any source save Quimby's thought, during an experiment with this end in view, was also clear from the fact that Mr. Quimby could in imagination call up the picture of a wild animal, and by concentrating upon this picture and making it as vivid as possible frighten Lucius by means of it. If the operator told his subject during the experiment that the animal was merely imaginary, this qualification made no difference; for Lucius was completely subject to the mental picture, and was unable to draw upon his own reason or entertain an explanation of the experiment. This result led Mr. Quimby to believe that "man has the power of creation," and that ideas take form. Then the question arose, What are ideas composed of? "They must be something, or else they could not be seen by the spiritual eyes." This led Quimby to inquire whether Lucius could see anything if he merely thought of something abstract, such as a general principle. "I found that if I thought of principles, he had no way of describing them, for there was nothing to see; but if I thought of anything that had form I could make him see it."

Sight, then, was equivalent to reality for Lucius. Yet in the operator's mind there might be merely a visual image. But if the supposed object had no existence outside of the mind of the operator and the subject's perception of it, why might not an alleged "spirit" in the case of spiritistic phe-nomena be a mere idea in the mind of people in the audience? An experiment convinced Mr. Quimby that this could be the case. Requesting any one to give him a name written on a bit of paper, Mr. Quimby passed the slip of paper to Lucius, who was sitting blindfolded by the committee. Lucius read the name aloud. Quimby then told Lucius to find the person. His account of this experiment continues as follows:

"My mode was to make him ask questions so that the audience could lead him along. So I said, 'Who is he, a man or a boy?' He said, 'A man.' 'Is he married?' 'Yes.' 'Well, tell me if he has children, and how many.' He answered, 'His wife has three children. 'Well,' said I, 'find him.' Lucius said, 'He left town between two days' 'Well find him.' He traced him to Boston, and by inquiring followed him to the interior of New York and found him in a cooper's shop. Now all this was literally true, and I suppose some one in the audience knew the facts, although neither the subject nor I knew anything about the man. I asked what became of the man. Lucius said the man was dead. 'Well,' said I, 'find him and bring him here.! 'Well,' said he, 'he is here, can't you see him?' Said I, 'Give a description' So he went on and gave a general description. But these general descriptions amount to nothing, for every one will make the description fit his case. So I said, 'I don't want that; if there is anything peculiar about the man, describe it.' 'Well,' said he, 'there is one thing. He has a hair lip.' I asked the question so that if there was anything peculiar the audience would create it"

What was the explanation of such an experiment? Mr. Quimby concluded that those in the audience who were pre-disposed to believe in spirits would infer that Lucius actually brought the man's spirit there. The proof was found in the fact that Lucius accurately described the man's peculiar appearance. But those who believed in thought-reading would conclude that Lucius had read from the minds of the audience his description of the man's appearance, and that the rest of the experiment was to be explained on the basis of clairvoyance. Once in touch with the personality of the man in question, as known by people present, Lucius could have read the rest, or discerned the mental pictures successively appearing as Lucius gained point after point essential to the description. Mr. Quimby's conclusion was that the mental image of the man was as real to Lucius as though the man himself or his spirit had been present. He became the more convinced that "man has the power to create ideas and make them so dense that they can be seen by a subject who is mesmerised" If an imagined person, or the mere memory image of a person was as real to the subject as an actual "spirit," why should one infer that a spirit was there?

Thus Mr. Quimby was led more and more steadily to the conclusion that all

effects produced on Lucius were due to the direct action of mind on mind, and that no other hypothesis was necessary. He found that he could influence Lucius either with or without Lucius's knowledge, and that Lucius was also affected in respects which were not intentional on his part. Again, be found himself able to give a thought to another's mind without mesmerism, for instance, by bidding a person stop when walking. Why, then, should he use either mesmerism or his subject? Why not follow out this discovery that ideas take shape in the mind, according to one's belief, and can be seen by the eye of the spirit? If one mind can influence another by creating a mental picture of an object to be feared, such as a wild animal. why may we not create good objects and benefit the minds of those we seek to influence? And if the same results can be produced by mere suggestion as by medicine taken with firm faith, why use medicine?

Referring to Mr. Quimby's lecture-notes, used during the period of his public exhibitions with Lucius, we find that he very gradually came to these conclusions when he saw that no other explanation would suffice. He not only read all the books on mesmerism he could find but familiarised himself with various theories of matter, such as Berkeley's, and with different hypotheses in explanation of the mesmeric sleep. Convinced that there was no "mesmeric influence" as such, no "fluid" passing from body to body but simply the direct action of mind on mind without any medium, he had also to become convinced that the states perceived by the subject were not due to imagination. He found, for example, that by creating a state in his own mind and vividly feeling it, Lucius felt the same and exhibited signs of its effect in the body. "Real cold" was felt by Lucius in response to certain suggestions. If imaginary, the subject would not have acted upon the ideas in question. Thus when Mr. Quimby handed Lucius a six-inch rule and pictured it in his own mind as a twelve-inch rule, Lucius would proceed to count out the twelve inches, and to him it was literally a twelve-inch rule. That is to say, the impressions received by the subject were real, not "imaginary," as real as would have been the actual things in question. An impression might indeed be produced on a subject's mind from a false cause, but the cause would then be real.

Nor was the state called clairvoyance imaginary. Mr. Quimby described it in this period of his thought as a "high degree of excitement which gives the mind freedom of action, placing it in close contact with everything, including past, present and future." If it were a merely fancied state the subject would not be able to visit distant places, describing people and things correctly. Nor would it be possible to see actual events in process and predict their results, as in the case of a captain located on board a ship bound for New York and then located in port later, the second time Lucius was asked to find that particular man.

There was every reason to accept these disclosures as real, for interested persons took pains to acquaint themselves with the facts. For instance, in the case of the ship above mentioned we have the evidence published in a newspaper at the time, reading in part as follows: "During Mr. Quimby's exhibition in this town on Wednesday evening, (14th inst.) his intelligent Clairvoyant was in communication with F. Clark, Esq., a respectable merchant of this place. The Clairvoyant described to the audience a Barque . . . called the Casilda then on her passage from Cuba to New York, minutely from 'clew to carving,' as seamen say. He then informed the company how far said Barque was from her destined port, and gave the name of vessel and port the distance we think was about 70 miles.

"On the next evening, he visited (in his somnambulism) the same vessel and said she had arrived off the Hook at New York, where she then was. On the Tuesday following this exhibition the merchants received a letter informing them of the arrival of this Barque (see our Marine Report) at the precise time stated by the Clairvoyant, who it will be recollected is Lucius Bickford [Burkmar], a young man 19 years of age.

"This was but one of several exhibitions of his visiting absent vessels of which he could have had no information, and describing even the master and people on board. We profess no knowledge of this wonderful science, but deem it a duty we owe to the public to publish every fact that may aid the progress of human knowledge."

It is interesting to note that this fair-minded newspaper writer, while heading his contribution "Animal Electricity," according to the popular notion prevailing at the time, 1844, expresses his opinion that "there is no more mystery in all this than there is in repeating a lesson committed." That is to say, he thinks these facts at a distance are discerned by "the mind's eye." He was probably convinced, therefore, by Quimby's argument in his lectures to the effect that there was no "fluid" passing between, no "magnetism," but mind operating on mind to put Lucius in possession of the clue he was to follow when locating a ship at a distance or describing her captain and crew.

Quimby tells us in one of his later articles that very early in his experiments with mesmerism he became convinced that Lucius could "see through matter." That is, a person in a clairvoyant state, with all his physical senses quiescent, can discern in another person every-state or condition ordinarily coming within the range of the five bodily senses. He was compelled to believe this, for the descriptions which Lucius gave proved it. He therefore adopted this as his point of view, namely, that the human spirit can intuitively see through matter.

His next interest, he tells us, in an article written in 1861, was to become a clairvoyant himself, that is, without mesmerism. For, having become convinced that "matter was only a medium for our wisdom to act through," he saw how matter could be transformed by attaching one's interest to higher ideas. This meant ridding the mind of all beliefs and opinions tending to create miseries and troubles, and dedicating the clairvoyant or intuitive powers to the welfare of the sick. Through his natural state, he tells us, as a being of flesh and blood, he could still feel as a patient felt. But in his higher selfhood or intuitive state he was governed by the spiritual ideal, "the scientific man." As this spiritual state can be attained by cultivating "the spiritual senses," which function independently of matter and see through matter, it is not of course necessary to make the body quiescent through the use of mesmerism.

Turning again to the period of his lectures, we find Quimby also stating his conviction that Lucius took his clue directly from the minds of others, by thought-reading followed by clairvoyance, and never from his own fancies. For Quimby found that the results attained through Lucius varied with his own progress. Thus the fears and notions which Quimby entertained as long as he believed in magnetism passed with his change of view. Instead of working himself up to the point of transferring fancied electricity to Lucius, he put all his efforts into creating a mental picture for Lucius to see in his mind. In either case it was plain that Lucius saw or did what was commanded when he gained the attention of his subject. Until the subject gave his full attention, nothing resulted. So in the case of clairvoyance, the subject would see any object to which his attention was called. If a failure occurred, the fault was the operator's not that of the subject.

Here, then was a highly important discovery. Quimby found that with his great powers of concentration he had great success in arresting the attention of his subject. This in brief was his control over him. But if certain results follow from arrested attention in the case of a person in the mesmeric sleep, why may not self-induced results follow upon attention in the case of any one of us? Does this not explain many of the ancient mysteries, and the self-induced states of Apollonius of Tyana, Mahomet and Swedenborg?

At this point Quimby's lecture-notes come to a sudden end, and we are left to infer that having reached these significant conclusions he was not interested to lecture upon them any further, but might better turn his results to practical account in healing the sick. For these notes show that here too he had reached the same conclusion which we noted in the foregoing, namely, that the results produced by physicians in treating the sick depend upon securing the attention of the patient in favor of a certain diagnosis and the proper medicine to be taken for the supposed disease. In fact he says, convincingly, that "all medical remedies affect the body only through the mind." The one who takes medicine must believe in medicine and anticipate the desired result. The result is then created by the believer.

Here, then, were interests enough to follow for a life-time. The human mind is plastic to ideas and imagery, and these take form according to belief. What enlists the attention long enough to produce. a distinct impression, has power to affect the body, and an idea accepted as truth is as good as reality in its influence upon the person believing it. Thus a person may be made to feel heat or cold, to be frightened by the mental picture of a lion, or be dispossessed of a desire to eat lemons. There is an endless range of possibilities. Be-lief in magnetism on the part of an audience tends to the production of anticipated magnetic phenomena, but the re-sults change when the hypothesis of a magnetic or electric "fluid" is dismissed. Spirits can be summoned up from the vasty deep, or precisely the same results may be created without their aid. A patient will proceed to create a disease according to a doctor's description of what he is likely to feel, or this process can be checked by diverting the attention in favor of some other idea.

Again, man has great power over his own states, and need not depend either on a mesmerist, a spiritist, physician or any other person. For strength of will proves to be, not the power of a fluid or current, but concentration upon an interest or object that has engaged the attention. There is nothing occult or uncanny in such power. There is no reason for yielding our minds to control, or for controlling the minds of others. Since a person may perceive the feelings of an-other by simply sitting nearby and rendering himself receptive, it is not necessary to put the mind into any special state, hitherto deemed a mystery. The great question is, What is that part of us which has power to penetrate beneath all errors and illusions, and learn what is true? What is truth in contrast with beliefs?

Quimby's mind was of the type that leads to science as opposed to mere belief. He had come in contact with facts at last, and learned how the human mind works under the influ-ence of suggestion. He sought one consistent explanation which could be followed through to the end and proved by practical experience. He took no interest in results following upon mere theories, such as those proposed by mesmerists and spiritists. There must be a deeper science than so-called medical science. Moreover, he was beginning to see that religious creeds were not much better. "What we believe, that we create." What then shall we create that is worth while?

We might expect him to raise the world-old problem concerning the reality of matter, especially as he had heard something about Berkeley's views. But he never mentions Berkeley again, after these notes of the period from 1843 to 1847. We might expect continued interest in such men as Swedenborg, but there is no reference to Swedenborg save this one, when it is a question of self-induced inner states. Quimby's brief studies when in quest of light on mesmerism apparently convinced him that there was little of value for him in books, and that he must explore for himself.

More-over, spiritualism came upon the scene to take the place of mesmerism in public interest, he was concerned to follow this to the end, too; and he must make his way alone by following experience. To the end of his life, so far as his notes and manuscripts can tell us, he remained sceptical concerning spiritistic phenomena, and confined himself to a study of the experiences taking place within the human personality in this world. This did not prevent him from acquiring a new view of death and of the relationship of the human spirit to God. But after 1847 we find his eyes definitely turned in the direction which led to the development of his "Science of Health:"

With reference to the rumor current in his later years that his views were unchanged, Quimby writes in 1862, "As I used to mesmerise, some think my mode of treatment is mesmeric. But my mode is not in the least like those who claim to be mesmerised, or to be spiritual mediums." Adding that he knows all about mesmeric treatment, after "twenty years" since he began the experiments which enabled him to see through it, he says that if he "had no other aim than dollars and cents," he would close his eyes, go into a trance, tell the patient how he felt and call some Indian to prescribe by making out the patient "sick of scrofula or of cancerous humor or some other foolish disease," and impress upon the patient the necessity of having medicine ordered by the spirits of his "own getting up." That is, he sees through the whole game played by mesmerists and mediums who mislead the people and take their money. "If I should do this, I should do what I know to be wrong." Instead, he tells his readers that he asks "no aid from any source but Wisdom.... Wisdom never acts in that way."

Again, in October, 1861, Quimby writes: "It is twenty years since I first embarked in what was one of the greatest humbugs of the age, mesmerism. At that time the people were as superstitious about it as they were two hundred years ago in regard to witchcraft."

What was the prime result of his investigations? That the human mind is amenable to suggestion, as we now say; that there are subjects capable of being put into a state which we now call hypnosis; and that the alleged magnetic, electrical or mesmeric effects are not mysterious at all, but are the results of the action of mind on mind. The alleged humbug was reduced to the operation of a principle to which we are all subject, the influence of thought. The supposed wonders of the clairvoyant state are capital instances of the activity of an intuition which we all possess. There is no such process as "mesmerism," therefore. There is no "magnetic healing." There is power of one mind to control another, to be sure, and this was surely remarkable in the case of Quimby and Lucius. But the clairvoyant or intuitive powers of Lucius were not generated in Lucius by Quimby these are latent powers of the human soul, and all minds have access to things, persons and events at a distance. All healing said to take place by mesmeric, spiritistic or magnetic influences occurs according to one principle: the only principle of healing in every instance whatever, natural and Divine, according to resident energies and unchanging laws. There could be no mesmeric or magnetic science of healing, any more than there exists a medical science: the one true science is spiritual. No one who sees this could ever be content to practise upon the credulity of the people, instilling suggestions into their minds under the guise of a "trance" or by the aid of hypnosis. Hence Quimby's work from this time on was to expose what he called the deception practised by physicians, just as he exposed priestcraft, the humbuggery of mediumship, and the fallacies of every sort of imposition turning upon the acceptance of opinion for truth.

Had Mrs. Eddy known this, she would have seen the futility of calling Quimby an "ignorant mesmerist" at any point in his career. An unenlightened mesmerist he was just as long as he adopted the prevailing theories, while trying them out. His own mind was free and his world of thought a free one from the time he saw that the right thing to do was to seek that Wisdom which "disabuses the mind of its errors." It then became necessary to draw a radical line of distinction between the "mind of opinions," subject to suggestions and in certain instances to hypnosis; and the "mind of Science," the "mind of Christ," possessed by the real self. It was a long road to travel from the point where Quimby started out, a believer in medical practice and a student of mesmerism, to faith in an inner or higher self immediately open to the Divine presence with its guiding Wisdom quickening the "mind of Christ." The guide throughout was love of truth, leading the way to inductions from actual experience. One of his patients who understood the prime results as he saw them fulfilled in Quimby's work among the sick has said:

"This discovery, you observe, was not made from the Bible, but from mental phenomena and searching investigations; and, after the truth was discovered, he found his new views portrayed and illustrated in Christ's teachings and works. If you think this seems to show that Quimby was a remarkable man, let me tell you that he was one of the most unassuming of men that ever lived; for no one could well be more so, or make less account of his own achievements. Humility was a marked feature of his character (I knew him intimately). To this was united a benevolent and an unselfish nature, and a love of truth, with a remarkably keen perception. But the distinguishing feature of his mind was that he could not entertain an opinion, because it was not knowledge. His faculties were so practical and perceptive that the wisdom of mankind, which is largely made up of opinions, was of little value to him. Hence the charge that he was not an educated man is literally true. True know-ledge to him was positive proof, as in a problem of mathematics. Therefore, he discarded books and sought phenomena, where his perceptive faculties made him master of the situation. Therefore, he got from his experiments in mes-merism what other men did not get,—a stepping-stone to a higher knowledge than man possessed, and a new range to mental vision."(1)

Quimby sums up his results in one of his tentative introductions, in which he says:

"My object in introducing this work to the reader is to correct some of the errors that flesh is heir to. During a long experience in the treatment of disease I have labored to find the causes of so much misery in the world. By accident I became interested in what was then called mesmerism, not thinking of ever applying it to any useful discovery or to benefit man, but merely as a phenomenon for my own gratification. Being a sceptic I would not believe anything that my subject would do if there was any chance for deception, so all my experiments were carried on mentally. This gave me a chance to discover how far Mesmer was entitled to any discovery over those who had followed him. I found that the phenomenon could be produced. This was a truth but the whys and wherefores were a mystery. This is the length of mesmerism, it is all a mystery, like spiritualism. Each has its belief but the causes are in the dark. Believing in the phenomenon I wanted to discover the causes and find if there were any good to come out of it.

"In my investigation I found that my ignorance would produce phenomena in my subject that my own wisdom could not correct. At first I found that my thoughts affected the subject, and not only my thought but my belief. I found that my own thoughts were one thing and my belief another.

If I really believed in anything, the effect would follow whether I was thinking of it or not. For instance, I believed that silk would attract the subject. This was a belief in common with mankind, so if a person having any silk about him, for instance a lady with a silk apron, the subject's hand would be affected by it and the hand would move towards the lady, even if she were behind him. So I found that belief in everything affects us, yet we are not aware of it because we do not think. We think our beliefs have nothing to do with the phenomenon. But anything that is believed has reality to those that believe it, and it is liable to affect them at any time when the condition of the mind is in a right state.

"Minds are like clouds, always flying, and our belief catches them as the earth catches seeds that fly in the winds. My object was to discover what a belief was made of and what thought was. This I found out by thinking of something Lucius could describe, so that I knew he must see or get the information from me in some way; at last I found out that mind was something that could be changed. I called it spiritual matter, because I found it could be condensed into a solid and receive a name called "tumor," and by the same power under a different direction it might be dissolved and made to disappear. This showed me that man was governed by two powers or directions, one by a belief, the other by a science. The creating of disease is under the superstition of man's belief. [Conventional] cures have been by the same remedy. Disease being brought about through a false belief, it took another false belief to correct the first; so that instead of destroying the evil, the remedy created more.

"I found that there is a Wisdom that can be applied to these errors or evils that can put man in possession of a Science that will not only destroy the evil but will hold up its serpent head, as Moses in the wilderness held up the errors of religious creeds, and all that looked upon his explanation were cured of the diseases that followed their beliefs. Science will hold up these old superstitious beliefs and theories and all that listen and learn can be cured not only of the disease that they may be suffering from but they will know how to avoid the errors of others.

"I shall endeavor to give a fair account of my investigations and what I have had to contend with and how I succeeded. I have said many things in regard to medical science but all that I have said was called out by my patients being deceived by the profession. The same is true of the religious profession. Every article was written under an excited state brought about by some wrong inflicted on my patient by the medical faculty, the clergy or public opinion. All my arguments are used to correct some false opinion that has affected my patient in the form of disease, mentally or physically. In doing this I have to explain the Bible, for troubles arise from a wrong belief in certain passages, and when I am sitting by my patient those passages that cause trouble also trouble me, and the passage comes to me with the explanation and I, as a man, am not aware of the answer till I find it out [intuitively].

"There is a wisdom that has never been reduced to language. The science of curing disease has never been described by language, but the error that makes disease is in the mouth of every child. The remedies are also described but the remedies are worse than the disease, for instead of lessening the evil, they have increased it. In fact the theory of correcting disease is the introduction of life."

Note

(1) J. A. Dresser in the "True History," p. 10.

Chapter Six - Intermediate Period

IT will be noticed that Lucius, when referring to some of Quimby's works of healing known as miracles, speaks of the fact that Quimby "worked over" patients unable to walk or move their arms. Apparently, manipulation was employed to some extent in such cases, possibly because the belief still prevailed that a "fluid" passed from operator to patient. We find confirmation of this in the biographical account already quoted from.

"He sometimes," writes George Quimby, "in cases of lame-ness and sprains, manipulated the limbs of the patient, and often rubbed the head with his hands, wetting them with water. He said it was so hard for the patient to believe that his mere talk with him produced the cure, that he did this rubbing simply that the patient would have more confidence in him; but he always insisted that he possessed no 'power' nor healing properties different from any one else, and that his manipulations conferred no beneficial effect upon the patient, although it was often the case that the patient himself thought they did." (1)

Again, we have the testimony of a patient who remained with Mr. Quimby for several years, meeting the new comers and conversing with them both before and after they received treatment. Mr. Dresser says, "In treating a patient, after he had finished his explanations, and the silent work, which completed the treatment, he usually rubbed the head two or three minutes, in a brisk manner, for the purpose of letting the patient see that something was done. This was a measure of securing the confidence of the patient, at a time when he was starting a new practice, and stood alone in it. I knew him to make many quick cures at a distance, sometimes with persons he never saw at all. He never considered the touch of the hand as at all necessary, but let it be governed by circumstances, as was done 1800 years ago." (2)

Bearing this explanation in mind, when we come to read Quimby's letters to patients, we will understand why he speaks as if he were putting his hand on a person's head at a long distance, that is, during an absent treatment. This was to engage the patient's attention and arouse faith. The explanation becomes perfectly intelligible, when we see the reason for it. There could be no reason for the bare statement, made many years after, that Quimby "manipulated his patients," without giving the above explanation, unless the one who said it wished to misrepresent the great spiritual healer.

The other typical misrepresentation, namely, that he was a spiritualist, was made in his own day, and is undermined by Quimby's adverse critique of spiritism as a whole. There was no reason for unfriendly feeling in this case. But the new therapeutist was popular in his later days, spiritism was struggling for recognition; hence it was natural for spiritistic mediums who claimed to do healing to include Quimby as one of their number. It was clearly impossible for Quimby to give assent, and to change to spiritism; for his researches led him to believe that all ordinary spiritistic phenomena could be reproduced without the aid of mediums and without recourse to spirits.

The sleep into which he put Lucius was akin to the "trance," as mediums knew it. The suggestions in this case came from people in the audience who visualized places they wanted the subject to visit, or held ideas in mind for Lucius to read. The phenomena could be explained by the action of mind on mind, in the flesh. Consequently, Quimby held close to the facts. Moreover, his own powers of receptivity and intuition were growing. By sitting near patients, he learned to diagnose their condition, and also learned to read their mental states. Therefore it was possible for him to make the complete transition from mesmerism and all psychical phenomena akin to it to the adoption of his spiritual method of treating disease, that is, by the aid of intuition or direct perception, through "silence" without mediumship.

On this point George Quimby writes, "He was always in his normal condition when engaged with his patients. He never went into any trance, and was a strong disbeliever in spiritualism, as understood by that name. He claimed, and firmly believed, that his only power consisted in his wisdom, and in his understanding the patient's case and being able to explain away the error and establish the truth, or health, in its place. Very frequently the patient could not tell how he was cured, but it did not follow that Mr. Quimby himself was ignorant of the manner in which he performed the cure."(3)

There is less documentary evidence to draw upon in the years after 1847, the date of the last experiment in mesmerism of which we have record, and the time when Dr. Quimby was in full possession of his silent method of healing. Naturally newspaper writers were less interested, for this new work was not at all spectacular, like the public exhibitions with Lucius. Moreover, it was harder to understand. For there was now no "subject," there were in fact no experiments, but simply the quiet development of a method in which Dr. Quimby depended upon his own impressions and intuitions.

So long as it was a question of alleged magnetism Quimby's work was subject to belief in the mysterious, and he himself was groping his way from belief in the medical faculty and in disease as an entity to a wholly different view. But when he comes to recognize the subtle influence of mind on mind, the power of what we now call suggestion, the expectant attention of onlookers, and his own ability to make an intuitive diagnosis in a wholly normal state, we find his thought moving in the realm of sure principles and fixed laws. His letters to patients indicate that he still gave much prominence to physical conditions, and advised his patients with reference to them. But that was because the patients must have concrete facts to interpret, substituting Quimby's new view for that of medical diagnosis. The patients ordinarily had no one to depend on save Dr. Quimby, since such healing was not then recognized. Hence they wrote frequently to him and reported their progress, that he might advise them anew.

Again, the experimental period was in a measure more intelligible to the public because the mesmeric activities turned upon the control of one mind by another. The excerpts quoted above have told us that Quimby had exceptional powers of concentration and remarkable control over his subject. The change which he passed through in the intermediate period was from the idea of merely human control to that of inner receptivity to Divine wisdom, and the dedication of all powers of concentration to the carrying out of spiritual ideals. This change was hard to follow, since few people believed in such direct access to higher wisdom, and all thoughts directed to another's mind were supposedly for the sake of controlling that mind. The prevailing interest in spiritism was no help, for that theory also encouraged belief in the mere action of one spirit on another; it did not trace guidance to the Divine mind. The teachings of the Church were not favorable, for Dr. Quimby's work centered interest upon the patient's own inner life at large, not upon the mere problems of sin and salvation. Therefore, the new trail had to be blazed alone.

Still further, Quimby's reaction against medical theory and practice in his experimental period was a reaction from all sciences based on external signs or appearances, matters that could not be proved. His most frequent reference is to "opinion" taken for truth, and his early articles are directed against all such suggestions or assertions. There must then be a true Science, so he reasoned, which is indeed verifiable. This wisdom will take" into account man's real as opposed to his apparent condition. It will not deny the actuality of human beliefs accepted as truth, while the spell is unbroken; it will break that spell and show people that an error regarded as truth is for the time being as real as life itself. It will therefore build upon psychological facts, but higher facts must gradually be brought into view.

The basis for this Science was laid in a measure by the discovery that the human spirit possesses senses or powers which function independently of matter. These "spiritual senses," as Quimby later called them, include not merely sight or clairvoyance but the power of detecting odors and atmospheres at a distance, the ability to read another's mind, and to travel in spirit, making oneself both felt and seen if the recipient of such a visit were himself clairvoyant. For the higher purposes now in view it did not very much matter whether Lucius had actually seen the condition of a diseased body or had merely read from the patient's mind, and from the minds of others present, what the patient or others merely thought was the disease; in either case the clairvoyant feat was significant. It established the fact that clairvoyance was possible without the aid of spirits; and, when Quimby found that he possessed the same powers, it established the fact that this clear-seeing is possible without mesmeric sleep. What was needed, therefore, was a higher, genuinely spiritual psychology. We find Quimby in his articles endeavoring to express that psychology, always greatly hampered by language and the fact that he had no co-workers save those who helped him to express his ideas.

But if the facts of spiritual perception gave the basis in part for a higher view of the human spirit, there was still another principle to be achieved, that is, the adding of the idea of "the Christ" as common to the works of healing of Gospel times and to those of the new day. There are no references to this idea in the earlier newspaper articles which have been preserved or in the earliest letters to patients. But when we turn to later letters and to the first articles written in the Portland period, in 1859 and early in 1860, we find this idea in full recognition as an essential part of the teaching then given. This shows that if it passed through a period of gradual development, that development must have been begun long before; since this view is not brought forward tentatively but with habitual conviction.

On the other hand, we do find references in letters from patients to Quimby's "Science," written with a capital "S." This would indicate that in conversation with patients Dr. Quimby was in the habit of talking about his "Science of Health" long before he put this view in writing and iden-tified it with the Christ. What we must presuppose, in order to have a complete view of his intermediate period up to October, 1859, is an insight which brought the principles under consideration into a single view, namely, the conception of the human spirit with its higher "senses," the idea of the Divine presence as guiding wisdom and healing power, and the identification of this wisdom with the Christ in terms of a demonstrable Science which all might understand.

We are not to suppose that Dr. Quimby quickly transferred his exceptional powers of control as formerly exercised over Lucius into immediate command of his forces so that he was never ill, never had any disabilities to overcome. For the transition began with the realization that he could readily take upon himself the feelings of patients, and that a way must be found to throw off these feelings. Already in Lucius's journal we find reference to the fact that Quimby sometimes found himself enveloped in mental atmospheres. Later, we find Quimby hesitating to take a patient with fits, because of the difficulty he experienced in keeping himself mentally free. In their letters, his patients sometimes inquire about his health, because they too realized that it was difficult for him to throw off his patients' troubles.

These difficulties are instructive to us, however, since they indicate that in thus gradually learning to keep his own spirit free by realizing the protective presence of "Wisdom," as he briefly called God's power with us, he passed through a period of analyzing his patient's feelings by making himself receptive, allowing those feelings to impress themselves upon the sensitive plate of his mind (his own illustration, drawn from his experience with photography), and then comparing them with the Divine ideal. For this contrast was essential to his Science. It led the way to his view that there is a part of us, namely, the spirit, that is never sick, never sins; but is what he called "the scientific man," the man of Christ or Science, in his articles on this subject. Had he not possessed exceptional sympathy, so sensitive a sympathy in fact that it was difficult at times to put a patient's atmosphere aside, he would not have developed so sure a view of the whole situation in the inner life. Even in the last years of his practice in Portland he found difficulties in this respect, and had to leave his practice for brief periods of rest at. his old home in Belfast. The sick often tended to overwhelm him. Yet one of the secrets of his remarkable cures is found in this willingness even to bear the burdens of the sick and sorrowing, that he might see through their miseries to the end and establish a science of right living which all might know and all could live by.

Those who, in recent times, have acquired the art of mental healing by standing apart from the patient and putting the mind through a series of affirmations, meanwhile keeping themselves comfortably free from all atmospheres, should hesitate to conclude that they possess a method superior to Quimby's, because he found difficulty in keeping free. Very few mortals are willing to undergo such sacrifices as the pioneer had to make to blaze the way for the use of his silent method in comfort and ease. At a distance it might seem as if the pioneer were lost in the woods of mental influences, not blazing a straight way through. But it is the one who has encountered all the difficulties and found the way through, who knows the sorrow and sufferings because he has borne them in sympathy, who can tell us the whole story. And, plainly, the affirmation or silent realization is only a part of the process as our pioneer developed it stage by stage in his journey. Had that part been sufficient he might have turned more quickly from his mesmeric experiments to the utilization of ideal suggestions as substitutes for medical and priestly opinion, he might have remained on the level of mind-to-mind projection of human thought. But his guidances led him far beyond all this to the conclusion that in taking the sufferings of patients upon himself he was learning the way of the Christ, coming to learn God's presence as love. There is one further point to note in reading the letters and accounts of the intermediate period, that is, the frequent references to the mind as if it were merely part of the body or identical with the "fluids" of the organism. Dr. Quimby has found that opinions and adverse mental pictures take such hold upon the mind that they produce what we would now call subconscious after effects. He has found that these disturbing mental states, believed in and increasing in power through fear and other disturbing emotions, bring about changes in the nervous system, in the circulation, and in other ways. But he lacks the common term, subconsciousness, and so is compelled to speak, now as if the mind were constituted of thoughts simply, again as if it were the mere nervous activities and the circulation of the blood. This is why he refers to the mind as "the name of something, and this something is the fluids of the body. Disease is the name of the disturbance of these fluids or mind." Later we shall see that by the term mind used in this sense Dr. Quimby always means the lower mental processes, never the real self. This is "the mind that can be changed," the mind that is subject to every wind of doctrine. Dr. Quimby was in possession of the facts we now call "subconscious," but could not readily name them. Consequently he often uses figurative language, as in his comparison of thought to the blossom of a rose. Again, he speaks of himself impersonally as "Dr. Q," trying in this way to suggest the impartial observer, puzzled at first to understand the new mode of treatment.

Dr. Quimby did not keep a record of his patients from the point of view of medical diagnosis or opinion, and we do not know just how soon after 1847 he began to give all his time to silent spiritual healing. But in 1861 he writes that he has sat with "more than three hundred individuals every year for ten years, and during the last five with five hundred yearly." By 1851, then, he was treating as many as three hundred patients a. year, and by 1856 the number had increased to five hundred. The greater years of his work in Portland, therefore, beginning in 1859, came after he had had abundant opportunity to test his method to the full.

What this method was we are now prepared to understand in a measure when we note that his early experiments had taught him how to converse with Lucius mentally, and had also shown him that there is a still higher way of communication. When he talked with Lucius it was by way of expressing a merely personal thought or wish, that is, telepathically, as we now say. Such thought-transference included also the transmission of suggestions involving imagery and emotion, such as the mental picture of a bear and the fear of a bear's presence would arouse. Quimby made this transfer effective by vividly creating the mental object in his own mind. Had he stopped there he would have rivalled some of the "applied psychologists" of our day who scorn the idea of anything spiritual.

But by discovering that there is an inner or higher mind, Quimby learned that spirit could talk with spirit. Such conversation did not involve the transfer of personal thought or emotion, but what we who believe in spiritual healing now call "realization," that is, the vivid picturing of the Divine ideal of man in perfect health and freedom. This spiritual process tended to arouse the same activity or spirit within the patient. It was not the influence of mind on mind, but the operation of spiritual power or Wisdom; for Dr. Quimby objected to the word "power" and always insisted that the real efficiency was Wisdom. That Wisdom is in all men, as Quimby says in his later writings on the subject of "God." It can be appealed to in all. It is the creative Mind within all. Man's part as healer is to establish the truth of this Mind. Hence Quimby dedicated his great powers of concentration to this vivid realization.

The apparent receptivity of the patient when sitting silently by Quimby, or waiting at a distance to feel an effect, was dependent of course on the patient's belief, which might mean that Quimby was regarded as a kind of wonder-worker, or that he was not supposed to know how he healed. But Quimby was not dependent on the patient's conscious attitude or faith.(4) He discerned the inner condition, and conversed with "the scientific man," looking for subconscious after-effects. What he then wrote or said to the patients depended on what he saw that they as conscious beings, with little understanding, were prepared to see. Hence he had often to content himself with brief statements concerning the bodily condition and the physical changes to be expected. But we learn from his more enlightened patients that the silent healing was a religious experience or spiritual quicken-ing, and that to them the great healer began forthwith to talk about the things of the Spirit.

It is this varied series of impressions produced by patients which account for the varied character of his writings, and on this point it would be well to hear from Quimby in his own words:

"The reader will find my ideas strewn all through my writings, and sometimes it will seem that what I said had nothing to do with the subject upon which I was writing. This defect is caused by the great variety of subjects that called the pieces out; for they were all written after sitting with patients who had been studying upon some subject, or who had been under some religious excitement, suffering from disappointment or worldly reverses, or had given much time to health from the point of view of the medical faculty and had reasoned themselves into a belief, so that their diseases were the effects of their reasoning. I have all classes of minds, with all types of disease. No two are alike. The articles are often written from the impressions made on me at the time I wrote.

"For instance, one person had a strong desire for this world's goods, and at the same time had been made to believe his salvation depended upon his being honest and steady. Hence his religion acted as a kind of hindrance to his worldly prosperity. This kept him all the time nervous, and he put all his troubles into the idea 'heart disease.' Another was a man who had a great deal of acquisitiveness and self-esteem, while all his acts were governed by public opinion. He wanted to be a great man by making himself wise at others' expense, or gaining every idea of value without paying for it. Hence he would often force himself into society where he was not wanted. His religion was always the last thing to think of. To him heaven and hell had no claims till he had gone through hell to make up his mind which place was the better for his practice. To cure these two was to show them the hypocrisy of their belief, and show that all men are to themselves just what they make themselves . . . So my arguments are always aimed at some particular belief, sometimes words, sometimes one thing, again another. . . . Hence what I write is like a court-record or a book on law with the arguments of each case. I take up a little of everything."

Notes

(1) New England Magazine, March, 1888, p. 272.
(2) "True History," p. 25.
(3) New England Magazine, March, 1888, p. 273.
(4) One of his patients assures as that when she visited Dr. Quimby, in 1862, she deemed him "an old humbug," and that she received his treatment at first merely because her mother insisted.

Chapter Seven - Early Writings

[These articles and letters are taken from a manuscript book containing copies of "pieces," as they are called, written previous to the first volume of articles, which was begun in October, 1859. Most of the pieces were written before 1856. They were copied by Miss Emma Ware from the originals, and are here printed without any changes whatever.]

THOUGHT, like the blossom of the rose, or tree, contains all the elements of the tree or rose. Now as the law of vegetation governs the tree or rose, so the law of mind acts upon the idea or spiritual tree, known by the name of good or evil. Now although this tree differs from all other trees in the garden of man, it cannot be detected except by its fruits, and as the fruits appear pleasant to the eye of the mind, and are supposed to make men happy, it is cultivated without knowing the peculiar properties it contains.

Now as this tree grows it sends forth its thought like blossoms, and as it is looked upon as a fruit much desired to make one well it is received with joy and cultivated in the garden of our minds. Now in the beginning of the creation of man this tree was a tree that differed from all others in man and was very like the tree of life. The fruits of this tree have been the foundation of all the philosophy of man ever since man was created.

Now as man's natural body contains the soil for this tree to grow, as the earth is the soil for the rest of the trees and herbs and creeping things that have life, it is the duty of man to investigate this tree and see what its fruits contain. The tree is to be known by its fruits. This tree is an idea like all other ideas in man, but differing in one peculiarity, happiness and misery. All the rest of the trees of knowledge contain right and wrong without any regard to happiness or misery. This is the difference between the trees.

Now as this tree can bear the fruits of other trees, it is another reason for its being cultivated, but to understand the tree or idea is to understand its fruits or thoughts.

I shall now call this tree an idea which contains happiness or misery and also truth and error. Now as error, like the serpent, is more subtle than any other idea in man, it acts upon the weaker portion of our thoughts and ideas, and engrafts them into the idea of happiness and misery. Now as this idea grows and sends forth its fruit, it is conveyed by error to other trees or ideas in others, and thus spring up false theories, false doctrines, etc. Now as this tree or idea sends forth such a variety of thoughts or fruit, it is like Joseph's coat of many colors, hard to tell what was the original color or idea. This throws man into darkness and doubt, and he wanders about, like a sheep without a shepherd, running after false ideas. Being blind he is not capable of judging for himself, and suffers himself to be led by the blind. Now as the tree of knowledge of good and evil was an idea of happiness and misery, it is easy to detect its fruits. All other ideas are spiritual and the fruits or thoughts are spiritual, and are not perceived till they come within our senses. We are very apt to get deceived by them, for they come like a thief in the night, when man is off his guard. Now as health and happiness is the greatest blessing that can be bestowed on man, and this was the original fruit of the tree, it can be very easily detected from the grafted fruit or ideas. The original fruit is spiritual and cannot be detected by the eye, for it does not contain even spiritual matter. Its qualities are sympathy, harmony and peace the fruit of the evil contains matter, and has form and can be seen and felt.

TO THE SICK IN BODY AND MIND

Dr. Q. has been induced by the great number of cases which have come under his care within the last twelve years, to devote his time to the cure of diseases. His success in the art of healing without the aid of medicine has encouraged many persons who have been suffering from sickness of long standing to call and see him for themselves. This has given him a very great advantage over the old mode of practice, and has given him a good chance to see how the mind affects the body. He makes no pretension to any superior power over ordinary men, nor claims to be a seventh son, nor a son of the seventh son, but a common every day man.

He contends there is a principle or inward man that governs the outward man or body, and when these are at variance or out of tune, disease is the effect, while by harmonizing them health of the body is the result. He believes this can be brought about by sympathy, and all persons who are sick are in need of this sympathy.

To the well these remarks will not apply, for the well need no physician.(1) By these remarks I mean a well person does not know the feelings of the sick, but the sick alone are their own judges, and to every feeling is attached a peculiar state of mind which is peculiar to it. These states of mind are the person's spiritual identity, and this I claim to see and feel myself.

When there is discord in these two principles, or inward and outward man, it seems to me that the outward man or body conveys to me the trouble, the same as one man communicates to his friend any trouble that is weighing him down. Now all I claim is this, to put myself into communication with these principles of inward and outward man, and act as a mediator between these two principles of soul and body; and when I am in communication with the patient, I feel all his pains and his state of mind, and I find that by bringing his spirit back to harmonize with the body he feels better.

The great trouble with mankind is this, they are spiritually sick, and the remedies they apply only serve to make them worse. The invention of disease, like the invention of fashion, has almost upset the whole community. If physicians would investigate mind a little more and medicine a little less, they would be of some service; but this inventing disease is like inventing laws: instead of helping man, they make him worse. Diseases are like fashions, and people are as apt to take a new disease as they are to fall in with any new fashion. Now if there was a law made to punish any person who should through any medical journal communicate to the people any new disease and its symptoms, it would put a stop to a great deal of sickness. Seven cases out or ten throughout the whole community of old chronic cases are the effects of false impressions produced by medical men, giving to the people the idea they have spinal disease, or heart or kidney or liver disease, or forty others that I could name, to say nothing of the number of nervous diseases.

Now all of these ideas thrown into the community are like so many foolish fashions which the people are humbugged by. I do not dispute but that any of these diseases may be brought about through the operation of the mind, but I do say if there was no name given to disease, nor its symptoms, there would not be one-tenth of the sickness there is at this day. I have taken people who have been sick with all of the above diseases, as they thought, and by describing their symptoms and state of mind without their telling me what the trouble was, and they have recovered immediately. A person sick is like a person in a strange land, without money or friends. Now there may be some one near by who would be glad to receive such persons, but they are ignorant of them. The sick are not in communication with themselves, nor any one else they feel as though no person could tell them how they feel.(2)

SPIRITUALISM AND MESMERISM

How does spiritualism differ from mesmerism? The word mesmerism embraces all the phenomena that ever were claimed by any intelligent spiritualists. The spiritualists claim that they get knowledge from the dead through living mediums.

Do not mesmerisers do this? Surely. Then what is the difference? In the ignorance of the people.

I will give some facts which have come under my own observation. When I first commenced mesmerising about sixteen years ago, the most of my experiments were of the following kind: after getting my subject in a mesmerised state I would try some simple experiment, for instance, imagine some person or animal which he would describe. I would then put him in communication with some person of the company, and let that person carry him to some place which he would describe. In these experiments it would often happen that he would get intelligence from some person of whom the company knew nothing. At other times the audience would like to have me send him after some one's lost friend. This I used to do but tried to make them understand that it was the reflection of their own thoughts.

In these experiments I had an opportunity to see and hear the different opinions and beliefs of mankind in regard to whether he really saw the person that he would describe or not. I found that my own opinion could have but little effect upon the mind of the audience. Their religious opinions would govern in most all cases. Sometimes when the experiments would embrace the friend of an infidel I would confuse him some; but I found that all persons were inclined to believe just about as their religious opinions were. I also found that my subject's religious opinions were just about like the person's opinions that he was in communication with.

If they professed religion to the world and were a hypocrite at heart, the subject would find it out, and the same was true of the subject. I had one subject who was very religious when awake, but when asleep was just the opposite.

I will here relate an experiment when on the Kennebec I had my subject in the sleep. I then requested any of the company to bring me the name of any individual dead or alive, and the subject would find him. A name was accordingly handed me. I passed it to the subject. He took the paper on which the name was written and read the name aloud. At this time the subject was blindfolded so that it was impossible for him to see with his natural eyes. I then told him to find the person. I will relate his own story.

He said, "This is a man." "Well," said I, "find him and talk with him." In a short time he said, "I have found him." I asked, "What does he say?" He answered, "He was a married man, had a wife and three children, was a joiner by trade; left his tool chest in a barn, and left between two days, went to Boston, stopped a time, left for the state of New York, worked there for three years, and then died; has been dead three years."

I told him to bring him here and describe him. He went on to give a general description of a man, and I told him that if there was anything peculiar in his appearance that differed from all others to describe it. "Well," said he, "there is one thing in which he differs from any one else in the room. He has a hair lip." This was the fact.

Now as there was no knowledge among the people of the principle by which this was done, the people were left to their own judgment. So I left them arguing, some trying to prove it. was the man's spirit, some calling it humbug and collusion. Others went away and told what they saw and heard.

This kind of experiment I was trying almost every day for over four years.

I then became a medium myself, but not like my subject. I retained my own consciousness and at the same time took the feelings of my patient. Thus I was able to unlock the secret which has been a mystery for ages to mankind. I found that I had the power of not only feeling their aches and pains, but the state of their mind. I discovered that ideas took form and the patient was affected just according to the impression contained in the idea. For example, if a person lost a friend at sea the shock upon their nervous system would disturb the fluids of their body and create around them a vapor, and in that are all their ideas, right or wrong. This vapor or fluid contains the identity of the person.

Now when I sit down by a diseased person I see the spiritual form, in this cloud, like a person driven out of his house. They sometimes appear very much frightened, which is almost always the case with insane persons. I show no disposition to disturb them, and at the last they approach me cautiously, and if I can govern my own spirit or mind, I can govern theirs. At last I commence a conversation with them. They tell me their trouble and offer to carry me spiritually to the place where their trouble commenced.

I was sitting by a lady whom I had never seen until she called upon me with her father to see if I could help her. The lady had all the appearance of dropsy. I took her by the hand. In a short time it seemed as though we were going off some distance. At last I saw water. It seemed as though we were on the ocean. At length I saw a brig in a gale. I also saw a man on the bowsprit, dressed in an oil-cloth suit. At last he fell overboard. The vessel hove to and in a short time the man sank. This was a reality, but it happened five years before. Now to cure the lady was to bring her from the scene of her troubles. This I did and the lady recovered.

I often find patients whose disease or trouble was brought on by religious excitement. I went to see a young lady during the Miller excitement. She was confined to her bed, would not converse with any person, lay in a sort of trance with her eyes rolled up in her head, took no notice of any person; the only thing she would say was that she was confined in a pit, held there by a large man whose duty it was to hold her there, and she said to me, "I shall never die, nor never get well." She had been in this condition for one year, refused all nourishment, and was a mere skeleton at the time I went to see her. This was her story when I got her so as to converse. I sat down by the lady, and in about an hour I saw the man she had created, and described him to her, and told her that I should drive him away. This seemed to frighten her, for she was afraid for my safety. But when I assured her that I could drive the man away she kept quiet. In three hours she walked to the door, and she recovered her health.

I could name hundreds of cases showing the effect of mind upon the body. Some will say it is spiritualism. Others will say it is not. When asked to explain where the difference lies, the only answer is, that the mesmeric state is produced by some other person than the subject, while the spiritualist is thrown into this state or trance by spirits. Now the fact is known by thousands of persons that this mesmerising oneself has been common ever since mesmerism has been known, therefore there is nothing new in that. So it is with questions put to any spiritualist.

Let us now examine the proof of its being from the dead. A person is thrown into an unconscious state: while in this state the spirit of some person purporting to come from the dead enters the body and addresses itself to the company, telling some story which the company knows nothing of.

When roused from the trance he is asked if he was con-scious of what he had been saying or doing. To this question they nearly all say, "No." The company is left in the same condition as in the mesmeric experiments. Some call it mesmerism, some spiritualism.(3)

LETTER TO A PATIENT

BELFAST, Nov. 4th, 1856.

Madam: Yours of the 2nd. inst. was received, and now I sit down to answer your inquiry in regard to your lameness. It seems to me that the skin on the knee is thinner and has a more healthy appearance. But you cannot be made to believe anything that is in plain contradiction to your own senses, and as your opinions have been formed from the evidence of persons in whom you have placed confidence, and facts have gone to prove these opinions correct, it is not strange that you should hold on to your belief till some kind friend should come to your aid and lead your mind in a different direction.

Now to remind you of what I tried to make you understand is a very hard task on my part; for as I said to you, some of my ideas fall on stony ground, and some on dry ground, and some on good ground. These ideas are in your mind like the little leaven, and they will work till the whole mind or lump is changed.

You have asked me many questions which time and space will not permit me to answer, but I shall write that which seems to be of the most benefit to you. In regard to your coming to Belfast, use your own judgment. The cure of your limb depends on your faith. Your faith is what you receive from me, and what you receive is what you understand. Now if you understand that the mind is the name of the fluids of which your body is composed, and your thoughts represent the change of the fluids or mind, you will then be in a state to act understandingly.

I will try to illustrate it to you so you can apply your thoughts to your body so as to receive the reward of your labor. As I told you, every thought contains a substance either good or bad, and it comes in and makes up a part of your body or mind, and as the thoughts which are in your system are poisoned, and the poison has come from without, it is necessary to know how to keep them [the thoughts] out of your system so as not to be injured by them.

Now suppose you have around you a sort of heat like the light of a candle, which embraces all your knowledge, your body being the centre and you having the power to govern and control this heat: you then have a world of your own. Now in health this globe of which your body is the centre is in harmony. The heat of this globe is a protection to itself, like a walled city, to admit none but supposed friends. Now as every person has the same globe or heat, each person is a world or nation of itself. This is the state of a person in health.

Now as we wish to change and interchange with other nations, so does our house like to enjoy the society of other persons, and as we are liberal we admit strangers to our city or world as friends. When this proclamation goes out our globe is filled with all sorts of people from all nations, bringing with them goods, setting up false doctrines, stirring up strife till the whole population or thoughts are changed, and man becomes a stranger in his own land and his own house-hold becomes his enemies. This is the state of a person in disease. Now as there is nothing in your own system of itself to disturb you, you must look for your enemies from the strangers whom you have permitted to come into your land.

TO A PATIENT

Mrs. Norcross.

MADAM : Yours of the . . . is at hand. But a lack of faith on my part to describe your case and explain my ideas to you so you could rightly comprehended my meaning is my only excuse for not writing before. But thinking you would expect an answer, I now sit down to talk with you a short time.

After reading your letter I tried to exercise all the power I was master of to quiet and restore your limb to health. But to give a satisfactory answer to you or myself was more than I was capable of. I therefore will disturb your mind or fluids once more, and try to direct them in a more healthy state by repeating some of my ideas which I repeated to you when here.

You know I told you that mind was the name of something, and this something is the fluids of the body. Disease is the name of the disturbance of these fluids or mind. Now as the fluids are in a scalding state, they are ready to be directed to any portion of the body. You remember I told you that every idea. contained this fluid, and the combination varied just according to the knowledge or idea of disease.

I will explain. Two persons are told they are troubled with scrofula. One does not know anything about it, and has never heard of the disease, is as ignorant as a child. No explanation is given to either. The other is well posted up in regard to all the bad effects of this disease. Now you can readily see the effect on the minds of these two persons. One is not affected at all till he is made acquainted with the case, while the other one's mind or fluids are completely changed and combined, so all that is necessary is to give direction and locate the disease in any part of the body.

I think I hear you say that a child can be troubled with scrofula, and they have no mind; then they have no body or fluids; for the fluids are the mind, as I said before. Your mother probably changed the fluids of your body, when an infant or at any early age, and some circumstance located it in your leg. Now as it is there you want to know how to get rid of it, and as it was directed there through ignorance you can't get rid of it without some knowledge.

Now as this disturbance comes like a fright or sensation, it is to be understood as a fright. Now as disease is looked upon as a thing independent of the mind, the mind is disturbed by every sensation produced upon the senses, and the soul stands apart from the disturbed part and grieves over it, as a person grieves over any trouble independent of the body. Now to cure you, you must come with me to where the trouble is, and you will find it to be nothing but a little heated fluid just under the skin, and it is kept hot and disturbed by your mind being misrepresented. (4)

Now I believe that I can impart something from my mind that can enter into that distressed state of the fluids and change the heat and bring about a healthy state. I shall often try to produce a cooling sensation on your limb, at other times a perspiration so as to throw off the surplus heat. If I succeed in helping or relieving you, please let me know. But do not expect another explanation. . . . If you think you would improve faster by coming to Belfast, please let me know, and I will get you a private boarding house, if desired. I think I can hear you say by this time that your limb feels better, if so I shall be satisfied.

MR. QUIMBY'S METHOD

It may be somewhat strange to you to hear something of the mode of curing disease by a person who does not believe in any disease independent of the mind. (5) I am acquainted with a person who does not give any medicine at all, and yet he is in the constant practice of curing persons afflicted with all diseases flesh is heir to. He not only discards medicine but disease also, contends that all disease is in the mind, and that the cure of disease is governed by a principle as much as mathematics, and can be learned and taught. His ideas are new, not like any person's I ever heard or read of, and yet when understood by the sick they are as plain and evident as any truth that can come within a person's senses. His ideas are compared to that which troubles the sick, not to persons well; for those who are well need no physicians. He is not a spiritualist as is commonly understood, believing that he receives his power from departed spirits. But he believes the power is general and can be learned if persons would only consent to be taught. (6) He has no mystery more than in learning music or any science which requires study and practice. It cannot be learned in a day nor in a month, yet nevertheless it can be learned. He has spent sixteen years [1840-1856] learning and yet he has just begun.

I will here state what has come within my observation. A friend of mine by the name of Robinsom, of N. Vassalboro, had been sick and confined to his house for four years, and nearly the whole time confined to his bed, not being able to sit up more than fifteen minutes during the day. Hearing of Mr. Quimby, for this is his name, he sent for him to visit him. He arrived at Mr. R's in the evening and sat down, and commenced explaining to Mr. R. his feelings, telling him his symptoms nearer than Mr. R. could tell them himself, also telling him the peculiar state of his mind and how his mind acted upon his body. His explanation was entirely new to Mr. R., and it required some argument to satisfy Mr. R. that he had no disease; for he had been doctored for almost all diseases.

His eyes were so swollen that it was impossible for him to see. His head had been blistered all over, and large black spots came out all over his body. Therefore to become a convert to his theory was more than Mr. R. could do. But Q. told him he stood ready to explain all he said, and not only that but to prove it to his satisfaction; for, said he, the proof is the cure, and R. was not bound to believe any faster than he could make him understand, and the cure is in the understanding.

So Mr. Quimby commenced taking up his feelings, one by one, like a lawyer examining witnesses, analyzing them and showing him that he [had] put false constructions on all his feelings, showing him that a different explanation would have produced a different result. In this way Quimby went on explaining and taking up almost every idea he ever had, and putting a different construction, till R. thought he did not know anything.

Mr. Q's explanation, said R. . . . "was so plain that it was impossible not to understand it. Not one of his ideas was like any that I ever heard before from any physician, yet so completely did he change me that I felt like a man who had been confined in a prison for life, and without the least knowledge of what was going on out of the prison received a pardon and was set at liberty. At about ten o'clock I went to bed, bad a good night's rest, and in the morning was up before Q. and felt as well as ever. Q. and I went to Waterville the next day. I had no desire to take to my bed, and have felt well ever since." This is R's own story.

[Quimby then goes on as if writing for a third person.]

I was well acquainted with Mr. R. and know these facts to be true. This is the case with a great many others where I was not acquainted with the parties, and I was induced to go to Belfast to see if he [Quimby] could talk me out of my senses, for I thought I had a disease. At least it seemed so to me, for I had had for the last ten years a disease which showed itself in almost every joint in my limbs. My hands were drawn all out of shape. My neck was almost stiff. My legs were drawn up, my joints swollen and so painful it was impossible to move them without almost taking my life. I could not take one step nor get up without help. It would be impossible to give any account of my suffering.

When I arrived at Belfast I sent for Mr. Quimby. He came, and after telling me some of my feelings said, "I suppose it would be pretty hard to convince you that you had no disease independent of your mind." I replied I had heard that he contended all disease was in the mind, and if he could convince me that the swelling and contraction of the limbs and the pain I suffered was in my mind, I would be prepared to believe anything.

He then commenced by asking me to move my legs. I replied that I could not move them. "Why not?" said he. Because I have no power to move them. He said it was not for the want of physical strength, it was for the want of knowledge. I said I knew how to move them but I had not strength. As he wished me to try, I made an effort, but without the slightest effect. He said I acted against myself.

He then went on to explain to me where I even thought wrong, and showed me by explaining till I could see how I was acting against myself. In the course of a short time I could move my legs more than I had for three years. He continued to visit me and I am gaining as fast as a person can. I have been under his treatment for two weeks, and I can get up and sit down very easily. I can see now that my cure depends on my knowledge. Sometimes he asks me if I want some linament to rub on my cords or muscles. I can now see the absurdity of using any application to relax the muscles or to strengthen them. The strength is in the knowledge. This is something that he has the power to impart. But how it is done is impossible to understand. Yet I know the knowledge he imparts to me is strength, and just as I understand so is my cure. (7)

Notes

(1) Dr. Quimby here changes from the third to the first person.
(2) Dr. Quimby's reference to "the last twelve years," would indicate that this "piece" was written between 1852 and 1855. It is his first statement concerning his spiritual method.
(3) Quimby gives evidence of his increasing clairvoyant and psycho-metric power in the above. This power made him more interiorly receptive than either a "medium" or a "subject," hence he had the clue to both. Moreover, he could cast out an obsessing idea.
(4) That is, in bondage to error. The sensation of heat under the skin has been misinterpreted.
(5) Dr. Quimby here speaks of himself in the third person.
(6) That is, it is from the infinite Spirit or Wisdom, as Quimby later called it; not from any "spirit."
(7) This is one of the first endeavors on Quimby's part to take up the point of view of a patient consulting him by showing how strange the new method seemed. It will be noticed that in his letters Quimby does not yet clearly distinguish between the mind, and the nervous activities and disturbed circulation of the blood. He needs an intermediate term to show that thought produces actual changes in the substance of the mind, and then subconsciously in the body. Later he uses the peculiar term "spiritual matter" to cover the activities which lie between, and says less about the changes in the "fluids." When he apparently identifies the mind with the fluids, in one letter, he is not then teaching materialism, but vaguely arguing for mental causation. The form "mind" is always used in a subordinate sense, with reference to that part of our life which is nearest the body. Dr. Quimby's higher term is "wisdom." Our wisdom is wholly distinct from the nervous "fluids" and troublesome mental states.

Chapter Eight - Contemporary Testimony

[Under date of July 8th, 1856, a former patient wrote a brief article entitled "An Important Discovery in the Healing Art," as if intending it for publication. The Ms. has been preserved, and from it we quote the following:]

THIS truly wonderful discovery is now practised by Dr. Quimby, of Belfast, a very respectable gentleman, for intelligence, agreeableness and integrity. He is able to cure without the use of medicine diseases which have baffled the skill of most eminent physicians. Of this we have evidence in his curing those who have been afflicted with sickness and pain for several years, without once knowing the cause of their sufferings, and were given up by their physicians as having a complication of diseases that were incurable. Having therefore to abandon all hope of a recovery and giving themselves up to die, they heard of Dr. Quimby and his successful mode of curing disease. Feeling no longer able to swallow the poisonous draughts administered for their relief, they with faith as a grain of mustard seed were at last induced to put themselves under his treatment. By the blessing of God they were in a short time healed of their infirmities. They also learned something of the nature and cause of disease, the effects of the mind upon the bodily functions, and how the mind may become a physician for the body, which is of more real worth than all the mines of

Golcond. For when in possession of this knowledge we learn to remedy our own ills, and no longer remain a prey to disease.

I now come to speak of myself and will give a short sketch of my own experience. For almost four years previous to my consulting Dr. Quimby I had been an invalid. In December, 1851, I contracted a violent cold, which brought on influenza, attended with a severe cough. Every part of me seemed wracked with pain, and it was with much difficulty I could move at all. This continued for some six weeks, when there was a change in my case which presented no favorable aspect. My physician was a man of considerable skill and experience, as I had received medical aid at his hand some two years previous, which produced the desired effect. I felt the fullest confidence that he would be successful a second time. But all his efforts proved unavailing, as the medicine I took only afforded me momentary relief. . . . My suffering at times was such as I shall not attempt to describe. I continued to take medicine, getting a little better and then worse until nearly two years of my sickness had elapsed . . . until August, 1854, when I was no longer able to walk, and obliged to lie down more than two thirds of the time . . . to the time of my consulting Dr. Quimby, October, 1855.

I had heard of his effecting wonderful cures in hopeless cases of long standing. Although I could not readily conceive the manner in which it was done, I did not doubt the truth of the assertion or think it absurd; but deemed it impossible for anything in like manner to be wrought in my case. I therefore listened with indifference to all I heard respecting his wonderful skill and superior knowledge until a few weeks previous to putting myself under his treatment. I had used every restorative recommended for my case, and all without benefit. I was at last compelled to give up trying, as it was only something simple I could take at all. I therefore concluded there could be no risk in applying to one who was represented to cure without the use of medicines, and hearing his mode of treatment spoken of in the best terms by many of the learned class.

I had the pleasure of seeing Dr. Quimby at my own home a few weeks before I was carried to Belfast. He gave me encouragement, said he could help me and soon enable me to walk again. This I thought was doing too much. I dared not believe. And yet I was impotent to know the truth . . . that I could not even fancy to be a reality . . . I set out on my journey with as much fortitude as could reasonably be expected of one so weak. . . I felt glad to lie down and rest myself after so fatiguing a journey. I was much dis-tressed, but wished to make as little ado as possible, for fear of alarming those who accompanied me.

Dr. Quimby made me a visit the same day, and expressed an opinion a second time that he could help me. In one week's time I was able by slight assistance from Dr. Quimby to walk down stairs. It was learning to walk a second time in life. I began to think, feel and act like a new being. Although I was very deficient in knowledge of the truth which was to set me free, I had already learned sufficiently to enable me to perform in one week what I had not done for the past fourteen months. I had never known what true happiness was before, so thankful did I feel for the pleasure of walking. Yet so sudden was the change and so speedy the recovery that it seemed like trying to do something altogether unnatural. During my stay at Belfast Dr. Quimby had more practice than he could well attend to, and several whose cases came under my own observation had long been considered hopeless were in a short time restored to their natural strength. By the leave of one young lady, Miss C., from Bucksport, I will narrate her sufferings and the help she received. She had been a sufferer for more than ten years, and had had fifteen medical attendants that were considered men of skill in their profession, who were at last obliged to admit her case as something which surpassed their knowledge of disease. She learning of my speedy recovery, desired to learn more particularly concerning it, and consequently came to see for herself. .: . Dr. Quimby examined her case and bid her be of good cheer, and thought he could help her. . . Strange as it may seem, in a little less than three weeks she was able to leave for home, and could walk two miles with much pleasure. She lives with a heart full of gratitude to God for the blessed means by which she was restored.

Ever since my return home my health has been improving, although very many thought my sudden cure was nothing to be relied on, and if I still persisted in taking exercise I might ere long be in as perilous a situation as when I first applied to Dr. Quimby. But they have become Convinced that it is reality, and think me almost a miracle in the history of disease. I have been able to attend a singing school during the past winter without experiencing the slightest injury. Permit me to say to those like myself when looking for a remedy that you have only to go to Dr. Quimby and "apply thy heart unto understanding, and thy ears to the words of knowledge. So shall the knowledge of wisdom be unto thy soul. When thou hast found it, then there shall be a reward, and thy expectation shall not be cut off."

I have deferred publishing this statement until the present time that all might know that I am now well, and suffer from none of my former difficulties, that I have recently gone to housekeeping and have "nothing to molest me, or make me afraid" as regards to my former difficulties. I desire always to bless the Lord, who has so wonderfully dealt with me, and also to express my deepest gratitude to Dr. Quimby, as the means employed to change my conditions. .

[A writer in the Bangor Times tells of the case of a Mrs. Hodsdon of Kenduskeag, who had been sick with a complication of diseases for two years. "Dyspepsia in its worst form, and a difficulty about the head, had utterly prostrated her, so that, for the two years, she had been unable to walk a step or to be moved in an upright position without fainting. Dr. Quimby called upon the sufferer, and in two hours the patient rose from her bed without assistance, seated herself in a chair and sat up two hours. She rested well that night, she steadily improved and in due time gained twenty pounds of flesh. All this came as the result of a single visit. The writer states that he has heard of other cases of remarkable relief, and he wonders what power there is behind Dr. Quimby's "gift." The testimony of others is mentioned regarding the "marvellous power" following Quimby's efforts. No theory is proposed, but the writer evidently agrees with one signing himself "Exeter" in the Bangor Jeffersonian, Feb., 1858, who declares that it is "too late an hour for the cry of 'humbug' in Mr. Quimby's treatment of disease. . . . People are beginning to inquire, 'Who and what is Dr. Quimby? By what strange agency does he cure disease which for years has baffled the skill of our most eminent physicians?'" Another newspaper writer of the period says,]

"We have been told that the 'age of miracles' is passed, but we have recently heard of several astonishing cures performed by a Dr. P. P. Quimby, which seem to border on the miraculous. How these cures are effected, it is impossible to say, as no visible means are employed. The most obstinate cases of disease have been made to disappear at the mere will, it would seem, of the Doctor. . . . Having heard of a remarkable recovery, we called on the patient, an intelligent young lady, who stated to us her case, and the manner of her cure, the facts of which she embodied, at our request, in the following letter."

PORTLAND, ME., August 29th, 1860.

Dr. Quimby, Dear Sir:

I have been sick since five years ago last July, having a great deal of pain in my back and limbs, "caused by blue pills taken two years before," physicians said, giving me "spinal disease." Very soon I was unable to walk, or even stand, and for months I was prostrate upon my bed and confined to a dark room, having neuralgia in the optic nerve, dyspepsia in its worst form, making me a great sufferer. After being for two years in the care of my uncle and brother, they decided medicine would not cure me, and took me to a Water Cure, at Hill, N. H. At this time I could not stand and was wheeled about in a wheel chair; my general health improved, and two years ago this fall I was able to walk about the room for two weeks only, and with this exception I have not walked in five years. The Water Cure physician decided there was no help for me there, concluding the spinal marrow was diseased.

Hearing of you, I set out at once to see you. Arriving at the United States Hotel in Portland, August 15th, A.M., I was carried up stairs to my room in my wheel chair, and in fifteen minutes after I saw you, Dr. Quimby, I was walking. I went down stairs to dinner without any assistance, and to my room again, and during the P. M., I took long walks of about forty steps and back again, and when you consider that in the morning of the same day, I could only stand for an instant, and take two or three steps with assistance, you will not wonder that I was wild with delight, or that I was to myself like one risen from the dead. The second day I walked on the street sixteen rods, and during the sixth day I walked four miles and a half, and in less than two weeks I walked into Portland from Falmouth, four miles. My disease is entirely gone, my back is perfectly well, and I have no fears of a relapse.

Yours with much esteem,

F. C. B.

Residence, Williamstown, Vt.

[To this testimony may be added that of Mr. Julius Dresser, restored to health by Mr. Quimby three months before and devoting himself to conversing with patients on "the Truth." Mr. Dresser saw Miss B. in her invalid condition, then walked and talked with her during some of the trips above mentioned, learning the facts of the case at first hand, and seeing that she was perfectly restored to health. The newspaper writer above quoted continues his account in the Evening Courier, Sept., 1860, as follows:]

Now, if this were a solitary case, we might ascribe the cure to the imagination, as it is well known that imagination has worked wonders in this way. But this is but one of a number of equally remarkable cases which have occurred here in our midst, and witnesses stand ready to bear testimony to the facts. One lady who had been severely afflicted with rheumatism, and for years was bent nearly double, a perfect cripple, unable to use her hands or feet, was in a short time restored to health, and is now a living, working evidence of the Doctor's skill. A gentleman, a friend of ours, had for years been afflicted with a hip complaint. He had for a long time been confined to his bed, and was brought so low his physicians had given him up, with the intimation he could live but a few days. It was purposed to call in Dr. Quimby. This the gentleman objected strenuously to, being bitterly opposed to anything like humbuggery, and the Dr. he considered one of the biggest of humbugs. His wife, however, insisted on calling in Dr. Q. He visited him and yesterday we met the patient on the street, going home to dinner, looking heartier than we have seen him for a long time. He considers himself entirely cured of the complaint. We told him people considered all these cures as humbugs. So did I, was his reply, but here I am, and if humbug can work such wonders, glory be to humbug, say I: and so say we. We might cite a dozen other cases, but we refrain. We have no other motive in mentioning these rare cures than to make our readers acquainted with the remarkable phenomena. We have but a slight acquaintance with Dr. Quimby, and have no interest in publishing his astonishing cures to the world. We have mentioned them as affording matters of curious speculation. We must confess there is something about them more than our philosophy ever dreamed of. (1)

[The next testimonial first appeared in the Lebanon, N. H., Free Press, and was then copied by other papers in Maine and New Hampshire.]

LEBANON, Dec. 3, 1860.

Just at the present time there is a good deal said about Dr. Quimby, of Portland, and it may not be considered amiss to mention the case of a young lady of this town who has been greatly benefitted by him. For nearly three years she has been an invalid-a great part of the time confined to her bed, and never left her room unless carried out by her friends. A few weeks since she heard of Dr. Quimby, and resolved to visit him. She did so, and after remaining under his care four days she returned home free from all pain and disease, and is now rapidly regaining health and strength.

The reputation of Dr. Quimby as a man who cures diseases has extended without the narrow limits of his own state, and the sick from various parts have learned to avail themselves of his services. The increasing respect and confidence of the public in his success suggests the day of miracles, and brings up a question as absurd as that of two thousand years ago, "Can any good come out of Nazareth?" Can actual disease be cured' by humbug? Dr. Quimby effects his cures without the aid of medicine or outward applications, and his practice embraces cases like the above, where all ordinary treatment has failed to relieve. These facts at first place him in the rank of the mysteries of a superstitious world, but there are few of his patients after a second interview who do not think the mystery is in them and not in him. . . . It is here that Dr. Quimby stands, his explanation and his cures go hand in hand. While his senses [intuition] are penetrating the dark mystery of the sick, he is in com-plete possession of his consciousness as a man. Not fearing to investigate the operation of the mind, be penetrated the region [where] nothing but magicians, sorcerers, witchcraft and spiritualists have ventured, and going far beyond them in his experiments, he arrived at the knowledge of the principle regulating happiness.

Therefore his curing disease is perfectly intelligent and is in itself a new philosophy of life. The foundation of his theory . . . is that disease is not self-existent, nor created by God, but that it is purely the invention of man. Yet it is so firmly established in our belief, and substantiated by so much wisdom that its existence as an independent entity is never questioned. In his treatment he makes a complete separation between the sufferer and the sickness; for the latter he has no respect, and while he is battling or destroying the faith or belief of which it is made, he respects the intelligence of the patient, which he leaves free and unchained.

It is impossible in a brief communication to do anything like justice to Dr. Quimby's system. Enough has been said to separate him from quacks and imposters. The case cited above is not a solitary instance of his skill in practising his science, and his increasing popularity with all classes shows that the confidence of the public is not misplaced.

ONE WHO HAS BEEN RELIEVED.

[Having heard that Quimby had restored a woman who had been dumb, an interested reader reported the results of investigations he had been prompted to make concerning this cure, which occurred during the same year, 1856, the patient being a daughter of Capt. Blodgett, of Brooksville. The patient had been suddenly deprived of her speech two years before.]

No cause was known, and the fact excited a melancholy surprise in herself. . . . She had not been sick . . . nor had any trouble of mind or body been known to have produced speechlessness. . . . One evening her speech was observed to be slightly impaired. She retired as usual, and on waking in the morning she found herself utterly speechless. From that time . . . she had not uttered an audible word. . . She is now in full possession of her former powers of speech. . . . One physician attributed the cause to a sort of paralysis of the vocal organs. ['The best medical aid had been sought without avail]. . . .

Mr. Q. says he employs no medicine of any kind for any complaint he is called upon to treat. His theory is . . . that all diseases of the body are caused by a derangement of the mind! And that the cure of all diseases may be effected, theoretically, by a restoration or rectification of the mind of the invalid, to its natural, proper condition. He has this faith, and when he succeeds in imparting it to the patient, the disease vanishes and the whole person is restored to harmonious natural functions. His formula of faith is confessedly that of the Saviour and the woman who touched the hem of his garment and became whole. The operation is purely mental. Mr. Q. discards this scriptural fact as a "miracle," but regards it as natural, as properly reproductive by those who have the right idea of diseases and their cure, and who have the faith to attempt to relieve human suffering. . . . He refrains entirely from any manipulation over the patients, such as are generally known to be the accompaniments of mesmeric experiments. He neither puts them to sleep nor biologizes them, but takes them as he finds them . . . explains the method he proposes for a cure. . . This is the way in which he says he restored this young lady to the power of speech with no other application but the power of his speech upon her mind. . . We have no reason to doubt the material statements in this case. . . . Mr. Quimby is not a "spiritualist" in any sense of the term. [Interest in this case led to the reporting of another instance by the same writer, that of a Miss Buker, afflicted with a hip disease, the conditions being described in much detail. In an utterly hopeless condition she consulted Mr. Quimby in Belfast, and the account continues as follows:]

She began immediately to improve, and has grown better every week to a wonderful degree. The disease has measureably departed from the hip, and the leg has resumed almost its natural length and strength. She threw aside her crutches a week or two ago . . . and now she walks with considerable ease and no pain, with the aid of only a small cane in one hand. She lifts her foot with ease, and bears her whole weight upon it momentarily while walking-a thing which until within a few weeks she had not been able to do for fifteen long years. The reader may imagine the enthusiastic congratulations in which she indulges at the cheering prospect she now has of being completely restored to health. She is apparently in the enjoyment of a new life.... Dr. Quimby has used no medicine or material appliances whatever, inter-nally or externally-he has not even seen nor touched the part afflicted. All he has done has been by acts of volition, conversing with his patient daily for about six weeks, "teaching her," as he says, "the use of her limbs and how to walk." He feels confident that he has obtained the mastery of the disease . . . he got the mind and most of the body of the patient on the winning side. He believes that their mutual "faith" will yet make his patient "whole." "He says he is not performing a miracle" but a "cure," by the exercise, in a novel way, of those powers of intellect and reason with which the Creater has endowed him in common with all intelligent beings. [This eminently fair-minded man appeals to his readers to visit the patient if so inclined and see for themselves while the actual process of restoration to health is going on.]

[More convincing to some will be the testimony of F. L. Town, assistant Surgeon, U. S. A., Louisville, Ky., who, in a communication over his own signature, March, 1862, wrote to a Portland paper concerning his observations and knowledge of the experience of a patient under Quimby's care. The editor, in introducing the letter says, "The Doctor himself came to the International Hotel . . . an invalid, so feeble that he had to be assisted in getting into the door, and afterwards to his room on the second floor. He was so terribly dyspeptic that he could eat no solid food, nor could he swallow cold water. . . . The Doctor left completely cured, in about six weeks from his coming to visit Mr. Quimby. . . . About the facts of the Doctor's remarkable cures there is no doubt; but there may be question about how they are done." Dr. Town's communication is as follows:]

Mr. Editor: I believe you have some knowledge of Dr. Quimby of the International and his peculiar mode of practice. By a chain of unforeseen circumstances. I have been led to know something of Dr. Q. and the modus operandi in the treatment of his patients. With a broad faith in the virtue of men I believe him to be an honest man in his profession, who practises as. he believes, and would not intentionally deceive anyone. His treatment is peculiar to himself and independent of all systems or forms of practice whatever. For that pretentious class, who in the guise of spiritualists, clairvoyants, and all other charlatans who with no previous study, or knowledge of the power or effect of the medicines they prescribe, seek to humbug communities . . . he has as little esteem, and holds himself as sensitively separate from them as the most orthodox practitioner. He has no sympathy or connection with them. Neither is his practice more nearly allied to that of the regular practitioner. He gives no medicine. . . .

The patient will find him unassuming in his manners, and no more ready to talk of his successes than other men of theirs. . . . He will explain to you his way of practice, give you the benefit of his treatment, entertain you with stereoscopic views of his theory or belief, and end off perhaps by explaining a few passages of Scripture. However, a man's belief is one thing, and his success in practice is another; this alone wins a favorable opinion and wise confidence. There can be no doubt that Dr. Q. has been the means of doing much good, as many patients from their homes, now in the enjoyment of health, are willing to testify. In some instances his treatment has been attended by the most unexpected and happy results, affording great and immediate relief, when hope almost had failed. These are not isolated cases, but none the less wonderful.

I will briefly relate the history of the following case, in which the ties of near consanguinity awakened the liveliest sympathy, and the happy termination of which was the cause of equal surprise and pleasure. A member of our family had, while in that transition period between happy childhood and budding womanhood, gradually lost the power of walking or standing, and for a number of years (some five or six) was wholly unable to make any use of her limbs whatever. There was no deformity, nor any discoverable lesion, but weakness, and all attempts to use them were attended by such excessive pain that they had to be given up. During this time she was confined exclusively to the house, as the jar of a carriage could not be borne; and often the tread of an incautious foot across the floor was productive of pain. She was visited by some of our most skilful practitioners, men of acknowledged ability and professors in popular colleges. They expressed a belief that in time a recovery might be hoped for.

Several years passed, and time brought no healing on its wings, but new causes of suffering. Her disease began to assume a much graver type-the eyes became morbidly sen-sitive to light, which increased to such an extent that the least degree of light seemed unbearable. The shutters were closed, curtains were drawn, and heavy blankets followed, tacked closely over the windows. The digestive powers became much impaired. The stomach, in failing to perform its office, sympathized with the rest of the system. . . . For five months the only nourishment that could be borne . . . was a few cups of milk and water drank during the twenty-four hours. In darkness, helpless and unable to take any proper food, she wasted away till she was but the shadow of her former self. Greatly prostrated and seemingly emaciated to the last degree, scarcely a hope was left for recovery.

Through the earnest representation of friends, Dr. Quimby was employed, certainly with the least expectation of any benefit. We were little prepared to witness the surprising and gratifying amendment that attended his visit.

The relief afforded was immediate, entire. All pain and irritation ceased, and the patient was convalescent. Light again began to shed its cheering rays through the room, for six months darkened. The digestive powers increased, and she was able to eat simple food. The use. of her limbs returned; and under a more generous diet, and as new strength gave power to them, she was able to walk. In a few months her weight more than doubled.... At that time, stopping at a distant city, I soon came home to witness these happy results. How great was the change! ... Like a child, she was again learning to walk. The hue of health was chasing from the cheek the pallor of sickness, whilst her returning smile and speaking eye told of the happiness within. Her whole aspect showed that she was indeed a new being.

Save an occasional drawback, which a visit of a few weeks to Dr. Q. set all right, she has steadily mended to the present, (nearly two years). The eyes are still troublesome, but improving; otherwise her health is apparently confirmed.

Other cases equally remarkable have come to my knowledge, whose history and symptoms were every way different. It is apparent that his influence is not confined to one class of diseases, and in no case could one safely predicate whether or not relief might be expected. However, all may not hope to be set at once in the broad highway to health....

Considering the means employed, and the diversity of the cases, Dr. Q.'s success is remarkable-whether it depends more upon the man, or he acts upon the first principle of that which, when better understood, shall be recognized as a new remedial agency ... time will tell.

These few remarks are made as an act of justice to Dr. Q.... Let us then in the exercise of Christian charity, if plain facts are before us, and we find an individual who can alleviate the pains of a single sufferer, strew flowers in his pathway through life, accept them as a verity and bid him Godspeed.

[Writing under the head of "The Art of Healing," another interested observer, signing himself "H.," communicates to the Portland Advertiser, Feb. 1860, his conclusions in the case of Quimby's practice. He says in part:]

Every theory admitting evil as an element cannot annihilate it. If disease is ever driven out of existence, it must be by a theory and practice entirely at variance with what we now put our trust in.... In every age there have been individuals possessing the power of healing the sick and foretelling events.... Spiritualists, mesmerists, and clairvoyants, making due allowance for imposition, have proved this power is still in existence. Like this in the vague impression of its character, but infinitely beyond any demonstration of the same intelligence and skill, is the practice of a physician who has been among us a year and to whose treat-ment some hopeless invalids owe their recovered health.

I refer to Dr. P. P. Quimby. With no reputation except for honesty, which he carries in his face and the faint rumor of his cures, he has established himself in our city and by his success merits public attention... He stands among his patients as a reformer, originating an entirely new theory in regard to disease and practising it with a skill and ease which only comes from knowledge and experience. His success in reaching all kinds of diseases, from chronic cases of years' standing to acute disease, shows that he must practise upon a principle different from what has ever been taught. His position as an irregular practi-tioner has confined him principally to the patronage of the ignorant, the credulous and the desperate, and the most of his cases have been those which have not yielded to ordinary treatment. (2)

[In introducing the following letter to the Portland Advertiser, the editor says; "We publish this morning a communication over the name of 'Vermont,' from a very intelligent young lady who, with her mother, was a boarder at the International Hotel during the most of last winter. The mother was a lady, we judge, of about fifty years, and the daughter about twenty. The mother had been treated for scrofula, which her physician thought was incurable. The daughter was simply afflicted with general debility. Both left restored to health. The lady, whose voice was restored, lost it nearly three years since by scarlet fever, and during that whole time had not spoken."]

One of the most noticeable characteristics of the present time is a growing distrust in the virtue of medicine, as in itself able to cure disease; and this state of the public mind- this demand for some better mode of treating the sick has either created or finds ready an army of new school prac-titioners of every possible kind, some sincerely desirous of doing good and firmly believing what they profess, while others are only too willing to impose upon credulity and benefit themselves thereby. Under such circumstances it would be extremely difficult for a true reformer, who not only sees the errors of the past and present, but dares to take entirely different views even of the origin of disease, to acquire for himself a reputation distinct from the many who also profess to have advanced far in the new paths they have chosen, though in reality having started from the same point that all others have in times past, they will in the end arrive at nearly the same conclusions. Even great success in the practice of his theory, might for a time be insufficient to establish public confidence, and prevent his being ranked with all the innovators of the day.

[This states in an admirable way precisely the difficulty Quimby encountered, classified as he was with humbugs, spiritualists, magnetic healers, and the like, although radically different from them. This writer goes on to say:]

Many people who have lost faith in the ancient school, are at the same time startled by such reasoning as Dr. Quimby uses with regard to disease. It is so contrary to the commonly received opinions, they hardly dare believe there can be any truth in it. They hear of remarkable success in his practice, but are then still more incredulous and say, 'The age of miracles has passed away, and this is too much to believe.' But 'seeing is believing' ... and after having opportunity to see some of the remarkable effects which Dr. Quimby has had upon obstinate cases of long standing disease, they are compelled to yield, though it may be reluctantly, that there is living truth in his principles-that he has cast off the shackles of opinion, which would narrowly enclose the limits of investigation.... They came to him suspicious, almost unwilling to believe what they saw, ignorant of his theory which, even after it was explained, they found difficult to understand, and therefore had to go through with this process of gradual conviction before they would receive its truths. So it may be said that he has to contend with those who would be his friends, as well as with his enemies.

The following outline of his theory was written after having passed through a similiar change of feeling, and may give some general idea-though a very imperfect one- of the principles which are so effective in opposing disease.

According to this new theory, disease is the invention of man. It is caused by a disturbance of the mind-which is spiritual matter [or substance]-and therefore originates there. We can call to mind instances where disease has been produced instantly by excitement, anger, fear or joy. Is it not the more rational conclusion that disease is always caused by influences upon the mind, rather than that it has an identity, and comes to us and attacks us?

Living in a world full of error in this respect and [educated] to believe that disease is something we cannot escape, it is not strange that our fear comes upon us. We take the opinions of men which have no knowledge in them for truth. So we all agree to arbitrary rules with regard to our mode of life, and suffer the penalties attached to any disobedience of the same. These diseases or penalties are real to us though they are the results of our own belief.

It is reasonable to infer from these statements that the only way to approach and eradicate disease must be through the mind, to trace the cause of this misery and hold up to it the light of reason, or disbelief in the existence of disease independent of the mind. Then the cloud like shadows vanishes as error always will when overpowered by the light of truth.

Dr. Quimby proves the truth of this belief by his daily works. The marvelous cures he is effecting are undeniable evidence of his superior knowledge and skill in applying it for the benefit of suffering humanity. He does not use medicine or any material agency, nor call to his aid mesmerism or any [spiritistic] influences whatever; but works upon scientific principles, the philosophy of which is perfectly understood by the patient, therefore [the patient] is not only rid of the present trouble but also of the liability to disease in the future. . . .

Accepting this new theory, man is placed superior to circumstances, easily adapting himself to any necessity. Free from all fear, he lives a more simple, natural and happy life. He is enabled to control the body and make it subservient to his will, instead of his being a slave, completely at its mercy, which he will be if he allows that it is subject to disease.

This truth is capable of extensive practical application in all the exigencies of life, and we learn to make constant use of it as we advance in knowledge. It helps us to place a just estimate upon everything, the value of life is enhanced, and as we have more of this true knowledge in ourselves we shall love and worship God, who is the source of all wisdom, more sincerely and intelligently.

[The following was inserted as an advertisement in a Portland, Maine, paper, Feb. 3, 1861, in gratitude for the work Dr. Quimby was doing.]

THE ANNIHILATION OF DISEASE

Disease is the great enemy of life. Even those who are free from it admit that they are liable to it and are in constant fear of the danger.

It is quite a new idea that disease cannot only be eradicated but annihilated, and might be questioned were it not daily proved by the practice of Dr. P. P. QUIMBY, of Portland, Maine, who has discovered an entirely new method of curing disease upon scientific principles, without the use of medicine or any material agency: also, without the use of mesmerism or any spiritual (3) influence whatever. He is constantly curing the more desperate cases of disease-paralysis, consumption, neuralgia yield to his control, and the deaf, blind and lame are made whole by a philosophy which is perfectly intelligent to themselves, and is able not only to rid them of present trouble, but also from the liability to disease in the future.

These statements are made without the knowledge of Dr. Quimby, for the benefit of any who, suffering from disease, have failed to find relief, and are left. without hope of finding assistance, by one who has been in that condition, but was saved by his cure from despair and death.

Dr. Quimby has, after years of patient investigation, discovered this new principle in metaphysics, which cannot fail to interest the well, and is of incalculable importance to the sick. But his superior knowledge and skill in applying it to the cure of disease is accompanied by such rare modesty of character that he has never taken any means to make himself known to the world, and therefore he is only known within the limits of the influence which his patients may hold in society.

As a token of gratitude to him, as well as for the benefit of any who may be suffering from disease, he is thus un-hesitatingly and publicly recommended.

[The name of E. Chase, Portland, is appended in ink to the following testimonial, clipped from the Portland Advertiser, 1860:]

Reader, did you ever see Dr. Quimby? You have heard of him. As a Doctor he is nondescript. He ignores all material medicines. He does not give the infinitesimal atoms of Homeopathy or bread pills. He repudiates all spiritual medicineship as he does the whole catalogue of pills and liquids recorded in the M. D.'s Materia Medics. These he asserts are all humbugs, and the works of darkness.

His patients come from the four winds of heaven . . . no, not from the South. The Doctor is a strong Union man; and would as soon cure a sick rattlesnake as a sick rebel. He has patients from all parts of New England, the Middle States, and the West. And his patients are all from the wealthier and educated classes. He has a large practice in this city and neighborhood. Most of his patients get well under his curative process, which differs from all other modes and theories of medical practice. (4)

We have been boarding at the International Hotel, in this city, during the last six weeks, and we have witnessed some remarkable cases; as have all the regular boarders. We express no opinion about the modus operandi; except to say positively that the Doctor's practice, if it do not cure, can do no possible harm, as he gives no medicines.

[The Portland Evening Courier also took to reporting instances of Dr. Quimby's cures and giving space to articles by patients. Some of the latter were by Mrs. Eddy, then Mrs. Patterson, and are reprinted in another chapter. Mrs. Patterson's sonnet, also quoted elsewhere, was called out by the striking cure of Capt. Deering. Commenting on this cure, a writer in the Courier says:]

Persons who know but little of the theory or practice of Dr. P. P. Quimby are constantly misrepresenting both. The Doctor has received hundreds of testimonials as to the permanency and wonderful nature of his cures. The following statement from Capt. John W. Deering, of Saco, written by himself, will have great weight with those who know Mr. Deering, and it is published as much to refute statements made by some interested persons to the effect that the Doctor acts as a spirit medium and mesmeriser, as for the testimony it offers in support of the healing power which the Doctor claims to exercise, even in cases called chronic, and given over by old-school physicians.

[The editor also takes pains to say that this wonderful cure, one of many equally remarkable and astonishing cures which have come to his knowledge, is evidence of Quimby's theory, as "original and entirely distinct from spirit mediums and mesmerisers. . . . Below will be found Capt. Deering's statement."]

"Early in August, 1862, I was attacked with a slight pain in the small of my back, and immediately my right leg commenced drawing up, so that in ten days, while standing on my left foot, I could but just touch my right leg on the seat of a common chair. All this time I suffered great pain in my knee pan. I was attended by two of the best physicians in York County, who applied blisters, leaches, and cappings to my right thigh, with no effect except to increase the pain.

"I became entirely discouraged, when I heard of Dr. P. P. Quimby; and after many solicitations on the part of my friends I yielded to their entreaties and visited him. After an examination, he told me that the cause of my difficulty was a contraction of the muscles about the right side. Physicians that I had previously consulted had treated me for disease of the hip. Almost despairing of a cure, but willing to gratify the wishes of my friends, I remained in the Doctor's care. Without calling on the spirits of the departed for aid, without mesmerism and without the use of medicines of any kind, he succeeded in completely restoring the muscles of my side and leg to their proper functions, and I am now as well as ever. I visited Dr. Quimby under the impression that he was some mysterious personage who had acquired a great reputation for curing diseases, and who must exercise some kind of mesmeric control over the will and imagination of his patients. But I am convinced that he is a skilful physician, whose cures are not the result of accident, but of a thorough knowledge and application of correct curative principles." (5)

SACO, Jan 8, 1863.   JOHN W. DEERING

[It is interesting, also, to note the zeal with which some took up the idea of absent treatment as a perfectly intelligible process in contrast with the difficult explanation offered by spiritists. The following is from a communication addressed to the editor of the Courier by a writer who signs himself, C. C. Whitney:]

"As spiritualism seems to be to many the only way of accounting for all phenomena of the present day, I thought it might be of some interest to your readers to state a case that came under my own observation, and I will leave the public to judge of the manner in which it was done.

"Two years ago last March, I sent to Dr. Quimby to visit my wife, then living in Wayne, in this state, who had been confined to her bed for over a year, and unable to lie on her left side, or raise herself in bed.

"The Doctor replied that he could not visit her in person, but would try an experiment, and wished me to keep him informed of his success. His plan was that on my receiving his letter be would commence to operate on her [absently,] and continue his visits till the next Sunday, when he would, between the hours of 11 and 12, make her walk. I received this letter Wednesday, and that night she was very uneasy and nervous, and the next day, Thursday, she was more comfortable, and turned over on her left side, a thing she had not done for nearly a year. She continued improving, and [I] sent the Doctor letters informing him of his success. On Sunday, not expecting her to rise, I attended church, and on my return I found her up and dressed. Between the hours of 11 and 12 she arose from her bed and walked across the room, returning to the bed, and then walked out into the dining room, and the next morning she took breakfast with the family, and continued to improve" (6)

[The letter goes on to say that the patient suffered a partial relapse a year later, and her husband, being in Portland, called on Quimby for help; the help was given without informing the wife, and her husband reports that it was with success according to Quimby's predictions. Evidently, there had been no opportunity in this case for Quimby to converse with the patient and give her advice regarding her health. The editor, commenting on the above instance, thinks it invites explanation from those who would attribute it to spiritistic influences. The editor was much impressed by the genuineness of the explanation offered by Quimby in such cases, namely, that it was intelligent use of therapeutic power, not the agency of spirits; for he learned from a woman in Lancaster, N. H., that at the time appointed by Quimby for visiting Mrs. Whitney absently, Quimby, then in Lancaster, remarked that he "must go to Wayne to visit a patient." After retiring to the parlor for an hour, Quimby returned and said he had "got the lady up from her bed, and that she walked, and three persons were present in the room who witnessed it. Upon writing Mr. Whitney, it was found that he and two friends, who had accompanied him home from meeting were present at that time, and saw her walk." This again shows the clarity of Quimby's perception at a distance, also the fact that what he gave as facts could be verified.

A writer in another Portland paper, name and date not given in the scrap-book, after pointing out the usual misconceptions gathering around Quimby's name and declaring that Quimby is "always conscious of what he says and does," adds that]

"He takes as a starting-point that disease was never created by God, but has been made by the false opinions which have been given and believed by man, and he contends that disease can be cured by simply explaining to the patient wherein he has been deceived. . . . He says that if he cures at all he knows how he does it, and that all the power he exerts is simply in what he says to the patient, while sitting with him. [This of course involved the silent realization known as a treatment.] . . The Doctor also contends that if he can cure an individual case . . . he can produce the same effect by addressing himself to many at the same time. He has [the intention] of publishing his ideas at some future time, and also the idea of treating disease publicly, when he feels that the people are ready.

[It will be noticed that the writers in the above excerpts from the press uniformly speak of the fact that Dr. Quimby practised according to a "new principle," not by giving medicine or by making any material applications, and not by the use of mesmerism or spiritism. These excerpts have not been selected and published here because they are favorable, but because they are frank statements of Dr. Quimby's practice as it impressed contemporary observers. The newspaper ex-cerpt which shows the least understanding of Quimby's practice is the following from the Bangor Jeffersonian, 1856. This excerpt was republished in "The Philosophy of P. P. Quimby," 1895. When the writer quoted below uses the term "animal spirit," he is using his own term, not Quimby's, for this term was not employed by Dr. Quimby. What Quimby taught was that the false ideas and mental imagery causing the disease were directly impressed on the plastic substance of the mind, which included what we now call the subconscious. Quimby did indeed find the soul, (not the "animal spirit,") partly disconnected from the body in certain extreme cases, when the patient lay at the point of death, and he conversed with the soul, or, as he says in most of his writings, "the scientific man." The statement quoted below shows that it was difficult for some observers to under-stand what Quimby meant.]

A gentleman of Belfast, P. P. Quimby, who was remarkably successful as an experimenter in mesmerism some sixteen years ago, and has continued his investigations in psychology, has discovered, and in his daily practice carries out, a new principle in the treatment of disease. . . . His theory is that the mind gives immediate form to the animal spirit, and that the animal spirit gives form to the body. His first course in the treatment of a patient is to sit down beside him and put himself en rapport with him, which he does without producing the mesmeric sleep. He says that in every disease the animal spirit or spiritual form is somewhat dis-connected from the body, and that when he comes en rapport with a patient, he sees that spirit form standing beside the body; that it imparts to him all its grief, and the cause of it, which may have been mental trouble, or a shock to the body, or over-fatigue, excessive cold or heat, etc. This impresses the mind with anxiety, and the mind reacting upon the body, produces disease. . . . With this spirit form Dr. Quimby converses, and endeavors to win it away from its grief, and when he has succeeded in doing so, it disappears, and reunites with the body. In a short time the spirit again appears, exhibiting some new phase of trouble.

[The following is one of the last newspaper references to Dr. Quimby and his work in Portland, after he had announced his intention of retiring from his practice there, that he might revise his writings for publication. It was written by a former patient.]

It is with feelings of surprise and regret that many of your readers receive the announcement, given in your advertising columns, that Dr. P. P. Quimby has determined to leave Portland. The Doctor has been in this city for nearly seven years, and by his unobtrusive manners and sincerity of practice has won the respect of all who know him. To those especially who have been fortunate enough to receive benefit at his hands-and they are many-his departure will be viewed as a public loss. That he has manifested wonderful power in healing the sick among us, no well-informed and unprejudiced person can deny. Indeed, for more than twenty years the Doctor has devoted himself to this one object, viz., to cure the sick, and to discover through his practice the origin and nature of disease. By a method entirely novel, and at first sight.

quite unintelligible, he has been slowly developing what he calls the "Science of Health;" that is, as he defines it, a science founded on - principles that can be taught and practised, like that of mathematics, and not on opinion or experiments of any kind whatsoever.

Hitherto he has confined his efforts to individual cases only, seeking to discover in them what disease is, how it arises, and whether it may not, with the progress of truth, be entirely eradicated. The results of his practice have been such as to convince him that disease, that great enemy to our happiness, may be destroyed, and that, too, on grounds and by a method purely rational; and he goes from us not to abandon the cause, we are rejoiced to learn, but to enter a broader field of usefulness, wherein he hopes not only to cure, but as far as he can, to prevent disease.

The path he treads is a new one and full of difficulties; but with the evidence he has already given, in numberless instances, of his extraordinary ability in detecting the hidden sources of suffering, we are led to hope he may yet accomplish something for the permanent good of mankind. An object so pure, and a method so unselfish, must, when understood, claim the favorable attention of all. We bid him God speed.

Notes

(1) The editor 'of a Lowell, Mass., paper prints a communication from Miss B. in which she gives the same facts cited above, and says, "The young lady who sends us the following . . . has relatives in this city whom she has recently visited. We have no question of the entire truthfulness of her statements, which we have heard orally and with more particularity." The communication is dated Oct. 22, 1860.

(2) This communication was reprinted in full in "The Philosophy of P. P. Quimby," p. 25.

(3) i. e. spiritistic.

(4) The writer puts in his own opinion when he speaks as if Quimby had only wealthy and educated patients. This was not true. According to his own statement above, "medical" should be omitted in the last sentence.

(5) What most impressed people who, like Capt. Deering, supposed Quimby would undertake to exercise some mesmeric control over their wills, was the fact that after making his intuitive diagnosis and giving his silent treatment he would put his patients in command of the curative principle and aid them to help themselves the first moment possible. This convinced them that he was no charlatan but a genuine friend to the sick.

(6) This case shows the clearness with which Quimby discerned a patient's condition at a distance, also his skill in telling how long his absent work would take before the patient would be up and about.

Chapter Nine - Letters From Patients

NORTH VASSALBORO, May, 26th, 1850.
Dr. P. P. Quimby,

DEAR SIR: I shall address you as the good Samaritan who came along and took me by the hand and opened my understanding, and took my disease from me in so remarkable a manner that I can say, Blessed be the name of the Lord for raising up such a servant as you are. It seems to me as though you took my disease, for it has never returned. But still I have many bad feelings to contend with, even to wrestling all day to the going down of the sun. I am still able to come out victorious over all bad feelings, for my health has been improving ever since you came to our house. I am now ten times as well as any living man could have supposed. I am able to walk over a mile a day without much inconvenience. [I have] only to think for a moment of the good Samaritan taking me by the hand and putting me on the road to health. . . . Only to think of my being almost four years a bed-keeper and now so well! Why, it is nothing short of a miracle. You can imagine how I am enjoying everything, sun, moon, earth, every living thing, never looked so grand, so beautiful or sublime. . . .

Your fame is still sounding as on the wings of the wind. Many questioners are asking about you. . . . I am saying it is the only true way whereby man can be healed. I am daily preaching your doctrines to the children of men. . . . I hope by strict attention to your rules to remain well.

[The letter concludes with references to sick people in the neighborhood who need Quimby's treatment. The writer describes the maladies he labored under for years and the difficulties he encountered in travelling about and overworking. His statements indicate that he is a man well along in years, and that he has now taken a new start in life, with the realization that he is in possession of an intelligible principle to live by. Quimby early began the practice of treating silently at a distance. The following extract is with regard to a woman who was clairvoyant enough to see Quimby in the case of one of his mental visits.]

Last Friday evening, Oct. 3rd, between 7 and 10 o'clock, mother and a niece of hers, who is here on a visit, were sitting together talking, and this lady says she saw you standing by mother, about to lay your hand on her head. Just at that moment mother left the room, before her friend had told her what she saw, so your visit was interrupted. What was quite strange was that this lady described some of your characteristics, in looks and appearance, very accurately, although you have never been described to her. Mother wishes to know if you were really here in spirit at that time.

[Fortunately, a letter was preserved in which Quimby, under date of Oct. 3rd, wrote to the patient in question that he would visit her on that day, the day he was seen by the stranger. This letter was not sent and the patient did not therefore know that Mr. Quimby expected to visit her in spirit at that time. But it is evidence that the visit was real on Quimby's part, and that it coincided with the time his presence was perceived by the stranger. In a letter written five days later, responding to the above, Quimby makes another appointment, adding, "If that lady is still with you, I will try to make myself appear to her eyes next Sunday, between 7 and 8 o'clock." This was in the days when it was still important to prove beyond all doubt that a person's presence could actually be perceived in this way, at an appointed time. Some would regard the instance in which Quimby was seen by a stranger without prearrangement as more significant than in the case of his plan to make himself "seen" at an appointed time.

The impression produced by some of Quimby's more remarkable cures is indicated by a letter dated, Exeter, Feb. 18, 1858, in which the writer, David Barker, speaks of the case of a Mrs. Crane, who is described as "perfectly happy and free from all pain and care." The writer goes on to say that the house is thronged by people anxious to witness a miracle, for a greater miracle was never performed since Christ raised Lazarus." A few days later, writing to Dr. Quimby, Mr. Barker says:]

Whether by accident or not, you performed as great a miracle in my mother's case as in Mrs. Crane's. You will remember stopping there with my brother two weeks ago tomorrow night and examining her ankle, which was so badly broken eleven years ago. She has only stepped on her toes since, and that with the aid of crutches. Her foot was nearly straight on a line with her ankle. Immediately after you left she found that the contracted cords in her foot were all relaxed, and that she could put her foot square upon the floor and walk well without the aid of crutch or cane. She was at my house today, and although nearly seventy years old she convinced me that you had given her the use of her foot by dancing a regular "pigeon's wing." The whole country is crazy to have you visit us again.

[Several letters were written to substantiate the case of Maria Towne, of Lancaster, N. H. The first is from her father and bears the date of March 18th, 1860:]

My daughter was attacked with lameness and unable to walk, nine years last December. The physicians called it a disease of the hip, and treated her for the same. She partially recovered in six months. In ten or twelve months she appeared to be quite firm. Five years last September she had another attack in the hips and limbs that has given her severe pain up to this time, and baffled the skill of our physicians. . . . She has constantly been under the care of the best medical aid.

Last August she was attacked with a weakness in the eyes, and unable to see; had been kept in a dark room since the twenty-fifth of August. She has subsisted for the last six months on the value of from four to two teacups full of milk in twenty-four hours. She has not walked any for the last five and a half years, with the exception of a few steps five years ago this winter.

Through the solicitation of a friend, we sent for Dr. P. P. Quimby of Portland, who came to her Saturday evening, March 17, at 9 o'clock. The next day at one P. M., she got up from her chair alone and walked ten feet without assistance. She can now bear some light in the room, and begins to see quite well. She walked from her room to the dining-room with very little help this evening, to tea, and ate quite a hearty meal without causing her any pain.

[The second letter, signed Harriet F. Towne, is apparently from the mother, and is dated March 21, 1860.]

Dr. Quimby

Thinking you would like to hear from Maria by this time, I hasten to inform you that she is in fine spirits, can have a little more light in the room; but cannot hold her eyes open any longer than when you were here. . . . She is all courage and walks a little every day, and enjoys her food very much. Maria wants to hear from you soon. Please write if that lady in Wayne walked last Monday, and if you come here often.   Maria imagines you do. (1)

[The third letter is from the father, under date of April 1, 1860:]

Dr. Quimby,

Dear Sir: Maria gains strength a little every day. She has gained in one week ending last Thursday two and a half pounds in weight. She walks across the room six or eight times in a day with a little help. Her appetite is good. Her eyes grow stronger, she can have considerable light in the room. . . . There are several here that are anxious for you to see them. One man that is very much troubled with the phthsic wanted me to ask if you had any control over that disease. . . .

[Then follows a letter from the patient herself who, after a visit to Dr. Quimby in Portland, writes concerning the one trouble now remaining, her eye-trouble, which she says is extremely obstinate. She finds that the eyes are better only when she is under Quimby's direct influence. Feeling entirely dependent upon her restorer for health and happiness, she is eager for more help from him. It was Quimby's endeavor to put his patients in possession of the healing principle so that they would not depend upon the "influence" they felt while sitting by him or receiving absent help; but this was a question of time, especially in the case of trouble with the eyes.

A patient who had been restored to health in a remarkably short time after years of invalidism in which she had been unable to walk, writes as follows after returning from Portland:]

HILL, N. H., Oct. 27, 1860.

My dear Doctor

How I do want to see you. I am well and happy. You can't imagine how the people stare at me here at the Water Cure. Dr. Vail thinks he will come and see you. I talk as much of your Science to him as I know how to. I wish I knew more. I want you to prove to me mind is matter, so I can to them. . . (2) I went to see one of the old-school doctors. He is coming to see you and see if he can learn your way. He . . . greatly rejoices with me. . . . I can't make the religious part go. I can't understand it. It doesn't seem to suit me. I go to church, though the preaching does not always suit me, to prayer meetings, and I pray as I used to. What do you think of me ? (3)

My uncle and brother, doctors in Lowell, were so anxious and had so many fears for me that I had to get out on the street soon as I could and go off on a walk four miles long. I went just as fast as I could, some of the time running, until all the fears were gone. They make my back feel strangely (the fears), and I can't seem to sit as erect.

I will send all I can to you. I will start some from this vicinity. I am a great sight to the people. . . . There are many more people ready to receive this theory than I had supposed. My uncle and brother did not seem to get any clue to it, and said they did not know what to think of it....

It does seem good to walk, and my heart is full of gratitude to you and God. I am so glad I went to see you. I can't express it.

[Nearly a year later, writing from Wilmington, Ills. this patient expresses the thought that her restorer has helped her since she left home, although she has had little to meet save homesickness. She says in part:]

I wish you would take away that longing for the East, at those times when I feel I would give all to see Dr. Quimby. I try to think you are not far away. I like to think of that place by you which is mine. I laugh over the "sittings" I had with you, don't you? when I think how dreadfully distressed I was lest you were wanting to cast me out of the way to give room for new friends. How funny that you should know how I felt all the while. How you can understand the feelings hidden within others are entirely ignorant of, appears to me quite mysterious. When I consider what you have done for me and others, and that you are continually doing greater and greater cures, I conclude I cannot tell what may not be done, and that you possess a knowledge far superior to any other person I have known or heard of. I am glad I ever came to you, almost glad I was sick to need your assistance, that I might know and feel these things. When one is raised from a long illness to perfect health, as it were instantly, do you not realize what a healthy person cannot? Would they want to help feeling glad, and that the man who did such a splendid thing for them was the nicest, best man in the world?

It does me good to know the Science is being appreciated, that you are successful. . . . I want to know if a knowledge of mind acting on mind will enable one to control an ungovernable child without using any means of punishment, and what you do in the next world with profane, drunken, stealing, murdering men-people commonly sent into eternal punishment?

I wish I could tell you how I feel. But it is the same as when I sat with you: an undefinable longing for something.

[Another letter of the same year begins by raising a problem:]

I wonder if everything that occurs through life that makes me sad has got to make me sick. Can't you tell me something about it, and give me some good fatherly advice? Something quite unpleasant has occurred since I was in Chicago that gave me a great deal of trouble night and day, and I find myself out of fix. . . .

Doctor, I often get your picture and I imagine I have regular sittings with you. They do me good, I do believe. But the picture is not equal to the live man.... You know the gratitude of my heart better than I can express it.

[Other letters written from time to time indicate that the cure was permanent, although there are slight matters requiring her healer's advice. Writing from her old New England home four years after she was cured, Miss X. says that everybody remarks how strange it is that she is so well. She also says:]

I have never lost a moment from sickness since I have been in school, nearly two years. I walk six and eight miles in a day, very often. . . . I feel so thankful I am well. If it had not been for you I would have been in my grave or much worse off long before now. I cannot tell you, Dr. Quimby, how much I think of you, and love you for what you have done for me. . . . When I went to school in Chicago my friends said in less than three months I should be sick. I wrote you and you said you would not let me, and I have not been. Now I want that knee of mine cured up. . . .(4)

[Another series of letters, dating from 1860 to December 25, 1864, begins with the description of the patient's case, a fibrous tumor about to be operated upon and other conditions as diagnosed by competent physicians, and traces the results from time to time, as the patient reports her progress. She, too, experiences difficulty in avoiding the recurrence of old symptoms, for her case was well known, the doctors are sceptical, sometimes angry, and she must maintain her faith against opposition. At times she can hardly call herself well, and so writes to Dr. Quimby to express her difficulties and receive his advice or help. The following letter is typical of those written to express gratitude:]

PLYMOUTH, Oct. 17th, 1858.

Dr. Quimby,

MY PRESERVER AND FRIEND: With feelings of gratitude and kind respect, I will write you, and inform you that I am able to walk as well as ever I could, a pleasure which I could not have enjoyed had it not been through your unceasing and untiring care and treatment. Words will not express my thankfulness to you, kind Dr., for the pleasures I am permitted to enjoy. When I contemplate my past helplessness, and know that to you I am indebted for all I do now enjoy, my heart is ready to burst in gratefulness.

I continue to improve in walking day by day, as you told me [I would], and now I can run up and down stairs (not as fast as you can, because you are so spry) but as well as most any one else. My friends receive me with wonder depicted upon their countenances, I assure you, to see me walking all by myself, was a joy to them indescribable, and believe me their whole tribute of praise is tendered to you. With all love and respect, I remain,

Your young friend, E. C.

Notes

(1) The "lady in Wayne" was one whom Quimby treated absently while in Lancaster attending Miss Towne. Such cases were interest-ing to patients as well as to onlookers, because they gave evidence of the great healer's power to make himself felt at a distance, and this was a new phenomenon in those days.

(2) That is, prove that mind is susceptible to opinions, leading to changes in the body, as Quimby explains in his writings.

(3) This is typical of people who tried to return to their old ways after coming in touch with Quimby and sensing his religious spirit. Quimby's emphasis was on good works, not on doctrine, and he directed attention to the Divine presence with all men as guiding Wisdom.

(4) These letters indicate that the chief difficulty encountered by former patients who depended solely on the new Science was in avoid-ing old fears and other mental associations readily called up when meeting sceptical friends.

Chapter Ten - Letters to Patients

PORTLAND, Feb. 9th, 1860.
To a Patient in Hill, N. H.

Your letter apprised me of your situation and I went to see [absent healing] if I could affect you. I am still trying to do so, but do not know as I can without sitting down and talking with you as I am at present. So I will sit by you a short time and relieve the pain in your stomach and carry it off. You can sit down, when you receive this letter, and listen to my story and I think you will feel better. Sit up straight. I am now rubbing the back part of your head and round the roots of your nose. I do not know as you feel my hand . . . but it will make you feel better. When you read this, I shall be with you: and do as I write. I am in this letter, so remember and look at me, and see if I do not mean just as I say. I will now leave you and attend to some others that are waiting, so "Good evening." Let me know how you get along. If I do not write, I may have time to call for that does not require so much time." P. P. Q.

PORTLAND, Feb. 9th, 1861.
To Mr. S.

Your wife's letter was received, and I was glad to learn you were all so much better. But your wife says you still cough: this is necessary for your cure, for you have no other way to get rid of that heat in the head called catarrh. Now, this heat seems to be a mystery to every one: everybody acknowledges it and tries to account for it. Some call it nervous, but when asked to explain that they fly to some other error.

'This letter shows what intimate connection Dr. Quimby established mentally with patients whom he treated absently. The reference to rubbing the head was to show that the absent help applied directly where needed. This tended to strengthen faith.

You know I told you that mind was spiritual matter. In order to illustrate my meaning so you will understand it, I will make use of an illustration that Jesus used. He said, when the skies are red, you know it will be fair weather. Now thought is something and this acts in space. For instance, the body is nothing but a dense shadow, condensed into what is called matter, or ignorance of God or Wisdom. God or Wisdom is all light. Your identity [consciousness] acts in these two elements, light and darkness, so that all impressions are [subconsciously] made in this darkness or ignorance, and as the light springs up the darkness disappears. One of these elements is governed by Wisdom, the other by error, and as all belief is in this world of darkness, the truth comes in and explains the error. This rarifies the darkness and the light takes its place. Now as this darkness is all the time varying, like the clouds, it is necessary that man should be posted about it as he would about the weather. For our happiness in this world depends a great deal on the weather. For the wisdom of man has got so far from the truth that even the weather is our enemy, so that we step out as though we were liable to be caught by a cold, and if we are then comes the penalty. All this error arises from ignorance. So to keep clear of error is to know who he is, how he gets hold of us, and how we shall know when he is coming.

To make you understand I must come to you in some way in the form of a belief. So I will tell you a story of some one who died of bronchitis. You listen or eat this belief or wisdom as you would eat your meals. It sets rather hard upon your stomach; this disturbs the error or your body, and a cloud appears in the sky. You cannot see the storm but you can see it looks dark. In this cloud or belief you prophesy rain or a storm. So in your belief you foresee evils. The elements of the body of your belief are shaken, the earth is lit up by the fire of your error, the heat rises, the heaven or mind grows dark; the heat moves like the roaring of thunder, the lightning of hot flashes shoot to all parts of the solar system of your belief. At last the winds or chills strike the earth or surface of the body, a cold clammy sensation passes over you. This changes the heat into a sort of watery substance, which works its way to the channels, and pours to the head and stomach.

Now listen and you will hear a voice in the clouds of error saying, The truth bath prevailed to open the pores and let nature rid itself of the evil I loaded you down with in a belief. This is the way God or Wisdom takes to get rid of a false belief: the belief is made in the heavens or your mind, it then becomes more and more condensed till it takes the form of matter. Then Wisdom dissolves it and it passes through the pores, and the effort of coughing is one of Truth's servants, not error's: error would try to make you look upon it as an enemy. Remember it is for your good till the storm is over or the error is destroyed. So hoping that you may soon rid yourself of all worldly opinions and stand firm in the Truth that will set you free, I remain your friend and protector till the storm is over and the waters of your belief are still.
P. P. Q.

PORTLAND, Feb. 8th, 1861.
To Miss S., Hill, N. H.

Your letter was received and I was sorry to learn that you thought you took cold. Perhaps you did, but you know all of my patients have to go through the fiery furnace to cleanse them of the dross of "this sinful world," made so by the opinions of the blind guides. Remember that passage where it says, "Whom the Lord loveth he chasteneth." As Truth is our friend, it rids us of our errors, and if we know its voice we should not fear, but receive it with joy. For although it may seem a hard master, nevertheless it will work out for you a more perfect health and happiness than this world of error ever could. So listen to it and I will try to set all things right.

Of course you get very tired, and this would cause the heat to affect the surface as your head was affected, the heat would affect the fluids, and when the heat came in contact with the cold it would chill the surface. This change you call "a cold." But the same would come about in another way. Every word I said to you is like yeast. This went into your system like food and came in contact with the food of your old bread or belief.   Mine was like a purgative, and acted like an emetic on your mind, so that it would keep up a war with your devils [errors, and they will not leave a person, when they have so good a hold as they have on you, without making some resistance. But keep up good courage and I will drive them all out so that you may once more rejoice in that Truth which will free you from your tormentors or disease. If you will sit down and read this letter, take a tumbler of water and think of what I say, and drink and swallow now and then, I will make you sit up so you will feel better. You must be [silent and receptive] just about as long as you used to be in Portland. Try this every night about nine o'clock. This is the time I shall be with Mr. and Mrs. S. You know that where two or three are gathered together in the name of this Truth, there it will be in your midst and help you. So try it and see if it does help you. If you do, let me know.

Hoping this letter will be of some comfort to you and the rest, I remain your true friend and protector till you are well, if I have the Science to cure you. So I leave you for the present and attend to others.(1)
P. P. Q.

PORTLAND, Feb. 8th, 1861.
To Mr. S.
In answer to your letter I will try to explain the color you speak of . . . so that you will forget it. Give me your attention while I explain. You know I told you about your stooping over: this stooping is caused by excitement affecting the head. This contracts the stomach, causes an irritation, sending the heat to the head. This heat excites the glands about the nose, it runs down the throat and this is all there is about it. It will affect you sometimes when you are a little excited, and you will take it for a cold. Remember how I explained to you about standing straight. Just put your hands on your hips, then bend forward and back.

This relaxes the muscles around the waist at the pit of the stomach. This takes away the pressure from the nerves of the stomach and allays the irritation. Now follow this and sit down and I will work upon your stomach two or three times in three or four days. It will affect your bowels and help your color. Tell your wife to sit down and give her attention and I will affect her in the same way. Please take a little water when you are sitting, say about 9 o'clock in the evening. . .(2)
P. P. Q.

PORTLAND, Feb. 9th, 1860.
To Miss K., Kennebunk, Me.
Your letter of the 5th is received. I am surprised that you do not remember that all my patients have "a cold" as they call it, when the belief is [of this character]. For instance, if you are told you have "consumption," this belief is matter under the direction of error, and as it is put into practice it changes the mind, so that the idea of consumption is thrown off from the belief. If you are excited by any other belief, you throw off all the misery that follows your belief. For instance, you are made to believe you are not so good as you ought to be: your belief puts restrictions on your life, and as it is a burden to you, it makes you throw off a shadow that contains the punishment of your disobedience. This makes you another char-acter, and you are not the happy child of Wisdom.

This was your belief when you called on me. As I struck at the roots of your belief with the axe of Truth, everything having a tendency to make you unhappy I tried to destroy.

So in the destruction there must be a change. This change must be like its father. So if you had grief, it would produce grief for the present. Finally the Truth would dry up your tears and you would rejoice in that Truth that sets you free.

So in regard to the "cold": if you had the idea of "consumption" when I drove that enemy of man out of your belief, this must produce a like cough, but it is all for the best. Remember that every error has its reaction, but an unravelling of error leads to life and happiness, while the winding it up leads to disease and misery.

All that is taking place in your case is just what I anticipated. SO it is all right. Keep up good courage and all will come out right. Tell Miss F. to keep good courage her cure is certain.(3)
P. P. Q.

PORTLAND, March 3, 1861.
To Miss T.

Your letter of the first was received. . . . I will now give you a short sitting and amuse you by my talk. But as you seem to want your head cured I will rub the top of it, and while doing this I will tell you what makes it feel so giddy.(4) You know I have told you, you think too much on religion or what is called religion. This makes you nervous, for it contains a belief, which contains opinions and they are matter, i. e. they can be changed. If opinions were not anything, they could not be changed. . . . All [so-called] religion is of this world and must give way to Science or Truth; for truth is eternal and cannot be changed. . . . So you see according to the religious world I must be an infidel. Suppose I am. I know that I am talking to you now does the Christian believe in [this talking with the spirit] ? No. Here is where we,differ.

Eighteen hundred years ago, there was a man called Jesus who, the Christian says, came from heaven . . . to tell man that if he would conform to certain rules and regulations he could go to heaven when he died; but if he refused to obey them he must go to hell. Now of course the people could not believe it merely because he said so . . . so it was necessary to give some proof that he came from God. Now what proof was required by the religious world? It must be some miracle or something that the people could not understand. So be cured the lame, made the dumb speak, etc. The multitude was his judge and they could not account for all that he did: then he must come from God. Now does it follow? . . . I have no doubt that he cured. But his cures were no proof that he came from God, any more than mine are, nor did he believe it. . . Jesus was endowed with wisdom from the scientific world or God, not of this world. Nor can he be explained by the natural man. . . . His God fills all space. His wisdom is eternal life, with no death about it. He never intended to give any [theological] construction to his cures; [they] were for the benefit and happiness of man. Men were religious from superstition, their religion was made of opinions, and as these were the light of the mind the opinion or light contained an idea: when the idea is lit up, it throws its rays and our senses [consciousness] being in the rays, they are affected by the idea. As their ideas affected the people, they were like burdens grievous to be borne; so the people murmured. . Jesus knew all this. No man was able to break the seal or unlock the secret of health. . . . Wisdom, seeing the groans of the sick, acted upon this man Jesus and opened his eyes to Truth. Thus the heavens were opened to him. He saw this Truth or Science descend, and he understood it. Then came his temptations: if he would listen to the people and become king they would all receive him. This he would not do. But to become a teacher of the poor and sick would be very unpopular. . . . He chose the latter, and went forth teaching and curing all sorts of diseases in the name of this Wisdom, and calling on all men everywhere to repent, believe, and be saved from the priests and doctors who bound burdens on the people. . . .
Hoping this will settle your head and make you easy on the subject of another world.
P. P. Q.
PORTLAND, March 3, 1861.
To Mrs. D.
In answer to your letter I will say that you know I told you that your disease was in your mind. Now your mind is your opinion, and your opinion is that you have scrofulous or cancerous humour. . . . This opinion shows itself in your system. . . . As I change this something or opinion, it must change the effect, . . . and in the change it will produce these feelings, because it is in the fluids. As this change goes on it must affect your head and also your side, and it ought to affect your stomach. This will bring on a phenomenon like a cold . . . this carries off all the false ideas and relieves your system of that bloat and heat. Keep up your courage. It is all right.(5)

PORTLAND, March 3rd. [1861].
T o Mr. R.
When your letter was received I went to your relief, but I cannot say that I affected you. But now I will sit down and try to affect your stomach so that you will not want to smoke. I feel . . . that if you were aware of the evil influence of the enemy that is prowling around you, enticing you to smoke, you would not harbor him one moment; but hurl him from you as you would a viper that would sting you to the heart. I know that opinions are something and they are our friends or our enemies. So the opinion you have of smoking is a false one and is an enemy to you. It is subtle like the serpent that coils around you like a boa constrictor till you feel its grasp around your chest, making your heart palpitate and sending the heat to your head. Then you will struggle to rid yourself of his grasp, till overpowered you become paralyzed. He will laugh at your folly when your fear cometh. Remember that "love casteth out fear," and fear hath torment. Science is love. Fear is disease: torment is your reward. So watch lest he enter your house while you are asleep and bind your limbs, and when you awake find yourself bound hand and foot. So remember what I say to you as a friend. P. P. Q.
March 3rd, 1861.
To Miss G.
I will now sit down and put on paper what I did at the time I received your letter. I went to you [in spirit] at that time and have visited you at times ever since. I wish now to let you know that I am still with you, sitting by you while [you are] in your bed, encouraging you to keep up good spirits and all will go right. If you cough, it is to get rid of the heat that has gone to your head.   P. P. Q.

March 10th, 1861.

T o Miss B.

Owing to a press of business I have not had time to answer your letter until now, but I often see you [in spirit] and talk to you about your health.(6) I feel as though I had explained to the spiritual or scientific man the cause of your trouble, which I may not have made plain in my letters to the natural man. But it may sometimes come to your senses, or you may see me: then I can tell you what I cannot put on paper. As for the cause affecting you now: I feel as though I had removed the cause, and the effect will soon cease, and you will be happy and enjoy good health. I wait to hear that my prophecies have fulfilled. But I shall keep a lookout for your health till I hear you say that you are well.

P. P. Q.

March 10th, 1861.

To Miss S.

In answering your letter I will say that I have used my best efforts to help you, and I feel as though I had [succeeded]. Now I will once more renew my promise not to forsake you in your trouble, but to hold you in the influence of this great Truth that is like the ocean. While your bark is tossed by the breeze or storms of error and superstition, while the skies are dark with error and you are moved by your cable or belief, feeling as though you may be blown on to the rocks of death, you may look to that Truth that is now beating against the errors and breaking them in pieces, scattering them to the winds and even piercing the hardest flinty hearts, grinding them into pieces. This Truth shall shine like the sun and burn up all these errors that affect the human race.

So be of good cheer and keep up your courage, and you shall see me coming on the water of your belief and saying to the waters or pain, "Be still," soothing you till the storm is over. Then when the sun or Truth shall shine, and the pure breeze from heaven spring up, slip your cable and set sail for the port of health, there to be once more in the bosom of your friends. Then I will shake hands with you and go exploring for some other bark that is out in the same gale.

P. P. QUIMBY.

March 10th, 1861.

To Mrs. W.

I have not been able to answer your letter until now. But I have often . . . talked to you. How much you have been aware of it, I cannot say. But I now see you and your husband sitting looking as easy as possible. I shall visit you as an angel, not a fallen one, but one of mercy, till you are able to guide your own bark.

It is true your husband can travel the briny deep, but he has never entered this ocean of this higher state. . . Our belief makes our bodies or barks, the sea is troubled, error is the rocks and quicksands where we are liable to be driven by the cross-currents while the wind of error is whistling in our ears. . . . Now keep a good lookout and you will see the breakers ahead. So brace up and see that your compass is right. Keep all snug and fast. Remember what I told you . . . not to lose control of yourself, but stand on deck and give your orders, not in a whining way, but bold and earnest. Then your crew will obey your orders. You will steer clear of all danger and land safe in the port of health.(7)

P. P. QUIMBY.

PORTLAND, March 19th, 1861.

To Mr. A.

Your change of mind when you got your religion was the effect of error, not of Truth. So you worship you know not what. But I worship I know what, and "whom you ignorantly worship, him declare I unto you.". . . This same Christ, whom you think is Jesus, is the same Christ that stands at the door of your dwelling or belief, knocking to come in and sit down with the child of Science that has been led astray by blind guides into the wilderness of darkness. Now wake from your sleep and see if your wisdom is not of this world. . . . To be born again is to unlearn your errors and embrace the truth of Christ: this is the new birth, and it cannot be learned except by desire for the truth, that Wisdom that can say to the winds of error and superstition "Be still!" and they will obey.

It is not a very easy thing to forsake every established opinion and become a persecuted man for this Truth's sake, for the benefit of the poor and sick, when you have to listen to all their long stories without getting discouraged. This cannot be done in a day. I have been twenty years training myself to this one thing, the relief of the sick. A constant drain on a person's feelings for the sick alters him, and he becomes identified with the suffering of his patients: this is the work of time. Every person must become affected one way or the other, either to become selfish and mean, so his selfish acts will destroy his wisdom . . . or his wisdom will become more powerful. . . .

It is not an easy thing to steer the ship of wisdom between the shores of poverty and the rocks of selfishness. If he is all self, the sick lose that sympathy which they need at his hand. If he is all sympathy, he ruins his health and becomes a poor outcast on a charitable world.   For the sick can't help him and the rich won't. (8)

[Whenever in his letters to the sick Dr. Quimby speaks of spiritism we find him sceptical concerning alleged messages from the "dead." In one letter he says, "As my mode of treating disease is entirely new to the world, the spiritualists claim me as a medium. I deny this, but believe that mind acts on mind, and that it is the living, and not the dead; so here is where we differ" He then goes on to tell about a woman who was greatly misled by an unscrupulous medium. The result was so serious that the woman left her husband in a fit of jealousy, and when Dr. Quimby was called had tried to take her own life by cutting her throat. After hearing all sides of the case, and finding the woman virtually insane, Dr. Quimby sat by her to restore her, her state being so violent that he had to hold her by main force. After four or five hours she was brought to her senses and so quieted that she fell asleep. Then followed Quimby's explanations to both husband and wife, showing how they had been misled, the explanation was convincing and a complete reconciliation followed. This instance shows the thoroughness with which Quimby searched matters out to the end. He endeavored to give a complete substitute for spiritism by showing how one mind can mislead another.]

[Sometimes Quimby declined to take cases of certain types, inasmuch as he was working alone and had the force of public opinion against him. What he says with reference to blindness in a letter to an inquirer in 1861, is significant. He says, "I should not recommend any one like your description to come to see me, for I have no faith that I could cure him. If a man is simply blind I have no chance for a quarrel, for we both agree in that fact. But if a person has any sickness which he wants cured and is partially blind besides, then I might affect his blindness, but that is thrown in. I never undertake to cure the well and if a man is blind and is satisfied I can't find anything to talk about; if I undertake to tell him anything he says, Oh! I am all right but my eyes. So he is spiritually blind and cannot see that his blindness had a beginning . . . I refuse to take such cases till my popularity is such that my opinion is of some force to such persons; for opinions of popular quacks are law and gospel about blindness, and so long as the blind lead the blind they will both fall in the ditch."]

[When asked if he could cure any one using intoxicating liquors, he answered by considering all matters involved. Quimby did not undertake to judge a man simply because he drank. For he wrote, "I judge no man. Judgment belongs to God or Science, and that judges right, for it contains no opinion. Giving an opinion is setting up a standard to judge your neighbor by, and this is not doing as you would be done by." He goes on to say that if some one under condemnation as a criminal who has taken to drink comes to him, he pleads his case by tracing every factor to the foundation. Convincing the man that he has been misled by his enemies and has taken to drink to "drown his sorrows," Quimby brings him to his reason, the victim of persecution abandons his old associates, and is ready to change his habits. But, says Quimby, "if he likes smoking or drinking, he is satisfied and wants no physican. If [he is] sick and I find that liquor is his enemy, then it is my duty to tell him so. If I convince him, he has no more difficulty." Quimby's caution in indulging in any opinion of his own is indicated in a letter, dated April 10, 1861, in which he says:]

An opinion involves more responsibility than I am willing to take. Moreover, an opinion is of no force . . . and it might do a great deal of harm. I always feel as though disease was an enemy that might be conquered if rightly understood. But if you let your enemy know your thoughts, you give him the advantage. Therefore I never give the sick any idea that should make them believe that I have any fears Making health the fixed object in my mind, I never parley nor compromise. Once when your sister remarked she never expected to be perfectly well, I replied that I never compromised with disease, and as she had been robbed of her health I should not settle the case except on condition of the return of her health and happiness. . . . When your sister came to me I found her in a very nervous state from the fact that she had lost her sister and expected soon to follow her. This made her very nervous and stimulated her to that degree that she appeared to be quite strong. As I relieved her fears she became more quiet. This she took for weakness. But every change has come just as I told her it would. [Thus Dr. Quimby gradually brought his patient into the affirmative attitude, so that she could see for herself.]

[Again, Quimby wrote as if conversing with his patient and meeting objections point by point, while still carrying on the treatment. Thus he writes to one not yet convinced of the efficacy of absent help:]

I will now sit down by you as I used to, for I see I am with you, and talk to you a little about your weak back. You forgot to sit upright as I used to tell you. Perhaps you cannot see how I can be sitting by you in your house, and at the same time be in Portland. I see you look up and open your eyes, and I hear you say, "No, I am sure I cannot, and I do not believe you can be in two places at the same time." I hear you think, not speak. . . . If you [understood], you would not doubt that I am now talking to you. . . . I have faith to believe that I can make you believe by my Wisdom. So I shall try to convince you that although I may be absent in the idea or body, yet I am present with you in the mind. . . . If you know that I am here, [in the case of present treatment] you attach your [thought] to the Christ or Truth and if you believe this you are saved from the uncertainty of seeing me in the body.

[Writing to another patient not quite clear on this point, Dr. Quimby states that when he receives a letter he always feels as though he were spiritually with the patient giving advice. Sometimes he seems to be present with several patients at once, because so many have come to him and are thinking of him. So, he says:]

I make a sort of general visit, as I used to when you were all in my office. But if I feel certain of one I make that one a text to preach from. So I believe if you can make yourself known to me by your faith I can feel you. Since I commenced writing you have come up before me so that I now recall you perfectly well, and I will give my attention to you.

[Speaking of his effort to convince a patient of "this great Truth," Dr. Quimby writes:]

When I say this great Truth I mean this light that lighteth every one that understands it. When I first sit by you, my desire to see you lights up my mind like a lamp. As the light expands, my [spiritual] senses being attached to the light, each particle of light contains all the elements of the whole. So when the light is strong enough to see your light in your darkness or doubts, then I come in harmony with your light, and dissipate your errors and bring your light out of your darkness. Then I try to associate you with . . . a substance that is separate and part from your senses.

[In still another letter on the same subject Quimby says that sometimes he cannot see a patient when he reads the letter asking for help, because the "errors" obscure his sight. The spiritual self in a person possesses spiritual light, independent of matter. But this is so associated with matter in the average person that it becomes attached to it. In its pure operation his light sees through matter in its various combinations. Common education has placed a barrier between people. Superior intelligence is required to see through this obstacle. To communicate with the spirit in person is to endeavor to reach that part which interiorly sees and hears and is independent of time and space. This part of ourself is not known by the natural man, in his dependence on ordinary sight and hearing. It is imprisoned by "the error of common belief." This belief is under the direction of people who are unaware that there is an intelligence independent of the body. Quimby shows that he wishes to talk with that part of the self which does not believe in the adverse suggestions to which one becomes subject through ignorance. If he can make himself felt apart from common means of communication, this experience will show that the self really possesses these higher powers. If his patient hears his inner voice, she should not put a false construction upon it or become frightened and close the inner door. For he must convince her that her supposed friends are her enemies, those who tell her "with long hypocritical faces and whining tones," that she "looks very feeble," and "not so well." "These are the hypocrites that devour widows' houses. For your science is your house, and as you are all alone you are a widow in the Science of Christ or Truth. Now Christ visited the widowed and fatherless in their distress, and told his disciples to do the same, and keep them pure and unspotted from the world of opinions. While you read this I am with you in your belief or prison, till I shall tear it down and raise you up."]

[Again, Quimby admits in writing to a man concerning his wife's case that he has sometimes judged for the moment by what the sick said about themselves, and advised them not to come; but on sitting with such patients he has found their trouble amounted to a "mere nothing." He has advised others to come, on the basis of their own description, and found them far worse than he expected. This has led him to give all people opportunity to take the chance and he will then do the best he can for them. If certain of curing one whom he has never seen he would at once advise favorably. But be will not venture to give a mere opinion. If however the patient herself in this case will write to Quimby, giving an account of her own case, he will devote an hour to her, and so write that she may follow her own leadings. In this way Quimby gave inquirers an opportunity to look beneath all opinions.]

[It is noticeable that in these letters, written in 1860 and 1861, Quimby shows that he has a clear conception of the "Science of Christ," or "Christian Science," a term which he employed later.]

[To a patient who tried to persuade Quimby to promise that he would heal her, he writes:]

You say in your letter that I told you so and so, and you hold me to what I said, just as though I might forget it. . . . Now these promises are the very things I am trying to get rid of. . . .   When my patients get me to make a promise, it seems to them as if that were all, and they never think they have anything to do for themselves. This is so common among the sick that I have become very cautious. . . . Now, do not hold me as P. P. Q. responsible to stop your cough, but hold the sick idea responsible for the cough. I must hold you, not Mrs. B. but the sick idea to its promises. . . . You must remember that Mrs. B. said she would keep up good courage, and not be afraid if she coughed a little. If I hear of your complaining about the cough, I shall hold you to your bargain. You see you are bound to keep the peace, to do all that is right so that health may come, and that you may once more rejoice. . . .

Notes

(1) Despite Dr. Quimby's great confidence in the Truth, he often wrote and spoke in this way, never making mere promises or claims. The use of the tumbler of water was to strengthen faith and aid concentration.

(2) Although the absent treatment given in such a case included much more than this letter indicates, Quimby, realizing the importance of expectant attention, mentioned specific results that might be looked for. He tried to make a patient self-helpful as soon as possible.

(3) The regenerative process was often emphatic in the case of Dr. Quimby's patients because his power was great, its action immediate. In another letter Dr. Quimby says, "To reverse the action is not a very easy task, but if you will wait patiently I cannot help thinking it will take place."

(4) This shows how little emphasis Dr. Quimby himself put on rubbing the head: he could do it as well absently! That is, it was merely "suggestion."

(5) Although Quimby speaks of disease as "in the mind," he speaks of the error or opinion as "something," and mentions the bodily effects without denying that such changes are produced in the physical system. But he turns the thought as quickly as possible to the regenerative changes presently to come.

(6) Quimby conversed with his patients in the same friendly way in spirit as during the talks which followed treatments in his office. He addressed the inner self, speaking what to him was the direct truth, in contrast with the patient's consciousness in bondage to opinion.
(7) Quimby habitually inculcated the affirmative attitude by employ-ing the terms familiar to his patients according to their occupation
(8) The resource, Quimby points out elsewhere, is found through knowledge that this Wisdom is from God; brings strength, guidance, freedom. Contrast Quimby's spirit as disclosed in this letter with that of later therapeutists who lacked his great sympathy.

Chapter Eleven - Letters to Patients and Inquirers (1)

PORTLAND, Dec. 7th, 1861.
Miss L.
Your letter was safely received, but my engagements have been such that I have not had time to give my attention to your case until now. Although we have lived side by side ever since we were children, we were ignorant of that power or Science that is necessary to smooth our ruffled path as we travel along the road to Wisdom, whence no child of Science returns to his former home of ignorance and superstition, You and I have a power called the inner man by the ignorant, but its true name is Wisdom or progression. This is the child of God, and although at first almost without an identity this little wisdom implanted in this earthly man or idea is held in ignorance till some higher wisdom frees it from its prison. YOU remember when your little pupils would stand by your side looking up to you for wisdom to satisfy their desires. You with your power like Moses went before them leading them through the sea of ignorance, they following your light as a pillar of fire, and in the clouds of darkness your light sprang up. As you traveled along, they murmuring and complaining, you like Moses fed them with the bread of Science and eternal life. You smote the rock of wisdom that followed them and they drank of the waters that came out of your teaching and this rock or Wisdom was Christ. You have a Teacher as well as I that goes before us teaching us Science. We become the child of the one we obey. You, like Moses, held up the serpent of ignorance before your little pupils and all who looked upon your explanation and understood were healed of their disease or ignorance; but the murmuring of your pupils would make you nervous and although you, like Moses on Mount Pisgah, could see the promised land, your heart failed you and you sank down in despair. In your discontented state of mind you call, as Job did, but no answer returns from your comforters, your doctors or spiritual advisers, who being blind guides find you . . . and fall upon you and rob you of all your wisdom. So here you are a stranger among thieves, cast into prison by the very ones you have always taken for your leaders on the road to health; you are bound with bands, sick and with no hope of ever being set at liberty.
Now your belief is like a bark and your wisdom attached to it, on the water of this world, for water is an emblem of error, so that the medical wisdom or ocean is where your bark seems to be moored. Here you are tossed to and fro, sometimes expecting to be lost, while the winds of spiritualism are whistling in your ear till they shake the bark to which your wisdom is attached. So the heavens are dark and the light of wisdom is extinguished in the opinions or waves of medical science.
As you are lying tossing to and fro you see me coming. When I say "me" I mean Science in P. P. Q., not the P. P. Q. that you used to see, but Wisdom in a body, not of flesh and blood, but a body such as Wisdom gives it; for Wisdom gives to every one a body as it pleases and to every science its own body. Your body or bark is of this world and your wisdom is in it, and I have come through your wisdom to get you clear of your enemies. So you may look out of the window of your bark while reading this and you will see me coming on the water of your life saying to spiritualism and the waves of the medical faculty. "Be still, and I will come on board of your bark, [quiet] your fears and return you once more to your own house whence you have been decoyed by these blind guides."
As disease is in accordance with the laws of man, a penalty is attached to every act so that every one found guilty must be punished by the law. As you are accused of a great many transgressions your punishment is greater than you can bear. So you sink under your trouble. I appear in your behalf to have you tried by the laws of your own country, not by the laws of these barbarians. So I will read over the indictment that stands against you. Here it is: You are accused of dyspepsia, liver complaint, nervousness, sleepless nights, weak stomach, palpitation, neuralgia, rheumatism, pains through your back and hips, lameness and soreness, want of action in the stomach. What say you to this indictment: are you guilty or not guilty? You say "guilty." But as I appear in your behalf I deny that you are guilty of the evils which cause this punishment. I want you to have a fair trail before the judge of truth, and if you have disobeyed any law of God or Science you must answer to Science, not to man. I will call on the hypocrite or doctor who goes around devouring widows' houses, and for a few dollars has got the people into trouble from which they cannot get out. He says you have all the above diseases.

On cross-examination when asked how he knows, his answer is [that] you told him. This is all the proof that he or any other doctor can bring. So by their false testimony you have been condemned for believing a lie, that you might be sick. Now as your case is one of a thousand I have, I have only to say a few words to your wisdom as judge. All disease is only the effect of our belief. The belief is of man and as Science sees through man's belief it destroys the belief and sets the soul or wisdom free.

I will now sum up the evidence. You have listened to the opinions of the doctors, who are blind guides crying peace, peace, till you have embraced all their wisdom. This has produced a stagnation in your system and what their ignorance has not done the spiritualists have tried to do. So between them both you are a prisoner, and in the same state as the people were in the days of Jesus when he said to them, "Beware of the doctrines of the Scribes and Pharisees; for they say and do not, they bind burdens on you that they cannot explain."

This keeps you nervous. So awake from your lethargy and come to the light of Wisdom, that will teach you that man's happiness is in himself, that his life is eternal, this life is Wisdom and as Wisdom is progression, its enemy is ignorance. So seek Wisdom and believe no man's opinion, for these opin-ions make you nervous. This causes a heat to go to your head making your head feel heavy and producing a dullness over your eyes. In fact [this opinion] causes all your bad feelings.

So if I can lift your wisdom above the error or mind then you will be free. But now this nervous heat is all through you and comes to the surface. When the cold strikes you it chills you. This you take for a low state of the blood. But it is a stagnation of your own self, not able to explain the phenomena that you are affected by. As you read this it will excite you to understand it. This is like a little leaven that is put into your bread or belief. It will work till it affects the lump and causes you to feel as though you had a very bad cold. Then it will work upon your system and affect your bowels.

Then you may know that your cure is at hand. So do not despair, only remember the signs of the times and pray that your flight may not be in the night nor on the Sabbath day when you are at meeting. So keep on the lookout and I think you will be better. If so let me know. When you read this letter I will be with you and you will not think it strange, for it will produce some strange sensations, sometimes joy and sometimes grief. But it is all for the best. So keep up good courage and I will lead you through the dark valley of the shadow of death and land you safe in that world of Science where disease never comes.

I will stop at this time. But remember as long as you read this and drink in these words. For this is my [wisdom] and to drink it is to understand. Do this in remembrance of me, not P. P. Q., but Science, till your health comes. I will leave you now and come again and lead you till you can go alone. If you will see fit to show this to Julia H., when you read it we shall all be together. You know what this Truth says that when two or three are gathered together in Science, Wisdom will be there and bless and explain to them.

P. P. Q.

PORTLAND, December 16th, 1861.

Miss B:

Yours of the 7th is received containing $2.00 as a fee for my services on yourself. As you have shown a spirit of sympathy that I never have received before, I certainly shall not prove myself one who will not return to another as I would that another should do to me. So I receive your two dollars sent in hope of a relief and return your money, believing it came from one who is as ready to give as to receive. I believe if two persons agree in one thing sincerely, independent of self, it will be granted.

I will now use my skill as far as I am able to correct your mind in regard to your trouble. The heat you speak of is not a rush of blood to the head but it is caused by a sensation on your mind like some trouble. This causes a weakness at times at the pit of your stomach. The heat in the second stomach causes a pressure on the aorta which makes the heart beat very rapidly at times. This you take for palpitation and it causes a flash or heat, which of course you take for a rush of blood to the head. But it is not so; it is in the fluids. As the clouds in the skies change when the wind blows, so the fluids under the skin change at every excitement. The skin being transparent reveals the color; this annoys you and the false idea that [the cause] is the blood that keeps up the fire. Now just take into your mind the [idea of the] spine as a combined lever of three parts, and you will see how to correct your [thought] so as to ease the pressure.... Now imagine yourself sitting in a chair with the lower lever or spine at right angles with your limbs. This [will] relieve the stomach, take the pressure from the aorta and put out the fire so there can be no heat. This will produce a change in your feelings and the change is the cure.

If you will sit down on Sunday evening I will try to straighten you up so as to relieve that feeling. [When] I succeed, if you feel that I am entitled to anything in the shape of a gift, it will be received if ever so trifling. Your sincerity towards me interests my sympathy in you, and if I relieve you I shall be very glad. You have taken the way to make me try my best. This is true sympathy to sympathize with those who make the first sacrifice. It is of no consequence if it be one cent or one hundred: the sacrifice is all. It shows your faith, and according to your faith so shall your cure be. This being a new experiment, let me know how I succeed and if I change your mind, the change is the cure. I send you one of my circulars which will tell you more of my treatment. It is easier to cure than to explain to a patient at a distance. But I am sure of the principle and feel confident that I shall cure at a distance. For distance is nothing but an error that truth will sometime- explode. If my faith and your hope mingle, the cure will be the result, so I will give my attention to you as far as my faith goes and shall like to hear how I succeed.　　　　P. P. QUIMBY.

Miss B

Yours of the 7th is received and I am glad to learn that I have relieved your mind by "my power," as you call it. But you misunderstand my power. It is not power but Wisdom. If you knew as much as I do about yourself you could feel another's feelings; but here is the trouble. What people call "power" I call Wisdom. Now if my wisdom is more than yours then I can help you, but this I must prove to you, and if I tell you about yourself what you cannot tell me, then you must acknowledge that my wisdom is superior to yours and become a pupil instead of a patient.

I will now sit down by you and tell your feelings. You may give your attention to me by [mentally] giving me your hand. I will write down the conversation that I hold with you while sitting by you. You have a sort of dizzy feeling in your head and a pain in the back part of the neck. This affects the front part of the head causing a heaviness over the eyes. The lightness about the head causes it to incline forward, bringing a pressure on your neck, just below the base of the brain, so that you often find yourself throwing your head up, to ease that part of the head. This makes it heavy so it bears on the shoulders, cramps the neck, numbs the chest, so that you give way at the pit of the stomach and feel as though you wanted something to hold you up. This cramps the stomach, giving you a "gone feeling" at the pit of the stomach. Now these symptoms taken of themselves are nothing. But you have had medical advice, or have got from some one else an answer to all these feelings. You are nervous. You think you have the heart complaint. Your blood rushes to the head. . . . [If] all these symptoms together would not make your face red, what would?

Listen to me and I will give an explanation of all the above feelings. I must go back to the first cause, say some years ago. I will not undertake to tell just the cause but I will give you an illustration. Suppose I (the natural man) were sitting by you, and we were alone. If I should go and fasten the door, and go towards you and attempt to seize hold of you, and if you asked me what I intended to do and I should say, "keep still, or I will blow your brains out," you would see that this would frighten you. I think your heart would beat as fast as it ever did. This explanation I do not say is true. For I suppose a case, [but a shock or] start contracts the stomach, the fright or excitement [generates] heat, [and the pressure] sets your heart beating, and throws the heat to your head, this heat tries to escape out of the nose causing a tickling in your nose and you often rub it because it itches and feels hot. It then tries to escape through the passage to the ears making your cheeks red and burn and causes a noise in your ears sometimes. This after a while subsides, the stomach relaxes and the heat passes down from the stomach into the bowels. .

Now follow the directions in the last letter and relieve the pressure on the aorta. This will check the nervous heat and relieve the excitement and then the heat will subside. The color is in the surface of the skin and has nothing to do with any humor or disease: it is nothing but excitement. As I told you in my last, I will be with you when you read the letters and you will feel a warm sensation pass over you, like a breath. This will open the pores of the skin and the heat will escape.

I send back the five dollars till the cure is performed. I don't like to be outdone in generosity and I am willing to risk as much as any one in such a cause as this. If I come off conqueror then it will be time enough for you to offer up a sacrifice. Till then if I accept a gift it is without an equivalent on my part. I feel as certain of success as you do, so I feel as though I run no risk. All I look for is the cure. You ask if I give any medicine. The only medicine I ever give is my explanation and that is the cure. In about a week let me know how the medicine works. Hoping to hear good news when next I hear from you, I remain,

Your friend,

P. P. QUIMBY.

PORTLAND, ME., Jan. 2nd, 1861.

To Mr. H:

In response to your letter I must say, that it is out of my power to visit your place in person at this time, from the fact that I have some thirty or more patients here on my hands, but if there comes a slack time I will come and let you know beforehand so you can meet me in Bangor.

Now a word or two to your wife. I will try my best while sitting by you while writing this letter to produce an effect on your stomach. I want you to take a tumbler of pure water while I write this and now and then take a little. I am with you now seeing you. Do not be in a hurry when you read this, but be calm and you will in a short time feel the heat start from your left side and run down like water; then your head will be relieved and you will have an inclination to rise. Be slow in your movements so that your head will not swim round. I will take you by the hand at first and steady you till you can walk alone. Now remember what I say to you. I am in this letter and as often as you read this and listen to it you listen to me. So let me know the effect one week from now. I will be with you every time you read this. Take about one half hour to devote to reading and listening to my counsel and I assure you you will be better. Now do not forget.

Yours, etc.,

P. P. Q.

PORTLAND, ME., Dec. 30,1860.

To Mr. J

As your wife is about leaving for her home, I take this way of expressing my ideas of the trouble she is laboring under, thinking you would like my opinion of her case. I think her friends are not aware of her true state. Hers is one of a very peculiar kind. She is not deaf in the strict sense of the word, but her condition has been brought about by trouble of long standing. When I say "trouble" I do not confine it to any neglect on the part of her friends, but trouble when young which made her nervous. This caused her to become low spirited till it has changed her system so that she is not the same person she was twelve years ago. I have given my attention to her general health, not to her deafness; for I think if she should come right in her mental or physical condition as she used to be, she would be well. You can see and judge of her appearance and buoyancy of mind. .

P. P. QUIMBY.

PORTLAND, ME., December 27th, 1860.

To Miss G. F

Your letter was received, and now I sit down to use my power to affect you. I will commence by telling you to sit upright and not give way at the pit of the stomach. If I felt that you saw me as plainly while I am talking to you as I see you, then there would be no use in writing; for you are as plain before my eyes as you were when I was talking to the shadow in Portland. For the shadow came with the substance, and that which I am talking to now is the substance. If I make an impression on it, it may throw forth a shadow of a young lady upright without that "gone place" at the pit of the stomach. . . . Remember that when I see you sitting or standing in the position I saw you in at Portland I shall just straighten you up. If you complain of the back, you may lay it to me and I will be a little more gentle. You may expect me once in a while in the evening. So keep on the lookout. See that you have your lamp trimmed and burning, so that when the Truth comes it shall not find you sleeping, but up straight, ready to receive the bridegroom. It seems that you understand this as I tell it to you. But for fear you will not explain it to the shadow, or natural man, I. will try to make you understand so it may come to the senses of the natural man. If I succeed, let my natural man know by a letter. (2)

Yours, etc.,

P. P. Q.

To Mrs. A. C. B:

In answer to your letter I will say that it is impossible to give an opinion of a case till I know something about it [apart from] my natural senses. If I myself cannot take another's feelings, my opinion is nothing. When I sit by a patient their feelings affect me and the sensation I receive from the mind is independent of the senses, for they [the senses] do not know that they communicate any intelligence to me. This I feel, and it contains the cause of the trouble, and my Wisdom explains the trouble, and the explanation is the cure. You must trust in that Wisdom that is able to unlock any error.   P. P. Q.

January 11, 1861.

To Miss G.

Your letter to Miss W. was handed to me for perusal to see what course I thought best to take. So I will sit down by you as I used to do and commence operations. Excitement contracts the stomach, not from fright but from being over-joyed at your recovery.... The food digests slowly and it will make you feel a little sluggish at times.   But it will soon act upon your system and relieve you of your trouble, for that is only nervous, and has nothing to do with the kidneys. . . . I will repeat the same till you are all right. Remember that I am with you when you read this and every time you read this you will feel my influence. . . .

P. P. QUIMBY.

PORTLAND, January 25, 1861.

To Mrs. Ware

By the request of E. and S. I sit down by you to see if I can amuse you by my explanation of disease. You know I often talk to persons about religion and you often look as though you would rather have me talk about anything else. Perhaps it would be better if you knew the cause of every sensation, but you would not want a physician.

Now you will want me to tell you how you feel, and if you will give me your attention I will try to explain. This heavy feeling that you have, accompanied with a desire to lie down and a sort of indifference how things go, comes from a quiet state of your system that prevents your food from digesting as readily as it did. But it will act upon you like an emetic or cathartic. Either way is right. So give no care to what you shall eat or drink, for Wisdom will cause all things to work for the best. If you want to eat, consult your own feelings and take no one's opinion. Remember that He who made us knows our wants better than man. So keep yourself quiet and I will reverse the action from your head, and you will feel it passing out of your stomach. Then do not forget to sit up as I used to tell you and remember not to believe what the blind guides say. They will come to you, and if your throat is a little sore, they will merely ask if you think this sore throat is the diptheria, looking as wise as though they had discovered the philosopher's stone. . . .

Remember what I tell you about this disease. For these hypocrites or blind guides are working in the minds of the people like the demagogues of the South. I do not say that you will be troubled by them. But I have kept on their track for twenty years and have not the slightest confidence in anything they say. I hear you now for the first time asking me if I believe in another world. Yes, but not in the sense of the clergy. I will try to explain my two worlds. You live in Chicago and I in Portland, and if it will not be blasphemy to call your place heaven, we will suppose you are in heaven and I in Portland. Now, if I am here sitting and talking with you I must leave the earth and matter and come to you. If I am with you, what is it that has left the body? It cannot be matter in a visible form, yet it is something. Listen, and I will tell you. You read that God made all living things that had life out of the earth, so that dead matter cannot produce living life nor anything else. As all matter decomposes, the dust or odor that arises from it was the matter that [the natural man] is formed of. As the child is of living matter, not wisdom, when it grows to a certain age it is ready to receive the breath of eternal life. The child was not eternal life. Eternal life is Wisdom as much above human life as Science is above ignorance. . . . Eternal life is Christ or Science, this teaches us that matter is a mere shadow of a substance which the natural man never saw nor can see, for it is never changed, is the same today and forever, This substance is the essence of Wisdom and is in every living form. Like a seed in the earth, it grows or develops in matter, and is as much under the control of the mother's Wisdom as the gold which is dissolved and held in solution is under that of the chemist. If the mother's Wisdom is of this world, the spiritual child is not under her earthly care. Nevertheless it is held in the bosom of its eternal Wisdom that will cherish it till it is developed to receive the science of Eternal Wisdom. Eternal Wisdom and eternal life are not the same. Eternal Wisdom cannot change but acts on eternal life, changes its form and identity. Eternal Wisdom teaches us that all matter is in itself a shadow and is no barrier. Matter is dense darkness. Spirit is light. If you are wise your body or wisdom is light, and just as you sink into error you become dense or dark. Therefore let your light shine, so that when this wind comes blowing round in the form of an opinion you may know it is merely the noise of a demagogue. Believe not, and you will live and flourish. If you can understand this you have the basis of my belief.

For fear I have not made my two worlds clear to your mind, I will say a few words more. The two worlds may be divided in this way: one opinions, the other Science. Opinions are matter or the shadow of Science. One is limited in its sphere, and the other has no limits. One can be seen by the natural eyes: the other is an endless progression. The one is today, and tomorrow is not. The other is an endless progression. One is always changing, the other is always progressing. The natural man never will know this truth, for he cannot see Wisdom and live; Wisdom is the natural man's death. So he looks upon it as an enemy, prays to it, pays tribute to it as though Wisdom were a man. He often uses it as a balance to weigh his ignorance in but never to weigh the difference of his opinions. He often quotes it, talking as though it were his intimate friend, while he to Wisdom is only known as a servant or shadow, all an imitation. Science is of another character. Science rises above all narrow ideas. He who is scientific in regard to health and happiness is his own law, and is not subject to the laws of man except as he is deceived or ignorant. No one after he knows a scientific fact can ignorantly disobey it. So with Science the punishment is in the act. With man's laws it is different; the penalty may follow the act or come after. With Wisdom the laws are science. To know Science is to know Wisdom, and how can a man work a mathematical problem intelligently and at the same time say he is not aware of the fact?

If we know the true meaning of every word or thought we should know what will follow. So a person cannot scientifically act amiss. But being misled by public opinion, we believe a lie and suffer.

I have gone so far that I have reduced certain states to their causes as certain as ever a chemist saw the effect of a chemical change. For instance, take consumption. I know the character of every sensation. Its father or author is a hypocrite and deceiver. I look upon it as the most vile of all characters. It comes to a person under a most flattering form, with the kindest words, always very polite, ready to lend its aid in any way where it can get a hold.

I will illustrate this prince of hypocrites. I will come in the form of a lady, for it has many faces and characters. I enter as a neighbor with the customary salutations and you reply that you seem very well. "Oh, I am very glad, for by what I had heard I was expecting to find you abed. But you can't tell anything by gossip. You do not seem quite so well as when I saw you last." "Oh, yes, fully as well," you say. "Well, you know there are diseases which always flatter the patient. I suppose you have heard of the death of Mr. " "No, when did he die?" "He died yesterday but was sick a long time. Sometimes he thought he was getting better, but I knew all the time he was running down. But you must not get discouraged because you are like him, for it is not always certain that a person in the same condition you are in has consumption."

Here I make you nervous and you are glad when I leave. Knowing I am not welcome in that form I assume another character. I must now appear as a doctor. I sit down and count your pulse, look at your tongue, take a stick and examine the phlegm that you have raised. Then leaning back in the chair draw a long sigh, and ask if you have a pain in your left side.

The doctor is like a dog that wags his tail while you feed him but when your back is turned will bite you. If superstition is to be put down by scientific facts, it is useless to mince matters. If a person is aiding an enemy, he is as guilty as the thief. I want you to know that every word that is spoken is either matter or Wisdom. Opinions are condensed into a belief. So, if I [as a typical doctor] tell you that you have congestion of the lungs I impart my belief to you by a deposit of matter in the form of words. As you eat my belief it goes to form a disease like its author, my belief grows, comes forth, and at last takes form as a pressure across the chest. The doctor comes to get rid of the enemy and by his remedies creates another disease in the bowels. He begins to talk about inflammation of the bowels. This frightens you. The fright contracts the stomach so the heat cannot escape, and causes a flush in the face which you call a rush of blood to the head. It makes you feel sleepy and weak; you lie down; then the stomach relaxes and the heat passes down into the bowels, this causes pains. You call it "inflammation."

All this is very simple when you know what caused it. This letter is an essay for you to read, so good-night. Let me know how it works.

P. P. QUIMBY.
IN REPLY TO A YOUNG PHYSICIAN (3)

Dear Sir

Yours of the 5th is received, and in answer I would say that it is easier to ask a question than to answer it. But I will answer your question partly by asking another, and partly by coming at it by a parable. For to answer any question with regard to my mode of treatment would be like asking a physician how he knows a patient has the typhoid fever by feeling the pulse, and requesting the answer direct so that the person asking the question could sit down and be sure to define the disease from the answer.

My mode of treatment is not decided in that way, and to give a definite answer to your inquiry would be as much out of place as to ask you to tell me all you know about medical practice so that I could put it into practice for the curing of disease, with no further knowledge [apart from what] I might get from you. You see the absurdity of that request.

If it were in my power to give to the world the benefit of twenty years' hard study in one short or long letter, it would have been before the people long before this. The people ask they know not what. You might as well ask a man to tell you how to talk Greek without studying it, as to ask me to tell you how I test the true pathology of disease, or how I test the true diagnosis of disease, etc. All of these questions would be very easily answered if I assumed a standard, and then tested all disease by that standard.

The old mode of determining the diagnosis of disease is made up of opinions of diseased persons, in their right mind and out of it, all mixed up together, and set down accompanied by a certain state of pulse. In this dark chaos of error [the doctors] come to certain results like this: If you see a man going towards the water, he is going in swimming; for people go in swimming. But if he is running with his hat and coat off, he is either going to drown himself, or some one is drowning, and soon. This is the old way. Mine is this.

If I see a man, I know it, and if I feel the cold I know it. But to see a person going towards the water is no sign that I know what he is going to do. He may be going to bathe, or may be going to drown himself. Now here is the difference between the physician and myself, and this may give you some idea of how I define disease.

The regular [physician] and I sit down by a patient. He takes her by the hand, and so do I. He feels the pulse to ascertain the peculiar vibration and number of beats in a given time. This to him is knowledge. To me it is all quackery or ignorance. He looks at the tongue as though it contained information.

To me this is all folly and ignorance. He then begins to ask questions, which contain nothing to me, because [this questioning] is of no force. All this is shaken up in his head, and comes forth in the form of a disease, which is all error to me, and I will give you the diagnosis of this error.

The feeling of the pulse is to affect the patient so he will listen to the doctor. Examining the tongue is all for effect. The peculiar cast of the doctor's head is the same. The questions, accompanied by certain looks and gestures, are all to get control of the patient's mind so as to produce an impression. Then he looks very wise, and so on. All the symptoms put together show no knowledge, but a lack of wisdom, and the general credulity of mankind rendering [people] liable to be humbugged by any person however ignorant he may be, if he has the reputation of possessing all medical knowledge.

Now, sir, this is the field you are about to enter, and you will find the hardest stumbling block from diplomas. Greek and Latin, and the like are all of no consequence to the sick. It is impossible to give you even a mere shadow of twenty years' experience. But I may be of some use to you. I will say a word or two on the old practice, (not taking much time,) that will answer all your questions on the old school; for the less you know the better.

Watch the popular physician. See his shrewdness. Watch the sick patient: nervous and trembling like a person in the hands of a magistrate who has him in his power, and whose real object is to deceive him. See the two together, one perfectly honest, and the other, if honest, perfectly ignorant, [the physician] undertaking blindfolded to lead the patients through the dark valley of the shadow of death, the patient being born [mentally] blind. Then you see them going along, and at last they both fall into the ditch.

Now, like the latter, do not deceive your patients. Try to instruct them, and correct their errors. Use all the wisdom you have, and expose the hypocrisy of the profession in any one. Never deceive your patients behind their backs. Always remember that as you feel about your patients, just so they feel towards you. If you deceive them, they lose confidence in you. Just as you prove yourself superior to them, they give you credit mentally. If you pursue this course you cannot help succeeding. Be charitable to the poor. Keep the health of your patient in view, and if money comes, all well; but do not let that get the lead.

With all this advice, I leave you to your fate, trusting that the True Wisdom will guide you-not in the path of your predecessors. Shun evil and learn to do good.

PORTLAND, Sept. 16, 1860.   P. P. Q.

A LETTER REGARDING A PATIENT

Dear Sir:

Yours of Aug. 27th was received, after a long journey through the state of Maine. I will give you all the information that I am aware I possess.

If certain conditions of mind exist, certain effects will surely follow. For instance, if two persons agree as touching one thing, it will be granted. But if one agrees and the other knows not the thing desired, then the thing will not be accomplished.

For example, the lady in question wishes my services to restore her to health. Now her health is the thing she desires. Her faith is the substance of her hope. Her hope is her desire, it is founded on public opinion, and in this is her haven, the anchor to her desire, public opinion the ocean on which her barque or belief floats. Reports of me are the wind that either presses her along to the haven of health or down to despair. The tide of public opinion is either against her or in her favor. Now, as she lies moored on the sea, with her desire or cable attached to her anchor of hope, tossed to and fro in the gale of disease, if she can see me or my power walking on the water, saying to her aches and pains, "Be still," then I have no doubt that she will get better.   The sea will then be calm, and she will get that which she hoped for her faith or cure. For her faith is her cure. . . . This is the commencement of her cure. I, like Jesus, will stand at her heart and knock. If she hears my voice or feels my influence, and opens the door of her belief, I will come in and talk, and help her out of her trouble.

PORTLAND, Sept, 17th, 1860.   P. P. Q.

TO A GENTLEMAN REQUESTING HELP WITHOUT A PERSONAL INTERVIEW

Dear Sir

In answer to your inquiry, I would say that, owing to the scepticism of the world I do not feel inclined to assure you of any benefit which you may receive from my influence while away from you, as your belief would probably keep me from helping you. But it will not cost me much time nor expense to make the trial. So if I stand at your door and knock, and you know my voice or influence and receive me, you may be benefited. If you do receive any benefit, give it to the Principle, not to me as a man, but to that Wisdom which is able to break the bonds of the prisoner, set him free from the errors of the doctors, and restore him to health. This I will try to do with pleasure. But if this fails and your case is one which requires my seeing you, then my opinion is of no use. Yours, etc.

Portland, Oct. 20th, 1860.   P. P. Q.

TO A CLERGYMAN (4)

Oct. 28th, 1860.

Dear Sir:

Your letter of the eighteenth was received, but owing to a press of business I neglected answering it. I will try to give you the wisdom you ask. So far as giving an opinion is concerned, it is out of my power as a physician, though as man I might. But it would be of no service, for it would contain no wisdom except of this world.

My practice is not of the wisdom of man, so my opinion as a man is of no value. Jesus said, "If I judge of myself, my judgment is not true: but if I judge of God, it is right," for that contains no opinion. So if I judge as a man it is an opinion, and you can get plenty of them anywhere.

You inquire if I have ever cured any cases of chronic rheumatism. I answer, "Yes." But there are as many cases of chronic rheumatism as there are of spinal complaint, so that I cannot decide your case by another. You cannot be saved by pinning your faith on another's sleeve. Every one must answer for his own sins or belief. Our beliefs are the cause of our misery. Our happiness and misery are what follow our belief. So as we measure out to another, it will be measured to us again.

You ask me if I ascribe my cures to spiritual influence. Not after the [manner of] Rochester rappings, nor after Dr. Newton's way of curing. I think I know how be cures, though he does not. I gather by those I have seen who have been treated by him that he thinks it is through the imagination of the patient's belief. So he and I have no sympathy. If he cures disease, that is good for the one cured. But the world is not any wiser.

You ask if my practice belongs to any known science. My answer is, "No," it belongs to Wisdom that is above man as man. The Science that I try to practice is the Science that was taught eighteen hundred years ago, and has never had a place in the heart of man since; but is in the world, and the world knows it not. To narrow it down to man's wisdom, I sit down by the patient and take his feelings, and as the rest will be a long story I will send you one of my circulars, so that you may read for yourself.

Hoping this may limber the cords of your neck, I remain, Yours, etc.,

P. P. QUIMBY

[The circular reprinted below is the one referred to in this letter. It was in circulation for some years before Dr. Quimby began to practise in Portland, and had blank spaces to be filled in by the name of the town and the location of Quimby's office.]

TO THE SICK (5)

Dr. P. P. QUIMBY would respectfully announce to the citizens of .... and vicinity, that he will be at the .... where he will attend to those wishing to consult him in regard to their health, and, as his practice is unlike all other medical practice, it is necessary to say that he gives no medicines and makes no outward applications, but simply sits down by the patients, tells them their feelings and what they think is their disease. If the patients admit that he tells them their feelings, &c., then his explanation is the cure; and, if he succeeds in correcting their error, he changes the fluids of the system and establishes the truth, or health. The Truth is the Cure. This mode of practice applies to all cases. If no explanation is given, no charge is made, for no effect is produced. His opinion without an explanation is useless, for it contains no knowledge, and would be like other medical opinions, worse than none. This error gives rise to all kinds of quackery, not only among regular physicians, but those whose aim is to deceive people by pretending to cure all diseases. The sick are anxious to get well, and they apply to these persons supposing them to be honest and friendly, whereas they are made to believe they are very sick and something must be done ere it is too late. Five or ten dollars is then paid, for the cure of some disease they never had, nor ever would have had but for the wrong impressions received from these quacks or robbers, (as they might be called,) for it is the worst kind of robbery, tho' sanctioned by law. Now, if they will only look at the true secret of this description, they will find it is for their own selfish objects to sell their medicines. Herein consists their shrewdness!-to impress patients with a wrong idea, namely- that they have some disease. This makes them nervous and creates in their minds a disease that otherwise would never have been thought of. Wherefore he says to such, never consult a quack: you not only lose your money, but your health.

He gives no opinion, therefore you lose nothing. If patients feel pain they know it, and if he describes their pain he feels it, and in his explanation lies the cure. Patients, of course, have some opinion as to what causes pain-he has none, therefore the disagreement lies not in the pain, but in the cause of the pain. He has the advantage of patients, for it is very easy to convince them that he had no pain before he sat down by them.   After this it becomes his duty to prove to them the cause of their trouble. This can only be explained to patients, for which explanation his charge is .... dollars. If necessary to see them more than once........... dollars. This has been his mode of practice for the last seventeen years. There are many who pretend to practice as he does, but when a person while in "a trance," claims any power from the spirits of the departed, and recommends any kind of medicine to be taken internally or applied externally beware! believe them not, "for by their fruits ye shall know them."

Notes

(1) These letters have been somewhat condensed to avoid repetitions.
(2) This letter shows how emphatically Quimby directed attention to "the scientific man" or real self, the self that already possesses the Truth or Science implicitly.
(3) Published in part in "Health and the Inner Life," p 61.
(4) Printed in part in "Health and the Inner Life," p. 60.
(5) Published in part in "The True History of Mental Science."

Chapter Twelve - Mrs. Eddy: 1862-1875 (1)

We have noted the fact that Mrs. Eddy, then Mrs. Patterson, was a patient under Dr. Quimby's care during the period of his practice in Portland. At that time Mrs. Eddy was recovering from invalidism of long standing. Hence she was greatly handicapped at first. She had firmly be-lieved in doctors and medicine, and accepted the conventional teachings in regard to disease. But while burdened with these allegiances she also possessed a strong desire to make the change to the new point of view as thoroughly and quickly as possible. To understand her relationship to Dr. Quimby and his teachings we need then to put ourselves appreciatively into the point of view of her inner life.

Dr. D. Patterson, Mrs. Eddy's husband, became interested in the new method of haling and urged his wife to consult Dr. Quimby. Two of his letters to Dr. Quimby have been preserved and are here printed in full.

DR. D. PATTERSON TO P. P. QUIMBY

No. 1

Rumney, N. H., Oct. 14, 1861.

Dr. Quimby,

DEAR SIR: I have heard that you intended to come to Concord, N. H. this fall to stop a while for the benefit of the suffering portion of our race: do you intend, and if so, how soon? My wife has been an invalid for a number of years; is not able to sit up but a little, and we wish to have the benefit of your wonderful power in her case. If you are soon coming to Concord I shall carry her up to you, and if you are not coming there we may try to carry her to Portland if you remain there.

Please write me at your earliest convenience and oblige, Yours truly,

(Address)   DR. D. PATTERSON,

RUMNEY, N.H.

No. 2

No 76 UNION ST., LYNN, MASS. Apl. 24th, 1865.

Dr. P. P. Quimby.

DEAR SIR: My wife arrived safely Sat. eve., and is greatly improved in her health, but says she did not settle with you. If you will send your bill by mail, I will send the balance due you by the same conveyance.

Yours,

D. PATTERSON.

The first of these letters is especially important since it gives the date of the request for Dr. Quimby's treatment. Dr. Quimby's circular (2) deeply interested Mrs. Eddy and as he was unable to leave his practice in Portland to visit Mrs. Eddy in New Hampshire, Mrs. Eddy wrote personal appeals from Rumney, and from a water cure in Hill, N. H., whither she had gone for treatment but without avail. It is plain that Mrs. Eddy had now reached the limit of endurance and the end of her faith in material methods of treatment. No record of Dr. Quimby's answer has been preserved, but doubtless he wrote to her with all the more interest and conviction in view of the fact that she had given up hope in all other directions. For under such conditions he anticipated the best results.

There is no record of the exact date of Mrs. Eddy's arrival in Portland, but one of Dr. Quimby's patients, still living, was present in the office when she came and distinctly remembers seeing the invalid assisted up the steps to his office. In the journal of Mr. Julius A. Dresser, under date of October 17, 1862, mention is made for the first time of this new patient, who manifested special interest in Dr. Quimby's teaching and was eager to converse with the patients who best understood the new theory. Mr. Dresser devoted the larger part of his time at that period to conversations with patients, and it was natural that he should talk at length with Mrs. Eddy. These conversations were highly important because they gave Mrs. Eddy her first connected idea of Quimby's great truth.

First of all, Mr. Dresser could speak with the conviction of one whose life had been saved at the point of death with typhoid pneumonia. Again, he had seen the results in hundreds of cases, since his own cure in June, 1860, and could substantiate whatever he said by describing the conditions and the appearance of patients when they first came for treatment and by telling how great were the changes wrought by Quimby's wisdom. Mrs. Eddy indicated her increasing interest in this "wisdom," and her desire to read a statement of it in Quimby's own words. Accordingly Mr. Dresser loaned her Vol: 1 of the manuscripts, as he possessed a copy in his own handwriting, this copy having been preserved with the others until the present time. (3)

The turning-point with Mrs. Eddy, as with all who came to Dr. Quimby, was of course the silent spiritual treatment which she received at regular intervals during her stay in Portland. Dr. Quimby always depended primarily on this silent work to bring about the fundamental or decisive change, to overcome the adverse influences and start the reaction in favor of health. In Mrs. Eddy's case there were years of invalidism to overcome, together with the beliefs and habits which bound her to another mode of life. Hence a gradual change in consciousness and attitude followed upon the remarkable effects of the silent treatment which lifted her out of her invalidism. To understand what Dr. Quimby accomplished for her we should not only bear in mind that the silent treatment took her past the decisive point, but note that the conversations were in their way no less essential, and that these were made good by the many opportunities to listen to the reading of manuscripts, to hear discussions and to read the manuscripts herself. We have the direct testimony of those who were present during the conversations and readings in the office to the effect that Mrs. Eddy showed unusual eagerness to acquire all she could through these exceptional opportunities. Indeed her zeal seems at times to have exceeded her understanding, for some of her letters indicate that she made ventures beyond her returning strength. She was nervously susceptible in type, easily took on the feelings or mental atmospheres of the sick. Hence the problem in her case was not merely that of the recovery of her health; it was to find a way to temperamental control so that he could apply the new "Science" and yet keep

free.

After her return from Portland to Sanbornton Bridge (1863) she was not sure of herself in all respects and found it necessary to send for absent treatment on occasion, but she had begun to care for the sick by Quimby's method. Later, at Warren, Maine, (1864) she acquired the power to detect others' feelings and atmospheres, had become accustomed to the feeling of Quimby's presence during absent treatments and had advanced to knowledge of that presence when there was no apparent reason for his coming.

It was at Warren that Mrs. Eddy gave her first public lectures expounding Quimby's views. She felt impelled to give these lectures because she found herself classified as a spiritualist and a public denial seemed necessary-she disclaimed any connection with phenomena involving rappings, trances; or any agency in healing the sick said to come from the dead, and contrasted Quimby's science of healing with Rochester rappings, spiritualism and deism in general. Her remarks attracted attention and a newspaper editor asked her for a communication on the subject.

Throughout this period, from the time of her acquaintance with Dr. Quimby by reputation and then as her healer in Portland and by means of "angel visits," Mrs. Eddy looked up to Quimby as the great discoverer and healer of the day, the one whose privilege it was to rediscover the truth which Jesus taught. She felt and expressed the profound gratitude and loyalty of one who had been marvellously restored to health. She made no claims for herself. She did not make light of Quimby's teaching or identify it with either mesmerism, magnetism or any other of the isms of the day, as we shall soon see more plainly, in her communication to a Portland paper. In fact, she showed herself more than an ardent disciple; she was eager to come to Quimby's defense, lest he should be misunderstood and classed with the isms and humbugs then current.

In order to depreciate Mrs. Eddy's indebtedness to Dr. Quimby, some critics have tried to make out that she was not cured by him. The recurrence of weakness seems to confirm this. Mrs. Eddy several times wrote for absent healing, and on one occasion felt it necessary to return to Portland for treatment. She frankly confessed that she had temporary recurrences of former troubles. But the critics who make this charge overlook the fact that she was at the point of death when she first went to Portland, and the fact that she was brought out of that condition so that she could walk, as she herself says in her communication to the Courier, unaided after only a week's treatment; and that Dr. Quimby gave her the therapeutic impetus and the wisdom which carried her through to the point where she herself began to understand and to demonstrate.

SONNET.

Suggested by Reading the Remarkable Cure of Captain F. W Deering (4)

For the Courier.

TO DR. P. P. QUIMBY

'Mid light of science sits the sage profound,
Awing with classics and his starry lore,
Climbing to Venus, chasing Saturn round,
Turning his mystic pages o'er and o'er,
Till, from empyrean space, his wearied sight
Turns to the oasis on which to gaze,
More bright than glitters on the brow of night
The self-taught man walking in wisdom's ways.
Then paused the captive gaze with peace entwined,
And sight was satisfied with thee to dwell;
But not in classics could the book-worm find
That law of excellence whence came the spell
Potent o'er all,-the captive to unbind.
To heal the sick and faint, the halt and blind.

MARY M. PATTERSON.

The confessions of weakness were evidences of the regerative work in process, as she realizes when it comes to her that to see the great new truth and to live by it consciously are two different things. For the mere restoration to physical health was only the beginning. There remained the great problem of a temperament which made her unduly aware of the ills and feelings of others. The problem of one's temperament is not to be solved in a week. Hence to Dr. Quimby she wrote as much of her weaknesses and failures as of her faith in his new Science that, seeing precisely where she stood, he might help her to take the next great step. Dr. Quimby always encouraged this frank statement of a patient's actual needs. Mrs. Eddy responded in full faith. Meanwhile her public lectures and her con-versations with interested persons showed how strong was her belief that Quimby possessed the true Science of the Christ. This faith is shown, for example, in the sonnet written at the time of one of Dr. Quimby's great cures, and in her article in a Portland daily paper.

The following is from Mrs. Eddy's article published in the Portland Evening Courier in 1862. It plainly shows the writer's real attitude toward her restorer.

"When our Shakespeare decided that 'there were more things in this world than were dreamed of in your philosophy,' I cannot say of a verity that he had a foreknowledge of P. P. Quimby. And when the school Platonic anatomized the soul and divided it into halves, to be reunited by elementary attractions, and heathen philosophers averred that old Chaos in sullen silence blooded o'er the earth until her inimitable form was hatched from the egg of night, I would not at present decide whether the fallacy was found in their premises or conclusions, never having dated my existence be fore the flood. When the startled alchemist discovered, as be supposed, an universal solvent, or the philosopher's stone, and the more daring Archimedes invented a lever where-withal to pry up the universe, I cannot say that in either the principle obtained in nature or in art, or that it worked well, having never tried it. But, when by a falling apple an immutable law was discovered, we gave it the crown of science, which is incontrovertible and capable of demon-stration: hence that was wisdom and truth. When from the evidence of the senses my reason takes cognizance of truth, although it may appear in quite a miraculous view, I must acknowledge that as science which is truth uninvestigated. Hence the following demonstration:-

"Three weeks since I quitted my nurse and sick-room en route for Portland. The belief of my recovery had died out of the hearts of those who were most anxious for it. With this mental and physical depression I first visited P. P. Quimby; and in less than one week from that time I ascended by a stairway of one hundred and eighty-two steps to the dome of the City Hall, and am improving ad infinitum. To the most subtle reasoning, such a proof, coupled, too, as it is with numberless similar ones, demonstrates his power to heal. Now for a brief analysis of this power.

"Is it spiritualism. Listen to the words of wisdom. 'Believe in God, believe also in me; or believe me for the very work's sake.' Now, then, his works are but the result of superior wisdom, which can demonstrate a science not under-stood: hence it were a doubtful proceeding not to believe him for the work's sake. Well, then, he denies that his power to heal the sick is borrowed from the spirits of this or another world; and let us take the Scriptures for proof. 'A kingdom divided against itself cannot stand.' How, then, can he receive the friendly aid of the disenthralled spirit, while he rejects the faith of the solemn mystic who crosses the threshold of the dark unknown to conjure up from the vasty deep the awe-struck spirit of some invisible squaw?

"Again, is it by animal magnetism that he heals the sick? Let us examine. I have employed electro-magnetism and animal magnetism, and for a brief interval have felt relief, from the equilibrium which I fancied was restored to an exhausted system or by a diffusion of concentrated action. But in no instance did I get rid of a return of all my ailments, because I had not been helped out of the error in which opinions involved us. My operator believed in disease independent of the mind; hence, I could not be wiser than my teacher. But now I can see dimly at first, and only as trees walking, the great principle which underlies Dr. Quimby's faith and works; and just in proportion to my light perception of truth is my recovery. This truth which he opposes to the error of giving intelligence to matter and placing pain where it never placed itself, if received understandingly, changes the currents of the system to their normal action; and the mechanism of the body goes on undisturbed. That this is a science capable of demonstration becomes clear to the minds of those patients who reason upon the process of their cure. The truth which he establishes in the patient cures him (although he may be wholly unconscious thereof) ; and the body, which is full of light, is no longer in disease. At present I am too much in error to elucidate the truth, and can touch only the key-note for the master hand to wake the harmony. May it be in essays instead of notes! say I. After all, this is a very spiritual doctrine; but the eternal years of God are with it, and it must stand firm as the rock of ages.   And to many a poor sufferer may it be found, as by me, 'the shadow of a great rock in a weary land'."

The day following the publication of the above article, it was criticized by the Portland Advertiser; and Mrs. Eddy then wrote a second article, replying to the criticism. In it appeared the following paragraph, referring to Quimby and his doctrine:

"P. P. Quimby stands upon the plane of wisdom with his truth. Christ healed the sick, but not by jugglery or with drugs. As the former speaks as never man before spake, and heals as never man healed since. Christ, is he not identified with truth, and is not this the Christ which is in him? We know that in wisdom is life, 'and the life was the light of man.' P. P. Quimby rolls away the stone from the sepulchre of error, and health is the resurrection. But we also know that 'light shineth in darkness, and the darkness comprehended it not.'"

"These excerpts" says J. A. Dresser, "are in plain language, and they speak for themselves. The statements are made with too evident an understanding of their truth to be doubted or questioned, or afterward reversed in any particular. It should be borne in mind that your speaker was there at the time, and was familiar with all the circumstances she relates and the views expressed. The devoted regard the lady formed for her deliverer, Quimby, and for the truth he taught her, which proved her salvation, was continued to be held by her from this time (the autumn of 1862) up to a period at least four years later; for in January, 1866, Quimby's death occurred, and on February 15 she sent to me a copy of a poem she had written to his memory, and accompanied it by letter."

This letter, which was published in full in "The True History of Mental Science," 1887, was both an expression of gratitude and a personal appeal. Knowing that Mr. Dresser was Quimby's most enthusiastic follower, Mrs. Eddy expressed the hope that he would take up the work of their much-loved friend. She then goes on to speak of a fall on the sidewalk which left her momentarily unconscious.

When she was brought to, she found herself in a crippled condition like that which Dr. Quimby had cured in 1862. The attending physician declared that she would never walk again. But so firm was her faith in Quimby's principle that she was out of bed in two days, with the declaration that she would walk. Nevertheless she found that the mishap had thrown her back into the old associations for the time being, also that her friends were helping her back into the spinal affection from which she had suffered so long. In this state of suspense between opposing forces she appealed to Mr. Dresser for help, according, to Quimby's method of silent spiritual treatment. If another person were in her condition she believed she could give help in this way, that is, if the other had not attributed intelligence to matter. But despite her strong faith that all intelligence should be identified with Divine power, she found herself weakening. Hence her appeal to one who had followed Dr. Quimby with such ardor and understanding.

The poem, which had been printed in a Lynn newspaper, is as follows:

LINES ON THE DEATH. OF DR. P. P. QUIMBY, WHO HEALED WITH THE TRUTH THAT CHRIST TAUGHT, IN CONTRA-DISTINCTION TO ALL ISMS.

Did sackcloth clothe the sun, and day grow night,
All matter mourn the hour with dewy eyes,
When Truth, receding from our mortal sight,
Had paid to error her last sacrifice?
Can we forget the power that gave us life?
Shall we forget the wisdom of its way?
Then ask me not, amid this mortal strife,-
This keenest pang of animated, clay,-
To mourn him less: to mourn him more were just,
If to his memory 'twere a tribute given
For every solemn, sacred, earnest trust
Delivered to us ere he rose to heaven.
Heaven but the happiness of that calm soul,
Growing in stature to the throne of God:
Rest should reward him who hath made us whole.
Seeking, though tremblers, where his footsteps trod.
LYNN, Feb. 22, 1866.   MARY M. PATTERSON.

It is interesting to realize how much depended on the answer to that letter. Had Mr. Dresser decided to take up Dr. Quimby's work at that time, no one would have disputed his right to do so or his worthiness, since he was the best fitted of Quimby's followers to succeed him. But, lacking the confidence to take over the work of a master hand, he expressed his unfitness and declined the opportunity which Mrs. Eddy's appeal put before him. There was then no resource far Mrs. Eddy save to apply the Quimby method in her own way.

On the other hand, as we have seen above, Mrs. Eddy was for sometime in the throes of proving Quimby's principle in her own way. With no healer to depend on, she had to look to that principle alone. She still remained loyal to Quimby. There is no reason for believing that her attitude toward him changed in any way until sometime in 1872. He was to her the modern representative of the great saving truths taught by Jesus. He had developed the method by which those truths could once more be applied to the healing of the sick. Her own necessity had proved the efficacy of that method anew. There was no reason for any revelation. There was no reason for any kind of claim in her own behalf. Her revelation was simply this: that when hard pressed she too could demonstrate the wisdom and power of the Science which Quimby had taught. It always comes to a person with the force of a revelation when one realizes that it is within one's power actually to apply a line of teaching which hitherto has seemed so wonderful that apparently its discoverer is the only person who can demonstrate it. This proof of his teaching was precisely what Dr. Quimby hoped his followers would make. For, as we have noted, he himself made no special claims. He knew that his teaching, fundamentally speaking, was eternally true. He knew that it was all to be found in the Bible. What he had discovered was a new key to unlock supposed mysteries which had been kept from the world throughout the Christian centuries. Years of experience were required on Dr. Quimby's part to work out this Science and to prove its efficacy. Quimby's followers really demonstrated it for themselves only so far as they added to the great work wrought for them by Quimby the personal proof which experience must give. Mrs. Eddy's case was no exception. A challenging experience gave her the conclusive evidence that the Science of the Christ had been brought to light once more.

Some allowance must always be made for the personal equation. Readers of the works of Rev. Warren F. Evans, the first author to produce a book on the rediscovered science of healing, have found in that writer's six volumes one type of interpretation of Quimby's teaching. Well versed in philosophy, the teachings of Swedenborg, and especially in the idealism of Berkeley, Evans put Quimby's views in terms of idealism, with scant emphasis on the realities of the material world. The interpretation made by Mrs. Eddy went farther in the same direction, that is, in her emphasis on the intelligence and power of spirit, as if the world of nature had no existence. The original sources of this interpretation, as based on Quimby's writings, have never been disclosed until the publication of the present volume.

The direct sources were "Questions and Answers," and Vol. 1 of the manuscripts, supplemented by notes based on the readings and conversations in Dr. Quimby's office. Given Mrs. Eddy's version of Christian Science as it is to be found in her various books, in "The Science of Man" and other small writings, and in the different editions of "Science and Health," including the first, the reader will be able to trace out her version of the Quimby theory from its inception. Given the present volume in its fulness, the reader will also see what the later version of Christian Science might have been had Mrs. Eddy enjoyed the benefit of all the Quimby manuscripts. For bo later writings are in various respects correctives of the view which underestimates the place and reality of the natural world.

It is not necessary to trace out the changes made in the writings which were in Mrs. Eddy's possession. The manuscript known as "Questions and Answers" is the typical instance. With great care Miss Milmine (5) followed all these changes throughout the period which intervened between 1866 and 1875, when Mrs. Eddy, then Mrs. Glover, lived in Maine and in Stoughton, Mass. She has shown how "Questions and Answers" gradually became "The Science of Man, by which the sick are healed, Embracing Questions and Answers in Moral Science, arranged for the learner by Mrs. Mary Baker Glover," 1870. She has disclosed the fact that this manuscript was still attributed to Dr. Quimby while Mrs. Eddy lived in Stoughton, but that Mrs. Eddy introduced a preface of her own which was later incorporated into the text, which in turn was put forth as Mrs. Eddy's (Mrs. Glover's) own during the period of her work in Lynn. Thus we have before us all the stages which led from entire fidelity to Quimby to the later attitude as expressed in "Science and Health" after the first edition. Then, too, in the New York Times, July 10, 1904, portions of "Questions and Answers" were printed side by side with passages from "Science and Health," together with a facsimile showing emendations in Mrs. Eddy's copy of the manuscript in her own hand. The article in the Times was conclusive evidence regarding this important transition from "Questions and Answers" to "The Science of Man." All that was needed to make the textual history complete was the publication in full of "Questions and Answers" in the present volume.

From all the evidence before us it is perfectly clear, that until sometime in 1872,

at the close of her intermediate period, Mrs. Eddy maintained her attitude of loyalty to Quimby as expressed in her letters, 1862-65, and her newspaper contributions and lectures of those years. We find her in the Stoughton period still attributing "Questions and Answers" to him without qualification. After that time, as Miss Milmine has clearly shown, changes in terminology were gradually introduced, and Dr. Quimby was no longer mentioned as the writer and discoverer. What followed is not for us to chronicle here.

For our present purposes it is a question of the gradual development of Dr. Quimby's own views, which have reached a certain stage of clearness only in the case of "Questions and Answers." Dr. Quimby was not at his best when thus answering questions, but rather when giving the silent treat-ment and conversing with his patients. While Mrs. Eddy was limited to a few manuscripts, in so far as she copied or rewrote them for her own purpose as a teacher, she had also had the benefit of that decisive silent healing and the touch with a quickening personality which gave her the directive impetus for her own work. This is the main consideration. And this ought not to be lost sight of in our interest in tracing the vicissitudes of such a manuscript as "Questions and Answers."

For better or worse, that manuscript is Quimby's. We may read it as a secondary expression of what Quimby believed, or we may read it to see just how it led to the development of the later Christian Science. One should guard against claiming too much either for this particular manuscript or for the use to which it was put by Mrs. Eddy. For no one who knows the facts from within has ever claimed that Dr. Quimby actually wrote Mrs. Eddy's book, "Science and Health." What has been claimed, and rightfully so, is that from Dr. Quimby in the period under consideration in this chapter Mrs. Eddy, then Mrs. Patterson, having been restored to health by the great healer, whom she publicly acknowledged as working by the truth which Jesus taught, acquired the essential ideas and methods which gave being to her version of Christian Science.

"Question and Answers," used as the basis for teaching for several years, was the connecting link. The "Science of Man" stands for another link in the chain of development, the first and second editions of "Science and Health" for other links. To understand all these in their connection is to understand the origin and the various expressions of the later Christian Science.

Chapter Thirteen - Questions and Answers

[In order to clear the way for real understanding of his theory, Dr. Quimby wrote in February, 1862, answers to fifteen questions put to him by one of his patients. Copies of this manuscript were kept on hand to loan to new patients, and some of the patients made their own copies. On the cover of a copy made in June, 1862, George Quimby has written, "Mrs. Patterson first saw Dr. Quimby in Oct., 1862, 4 months after this was written. Questions and Answers. Portland, June, 1862" George Quimby loaned a copy of this manuscript to Miss Milmine when she was tracing out the various changes made in "Questions and Answers," as recorded in her "Life of Mary Baker G. Eddy." (1) This manuscript is not so clear as the brief articles printed in the following chapter, and known as "Volume I," also loaned to patients and Mrs. Patterson-Eddy. It is printed as originally written, with a few changes in punctuation and capitalization to conform to writings of the same year. Obscure points will be made plain by selections from later articles, in Chapters XV-XVIII.]

QUESTION 1. You must have a feeling of repugnance towards certain patients. How do you overcome it and how can I do the same ?
Answer. In order to make you fully understand how I overcome the repugnance it will require some little explanation of my mode of curing, for my cures are in my belief or wisdom, and the patient's disease is in his belief or knowledge. Now my wisdom is not knowledge, for what a man thinks he knows is knowledge or opinion, but what is wisdom to a man, he has no opinion about. As God is Wisdom, Wisdom is Science and we call the proof of getting Science knowledge, belief or reason; but when the answer comes, our knowledge vanishes and we are swallowed up in God or Wisdom. The sick are strangers to this Wisdom, being led by false guides without it, who have eyes and see not, ears and hear not, and hearts that cannot understand, therefore like strangers they are at the mercy of every one's opinion. Having a strong desire for wisdom or health, they call on every one for their food or wisdom. So when they ask for bread they receive a stone, or for water they receive vinegar, and thus they are driven like sheep to the slaughter, not daring to open their mouths. This is the state of the patient who asks the above question. My wisdom sees their condition, feels their woes and comes to the rescue, but to get them from their enemy is often an arduous task. The repugnance of which you speak is not towards their personal senses, but to the ideas their senses are attached to. As the ideas are knowledge to them, they are a person besides themselves and it is the identity disease that I first come in contact with. This is what I have to annihilate, and at first I sometimes feel a repugnance towards the sick such as a man will feel in entering a penitentiary to rescue a victim, who has been innocently confined, the disturbance of the rescue sets the house in an uproar, the victim not knowing the cause is as much frightened as her enemies. But when I succeed in destroying her enemies or opinion and get her to wisdom or [her real] self she receives me as one who has saved her from the jaws of death. This to her is health and happiness. You say how can I do the same? If you believe this Wisdom is superior to opinions, and that opinions are nothing but error that man has embraced, then when you come in contact with a person diseased, your wisdom will throw the mantle of charity over their errors, if it is for the restoration of their health. But if the repugnance arises from some unknown cause, examine yourself and see if the fault lies at your own door. If not you may be sure it is some false opinion in the person that troubles them. So to overcome their evil or error, pour on coals from the fire of love or charity in the form of right reason till you melt down the image of brass that is set up in their minds, and they will leave their errors and embrace the truth.   This is heaven.
2.   "You say when you know a thing, it is not an opinion. I can understand that, but how may I be really sure I know a thing? I have felt perfectly sure of a thing and still afterwards found I had been in error, or had been mistaken."
Knowledge, as I have said, is not wisdom, but it may be harmony and it may seem like wisdom. Yet there is a discord. So discord is harmony not understood. To know how to correct this harmony or knowledge that it may be wisdom is the question to consider. The first part of your question where you say "I can understand that" is contradictory to the last sentence, showing that you do not understand. Here is the discord. You say you have been perfectly sure of a thing and yet found you have been mistaken. Now if your wisdom had been perfect, in the thing you thought you knew, it would have revealed the discord or error. So to purify yourself from error so that you may know the truth or Wisdom, is a

process of reasoning outside of matter, for there is no wisdom in matter. So that when you have arrived at a truth, if you find it attached to a belief, you may know it is not a truth, for it may change; but this is a truth, that a belief may be changed. God is Truth and there is no other truth, and if we know God the same is known to us. I will now try to attach your senses to God, not the God of this world or Christian's God; but the God of the living, and not of the dead. My God is my standard of truth, and as I know God the same is known to me. I know I am writing this if I know anything; but to know that I shall finish it admits a doubt and to know that you will understand it admits more doubt. This doubt is not wisdom but belongs to that class of man's inventions called reason, knowledge, etc. God is not seen in this question, perfect, except as far as I see, but He is seen in the clouds of my knowledge. When you read this if you understand it, then you will see God face to face but not as Moses did. I await your answer, to know whether He does appear to your understanding; if so then here is your proof that you are born of God in this one thing then you cannot know anything more so far as this question goes. Man's God is all the time listening to his prayers and setting all sorts of trouble. My God does not act at all, He has finished His work and leaves man to work out his happiness according to his own wisdom. I will give you the attributes of my God. The Wisdom or God is in this letter, and if you understand, you will hear His voice saying I understand this. So the understanding is God, for in that there is no matter, and to understand is Wisdom, not matter, and to know wisdom is to know God, for that is Wisdom. I will give you some ideas of God, reduced to man's knowledge. All science is a part of God, and when man understands Science the same is known to God; but the world's God is based on man's opinion and right and wrong is the invention of man, while God is in their reason, but not known. Here is an illustration. The bells are ringing. I walk to church and take a seat. The minister opens the Bible and reads the text from John. The fact of going to church, and seeing the minister is known to me, but there might be a doubt in regard to the Bible, for it might be another book. This last I admit with a doubt, and also the verse and chapter is a doubt. He reads the thirteenth chapter of John, 36th verse, where Peter says, "Lord, why cannot I follow thee now? I will lay down my life for thy sake." All the above as far as words go is true, but when he comes to explain where Jesus went, when He came back, or if He went at all, and why His wisdom was knowledge, he reminded me of Paul's words: "All men have knowledge, knowledge puffeth up, charity or wisdom edifieth." I could see nothing but an opinion of what he had no wisdom, a parable of something which he might know as a belief but not wisdom. The explanation of the Bible is founded on man's opinion, and not on Wisdom. The Bible contains Wisdom, but it is not understood, and to prove a thing is to put your proof into practice, for all men can give an opinion. Jesus came into the world not to give an opinion, but to bring light into the world upon some-thing that was in the dark. What was it? where was it? how did He describe it? and what was the remedy? He tells the story Himself, where He called His disciples together and gave them power or wisdom. Now if it was power and not wisdom, then He knew not what Wisdom was. So far as I can see, it admits a doubt, but I have no doubt of what He meant to command them to do.   In Math. Ch. XI. He went to preach, and put His preaching into practice. John was cast into prison for preaching the coming of some one who would put this great truth into practice, so he sent one of his dis-ciples to Jesus to inquire if He was the one that was to come, or do we look for another. Now what was He to come for? Jesus answers this question when He said, "Go tell John the things you have seen and heard, how the blind receive their sight, etc." After telling how John or this truth had suffered, how it had been put down by force, He made a parable of the ignorance of his generation. "We have piped unto you and ye have not danced." Then giving a statement about error, He says "Oh Father, Lord of heaven and earth, because thou hast hidden this truth from the wise and revealed it unto babes," even so is it. All things concerning these errors are revealed unto me by my Father. No one knows the truth but the Father, save the son, Jesus, and those to whom He shall teach this truth. Then He says, "Come unto me, all ye that labor and are heavy laden and I will give you rest, take my yoke upon you and learn of me, for my burden is light." You see that His labor was with the sick, and not the well, and all His talk was to explain where the people had been deceived by the priests and doctors, and if they learned wisdom they would be cured. The knowledge of man puts false construction on his wisdom and gets up a sort of religion which has nothing to do with Jesus' truth. There is where the fault lies. If you do not believe the Bible as they explain it then you are an infidel. So all who cannot believe it as it has been explained, must throw it away. I do not throw the Bible away, but throw the explanation away, and apply Jesus' own words as He did and as He intended they should be applied, and let my works speak for themselves, whether they are of God or man, and leave the sick to judge.

3.   "Our spiritual senses are often more acute than our natural ones. What is the difference ? What do you call the spirit-world?"

I will try to explain the difference between spiritual and natural senses. If I had never seen you and wished to write you a letter on some worldly affair, I should address your natural senses, and you would attach yourself to my knowledge. Suppose you believe what I say, then your belief is founded on my knowledge. This belongs to the natural world and your happiness or misery is in your belief. But I have sat by you and taken your feelings, these are [disclosed by] your spiritual senses, not wisdom but ideas not named or classified. In the spiritual world there are things as they are in the natural world that affect us as much, but these are not known by the natural senses or wisdom. The separation of these is what Jesus calls the Law and the Gospel. The natural senses are under the law governed by the knowledge of the natural world, subject to all the penalties and punishments man can invent. The spiritual senses have their spiritual world, with [knowledge of] all the inventions of the natural world, but the communication [relationship] is not admitted by the natural man except as a mystery. There is just as much progress in the spiritual as in the natural world, and the Science I teach is the wisdom of my God [applied] to the senses in the spiritual world. So it requires a teacher to teach the wisdom of God in the spiritual world, as well as that spiritual wisdom that has been reduced to man's senses in the so-called science. Paul says "How shall they believe in him of whom they have not heard? And how shall they hear without a preacher?" And how shall they teach unless they be sent or understand how to teach? I am now talking to your spiritual senses, standing at your door, knocking with my wisdom at your heart or belief for admittance; if you can understand, then I will come in and drink this Truth with you, and you with me. This is the spiritual world or senses. Suppose you are sick, and feel you need a physician; then is the time you in your spirit will call on me, or my spirit, and when I come if you know my voice or understand, you will open the door, and when you do understand, I am with you.

4.   "Is not one's own experience wisdom to him in a certain sense ?"

Wisdom is not knowledge but the answer to our knowl-edge. But in error knowledge is wisdom, till Wisdom comes. For example: Suppose I make a sound, that is not wisdom but a sensation. Suppose you try to imitate it, this process is called knowledge or reason. When the sound is in tone with me, this is wisdom not understood. So we call it wisdom, but when we can make the tone intelligently and teach it to others, then the tone is the effect of wisdom, and wisdom comes out of the discord. Wisdom is always the same, it is the point of all attraction, and everything must come to this, it is harmony. This is the Christ. True Wisdom contains no matter, false wisdom is the harmony not understood. I will illustrate: Suppose you tell me a story that you say is true, but you get your information from another. I believe it and to me it is wisdom, but you see it is not wisdom, for there is a chance for deception. But Wisdom leaves no loophole, it can be tested. This was the contra versy of Jesus. The priests thought their opinions were wisdom, but He knew they were false. To test their wisdom was to put it into practice, so every one was to be known by his works, whether they were of God or not. Jesus showed His wisdom by His works, for when they brought Him the sick He healed them. So did others pretending the same way. If Jesus knew how He cured, then the kingdom of heaven had come to their understanding; but if He did not, then He was just as ignorant as they were, and the world was no wiser for His cures. His wisdom was from above, theirs from man's ignorance. These made the two worlds, Science and error, and as man has borne the one, he shall also bear the other.

5.   "Is it possible for one to condense his spiritual self so as to be seen by the natural eye of others as Jesus did?"

This question is not properly stated. Jesus never said He had a spirit, but said, "spirit hath not flesh and blood, as you see me have." There was the rock that they split upon. Jesus' wisdom knew that it was not in the idea body: their knowledge made mind in and a part of the body. So each reasoned according to their wisdom. Their wisdom was their opinion about what persons had said a thousand years before without any proof but merely as an opinion; this they called knowledge. Therefore Jesus' wisdom or Christ was a mystery to them. So when Christ or Wisdom spake through Jesus saying, "though you destroy this temple I will build it up again," this that spoke was the wisdom, so the builder was not destroyed, but the temple. But they believed as all the Christians of our day do, that the temple and the builder were the same; so that when the former was destroyed, they had no idea of what Christ intended to do. Here comes in your question. The Christ that acted upon the idea "Jesus" admitted flesh and blood as well as His enemies, but His wisdom knew it was only an idea, that He could speak into existence and out. So when they destroyed the idea "Jesus" they destroyed to themselves Jesus Christ, or mind and matter. Now when this Wisdom made Himself manifest to them, they thought He was a spirit, for they believed in spirits, but Christ to Himself was the same Jesus as before; for Jesus only means the idea of flesh and blood or senses, or all that we call man. Now, Christ retained all this and to Himself He had flesh and blood. This was to show that when you think a person dead he is dead to you, but to himself there is no change, he retains all the senses of the natural man, (2) as though no change to the world had taken place. This was what Jesus wanted to prove. Man condenses his identity just according to his belief; this all men do, some more than others. I cannot tell how much I can condense my identity to the sick, but I know I can touch them so they can feel the sensation. To me I really see myself but I cannot tell about them. I will try to prove the answer to you. When you read this I will show you myself and also the number of persons in the room where I am, writing this. Let me know the impression you may have of the number. This is the Christ that Jesus spoke of. How much of the Christ I can make known to you, I wait your answer to learn. Read the 16th Chap. of John; He speaks of this truth that shall come to the disciples as I am coming to you. (3)

6.   "If I understood how disease originates in the mind and fully believe it why cannot I cure disease?

If you understand how disease originates, then you stand to the patient as a lawyer does to a criminal who is to be tried for a crime committed against a law that he is ignorant of breaking, and the evidence is his own confession. You know that he is innocent, but you can get no evidence, only by cross-questioning the evidence against him. Disease has its attending counsel as well as truth or health, and to cure the sick is to show to the judge or their own counsel that the witness lies. This you have to show from the witness' own story, then you get the case. The error is on one side and you on the other, and out of the mouth of the sick comes the witness. I will first state a case. A sick person is like a stranger in his own land, or like an ignorant man not knowing what is law or right and wrong according to law. Both are strangers and both are liable to get into trouble, so each is to be punished according to the crime he has committed. Now the man, ignorant of state laws wants a horse, seeing one he takes it, not knowing that he is liable to any punishment, but as a matter of conven-ience, and when he has used him as much as he pleases he lets him go. Now, he is arrested for stealing, and being ignorant he is cast into prison to await his trial. I appear against him as state's attorney, and you appear for the prisoner. All the testimony is on my side, but if you are shrewd enough to draw from me an acknowledgment that the law cannot punish a man that is ignorant of the law (and not know it) after I have shown the testimony and made my plea, then if you can show that the prisoner has been deceived, and led into the scrape by me, I having received pay from him, then the court will give you the verdict, and arrest and imprison me. A sick person is precisely in this very state. The priests and doctors conspire together to humbug the people, and they have invented all sorts of stories to frighten man and keep him under their power. These stories are handed down from one generation to another till at last both priest and doctors all believe they are God's laws and when a person disobeys one he is liable to be cast into prison. Suppose you are a doctor of the law of health as it is called, and you call on her and commence explaining the necessity of being acquainted with the laws pertaining to health. She being ignorant or like a child sees no sense in your talk; but you continue to explain, and as she grows nervous you keep it up till she shows some sign of yielding to your opinion, then you tell her she has the heart disease, or lung disease and it will soon be found out, and then she will be punished with death at any time that the Judge sees fit to call her. In her fright, she acknowledges she is guilty, then you enter a complaint against her. She is arrested and cast into prison, there to await her trial, you are the devil or error's attorney and she is the judge; she is brought into court to be tried by error's tribunal. Now I appear, for I have heard her story, unknown to the judge or attorney. I have the evidence and see that the very attorney against her is her disease and the author of her trouble. This I keep to myself, till I draw from the judge that a person cannot be tried for a crime which they were forced to commit. This being done, I commence my plea for the victim and show that she has never committed any offense against the laws of God and that she was born free, etc. Then I take up the evidence and show that there is not one word of wisdom in all that has been said, also that she has been made to believe a lie that she might be condemned. In this way I get the case. Disease being made by a belief, or forced upon us by our parents or public opinion, you see there is no particular form of agreement, but everyone must suit his to the particular case. Therefore it requires great shrewdness to get the better of the error: for disease is the work of the devil or error, but error like its father has its cloven foot and if you are as wise as your enemies you will get the case. I know of no better answer than Jesus gave to His disciples when He sent them forth and told them to preach the truth and cure. Be ye wise as they were, or serpents, and as harmless as doves, that is, do not get into a rage. In this way you will annoy the disease and get the case. Now if you can face the error and argue it down, then you can cure the sick.

7.   "I can see this belief places man entirely superior to circumstances, but will it not therefore take away all desire for improvement and cause invention to cease, and the whole go back rather than progress, and cause us also to become indifferent to friends and social relations, and say of everything that it is only an idea without substance, and so take away the reality of existence ?"

The answer to this is involved in the last. You can answer it by your own feelings, when you plead the case of the sick, condemned by the world, cast into prison with no one to say a cheering word, but left to the cold icy hand of ignorance and superstition, who have no heart to feel and whose life depends on its destruction. If you can be the means of pleading their case and set them free from their prisons or superstitions and error, into the light of wisdom and happiness, there to mingle with the well and happy, knowing that you were the cause of so much happiness, would it not be enough to prompt you to continue your efforts for the salvation of the sick and suffering, till the great work of reformation is completed? You may answer for yourself, and say if it does not place man superior to the interests of this world, and instead of taking away the reality of existence it makes man's existence an eternal progression of joy and happiness, and its tendency is to destroy death and bring life and immortality to light.

8.   "Suppose a person kept in a mesmeric state, what would be the result? Would he act independently if allowed? If not, is it not an exact illustration of the condition we are in, in order to have matter which is only an idea seem real to us, for we act independently?"

I think I understand your question. God is the great mesmeriser or magnet,(4) He speaks man or the idea into existence, and attaches His senses to the idea and we are to ourselves just what we think we are. So [man] is a mesmerised subject, they are to themselves matter. You may have as many subjects as you will and they are all in the same relation to each other as they would be in the state we call waking. So this is proof that we are affected by one another, sometimes independently and sometimes governed by others, but always retaining our own identity, with all our ideas of matter and subject to all its changes, as real as it is
in the natural or waking state.

9.   "What do you think of phrenology?"

As a science it is a mere humbug. It is at best a polite way of pointing out the soft spots of a man's vanity.

10.   "What is memory, or that process by which we recall images of the past?"

I have explained memory in that class of reason called knowledge. It is one of the chemical changes to arrive at a fact, matter being only a shadow. When the senses are detached from it we forget the shadow, till it is called up by another. This is memory. If there was no association there could be no memory and those that have the greatest amount of association, and least wisdom have the greatest memories. Those who rely on observation and opinion as the laws of reason have great memories, for their life is in their memory. But the former retain their reason as it is called and are forgetful of events. Memory is the pleasure or pain of some cause or event that affects our happiness or misery, or it is something ludicrous. For instance, a judge hearing one tell another "his coat-tail was short," and the other replied "it will be long enough before I get another" attempted to repeat the joke, but he forgot the sympathy or music in it, and said, "a man told another his coat-tail was short, and he replied, it would be a long time before he got another one." The company failed to laugh and he said, "I do not see anything to laugh at myself, but when I heard it I laughed heartily" Memory is the effect of two ideas coming in harmony so as to produce an effect that leaves a scene of some idea either ridiculous or otherwise embracing so many combinations that it brings up the scene. Memory is one of the senses of man and will exist so long as the idea matter exists. (5)

11.   "What became of the body of Jesus after it was laid in the ground, if you do not believe it rose?"
Jesus is the idea "matter," so those that believed that Jesus Christ was one believed that His body and soul were crucified. Now came their doubts whether this same idea should rise again. Some believed it would, others doubted. So far as Christ was concerned, all their opinions had no effect. Christ was the Wisdom that knew matter was only an idea that could be formed into any shape, and the life that moved it came not from it but was outside of it. Here was where their wisdom differed. The disciples believed that the wisdom of man would rise out of the error or idea "man," or matter, and matter comes under the head of memory. How far their idea of Jesus went I am unable to say. Some said He was stolen, others that He rose. There is as good reason for believing one story as another. Now, Jesus said nothing about it. Now, I take Christ's own words for truth when He said touching the dead that they rise, "God is not the God of the dead, but of the living." He knew that they could not understand, but to Himself Christ went through no change. To His disciples He died. So when they saw Him they were afraid because they thought He was a spirit, but Christ had not forgotten His identity Jesus, or flesh and blood. So He says, "a spirit hath not flesh and bones as you see me have." If Christ's believers of this day could have been there with their present belief, I have my doubts whether they could have seen or even heard any sound. Yet I believe Christ did appear and show Himself as dense as their belief could be made, but their unbelief made the idea so rarified that it was a spirit. These are my ideas of the resurrection of Christ. But Jesus [according to] the world's idea (if the people were as they are now) was without doubt taken away; at any rate, their idea man never rose. Christ lost nothing by the change.   Every person rises from the dead with their own belief, so to themselves they are not risen and know no change, and the dead as they are called have no idea of themselves as dead.

12.   "Do we receive impressions through the senses and do they, acting upon the mind, constitute knowledge?"
This question is answered by Paul to the Romans, although he did not use the same words. This belief means faith, the peace in the truth was through their belief. Hope is the anchor made fast to the truth, belief is the knowledge that we shall attain this truth, so that we glory in the tribulation or action of the mind, knowing that it brings patience and patience confidence and confidence experience, that we shall obtain the truth. Knowledge is opinions, so when an impression is made on the mind it produces a chemical change, this comes to the senses and opens the door of hope to the great truth. This hope is the world's knowledge or religion that is used like an anchor to the senses till we ride out the gale of investigation and land in the haven of God or Truth.

13.   "How is matter made the medium of the intelligence of man?"
There are two ideas, one spirit and one matter. When you speak of man you speak of matter. When you speak of spirit you speak of the knowledge that will live after the matter is destroyed or dead. This is the Christian's wisdom. With God in all the above is only opinions and ideas without any wisdom from God or Truth. All the above is embraced in his idea as an illusion that contains no life but lives, moves, has its being and identity in his wisdom. So that to itself it is a living, moving something with power to act to create and destroy. Its happiness and misery are in itself. So when its shadow is destroyed to B and C he is dead. A loses nothing but is the same as before, but to B and C he is dead. So the shadow is the medium of truth and error, to error it is matter but to Truth it is an illusion.

14.   "Do I err in thinking knowledge the effect of some influence on the mind, instead of something independent of the whole individual?"
Knowledge is the effect of an influence on the mind and is the medium that carries the senses to this great Truth.

15.   "Can any one bear any amount of excitement and fatigue without a reaction?"
No, no more than a mathematician can solve every problem without a reaction, but as he becomes master of the science, the reaction diminishes, till all error is destroyed.

Dr. Quimby's writings are not to establish any religious creed or bolster up any belief of man, but they are simply the out-pouring of a truth, that sees the sick cast into prison, for no other cause than a belief in the opinions of man, there to linger out a miserable existence, driven from society into the dark cell of disease where no friend is allowed to enter to soothe their woes. The knowledge of this condition is known to him from their own feelings and calls forth his plea in their behalf. He stands to the sick as an attorney to a criminal, a friend. This is what he believes Jesus intended to communicate to the world when he said, "they that are well need not a physician, but they that are sick." So he pleads their case and destroys their opinion, breaks the bars of death and sets the prisoner free. This was Jesus' religion, that he believed, taught, and practised. (6)

Notes

(1) See Appendix, "The Quimby-Eddy Controversy." 166
(2) The italics are Quimby's.
(3) That is, Dr. Quimby will make himself known by means of an "absent treatment," and this will show the questioner how far Quimby can project his spiritual self.
(4) Quimby says this to try to bring meaning from an obscure question. He uses no such expression in his other writings.
(5) Elsewhere Quimby calls matter much more than a "shadow" or "idea."
(6) This paragraph was added by Dr. Quimby for the sake of the general inquirer.

Chapter Fourteen - Christ or Science

[The articles published under this head constitute Vol. I of the Quimby writings. They are published here in the order in which they were copied from the originals, as written, save for a few changes made under Quimby's super-vision, and slight condensations. They are printed in this order instead of being arranged in connection with other pieces on the same topics, because they were the first papers containing a statement of the general theory, and the copy-book containing them was sometimes loaned to patient-students, including the one who made liberal use of their contents.
In these studies Quimby speaks of mind, in the ordinary sense of the term, as a "substance" which can be changed, in which thoughts are sown as seeds. Mind is put in contrast with intelligence or Wisdom. Thus intelligence is said to possess an "identity" or reality which mind does not have. The next step is to show that the human soul has clairvoyance or intuition, independent of the natural senses. This fact Quimby had proved by repeated experiments in diagnosing the sick.
The term "matter" is used in a peculiar sense throughout, to cover the processes of change attendant upon suggestion and taking place subconsciously. "Thoughts are things," later writers have said.
One of the copybooks containing these studies has emendations in pencil, made under Quimby's directions by Miss Sarah Ware, in preparation for a book. The following introductory note by Dr. Quimby is written on the page opposite the first article. It is given here word for word as written.]

It will be necessary to give the reader some idea of what suggested the following article, headed Mind is Spiritual Matter. I found that by the power of my own mind I could change the mind of my patient and produce a chemical change in the body, like dissolving a tumor. Now the word mind is not the substance, only the name of the substance that can be changed. The world makes mind intelligence, i. e., direction. I put no intelligence in it, but make it subject to intelligence. The word fire, for instance, doesn't mean the substance to be consumed but the process of consuming it. So mind is the name of a spiritual substance that can be changed. We speak of a cold fire or a hot fire, yet we do not mean that the fire itself is cold or hot, only that we make it hotter or colder; yet it is fire, subject to our direction. Wisdom I do not use in this piece. I call the power that governs mind, spirit. But you will see that I recognize a Wisdom superior to the word mind, for I always apply the word mind to matter, but never apply it to the First Cause.

MIND IS SPIRITUAL MATTER

Thought is also matter, but not the same matter, any more than the earth is the same matter as the seed which is put into it. Thought like the seed germinates and comes forth, like the tree, in the form of an idea. It then waits like the fruit to be eaten. Curiosity is excited and wants to be gratified; it tastes and then inquires; the answer comes and the spirit is affected in proportion to the answer. Illustration: A thought is sown in the mind while asleep or ignorant, it grows and comes forth. The curiosity tastes; it produces a strange sensation in the throat. The spirit inquires, the answer comes, Bronchitis. The spirit is disturbed and tries to rid itself of its enemy. This disturbance is the effect called disease. Now if no name had been given or fears excited, the idea or tree would have died of itself. -Oct. 1859.

WHAT IS DISEASE?

Disease is what follows the disturbance of the mind or spiritual matter. When I speak of disease I do not mean to confine the word to any particular phenomenon or disturbance of the mind, but that mind is disturbed like the soil of the earth ready to receive the seed. This disturbance contains no knowledge or thought, any more than a house on fire which disturbs the inmates or spirits, who flee out, not knowing the cause. It embraces mind without truth or error, like weight set in motion with-out direction. Weight like mind could never set itself in motion, but being set in motion it is called mechanical power. So is mind set in motion spiritual power. Both are governed by laws of truth or error, the fruit shows which of the two powers governs. If it is directed by the wisdom of God no bad results can follow, but if directed by error and ignorance, as ignorance is the enemy to truth, the truth will show which governs. As there is no knowledge in error, it sometimes happens that some results follow, as it did in the case of selling Joseph to the Ishmaelites. They, it is said, meant it for evil, but God meant it for good. Truth does not work in that way (that is, by accident). Truth works by laws, like mathematics;-error like chance.

The answer may come right, or may come wrong (in error) either way it contains no law by which the world is wiser. Ignorance is its life and truth its death. So by error comes disease or death. But by the destruction of error comes the introduction of Truth or Science, or health; and as error is matter or mind, it is the instrument of its own destruction. The matter is not annihilated, but the opinion is.

The combination which shows itself in persons in the form of an opinion, indicates its character by a peculiar show of wisdom superior to its followers, and when disturbed by Wisdom or Truth, it dies, but when not opposed, its opinions are sown into the minds of others, like seed in the ground, which comes forth in some form.

This form which follows the disturbance of the mind the doctors call disease. Here is where all the error lies; they take the effect for the cause. We confound the error and truth together; we take an opinion for a truth. This is an error, for what we know we have no opinion of. Knowledge is the destruction of an opinion or disease. Disease is what follows an opinion, it is made up of mind directed by error, and Truth is the destruction of this opinion.

These ideas, and hundreds of others, have been given to explain the effect of the mind. All admit the mind one thing and disease another. This theory that mind is one thing and disease another, has left the people in darkness, and caused more misery than all other evils put together. It has always been admitted that a theory that cannot be put in practice is not good.

Mind is a spiritual matter which, being agitated, disturbs the spirit. This disturbance contains no knowledge of itself, but produces a chemical change in the fluids of the system. These disturbances may be produced in various ways, for instance, by a shock on the mind, by the death of a friend, or by religious excitement, witchcraft, etc. All of the above contain what is called knowledge, which is communicated to the spirit and sets it to work to form disease, after the form the spirit gives the mind. The mind being the matter under the control of the spirit, is capable of producing any phenomenon. -Oct. 1859.

HOW DOES THE MIND PRODUCE DISEASE?

I will give the symptoms of a person who called on me to be examined. The upper part of his body above his hips felt so large that his legs were not strong enough to carry the weight, therefore he complained of weakness in his knees. This idea of weakness was in his mind, for there never was any strength or knowledge in his knees of themselves, any more than there is power in a lever of itself. If the lever, or legs, had to create its own power his body would never move. Therefore, if his body ever moved, it must be by some power independent of his knees or legs. There is such a thing as pressure, but pressure is not power, for it contains motion and motion is another element.

These two elements together we call mechanical power, so mind agitated is called spiritual power. Neither matter nor mind contains any knowledge. As this man's mind was in a state in which it contained motion or error, (for error is motion, not knowledge), it was not all pressure. As health is the enjoyment of all our faculties, any foreign substance trigs the wheels so as to retard the motion, so error trigs the mind or retards the motion. This was the state of this man's body. To put this man in full possession of his faculties is to remove the burden that binds him down. These burdens are the effect of error having control of the mind. These errors are made of mind or matter first formed into an opinion, then comes reason, then comes disease or death, accompanied by all the misery the idea contains.-Oct. 1859.

MIND IS NOT INTELLIGENCE

Intelligence contains no thought, nor opinion or reason. Mind contains them all. Disease is the offspring of the mind, not of intelligence. All the above is the result of a chem-ical change, to bring about and develop some scientific law that will put man in possession of a knowledge of himself, so that he will avoid the evils which man [through his ignorance] is subect to.

Thoughts are like electric sparks. Knowledge classifies and arranges them in a language nearer itself so as to use them for a medium with which to communicate an idea to another. This is the state of all men. Under this state of mind all the laws of science have been developed. Every day brings to light some new idea not yet developed, but bursting forth to the natural world. During this process, the mind undergoes very powerful changes which affect the body, even to the destruction of the same. But this destruction contains no wisdom, it is only the destruction of the idea. The effect still agitates the mind till its end is accomplished. Then the mind returns to its quiet state, and the law is understood. While all this is going on, as in all sciences, ideas come forth and the minds are affected, and try for the prize; for instance, the idea of navigating the air. All minds are excited. Experiments are tried; accidents, as they are called happen, and lives are lost to this world of error. But that which governs life cannot be lost; but must mingle in with the idea of progression-not losing its identity. What man loses in weight or matter, he makes up in science or knowledge. Therefore, accidents as they are called must happen, and we say, woe to them that are affected; it would have been better, as we think, if they had never been born. This would be true, if it were the end of their existence. Now as these laws develop themselves, is the trouble in the laws or in ourselves? Accidents are the errors or diseases. Correcting these errors and establishing the Truth or Science is curing the disease or establishing the law.

I have said that when any new idea comes up a class of persons enter into the investigation of it, but very few are ever able to put the idea into practice, or get the prize, though most all can understand something of the theory. There is a vast difference between talking a theory, and talking about a theory. Talking about a theory is like talking about a science we do not understand; it contains no wisdom. Wisdom contains no opinion or selfishness; and, like charity, has no ill will towards its neighbor, but like the rays of the sun, is always ready to impart heat to all who will come to the light.

To cure a disease is to understand the law by which that disease was produced. To make it more plain, I will suppose a case. In supposing a case the person you address must suppose himself perfectly well. Now as thoughts contain a substance set in motion by error to form an idea, this sub-stance acts upon another like a galvanic battery, and keeps up a deposit of thought till the idea is formed in the mind. These thoughts may arise from different causes. I will select one. Suppose you become acquainted with a person, the first impression is a shock from his mind, this shock is kept up till an idea is formed in your mind.   The motive or disease is in the idea of the person from whom you receive the shock. To you it contains no knowledge.

You receive it as a sweet morsel that you can roll under your tongue. You nurse and foster it in your breast till it becomes a part of yourself. You form a strong attachment for it, and as it contains the character of this father, you become attached to the author. When the idea becomes developed and you find what it con-tains, you see you have been fostering a viper, that will sting you to the heart. Grief, passion, fear and love, take possession of your mind; reason enters into the combination, and a warfare commences. Hatred takes the place of love, truth the place of ignorance, firmness takes the place of weakness, and a battle ensues. As truth works through this error or disease, wisdom and happiness take its place, the evil is cast out, the author or idea is despised, and the mind is changed. You see the deception. Your knowledge is the enmancipation of the error, and all that followed it, the Truth sets you free and happy, which is the cure.

Now sensations can be learned (1) before they affect the body or produce disease, so that they [will] fall harmless at your feet. It is necessary that all persons have a teacher, till they can teach themselves. The question then arises, How can a person believe in one whom he has never heard, and how can he learn without a teacher, and how can one teach without he is sent?-Nov. 1859.

IS THE CURING OF DISEASE A SCIENCE?

I answer, yes. You may ask, Who is the founder of that Science? I answer, Jesus Christ. Then comes the question, What proof have you that it is a science? Because Christ healed the sick, that of itself is no proof that He knew what He was doing. I answer, If it was done, it must have been done by some law or science, for there can be no such thing as accident with God, and if Christ was God, He did know what He was doing.   When He was accused of curing disease through Beelzebub or ignorance, He said, "If I cast out devils or diseases through Beelzebub or ignorance, my kingdom or science cannot stand; but if I cast out devils or disease through a science or law, then my kingdom or law will stand, for it is not of this world" When others cast out disease, they cured by ignorance or Beelzebub, and there was no science in their cures, although an effect was produced; but not knowing the cause the world was none the wiser for their cures.

At another time when told by His disciples that they saw persons curing or casting out devils in His name, and forbade them, He said, "They that are with us are not against us, but they that are not with us, or are ignorant of the laws of curing, scattereth abroad, for the world is none the wiser." Here, you see, He makes a difference between His mode of curing and theirs. If Christ's cures were done by the power of God, and Christ was God, He must have known what that power or science was, and if He did, He knew the difference between His science and their ignorance. His Science was His Kingdom therefore it was not of this world, and theirs being of this world, He called it the kingdom of darkness. To enter into Christ's Kingdom or Science, was to enter into the laws or knowledge of curing the evils of this world of darkness. As disease is an evil, it is of this world, and is in this kingdom of darkness. To separate one world from the other, is to separate the truth from the error, and as error is death and truth is life, the resurrection of one is the destruction of the other. (2) -Nov. 1859.

IS DISEASE A BELIEF?

I answer it is, for an individual is to himself just what he thinks he is, and he is in his belief sick. If I believe I am sick, I am sick, for my feelings are my sickness, and my sickness is my belief, and my belief is my mind. Therefore all disease is in the mind or belief. Now as our belief or disease is made up of ideas, which are [spiritual] matter, it is necessary to know what beliefs we are in; for to cure the disease is to correct the error, and as disease is what follows the error, destroy the cause, and the effect will cease. How can this be done? By a knowledge of the law of harmony. To illustrate this law of harmony I must take some law that you will admit. I will take the law of mathematics. You hear of a mathematical problem, you wish to solve it; the answer is in the problem, the error is in it, the happiness and misery are also in it. Your error is the cause of your sickness or trouble. Now to cure your sickness or trouble, is to correct the error. If you knew the real state of things, you would not call on a person who knows no more than you do, if you knew that fact.-Nov. 1859.

LIFE AND DISEASE

True life is health, knowledge, and happiness. Death is disease, error, misery and pain; all in this belief. Each of the above is called our knowledge, and to believe in one is to disbelieve in the other, for our life is in our belief. Death is the destruction of the one, and the life of the other, or the disbelief of the one, and the belief of the other. Christ came to destroy death or belief, and bring life and immortality to light, and this life or belief was in Christ. They that lost their life or belief for his sake should find it. Upon this rock I build my faith, and the gates of death cannot change me. Now your life is in your belief, and you are known by the fruits. As I impart my Truth to you, it is your life or health. As you receive my life you die to your own. My life in you grows to a truth and this is your health or happiness.-Nov. 1859.

DISEASE

What is disease? It is what follows the effect of a false direction given to the mind or spiritual matter. The body is composed of matter, not mind, but when agitated, that part which is called heat, and is thrown off, is mind or spirit. It is not intelligence, but a medium to be used according to the direction given it, by a power independent of itself, -like that direction given to mechanical power. The effect of this direction (call it what you please) on the body, is to destroy itself, for its life is its own destruction.-Dec. 1859.

LOVE, 1

What is the strongest feeling in man or woman? Love for the sake of love for others. For this love they will lay down their lives, when directed by knowledge, for no passion can follow true love. What makes what is called animal passion? Ignorance of ourselves, not understanding the truth. Love contains no fear; ignorance puts a false con-struction on love. Here lies all the trouble. Love and ignorance are the mother and father of all error or disease. Now to know ourselves is to know the truth of this problem. Love is an element of itself, without any form; it has no length or breadth, or height or depth; it neither comes nor goes, it fills all space, and melts all error down that comes within its power. Its power is its heat, its heat is its love, it is heaven. For this love Christ laid down His animal life or passions for mankind, that they might understand themselves and be saved from the endless hell of misery that follows our ignorance of this power or love. On these two powers, love and ignorance, hang all the law and the prophets. The gospel is love, the law is error; therefore when you are under the law, you become subject to the laws and penalties. When you are freed from that law, it has no power over you. This law of love is that love in mankind that is working in us or our error to bring us to truth and set us free from the law of sin or death. The laws of love are the destruction of the laws of error, and they make us a law to ourselves. This law of love has no penalties or prisons; but, like the bird that flies in the sky, is not troubled with earthly laws, but is a law to itself. Its purity is its buoyancy, its ignorance is its weight or stupidity. Each is governed by a sort of intelligence, like science and ignorance. As ignorance and superstition are what are under the law of error, Science and Truth are their opponents, and the mind is the medium of them both, like the telegraph-wire a medium of truth and error. Love is a substance like food that comes from heaven to feed the soul. Er-ror is matter, and contains reason and all the faculties. Love is the true answer to our desire; in our desire is our hope, and when we get that which we hope for, it contains nothing but true knowledge or love, no sorrow, nor pain, nor grief, nor shame, nor fear.-Dec. 1859.

WHAT IS MY THEORY?

The question is often asked, if I am a spiritualist. My answer is that I am not, after the manner of the Rochester rappings, but I am a believer in the spirits of the living. Here seems to be a difference of opinion. The common opinion of the people in regard to the dead I have no sympathy with, from the fact that their belief is founded on an opinion which I know is false; yet I believe them honest but misled for the want of some better explanation of the phenomenon. We see men, women, and children walking around, by and by they pass away from us, and their bodies are laid in the earth. We look on the scene and pause. A cold icy sen-sation passes through. our frame. We weep from our ignorance. We have seen the matter in a form moving about as though it contained life. Now it lies, cold and clammy, and our hope is cut off. Perhaps it is a son or daughter, in whom we have had hopes, raised to the highest extreme, of seeing them stand before the world, loved and respected for their worth, now gone forever. Doubts and fears take possession of oar minds. We want to believe that they will know us, and in this state of mind, we often ask this lump of clay if it does know us, but no answer returns, we weep and repeat the question. No answer comes, and in a convulsive state of mind we leave and retire to some lonely spot to pour out our grief. Some kind friend tries to console us by telling us that our friend is not dead, but still lives; by talking what they have no knowledge of, only a desire that it may be so.
Their sympathy and ignorance mingle in a belief, and we try to believe it. This is the state of the people in regard to the dead. Their belief arises from the necessity of the case, but it keeps them in ignorance of themselves, and all their life subject to bondage.
Now where do I differ from all this belief ? In every respect. My belief is my knowledge, my knowledge is my practice, and my practice gives the lie to all my former belief. I believed as all others did, but my theory and practice were at variance with each other. I therefore abandoned all my former beliefs, as they came in contact with my practice, and at last followed the dictates of the impressions made on me by my patients. In this way I got rid of the errors of the world and found an answer to all my former opinions. These former opinions embraced all sorts of dis-ease, and ideas that contained error, disease and unhappiness, which led to death. The unravelling of my old opinions gave me knowledge of myself, and happiness the world knew nothing of, and this knowledge I found could be taught to others. It teaches man that he is not in the body, but outside of it, as much as the power is outside of a lever; and the body is to the soul as the steam engine is to the engineer -a medium without knowledge or power, only as it is given by something independent of itself.-Jan. 1860.

CLAIRVOYANCE

Clairvoyance is a state of existence independent of the natural senses or the body, which has no matter nor reason, but is perfect knowledge. Thought-reading is a lower order connected with mind, but superior to the natural man. This state is what would be called spiritualism, and contains the knowledge and reasoning of this world. Clairvoyance is a higher state entirely disconnected with the natural man, but can communicate information through him while in a dreamy or mesmeric state which the company cannot know. This principle is in every man. (3) The understanding of it is eternal life. This eternal life was in Jesus, and was Christ. It has manifested itself in various forms in all ages of the world, whenever Science has been discovered. This ignorance of the world with regard to this higher state of knowledge looks upon the manifestions of the thought-reading state as the highest development of man. This state dies and the clairvoyant state rises from the dead. It is all that is left. It can act on mind. It has an identity, and never knew of its beginning nor ending. It is all the intelligence in man. (4)

LOVE, II

The identity of woman's soul can be compared to a fire, which throws an equal heat on all around. This heat is pure love, containing no knowledge, no selfishness, but is like the love of a mother for her child. This love is little understood, and causes doubts and questionings. It is an element of itself, containing no matter and asks nothing in return. Ignorance and superstition put false construction on this love, and think intelligence is contained in it. Its language is itself. It speaks not as man speaks, for it contains no error. It answers our inquiry by an impression which cannot be misunderstood, if man knows himself. This love is what leads man to truth. When I speak of man, I speak of the errors and ignorance of the world, and the heat that arises from this error contains the character of its author. When these two elements meet, which I will call man and woman, then comes the temptation, and as love never makes war for gain, it knows no evil. As error contains selfishness, dishonesty, jealousy, and disease, it cannot see truth or love in any element differing from its own, it therefore judges others by its own standard. This element, when excited by love to lead us to truth contains all kinds of disease and error. All mankind embrace both elements, and the separation is the resurrection from error into truth. As we learn the truth, we discard the error. True knowledge is in true love. False knowledge is in error. As God is in the former, He contains no matter. As man is the latter, he is made up of truth and error. Now as there is a gradual progression from error to Wisdom, our identities act in the two elements of pure and combined love; for man has two elements, and is subject to the one which he obeys. The question arises, Are these elements capable of separation? I answer, yes, by the mother for her infant, but not understandingly. She was a law to herself, and did the things contained in the law, without a knowledge of that law.-Dec. 1859.

HOW DR. QUIMBY CURES

Every phenomenon in the natural world has its birth in the spiritual world.(5) The world gives credit where it is not due, mistaking noise for substance. No man should have any credit over his fellow men unless he shows some superiority over the errors of his age. To show that he is superior is to reduce to a science some phenomenon which has never been explained, music for an example. Before music was reduced to a science there was a phenomenon. People could whistle and sing, but no one supposed that the one who made the most noise was entitled to any credit above the rest. Credit was due to him who first reduced it to a science.

Take diseases. The world is full of sickness, arising from various causes,-the phenomenon exists in the natural world, while the causes originate in an invisible world. Doctoring is confined to the natural world, and [it attributes] the causes of the disease to the natural world.

Dr. Quimby, with his clairvoyant faculty, gets knowledge in regard to the phenomena, which does not come through his natural senses, and by explaining it to the patient, gives [another] direction to the mind, and the explanation is the science or cure. To illustrate: suppose a patient calls on Dr. Q. for examination. No questions are asked on either side. They sit down together. He has no knowledge of the patient's feelings through his natural senses, till after having placed his mind upon them. Then he becomes perfectly passive, and the patient's mind being troubled [this] puts him into a clairvoyant state, together with his natural state, thus [he is in] two states at once; when he takes their feelings, accompanied by their state of mind and thoughts. A history of their trouble thus learned, together with the name of the disease, be relates [this] to the patient. This [state which he discerns] constitutes the disease and the evidences in the body are the effects of the belief. Not being afraid of the belief he is not afraid of the disease.

The doctors take the bodily evidence as disease. Disease with him does not come to the natural senses, therefore he cannot explain to the well his mode of treatment. The well take no interest, and his theory is of no use to them. Then what use is it to the world? To give the sick such confidence that they will not be frightened by the opinions of the world, for disease is an imprudent opinion. He throws the [patient's] feelings off, and imparts his feelings (6) which are perfect health, and his explanation destroys their feelings or disease. His theory in this respect differing from any other, is the result of the success of his practice. Therefore when he is with the sick, they feel safe. He is like a captain who knows his business, and feels confident in a storm, and his confidence sustains the crew and ship when both would be lost if the captain should give way to his fears. Dr. Q. comes to the sick as a pilot to the captain of a ship in a storm or fog, when dangers thicken and inevitable destruction threatens. He learns the trouble from the captain, and quieting the crew by his composure inspires them with confidence, gives other di-rections, and brings them into harbor.-Jan. 1860.

ANOTHER WORLD

What did Jesus mean to convey when He said all men had gone out of the way, that there was none doing good, no not one? It is generally understoood that man had wandered away from God, and had become so sinful that he was in danger of eternal banishment from the presence of God, and unless he repented and returned to God, he would be banished from His presence forever. This being the state of mankind, God, seeing no way whereby man could be saved, gave His only Son as a ransom for the redemption of the world; or, God made Himself manifest in the flesh, and came into the world, suffered, and died, and rose again, to show us that we should all rise from the dead.

This is the belief of most of the Christian world. Its opposers disbelieved all the above story but death. They can't help believing that man dies, and they have a belief that there will be some sort of hocus-pocus or chemical change, that the soul or spirit will jump out at death, and still have an existence somewhere. After the soul is set at liberty, it can go and stay just where it pleases. Others believe it goes to God, there to be in the presence of God, and be a saint and sing hallileujah forever.

The above embraces all of mankind's belief, and in this belief people feel as though Jesus Christ was the author and finisher of their faith. These beliefs embrace all the horrors of a separation from this world, and a doubt whether man will obtain that world beyond this life.

No person is in danger of this change but the sick, for if a person is well he can't be dead, and if he does not die, he is in no danger of heaven or hell, therefore to keep well you keep clear of both. This was just about the same belief that the people had before Christ began His reform.

I will try to show that Jesus never taught one single idea of all the above, but condemned the whole as superstition and ignorance. He not only condemned the idea of a world independent of man, but proved that there was none by all His sayings and doings. He looks upon all the above theories or beliefs as false and tending to make men unhappy. These beliefs Jesus came to destroy, and established the Kingdom of God or Truth in this world. The two beliefs are in ourselves and we become the servant of the one we obey. The embracing Of the true Christ is the resurrection from the dead. The dead know nothing. To be dead in sin or ignorance is [to be in a state of] separation from God or Truth. To know God is to know ourselves, and this knowl-edge is Christ or Truth. What is the difference between Christ's belief, and the world's belief? Christ had no belief. His Kingdom was an everlasting Kingdom, without beginning or end. It is a Science based on eternal truth. It does not contain an opinion or belief. It is all knowledge and power, and will reign till all beliefs and error shall be destroyed. The last error or belief is death or ignorance, the Truth and Science will reign till ignorance is destroyed. Then the son or law shall be subject to God.-Jan. 1860.

YOUR POSITION

What is your position in regard to the world, or the errors of the world? You cannot embrace both. If you embrace the world you embrace its errors, and become a servant to its laws, and the spirit or truth departs to the God that gave it. But if you hold on to the Truth the world is in subjection to you, and instead of becoming a servant you become a teacher of Truth to the world, to lead other minds to the Truth.

Instead of your happiness being in the world, the world's happiness is in you. Here is your true position, and this is the struggle you will have to go through. Shall the world lead you, or shall you lead the world? This is the point that is to be settled in your mind.

Now I will give you the signs of the times. Many shall come in the name of the Truth, and say, do this, or do that music, dancing, and all sorts of amusements. But Truth says beware, be not deceived, seek first the truth, and all the above will be a pleasure to you. To know whether you are born of the truth, the truth shall show just your position in the world. Then you can take the lead, and the world will listen to you. Then the kingdom of this world has become subject to the kingdom of heaven, or error has become the subject of Truth. This is a trying scene to go through, it seems as though you must leave all the world's pleasure, and seclude yourself from society. But this is not the case; you will like society all the better. For where the carcass is there will all the eagles be gathered, so where error is, truth will go, to lead the captive free. This will make you love amusement for the sake of doing good. Then you will rejoice with those that rejoice and weep with those that weep, and your happiness will be their happiness. Then you will be loved and respected for your love or knowledge, then you will draw around you those minds that are in harmony with yours. Then will the old ideas or errors of the world come and knock at your door for admittance, but the truth will say, "Depart ye cursed, for when I wanted truth ye gave no answer, when ignorant or naked, you gave me no truth or clothes, therefore depart ye cursed, into everlasting darkness, where ignorance and error dwell."-Dec. 1859.

MY THEORY

All effects produced on the human frame are the result of a chemical change of the fluids with or without our knowledge, and all the varieties and changes are accompanied by a peculiar state of mind. If the mind should be directed to any particular organ, that organ might become deranged or might not. In either case the trouble is in the mind, for the body is only the house for the mind to dwell in, and we put a value on it according to its worth. Therefore if your mind has been deceived by some invisible enemy into a belief, you have put it into the form of a disease, with or without your knowledge. By my theory or truth I come in contact with your enemy, and restore you to your health and happiness. This I do partly mentally and partly by talking till I correct the wrong impressions and establish the Truth, and the Truth is the cure. I use no medicines of any kind, and make no applications. I am no spiritualist. . . . I am not dictated to by any living man, but am guided by the dictations of my own conscience, as a lawyer is in pleading a case governed by the evidence. A sick man is like a criminal cast into prison, for disobeying some law that man has set up, I plead his case, and if I get the verdict, the criminal is set at liberty. If I fail, I lore the case. His own judgment is his judge, his feelings are his evidence. If my explanation is satisfactory to the judge, you will give me the verdict. This ends the trial, and the patient is released. -Dec. 1859.

ESTABLISHING A NEW SCIENCE

What has a man to contend with who undertakes to es-tablish a new science? He has the opposition of all the opinions of the world in regard to it, and all their influence. He will be misunderstood by fools, and misrepresented by knaves, for [his science] will tear down their fortress or belief, and they will use all their skill and deception to defeat their enemy. Their weapon is their tongue, and the tongue of a hypocrite is of all weapons the most deadly to truth; for it can assume the form of an angel, while it is sapping your very life's blood from your soul. Its life and happiness are its own torment. Ever since the world began, Science has had this enemy to contend with, and some very hard battles have been fought before error would leave the field. Even when forced to retreat into darkness it would come out. . . . Therefore, science must keep awake for its own safety. These two powers are in every person, and each one's happiness or misery shows which one he is under subjection to. If well and happy, it is no proof that he has been through this war of science and arrived at the truth, but that from some cause, he is satisfied to become the friend of both powers. In this way he is a kind of know-nothing; but his position is not safe, for his enemy knows his position, and only lets him remain while he will keep still or quiet.

What has Truth accomplished? A great deal. It has planted its standard in this battlefield. The standard of mathematics waves its banner to the truth. These monuments of Science, like Solomon's Temple, are the place where truth comes to worship, and the true priests are those who can teach these sciences understandingly, and the masses are those whose belief is founded on these teachers' opinions, without knowing the Science or Truth, but whose faith is pinned on another's opinion or sleeves. This credulity of the people prompts men to selfishness, and there arise false teachers, whose aim is to deceive the people and make themselves famous. They throw discredit on their ideas, and render them unpopular, so that if the same standard should be adopted by a true priest, he would have much opposition to meet with in the minds of those who have been deluded and imposed upon by hypocrites. This places a man in a very bad situation to defend himself, and all the influence he gets is from those he cures, and they dare not stand up and face the world and sustain their position, for it is so unpopular that their reputation is at stake. This is the state the two armies are in, when the leader plants his standard of Science with this inscription, The Science of True Religion is Health, Happiness, and Deliverance.-Dec. 1859.

TWO SCIENCES

There are two sciences, one of this world, and the other of a spiritual world, or two effects produced upon the mind or matter by two directions. The wisdom of this world acts in this way: It puts its own construction on all sensations produced in the mind, and establishes its knowledge after the effect is produced. For in a child feels a pain in its head, the child has no idea what it is, and if the mother is as ignorant of its origin as the child no effect of any moment is produced. But the wisdom of the world arrives in the form of a lady. She hears the account of the pain from the mother, and assuming a wise look gives her opinion in regard to the trouble, and says the child is threatened with dropsy of the brain, because she shows the same symptoms of another child who died of that disease. This account excites the mother, whose mind acts upon the child. The explanation of the wise lady gives direction to the mind, and presently the work commences to show that she is right. A doctor is called who is as wise as the lady, and not being willing to be outdone by her he puts in a few extras like congestion of the brain, says the lady was right but did not get the whole of the matter. So he has two chances after the child is killed to prove his superior wisdom over the lady.

It sometimes happens that a controversy arises between the two parties, each trying to establish their own opinion so as to have the disease turn their way. In the meantime the patient is left to her own self and gets well. This is all the good result I ever saw from such a controversy. The patient is a mere tool in the hands of these blind guides who attempt to cure her. While this controversy is going on, seeing that all each party wants is to establish their own way, the mother sends for me in her dilemma. I arrive and a fire-brand is thrown in between the combatants. I contend that the child has no dropsy of the brain, but only some slight shock upon its mind, and quieting the child is all that is necessary for a cure. Here the controversy ends. If the mother employs me I prove my theory and the child gets well. If they prove theirs they kill the child, and an examination is made which establishes their theory, and I am a humbug or quack. If I take the case, and the child gets well, the child was not sick, only a little nervous.—Dec. 1859.

CHRIST AND TRUTH

Eighteen hundred years ago, while Jesus was disputing with the Pharisees upon the old scriptures, He asked the question, what do you think of Christ or this Truth? Has it a father, if so, who is be? They answer, "David," or this truth is David's ideas or theory. Jesus said, "If David is the father of this Christ (or theory, or ideas, or truth), why did he call it Lord, if it was his son?" 'Here they both admitted a truth independent of the natural man. The Pharisees believed it was the offspring of David, and therefore called it David's son or theory. Jesus knew it was not of this world, but of God or Truth, hence that it could be reduced to a Science. This has been the rock upon which the people have split. This is the thing to decide, whether there is a knowledge independent of man, or whether it is the offspring of an organized being. Jesus called this truth the Son of God. Peter called it Christ. The people's ignorance confounded the two together, and called it Jesus Christ. This last construction has given rise to all the religious wars and bloodshed since the Christian era. Decide this question and you shut the mouths of all the lions of the world.

Now let us look at the controversy of the two parties. This makes the two worlds, ignorance the one, and Truth or Science the other. These two powers act upon every man. One is identified with the body and a part of it. Jesus gave some of the traits of that power when He said that it is of the earthly man, and when He said, "Out of the heart proceedeth all kinds of evil thoughts." These thoughts are matter, and are the result if error, superstition and ignorance, without any knowledge of God. Science is the opponent of the above, and as it accounts for all phenomena, ignorance is destroyed. Science has had to fight this battle with the world of error and ignorance before it could establish its standard, and take its position above the natural man. Then it is acknowledged and worshipped in spirit and in truth. Before it becomes a science it is under the law of ignorance and superstition, directed by blind guides leading the blind, through the knowledge of this world, and this wisdom Jesus calls foolishness with God (or Science). Now to separate these two, so that the wisdom of this world shall become subject to the knowledge of God, is not an easy task. Almost all who have ever tried to do so have lost their lives.

I will not go back further than John the Baptist. John saw that the time was very near when his truth or Christ was to become a science, therefore he says, "As the truth is laid at the root or foundation of their theories, every tree or supposed science that cannot stand the test of true science must be hewn down." Therefore his belief was like water that could wash away some of their errors, but when the Truth or Holy Ghost should come than it would be reduced to a science. At this time Jesus had not received the Holy Ghost so as to explain it. Therefore He went with others to John to be baptized or hear John's ideas, and when Jesus asked John to explain to Him, John modestly replied, "I have need to be baptized or taught of you." Jesus declined explaining, so John then went on to tell his ideas or belief. Jesus entered into his water or belief, and understood it, and when He came out of the water, the Heavens were opened to Him alone, and the Holy Ghost descended like a dove and lit on Jesus and a voice said to Him alone, "This is my beloved Son (or Science), in whom I am well pleased." This Science had no name till Peter gave it the name of Christ, as an answer to the question put to him by Jesus-"Whom do the people say that I, this power, am ?"-Peter answered, "Some say, Moses, etc." Jesus then said, "Whom say you that I am?"-not Jesus, as is supposed, hut this power; for all the persons that Peter had named were dead, so of course Jesus did not include Himself, but His theory. Peter answered Him "Jesus, the Christ, the living God (or Science)." This Science he called Christ. Then Jesus said, "Flesh and blood hath not revealed this to you." It must have come from the same power that Jesus had. Therefore He said, "Upon this rock or truth I will build my church or theory, and the gates of error and superstition shall not prevail against it." This truth or Christ is what Jesus taught. This broke the locks and bars, opened the prison doors and let the captive free from the old superstition and ignorance. By this power He healed all manner of diseases, cast out devils, established health and happiness, brought peace and good will to man.

This theory came in contact will all other theories, for there were false ones and Christ warned the people against them. He said there were false Christs and told them how to distinguish between the false and the true. Now as Jesus became popular with the people, the chief priests, and the doctors or scribes sought how to put Him down, and they tried in every way to catch Him. At one time while in the temple the chief priests and elders of the people came to ask by what authority He did these things. Jesus answered them by asking them a question which, if they answered, He would tell them how He performed His cures. The baptism of John, or his theory, was it from Heaven or of man? And they reasoned among themselves, saying, If we say, from Heaven, He will say, "Why then did ye not believe it?"-for they had killed John as a prophet. And so they answered, "We cannot tell." "Neither can I tell you how I do these things."

As it never has been explained how Jesus did these things, the people have looked upon them as miracles. But to suppose Jesus performed a miracle is to suppose Him ignorant of the power He exercised, and if so He was just as much a quack as those He condemned; for He said, when accused of curing through ignorance or Beelzebub, "If I cast out devils through Beelzebub, my theory or kingdom cannot stand, but if I do it by Science, it is not of this world, but of God, and it will stand." Here He makes a difference between ignorance and knowledge. Again, if Jesus was ignorant of His power, and did not know how to explain it to others, why did He tell His disciples to go out in all the world and heal all manner of disease? If ignorant of what He said, and gave no explanation of His manner of curing, He was as ignorant as they. But I am certain that He knew more than His disciples could understand, and as soon as Jesus was crucified, the cures ceased to be done by a Science, but went back into the hands of priests and magicians, and have been a miracle ever since, and the Christ that. prompted Jesus' acts is not known at all. That Christ never did any doctoring, nor offered up prayers, nor creeds. It never belonged to this world, nor talked about any kind of religion. It talked itself. Itself was its life, and its life was the healing of the sick and distressed. It takes the feelings of the sick and knows their wants, and restores to them what the world has robbed them of. This is the Christ that was crucified eighteen hundred years ago.

Now the only thing we hear is what was said about Him. Yet He is in the world but has no identity as a Science.-Jan. 1860.

DIFFERENCE BETWEEN MY BELIEF AND OTHERS

Where does Dr. Q's. mode of practice differ from that of others? In every particular. Disease is admitted by every one (though there may be a few exceptions) as a something independent of the mind. Dr. Q. denies all this and asks for the proof of it.

Disease is a departure from life. Now, bow can a man lose his life, and know it after it has taken place and at the same time, not know it? For if health is life, and a departure from it death, how can this change take place, independently of the mind? For if the mind is not that which undergoes the change how can it suffer death? . . . We are called upon to prepare for this change from life to death, or from health to disease.

People understand this theory pretty well, for they prove it in a very few years to the satisfaction of both parties. This was the state of the mind when Christ came to destroy this theory of disease and death by showing the Truth, which was and is life. And no person was in any danger of hell, except those who were sick, for the well need no physician. Therefore to keep well was to keep clear of hell, and to get into it was to get sick, for sickness led to death, and death led to hell.

Therefore as long as man is well, according to this theory, he is safe. Now as Christ was the sick man's advocate, He warned the people against believing either of the two advocates of health or disease. He said to the people, "Beware of the doctrine of the Scribes and Pharisees, for they undertake to tell of what they know nothing about, and they bind burdens in the form of disease or opinion, and lay them on your shoulders, which are grievous to be borne, and which must lead to death, or the departure from life or health." To keep in health, and keep clear of death, was to understand ourselves, so that their opinions cannot harm us. Now, in all the above belief or theory, there is not the slightest intimation of any knowledge independent of mind. It is true that some people have a vague idea of something independent of the mind, but the person who dares express such an opinion is looked upon as a sort of lunatic or fool. Phenomena are constantly taking place, showing that there is a higher order of intellect that has not yet been developed in the form of a theory, but which can unravel the old theory, and bring in one that will lead man to health and happiness, and destroy the idea of disease and death. Dr. Q's theory, if understood, also goes to correct this error that is depriving so many of the life and happiness of mankind. His belief is his practice, and his practice gives the lie to the old beliefs.-Jan. 1860.

TRUE AND FALSE CHRISTS

I will try to explain the true Christ from the false Christ, and show that "Christ" never was intended to be applied to Jesus as a man, but to a Truth superior to the natural man -and this Truth is what prophets foretold. It has been called by various names, but is the same truth. There is a natural body of flesh and blood -this was Jesus. His mind like all others was subject to a law of truth that could be developed through the natural man. This power Jesus tried to convince people of, as I am trying to convince people that there is such a state as clairvoyance, that is, that there is a power that has an identity and can act upon the natural man, which the natural man is ignorant of. When this power acts upon his senses it acts in the form of an idea or thought. The natural man receives it like the servant, but acts as though he was the father of the idea. The world gives him credit for this superiority over the rest of his fellow men.

But unwilling to admit this power, the world attributes it to some unknown cause, as the best way to get out of trouble. People would rather have it a miracle than a science, for otherwise it would lower them in the estimation of themselves and cause their own destruction, as all truth destroys error. This belief that there is an intelligence independent of ourselves has always been admitted, but attributed to some miraculous power from another world.-Jan. 1860.

YOUR TRUE POSITION

Question: "I understand you to say, sometimes that mind is matter, and at another time you separate the two by showing that the mind leaves the body and goes to a distant place, sees and describes objects that are not known to any person present." Answer: Certainly and I will give you the proof. The mind is the medium of a higher power independent of the natural man that is not recognized. When we speak of mind we embrace this power, as we often do in speaking of a lever, supposing the power to lie in the lever, not thinking that the lever contains no knowledge or power.

This natural mistake is attributed to our ignorance of mathematics. The same mistake exists with regard to mind and matter. The body may be compared to dead weight, the mind to a lever. Error puts knowledge into the lever. Here is where the mystery lies. The natural man cannot see beyond this standard, and as all our happiness or misery is in what follows our acts, it is not strange that we are all the time getting into trouble. Now, separate the power from the lever or mind, and the mind becomes subject to this independent power, and acts upon another's mind in the same way that the natural man may suggest to his friend the best way of apply-ing his power to a lever to move matter. As our bodies are the machine to be moved like the locomotive, and our mind is the steam, the whole must be kept in action by a power inde-pendent of itself, for the steam contains no knowledge, any more than the body or engine. Now all men will admit the two elements. These two powers are not understood or admitted to have an existence independent of the lever or mind. These two powers govern the mind and body as the engineer governs the steam-engine. Knowledge of ourselves as spiritual beings separates both.-Jan. 1860.

MY RELIGION

When I talk to the sick I talk my theory, when I talk to the well I talk about it. It is so with my religion, I have no religion independent of my acts. When I am religious, I talk it and put it into practice. When I am not putting my religion into practice for the benefit of the sick and those whom I can help, then if I talk I am talking about something. Here is a distinction that may at first seem curious to some, but if you will look at it rightly you will see that there is more in it than you would at first suppose. One of Christ's followers made a remark like this in regard to the same distinction, only he called their talk or belief, Faith, which is religion put in practice. He said, show me your religion or faith independent of works, and I will show you may religion or faith by my works. There is no such identity as goodness by itself.-Jan. 1860.

HAPPINESS

What is happiness? It is what follows any act of the law of science, but it is not always understood. Sin and misery are the effects of our belief put in practice, governed by the law of sin and death. Man is the medium of the two laws; the one, chance or ignorance, which is of this world; the other, God or Science, which is of a higher. The wisdom of one is called the law, the knowledge of the other is the Gospel. These two laws enter into all our acts. Mathematics contains the two laws. The solving of a problem does not establish the science, although it may be right, but it develops a phenomenon for a more wise and excellent law so that the world may be benefited by it. So by establishing the law of science we destroy the law of ignorance. This holds good of all the laws of science, the introduction of the one is the destruction of the other, to all who understand. To such there is no offering up of sin or sacrifices, but a fear of judgment because of wrong-doing. This keeps us on our guard. Now, it has not entered into man's heart to conceive a more excellent law whereby man may be saved from the sins or errors that bind him down by the laws of sin and death. To introduce a Science that can explain the errors that keep us in trouble is what prophets foretold and wise men have looked for ever since the world began. This knowledge has been called by various names. It was called the New Jerusalem that came down from heaven, and it was called the kingdom of heaven. This is the law that was written in the heart; it is the knowledge of ourselves that can see the evils of our own misery.
It may be asked, how can we distinguish between the two, for every one has a right to his own opinion? That is true, but science does not leave it answered in that way, but proves it so that there can be no mistake. Now as disease is an error, so the mind, as in any error, must be corrected by a power independent of itself, and this power must be governed by a science in all cases; though it may not be necessarily understood by the person applying this power. As Science, like God, never acts except like a balance which judges correctly, it contains no [mere] thought or reason, but judges every one according to his worth. As error is a chemical action and contains all of the above, it is like two rogues, at war with itself. There is an old saying, and a very good one that, when two rogues fall out an honest man gets his due; so when error is at war, it develops some truth. As the degrees from total darkness or ignorance are progressive, they embrace all kinds of talent, like teachers from the lowest classes of this world to the highest of the spiritual world. All science to the nat-ural world is looked upon as mystery, witchcraft, sorcery, etc., because the natural world cannot see anything beyond itself. But there is a mind that can teach it, and another that can learn it, and so on till it reaches Science. Then comes the end of the world of error, and the introduction of a more excellent law of, God. As a person's happiness is the effect of his knowledge, to be good is the fruit of Science. All religion that embraces creeds is of this world, and is governed by laws, and contains rewards and punishments; therefore holding out inducements to be good with one hand, and retribution with the other, is not the religion of Christ. He is in us, and a part of us, and to know ourselves is to know Christ, and to preach Christ is to help each other out of our troubles, destroying the enemy that has possession of us.
The laying down of your life for your friends is not so easy a matter as some might think. It is easier to talk about religion than to talk it. To talk it is to put it into practice, and to put it into practice is to give it to those who ask, for to give them a stone when they ask for bread is what any one can do, as then you part with nothing. To give to every one that asks of you some spiritual food or knowledge, that will cool their feverish tongue, or soothe their excited brain, and

lead them like the true shepherd to their home or health, where they can rejoice with thir friends, is not so easy as to sit down and thank the Lord that you are not like other men.

To be a follower of Christ is not an easy thing, but to be a representive of the kingdom of heaven is not very hard, it only requires one to become as ignorant as a child.

To call yourself a follower of Jesus, is to call yourself a pattern of goodness, and that was more than Jesus did of Himself, for He never sounded the trumpet of His own praise. We are all called upon to become followers of Jesus so that the world may be benefited by His truth. This is our happiness and the happiness of others, for we are all workers for the same truth. Therefore dismiss error, and embrace the true Science, and fight the enemy of health, like a soldier of Science.-Feb. 1860.

PRAYER, I

Can any good come out of prayer? I answer yes, but not in the sense that is supposed. A phenomenon can be produced in the same way that is brought about by mesmerism, but there is no knowledge in the church-prayer. It is the effect of superstition and ignorance. It is not of Christ, but from a mind ignorant of self and God. No man prays except the one who wants a favor, to be rewarded for more than he deserves, or one who has more of this world's goods than his neighbor. Witness the effect of the prayer on this world, those who pray to the earthly man, who belong to the lowest class of mankind. No man of character will beg or pray for the sake of gain.

True prayer is the desire of the heart, and if the heart is right the prayer will be answered. For as the heart is only the figure or emblem of knowledge, a true heart must have scientific knowledge, and a corrupt heart must be full of superstition and ignorance, deceit and hypocrisy.

It is generally admitted that prayer is of divine origin, but if it is to be offered to God this is not the case. If it is of the devil, I will admit that it is as old as its father, for we read that the devils prayed, as when the devil wanted Christ to worship him. So do all men of narrow minds like to be worshipped for what they have no claim to. One great argument offered in favor of prayer is that Christ said, "He who humbles himself shall be exalted." What is required of a person to humble himself is to get down on his knees and hold up his bands, and in a hypocrital cant ask of God some favor which he is not entitled to. But God rewards everyone according to his acts, and He knows our wants before we ask. So to ask of a Being whom we acknowledge knows our wants is either to curry favor or flatter Him with the idea that we think He will be pleased to see how much we honor Him. This is the wisdom of this world, but not the wisdom of God. God asks no such worship. To worship God is to worship Him in spirit and in truth, for He is in the truth, not in the error. Our reward is in our act and if we act rightly and honestly we get the reward. If we act selfishly we get the result also. He who expects God to leave Science and come down to ignorance and change a principle for a selfish motive to please Him, is either a knave or fool and knows not God. God is like the fire which throws heat or love on all around. Those who will can enjoy the heat or love, but if we choose to stand out in the cold, we cannot expect exclusive privileges; for God has no respect to one over another. I have no account with God, He pays me as soon as my work is done, and I do not ask favors of Him apart from His principles. If I act wrongly He will not step out and correct me. I must do it myself. If I act rightly I get my reward, for our happiness or misery is in our acts, and as we are a part of each other, our happiness is in our neighbor, and to love our neighbor as ourselves is more than all burnt offerings and sacrifices. If you understand this, Jesus said, you are not far from the kingdom of heaven. Jesus had no sympathy with the hypocrites' prayers. He warned His disciples and the multitude against all such prayer. His prayer was that God would forgive them for they knew not what they did. A desire to know God, is a desire to know ourselves, and that requires all our thoughts to come into that happy state of mind. That will lead man in the way to health. This is a science and is Christ's prayer-March, 1860.

PRAYER, II

I look on church-prayers as I do on all other errors that have been invented to govern mankind and keep the people in ignorance of themselves and God. You may ask if I would destroy prayer. No more than I would the law for murder or theft; but I would put into man a higher law that would teach him to worship God as a God of science and knowledge. This law would put the law of ignorance to death. For prayer is the law of man, not of God, and makes God nothing but a mere sorcerer or magician to frighten the ignorant and superstitious. It puts Jesus on a level with the jugglers of His day. The construction upon the parables shows the state of intelligence of the church. It makes Christ's mission here of but little account to the world of science.

Take for instance the parable at the wedding. The turning of water into wine is quoted as some great thing, as though God took this way to convince man of His power. But if there could not be a better explanation of this parable than the church gives, Christ is merely a magician.

Why should the explanation of Christ's mission which was to heal the sick, destroy death, and bring life and immortality to light, be left to persons who have no sympathy for the sick, but who by their interpretation of Christ keep man sick and ignorant of himself? Of what advantage has Christ been to the sick, according to the common opinions of man-kind? Does the priest relieve them of any burdens? If not, where is the benefit of the church-prayer? It is in contradiction to Christ's own teaching. What was Christ's idea of prayer? He called it hypocrisy and a blind guide to lead the blind. He warned the people against those who prayed in the streets, told them to obey all the laws, but not to believe in the doctrines, for they laid burdens on the people grievous to be borne. Now, if these burdens were their belief Jesus must explain them away, to relieve them, and his explanation was their cure. Therefore He said to them, "Come unto me all ye that are weary and heavy leaden, and I will give you rest." Jesus's explanation was his religion, but their religion contained all the superstition of Egyptian darkness, prayers, sacrifices, and burnt offerings.

Jesus did not condemn any of the above, but He had a knowledge of the errors

that man is subject to and His mission was to bring science to light, in regard to our ignorance or darkness, and put man into a state where he might, by re-lieving the sufferings of his fellow men, be of some advantage to himself and to the world. His religion was not of this world, and the world knows Him not. Christ is God or Science, and to know God is to know Science and put it in practice so that the world can be benefited by it. This tells the rules of action. They are not left to the natural man, but they must prove themselves on some subject that is in need of it. The same subject is in the world now that was at the time when Jesus put His theory into practice. He gave His disciples knowledge to put the same into practice for the benefit of mankind.

Who art thou, O man, that shall say to the poor and sick, lame and blind, that the person who can help you is a "hum-bug" or acting under the direction of the devil? If the devil will take your aches and pains and relieve you, cling to him, and at the end of your disease you will see that this devil is the same one who was crucified eighteen hundred years ago, by just such enemies to the sick as they have now. I, for one, am willing to be called a humbug by all such people. I have the same class to uphold me that Jesus had, the sick. The well opposed Him, and the well oppose me. I do not set myself up as an equal with Jesus, or any other man, but I do profess to believe in that principle that Jesus taught, which I call Christ. That I try to put into practice as far as I understand it, and the sick are my judges, not the well; for as the well need no physician they cannot judge me. Neither am I willing to be judged by the creeds till they can show that their belief is above their natural power. I shall not take their opinions of what they know nothing about. I will draw a line between the professor of Christ and myself, and leave the sick to pass judgment. As I have the Bible I have the same means of judging as any one, for every one has a right to his opinion concerning it. But there is no truth in an opinion unless it can be put into practice as Christ put His in-to practice. Then it becomes a fact.

What does Jesus Himself say of this power? He admitted it, for He says, "of myself I can do nothing," thus admitting a power superior to Himself; and also when asked a question by His disciples, He said, "No man knoweth, not the angels in heaven, neither the Son, but My father only." At another time when asked by a scribe who had been listening to Jesus, while He reasoned with a Sadducee, "What is the first commandment of all?" Jesus answered "The first commandment is Hear, Oh, Israel, the Lord our God is one Lord." Here He admits a supreme power, and says, "Thou shalt love the Lord thy God with all thy heart, and thy neighbor as thyself."

The young man said unto Him, "Well, Master, thou hast said truly, for there is one God, and there is none other than He, and to love Him with all thy heart and soul is more than all burnt offerings and sacrifices." Jesus saw that he had answered discreetly and He said unto him, "Thou art not far from the kingdom of God." These questions and answers were given before the whole multitude, and I see no reason for disputing Jesus' own words by putting a misconstruction on some passage, and making Jesus something that neither He nor any one else ever thought of. He was accused of making Himself equal with God, but that was their ignorance, which gave that construction, and if I had not been accused of the same thing a hundred times, I might put the same construction on Jesus as others do. But I can see, and show to the sick beyond a doubt, the difference between Jesus and Christ, and the difference between the two words gives a very different meaning to religion. The church's construction makes our acts and lives one thing and our religion another. Jesus made our acts the effect of our knowledge and in proportion as we understand Science we understand God, and acknowledge Him in truth. This Science separates us from this world of sin and death and brings life and immortality to light, and this life was what Jesus taught. Ignorance of Christ or Science put "Jesus" and "Christ" together and said "Jesus Christ." For superstition could not account for any of the cures that Jesus made except they were from heaven, and although Jesus tried all in His power to convince them to the contrary, He could not. The religious people of Jesus' day like the Christians of this day, made heaven and hell places independent of man, and although some may deny it their acts give the lie to their protests.

All people pray to a being independent of themselves, acknowledging a state or place where God is, and when they pray, supposing that He listens, ask Him to hear their prayers and relieve their wants. This is precisely what the heathen did, and Jesus called them hypocrites and condemned them, for He said this offering up of prayer and sacrifices year after year could never take away sin or error, so Jesus embraced Christ or Truth and laid down His own life for the happiness of mankind. Before this the world knew not Christ or Truth. This truth Jesus taught, and His teaching was the healing of the nations, and if His truth had not been mis-construed, the world at this time would have been rid of thousands of errors it now has. This was Jesus' truth, which was to the people a mystery, and seemed to embrace a belief merely, for a truth to a person who cannot understand it is a belief. But Jesus labored to convince the people that it was a science, that the fruits of it were seen in His practice, and that it could be taught; for He made a difference between His cures and His disciples' cures, and the cures of the rest of the world.

The magicians and sorcerers cured by their belief. They thought their power came from a spirit-world, and they acted upon this belief. They believed that disease was sent into the world to torment mankind. The priests had the same belief. Each one's prayer was to his own God, to keep him clear of his enemy. The priest held up to the people the idea that they must do something different from living honestly and dealing with mankind as though we were one family, that a certain belief was necessary to keep us clear of hell, which itself had been invented to torment man. This doctrine kept the people in ignorance of themselves and made them nervous, giving rise to belief in evil spirits. As people are all the time inventing ideas for their own interest, it finally led to the intro-duction of the medical faculty. Now it seemed to cover all the ground that ignorance and superstition wanted, it put the masses into the power of the two classes, the priests and the doctors. The priests would offer up prayers to their God for the salvation of souls, and the doctors would offer up prayers for their business. The people are, in the mean time, in the condition that the prophet told of when he said, "The prophets prophesy falsely, and the priests can rule by their means, and the people love to have it so, but what will they do in the end thereof ?"

Jesus wanted to introduce this Science, which He called Christ, which gave the lie to all the old opinions of Jesus' day. He had no heaven or hell out of man, no happiness, or misery outside of us. His God was in Him and in us, and His prayers were in Him and in us, and His life and ours was this Christ, the law which He put in all of us. If this law could be understood, it would rid us of all the evils that are bound on mankind. It would not keep man in ignorance of himself, but would exalt him in the natural world. It would rid him of the superstition of the world, would make men worship God, not as one who could be flattered by our hypocrisy, but as a God of science that gives to every man just what he learns. Those who seek Him in prayer desiring to learn His laws will be rewarded in proportion to their labor. He asks no prayers for His good, and a prayer made up of words is lost unless accompanied by good to some one, and if we do good to one another our prayer is in the act. When Jesus said to the righteous, "Come ye blessed for I was naked and you clothed me," they were not aware that they had done any good, but He said, "Inasmuch as you did it unto the least of these my brethren you did it unto me," or God, and in His answer to the wicked, "Inasmuch as you did it not to them, ye did it not to me," He put the good and bad in acts, and not in the words. So true prayer is in our acts, false prayer is in our words, and by their fruits you shall know them. For He said, "Not all those who say, Lord, Lord, shall enter into the kingdom of heaven or Science"; not those who say, "I understand it," but those who put it into practice so that the world shall be the wiser for the knowledge. If this is so, "it is easier for a camel to go through the eye of a. needle, than for a rich man," or one learned in this world's knowledge to embrace this Truth or Christ.   But I say to all, strive to understand.- March, 1860.

HOW I HOLD MY PATIENTS

The question is often asked, how I hold my patients, when I give no medicine, and make no applications. I answer, it is through my knowledge. Then you may ask me where I differ from; others. In everything so far as disease and what produces it is concerned. All persons believe in disease and their belief is in the thing believed. For instance, take consumption. People are not aware that consumption has an identity, as much as a serpent or canker worm, that it has life or a sort of knowledge. (7) It is liable to get hold of us, and if it does we cannot shake it off, as Paul did the viper, from his hand. All diseases have an identity and the well are likely to be deceived. But these diseases are in the mind as much as ghosts, witchcraft, or evil spirits, and the fruits of this belief are seen in almost every person. These beliefs show what the people are afraid of, and what they have to contend with, and make it necessary for them to have help in driving off their enemies. For if a person cannot conquer his enemy or disease himself, he must have help.

Now the people involved admit the existence and superiority of their enemy or disease, and commence making war with him by first firing calomel, and if that does not start him, the next is blistering, or burning. This only enrages the enemy, and a regular battle commences. Finally a council of physicians is called, a suspension of arms takes place, a compromise is made, health yields up all claims to happiness and enjoyment, and the victim has the privilege of going about a cripple and an outcast the balance of his natural life, knowing all the time that he is liable to be caught by any of his enemies, at any time, either asleep or awake. This keeps him in a nervous state of mind, not fit for any business, like a man who is in prison, under sentence of death. This is the state of this world.

Now, is it strange that a person is known by this character, and is afraid of this state of mind or disease? And when one who has the power of restoring health and destroying these enemies comes up to another who is tormented by these devils, is it strange that he likes him and feels safe in his presence, until he himself is perfectly free? This feeling is not always known by the sick, but it is felt. It cannot be understood, for its language is its feelings, and it cannot talk till it learns to speak through the senses. It knows and feels its friend, and clings to him as a child does to its parent before it can walk; it is led by sympathy till it can go alone and can understand that it has power over its enemy. Then its knowledge is its cure. Till then it feels the want of some one who can protect it from its enemy. Now my wisdom is their protector and my explanation is their cure. My wisdom is accompanied by sympathy for their troubles, and like a shepherd who leads his sheep I lead the sick home to health and deliver them to their friends. Then I leave them happy, and feel that they appreciate the benefit I have been to them. This money cannot buy. This is what holds my patients. It is what none but the sick can appreciate. The well know nothing of the feelings of the sick, therefore to them it is a stumbling block, and to the doctors foolishness. -March, 1860.

HOW I CURE THE SICK

I will illustrate to you the way in which I cure, or correct the sick. You know I talk parables. To the well this is of no consequence, for they cannot see any sense in my talk. So it is in every science with those who are ignorant of the meaning the person wishes to convey. This was the trouble Jesus had to contend with. All His knowledge must be explained by parables, for the people's belief was in the thing believed. To reduce their belief to a science was a very hard task, for it had to be done by parables of things that each person could understand. When He talked to the multitude it was about the Science or principle that was intended to be applied to each person's individual case.
The parable of the sower illustrated the principle like an illustration regarding some science. It was not intended to be applied to any individual case, therefore when the disciples heard the parable, they did not understand it, and wanted an explanation. Now His explanation to them is as much of a parable to the rest of the world as His parable to the multi-tude was to His disciples.
So a parable of mine is of no use to the well, for it is not intended for them, and must be varied to suit the case that calls it out. Like a lawyer's argument, it depends upon the case to be tried. So it is with the sick, each must have his case explained to himself. The Science can be explained to the well, but not by the same parables that are necessary to be applied to the sick.
I will illustrate. A lady called on me whose feelings were as follows: She felt so weak that she could not keep from stooping over, it was with difficulty that she could sit up. This feeling I could feel but the woman who was with her could not detect it. To cure her and make her sit up, the work must be done by an explanation she could understand, by a parable, because the patient's identity was in her belief.
Her body had an identity apart from the earthly body, and this sick (spiritual) body is the one that tells the trouble. This body seemed to be holding up the natural body, till it was so weak it could barely sit up. This spiritual body is what flows from, or comes from the natural body, and contains all the feelings complained of. It speaks through the natural body, and like the heat from a fire has its bounds, is inclosed by walls or partitions as much as a prison. But the confinement is in our belief, its odor is its identity; its knowledge is in its odor; its misery arises from, false ideas, and its ideas are in itself, connected with its natural body. This is all matter, and has an identity. The trouble, like sound, has no locality of itself, but can be directed to any place. Now as this intelligence is around the body, it locates its trouble in the natural body, calls it "pain" or by some other name. Now the sick person is in this prison, with the body, which body feels as though it contained life. But the life is in the spiritual body, which being ignorant of itself places its own identity in the flesh and blood. This is because the heat which arises from the body contains the identity, and the soul puts such a construction upon the pain as has been taught, and thinks its trouble is in and part of the natural body. This is the prison which Christ, not Jesus, entered, and broke the walls by His word or power and set the captive free. At this door He stands and knocks, and if we will let Him in He will explain away the error or forgive the sin, and save the soul. He will deliver us from our earthly hell made by the wisdom of the world-March, 1860.

DO PEOPLE REALLY BELIEVE WHAT THEY THINK?

To some this may seem a strange question but it involves more of our knowledge than we think it does.
Our belief involves all our religious opinions. Our opinions are the foundation of
our misery, while our happiness is in the knowledge that follows the solving of the problem or error.
To illustrate, when solving a problem you have an opinion, and are in trouble about it. But when the answer comes the happiness accompanies it. Then there is no more death, or ignorance, sorrow or excitement. Error and ignorance have passed away, all has become new, and we are as though we never had been. We have all the happiness we want; the misery is gone, and the spirit returns to the Great Spirit, ready to solve another problem.
Now the problem I wish to solve is what I first named. Do we really believe in
what we think we do? I answer, "No," and shall show that we deny what we profess to believe in almost all we say and do, thereby proving ourselves either hypocritical or ignorant. We profess to believe in Christ, that He is God, that He

knows all things, and is capable of hearing and answering our prayers. We also believe that man is a free agent, that he is capable of judging between right and wrong, and believe that if man does not do right he will be punished. When asked for proof of all this, we are referred to the Bible. When we ask an explanation how Christ cured, we are told it was by miracle. If we ask if Christ did not know all things, the answer is, "Yes." Then did He not know what He was about, what He did, and how He did it? "Yes." Then if you ask how He knew, the answer is, "It is a miracle," or "The ways of God are past finding out," -and thus you are left in the dark. Now those who reason this way will not accept any fact based upon any other way of reasoning. You must bring the strongest proof to convince them of a fact produce in the same way, otherwise they will not believe. The fact is they don't reason or compare at all, and admit what they have not the slightest proof of, except the explanation of some person of doubtful existence.

Now, when I show that I can produce a phenomenon that to all appearance is just like some produced by Christ, and in the living, who speak for themselves, I should like to know by what authority anyone dares to say that it is not done in the same way that Christ did His works. If they cannot tell how I do it, or how He did it, how do they know but that it is done in the same way? Their only objection can be that it happens to be contrary to their own opinion, which is not worth anything, and they admit it; for they will say it is a miracle to them. This makes them what Jesus said of such guides. He called them blind guides leading the blind, and warned the people against them. He called them whited sepulchres, and all kinds of names, and the world has been led by such guides every since. Jesus told the people how they should know them. He said, "Not all who say Lord! Lord! shall enter into this theory or kingdom, but he that doeth the will of the Father that sent him." Now what do they do that Jesus did? Nothing. You cannot point to one act that Jesus did that these guides do. All who do good ac-cording to Scripture imitate the Pharisees in every respect. He called them the children of the devil, and He said their father (or error) was a liar from the beginning. Jesus judged them by their works, and told the people to do the same; for He said, "by their fruits ye shall know them."-March, 1860.

JESUS AND CHRIST

When Jesus asked Peter, "Whom do the people say that I am?" Peter and the disciples said, "Some say, John the Baptist, some Elias, and others Jeremiah or one of the prophets." Now all of these were dead, therefore they did not mean to confound the man Jesus with them. But they believed the spirits of these men came back and entered the living, and talked to the people. Jesus knew that this was their belief, and they knew it. When Jesus asked His disciples the question, He never intended to convey the idea that He wanted to know who He, Jesus, was, but who this power was. They thought it must be the spirit of some person who had been on earth, and when Peter said it was the Christ or God: Truth or Science, this was a new idea, and Jesus an-swered, "Flesh and blood hath not revealed this explanation to you," and upon this explanation He, Jesus, would build His Christ or Church, or Truth, and the gates of error could not prevail against it. He, that is, Jesus, would give Peter the keys or explanation so that he could understand and practise it for the benefit of mankind. This knowledge would give him power to loose those who were bound in heaven or in the mind, and loose those bound in the earthly body. The idea that the man Jesus was anything but a man, was never thought of. Jesus never had the least idea of such an explanation.

The prophets had foretold a Messiah that should come, and when the child Jesus was born, the people believed that David's spirit had come and taken possession of his body, so they called Jesus the son of David. But they meant to be understood that it was David's spirit speaking through Him, Jesus, and some called Him the Son of Man.

Now, every one admitted the power that Jesus bad, but there was a difference of opinion in regard to it. All men have a power, but to have a power superior to the natural man, has been a question ever since the world began. Upon this question the people split. To believe it is to believe in a power the natural man cannot explain. If Jesus had a power, we must admit a knowledge superior to it, that governs and directs it, and if we do admit it where does it come from? All will answer, from God. All will admit that there is another power that affects man for evil. There must then be a sort of bad knowledge, or false Christ that governs it. How are we to know the good from the bad? Only by the fruits or direction. If we must take an opinion we have no standard; for every one has a right to his own opinion, and by doing so we throw away Christ's teaching when He says by their fruits men are to be judged. We judge them by their works. What are the works? I suppose Jesus knew what He meant, and He meant to give His disciples the true idea when He called them together and gave them power to heal all sorts of diseases, and cast out devils. Did He mean to give power without any knowledge how to apply it, or did He give the knowledge with the power? If He gave the knowledge so that it could be applied, are not the ones who apply it better acquainted with the power than those who are ignorant of the power and the knowledge?

I will try to illustrate what Jesus meant by these powers, when He was accused of curing by ignorance. You may have seen in the paper an account of a young lady being cured by the prayers of a Mormon preacher. I have no doubt that he raised her up through his prayers, and the belief in Mormon-ism would naturally be established in the young lady's mind. This cure, as far as it goes, is to establish Mormonism. Now if the Mormons established all their belief and that is right, why do not all people who believe in prayer embrace Mormonism and all the Mormons preach?

87

When the disciples said to Jesus, We saw men casting out devils in Thy name and forbade them, He said, "Forbid them not, for they that are with us are not against us, and they that are not with us scattereth abroad." Here Jesus showed the difference between His knowledge and theirs in using this power. The others cured, but the world was no wiser for their cures, so they scattered abroad. The cure was right, but it was done through ignorance.

This is the way with prayer. Prayer contains no knowledge and only leaves men in ignorance and superstition. Seeing this account in print, and knowing how it was done, I thought I would try the same experiment on a lady, myself, according to my way of curing disease. I have no creed or belief. What I know I can put into practice, and when I put it into practice I am conscious of it, and know what will be its effect. I sent to the lady (the subject of my experiment) who lived out of town, a letter, telling her I would try my power on her from the time I commenced the letter which was Sunday, and visit her at different times till the next Sabbath, and on the next Sabbath I would come between the hours of eleven and twelve, and make her rise from her bed, where she had been confined by sickness, unable to walk for nine months. At the time appointed I went and used my power to restore her to the use of her limbs and to health. On the Wednesday following my letter, her husband wrote me that on Monday night she was very restless, but was better the next day. On the Monday following that, I received a letter saying that at the time I appointed for her to rise from her bed, she arose from the bed, walked into the dining room, and returned, and laid down a short time. She then arose again, dined, and also took tea with the family, rested well that night, and continued to do well. Now I suppose all of this transaction would be accounted for by the religious community by the power of the imagination of the patient. Suppose you do give it that explanation. How was the lady cured by prayer? On the same principle, I suppose. If so, how was it with the centurion who came to Jesus, saying that he had a servant lying sick with the palsy, grievously tormented? Jesus said unto him, "I will come and heal him." The centurion said, "Speak the word only and my servant shall be healed." Then Jesus told him to go his way and the servant was healed in that self-same hour. Now who cured the servant? Jesus, or the centurion, or the servant's own imagination? Settle this question among yourselves.

Another case: When Jesus came into Peter's house, He saw the mother of Peter's wife lying sick with a fever. He touched her and she arose and administered unto them. Now if you cannot tell how this was done, and yet admit it, you must admit a power that you cannot explain or understand, and if you cannot understand it, it is an unknown power. To attribute to any individual this power from which you hope to derive benefit is to worship an unknown God or principle. This principle which you ignorantly worship, this I declare unto you by explaining it.-March, 1860.

WRONG USE OF WORDS

We often use words, putting upon them a wrong construction, and think that a person is bound to believe what we say because we say it. For instance, you often hear a scientific person make this assertion, that there is no such thing as weight, that weight is attraction, that its true scientific explanation is attraction. Now this is easy to say, but hard to prove. You cannot convince a man of ;what does not come within his senses, and he will not believe it because some one says so. Neither party is right, and both are nearly right. If you place the two weights in an exhausted receiver they will both fall at the same time. This proves attraction. Take them into the open air, and then the iron weight will fall the faster. Now is it attraction, or must you introduce another word? Why do they not fall in the same time as in the receiver? Because they have to fall through a medium called atmosphere or air. This medium is more dense near the earth, but as it recedes from the earth it becomes less dense, and bodies are weighed or measured in this medium. So attraction is of no use except to show that all things have a tendency towards the earth. To suppose that the attraction is in the thing attracted is wrong, and so is the idea that the weight is in the matter attracted. The word weight is the name of matter in motion, for when there is no motion it is called pressure. Weight in motion makes mechanical power, and as velocity increases weight diminishes until weight is lost in velocity, then the whole is under the law of attraction.

Now as the human body is matter and mind is weight, the natural man knows no law of attraction, any more than the metal knows of the attraction that governs it. The law or science that governs man is as much in the dark to the natural man as attraction is to weight. Attraction knows weight is ignorance. As the mind is like the weight, and the soul or truth is like the attraction, as we gain in knowledge we lose in mind or ignorance. So as perfect velocity casts out weight, perfect knowledge casts out mind or ignorance, and truth reigns in all. God is the attraction of both. Ignorance, like the brute, sees no higher law than itself, therefore the ignorant act in accordance with their belief. Man, who is a little above the brute, has discovered that there is a law of attraction, and that same knowledge sees in man a higher and more intelligent law of knowledge that the natural man knows nothing of. This teaches man that as he loses in ignorance by embracing the truth he leaves this world of error, and as he learns Science he disregards error till all error is swallowed up in truth. Then one shall not say to another, "Know you the truth?" but all shall know it from the least to the greatest. Then disease shall be destroyed and truth shall reign all in all.-March, 1860.

HARMONY, I

Can two persons be in harmony except they be agreed? If you are affected by any person in a way that produces fear, you cannot be in perfect harmony with another till the fear is cast out. If it is from some idea that affects your character, you will be imprisoned in the idea till free from it. The idea may or may not be accompanied by an individual, but if it is so accompanied you will be affected by that person in your sleep, the same as in your waking state. One of these effects is attributed to the natural mind, and the other to the spiritual mind, but both have the same effect on health.

But as my knowledge contains no matter I am free from your prison, and as I break or destroy the prison or person that holds you, you come out of that spiritual idea and come to me. You will have no fear, and if you dream of me you will not be afraid. I am your protector, but till you know who I am you may be afraid because you have been deceived so many times. You look upon all sensation with suspicion, and you suspect yourself. The ignorance of yourself is the worst enemy that you have, to contend with; for its character is public opinion, which is taken for truth.

To separate us from what we look upon as truth is not a very easy task, for sometimes we think we like the very thing we really hate. This keeps us in ignorance of ourselves. When we would do good evil is present with us. It is not ourselves but the evil that dwelleth in us. This evil comes from the knowledge of this world, and as this world is made up of flesh and blood, no true knowledge is in it. To separate us from the error, and bring us into harmony is to explain the false idea away, and then all sorrow will pass away, nothing will remain save the recollection of what is past, like a dream or nightmare, and you will not be likely to get into the same error again.

All sensation, when first made, contains no direction, but is simply a shock. Error puts a false construction or opinion upon it, and speaks disease into existence. The mind is then imprisoned in the idea, and all the evils that follow are what are called disease. I shall speak of two kinds of disease. One is called by the doctors, local, the other nervous. I make no difference as far as the effect of the mind is concerned.

Nervous diseases are the effect of the regular's opinion reduced to a belief, and so are all others. I will state two cases to show the difference. A person is exposed to the cold. Ignorance and superstition, have reduced [this sensation] to a disease called cold or consumption. This is set down as a real disease, and so it is, but it is based upon an ignorant superstitious idea. This is one of the errors of this world, judged by this world and proved by the effect on the body. This is called "real, and no mistake."

Now, tell another that there is a serpent in his breast, or a hell that will torment him in case he does not dream just such dreams or believe just so, and when you have succeeded in making the person believe this, seeing him tormented and miserable you turn about and accuse him of being fidgety or nervous. All the sympathy he gets is to be told that he is weak-minded for believing what doctors and ministers have told him, and warned him against for years. This is the judgment of this world's belief. To condemn all this folly is to disbelieve in all peoples' opinions that tend to make one sick or unhappy. Let God or Truth be true, and all men liars. If two ideas come in conflict in you, investigate the wrong and you will find that it is from some one's opinion. You have tried to carry it out, to your own destruction. You have taken some effect for an element. This makes all the trouble. Error can produce no element, but can only create disease and misery. Elements are like true love or Science. They contain no evil except when hatred or passion is put in. Then they may take the name of the author of the evil. For instance, you may love a person, and he may love liquor, you may be induced to drink; your love for the person may be transferred to the liquor, and you may become a drunkard. Now to cure you is to have some one interest you in those who have a distaste for liquor, and in that way, if you follow your friend, and if he

knows what be is about, he restores you to health and happiness.—April, 1860.

HARMONY, II

When two persons are in harmony in regard to a fact, they are as one, for there is no jar. The fact may be of truth. or error, but if they are of the same opinion in regard to it, then they harmonize. If the harmony is pleasure, it is well, if it is trouble, it is harmony with them and discord with something else. Error cannot be in harmony with truth. Ignorance is as a blank, error is the working of ignorance to arrive at harmony or truth. Truth can govern this chemical change in ignorance to bring it in harmony with science. Truth contains no happiness, no misery, but is that power that governs all things according to itself. This truth is in all men, but it is not in the brutes, for it is not matter but the knowledge of creating matter or destroying it. Therefore, fear not that power that can destroy the body and nothing more, but fear that power that can destroy both body and soul. The power that can destroy and create matter, is the destruction of the life of error. Ignorance says in its heart there is no such power. Error knows that there is but is ignorant of its locality. To ignorance this power is an unknown God. The knowledge of this power is the harmony of one person in trouble with another in truth and happiness.-April, 1860.

DIFFERENCE OF OPINION ABOUT THE DEAD

Why should there be such a difference in opinion in regard to the dead? It is of the body, I suppose. If the body is matter, has matter life? If it has then the life is a part of the body, and if the body dies the life dies also. If you mean that this is the end of man, what lives after the life and body die? You will say, the soul. Where is the soul? Has any one ever seen it? or is it an opinion? The fact is that the theory of the body and soul is not in keeping with the progress of truth or science. It leaves everything in the dark. It gives no proof of any phenomenon, but assumes that man must take an opinion of some one about which no proof can be shown, unless you admit an opinion of something that took place five thousand years ago, and was renewed eighteen hundred years ago. Jesus tried to establish the kingdom of truth in man so that men could teach it, but man was not developed

enough to receive it.

It is sometimes supposed that the wisdom of God or Science is made manifest in some simple girl or man. This is the case, and phenomena are constantly occurring, which baffle the world's wisdom to explain. . . . I can prove that mind is spiritual matter, that there is no matter without mind, and that death is nothing but an opinion or state of mind made up of matter which can be destroyed like any other opinion. It is true to the soul that is in matter, but to the Science that is out of the matter it is nothing but an idea. The word matter is applied to man in his lowest state, just a little above the brute. . . .

It is not to be supposed that every man who walks upright is to be set down as a scientific man, nor is it true that every one who calls himself scientific is so. But it is he who can show himself so to the world by his acts, who can explain some truth, thereby putting the world in possession of a fact that it has been ignorant of, increasing the wisdom and hap-piness of mankind. This is the case with Science.

Now, if death can be explained away so that man can be put in possession of life eternal, the world will be put in possession of a fact it is now ignorant of. This I will try to do. What is life? It is admitted that it is something. It is consciousness of existence, and death is the fear of the annihilation of that consciousness. The natural man never sees anything beyond the idea of his belief. Therefore he lives in death and is all his life subject to his own belief. Convince man that there is something independent of this belief that is true, that there is no such thing as matter only as it is spoken into existence, and he will then see that mind is the matter or error that is his belief. As his belief changes the matter or opinion will change, and when a chemical change takes place the mind or opinion will be destroyed and truth or Science take its place. Then Science will stand out from mind or matter and show how mind can be made the medium of any soul to bring about any belief. When man arrives at that then death will be swallowed up in Science. Then the world will rejoice in the Science that teaches man that he can be moulded to any belief taking a form to suit its author, and that all misery is in ourselves arising from some idea that our soul is in like a prison. The destruction of the prison is the destruction of our belief, and the liberation of our soul from bondage is life eternal. This is God or Science.-April, 1860.

RESURRECTION

It has been generally taught that there is a resurrection of this flesh and blood, or that this body should rise from the dead. Now if death is anything independent of ourselves, then it is not a part of our identity, and if death is the annihilation of life, then life dies and if your life dies it is not life. This absurdity arises from the fact that man began to philosophize before he understood himself. Man is superstitious from ignorance. He sees through a medium of ignorance called matter, therefore he sees nothing outside of his belief. His reason is a part of his belief, therefore he is to himself just what he thinks he is. But his belief makes his life and death of the same identity. Therefore when he speaks of life he speaks of saving it or losing it, as though it were matter and must go through a chemical change before it could go to heaven or be separated from itself. Thus we are taught to believe that our lives are liable to be lost and cast into some place of torment, if we do not do something to save the soul, as though life were a thing independent of ourself, and we must look out for it or lose it. Absurd as this is, it is the belief of all mankind, infidel or Christian. Therefore we are taught to believe that Jesus came to make all right, suffered and died and rose again, to let men know that they should rise. Let us see what was really accomplished by His mission according to His followers' opinions of Him. We are told that man had wandered away from God, and had become so wicked that it was necessary that something should be done, or he would be in danger of being banished from God's presence. What was required of him in order to be saved was to repent and return to God, only believing that he should never die. Therefore, his life depended on his belief, for if he did not repent or change his mind, he would be damned. Now, what are we called upon to believe? In the first place, you must believe that Jesus, the man, was Christ or God, and that He died on the cross, and that the man Jesus rose from the dead and went to heaven, there to appear before God and sit down with God in heaven.

If we believe this we will be saved. If we do not believe it, we must be damned. Now you see that our lives are in our belief, and our belief is made up of some one's opinion who knows just as much as we.

I, for one, do not reason in that way. I know that man has two identities, one in this state called Christian or diseased, and one in the spiritual or scientific state. Death and life are the two identities. Life is the knowledge of our existence, which has no matter. Death is the name of that state of mind that reasons as man reasons. The life of this state depends on its reason. It reasons that life is in it and a part of it, and at the same time acknowledges that life is something that can be lost or saved, and reasons about it as one man reasons with another. Death reasons also with the idea that it is saving its life, and invents all sorts of diseases which destroy its state of self. It prays to be saved, it fasts and observes forms and ceremonies. It is very strict in its laws to protect its life. Knowledge is its destruction, so it fears God or Science. Its life is not destroyed but its opinions are, and its opinions are matter. The destroying of its opinions is death, but not annihilation of matter, but of error. The matter returns to its former condition ready to be formed into some other idea. These beliefs are from the knowledge of this world, and are the inventions of man; but the wisdom of this world is foolishness with God or Science. This world is made up of the above beliefs and is subject to a higher power.

The wisdom of God does not go into the clouds to call truth down, nor into the deep to call God up, but shows us that God is in us, even in our speech. It sees matter as a, cloud or substance that has a sort of life (in the appearance). It sees it move around. It .also sees commotion, like persons moving to and fro upon the earth. It can come into this state called "this world" and reason with its followers who are in this world, imprisoned by a belief. To be clear from this world is to know that an opinion is not knowledge, and when this is found out the opinion is destroyed and Science takes its place. I am now speaking of the wisdom of this world.

You see your friend walking about, and you talk with him. Finally he dies, as you would say. Now his identity with you is that he once lived, but is now dead. You do not know but he may live again, though this is only an opinion. You follow him with the same idea or belief. So you never enter into the world of Science, for flesh and blood cannot enter Truth, it cannot understand the separation from this world or belief.

Where do I stand ? I know that all the above is the reasoning of matter, and when people learn the truth, they will make matter subject to Science. Then the wisdom of this world will become subject to the scientific world. This world calls the world of Science a "gift." To call it a gift is to say that those who practise it for the benefit of man are either ignorant of this Science, are humbugs, or are fools talking about what they do not know. Those who call Jesus' knowledge of this Science a power or gift place him on the same level with all the sorcerers of his day.-April, 1860.

[This is a supposed "communication" from one said to be "dead," to show how little reality there is in death.]

"William, will you give me your idea of death?" "I can give you my opinion, but you will say an opinion is no proof, and therefore is of no force." "Well, tell me what you think." "Well, if you want me to tell you what I have no proof of, and what is only my opinion, I suppose I can do it, if it will be of any use. You remember when I was sick in bed, and one night when you were sitting by me, you know I was very weak, and you all thought I was worse, and I thought so. Mother thought I would die, and I thought sometimes that I should; and don't you remember that I told you to put me to sleep?" "Yes." "Well, that was to get rid of that feeling, and when I went to sleep I felt a little nervous, I suppose, and I had a dream that I never told of before, because it troubled the family and made them feel badly. I dreamed that I was dead; and you wanted me to go to Bangor and stay till the trouble was over, and I seemed to go there, but I knew all about it. But as it was a dream, and the association made' me feel so badly, I could never speak of it to mother, for it seemed they had the same dream, so I kept it to myself." "How long did you sleep?" "Till the trouble was over, and when I woke up, it seemed like a reality." "Did you have any sort of knowledge in this sleep of your opinion while awake?" "Yes, I reasoned I was with you, just as you and I used to be when you would talk me to sleep before, but I never was conscious, before, of the idea of death having so much effect on a person, for I could reason with myself, and I am satisfied if I had been taught to believe as some people do, my belief would have governed my dream, and I should have been ten times more unhappy; for when I woke up it did not affect me so long, from the fact that I knew it was only an opinion, and you say that is no proof, and I always remembered that. But I know how to pity those who take an opinion for a truth, for an opinion is as real to the person who believes it as though it were true. As I have reasoned myself into a belief that man never dies, I shall not try to give myself any trouble about others' belief. If people believe that they die, and their spirits come back and talk with their friends, I have no doubt but what they do. But it is their opinion and that is of no consequence, except to lessen their belief that there is such a state as death; per-haps it gives them some happiness. But as far as I am concerned I am satisfied with my belief." "Suppose I should believe that you were dead?" "Suppose that you should, would that make it so?" "No." "Suppose I should believe that you were dead, what would you say to that?" "I should say, if I knew anything, I know I am alive." "Well, can't you be as charitable toward another as you would like them to be towards you?" "Yes, but I can't believe that you are dead." "Did you ever know a dead man to speak?" "No, but you know that we all believe that the body dies and the soul lives." "Yes, but did you ever see a soul?" "No." "Then why do you believe the soul lives, when you say an opinion is of no force? Have you any proof that a person is alive, when you see him dead?" "No, only my belief." "You say that your belief is of no force, for it contains no proof, is it not so?" "Yes." "Well, suppose 1 admit that I am dead, will that make you any better satisfied?" "No." "Well, what shall I admit." "I don't know, but I wish I really knew whether I was talking to you." "Don't you believe your own senses?" "Certainly, but you don't come within my senses." "Why not?" "Because I can't see you." "Then because you think you ;can't see me, I am dead?" "Yes." "Can you see John?" "No." "Is he dead?" "No." "How do you know?" "I think he is alive." "That is nothing but an opinion which you say is of no force." "Will you give me your opinion about it?" "I have no opinion about it. I know that I am here now, and that is all I care about it. If I am dead, it is news to me: I don't know any more about it than Lucius knew when he was asleep, that he was asleep. So if death is only a mesmeric sleep, it is not much to go through."- Dec. 1859.

MY USE OF THE WORD MIND

You know I have tried to prove that mind is spiritual matter; and if I have proved that, I will now show you that matter is life. This you will admit so far as vegetation is concerned. Now see if animal matter is not life. If so you see that man is made up of life. His body is particles of animal life condensed into a form or idea, called man, or a living being of life; not Science, but life is governed by Science. Now what is man when he is not man? for you say man dies. What is Science? Is it that wisdom which controls life? Is it not life? If it is then there is no word to define it, for life is matter, and matter is life. Animal life is in flesh and blood, so flesh and blood is not Science, but Science controls it. What are Wisdom's attributes? Has it an identity? The wisdom of man has an identity in a living form. Can you give any definite idea of what people mean by "the soul?" The one who invented the word must have applied it to an idea that never had an existence, for soul is always applied to life. We read of "fat souls" and "lean souls," and "saving souls and losing souls"; so that word cannot explain man when he is not man. When he is not man he is not soul, so we must get some other word to define what man is when he ceases to be matter.

I will now try to explain what man is, and what he is not; and show that what he is, he is not, and what he is not, he is. I will illustrate the two men so that each shall be a separate and distinct identity. I will take for my illustration the man as we see him, and Science as the man who cannot see through the natural man (for Science cannot be seen, only its effects) and show how they differ. The natural man is made of flesh and blood; Science is not. Man has life; Science is life. Man has sight; Science is sight. Man has feeling; Science is feeling. Man has all of the five senses; Science is all of the five senses. Man of himself cannot do anything; Science can do all things. Man is of matter; Science is not. Then what is man, independent of Science? Nothing but an idea of life and death. Then where does he differ from the brute, where does Science make the distinction? It makes no distinction. Who does? The first cause or God. How? In attaching Science to the identity called man. Then does Science have an identity? Yes. What is it? Wisdom or God. When you give it all its qualities, what kind of person is it? It is the Scientific man, not of flesh and blood, but of that world where error never comes. It speaks through man. What does? Its life or the wisdom of God. How does it get its food? By the sweat of its brow, or the development of itself. Where does it differ from the natural man? In everything. Show by illustration. The natural man is nothing but an idea which Science uses to illustrate some fact or problem that is for the development of Science. Then what does man gain or lose by death as it is called? Just as much as any matter that is always changing. (8)-Aug. 1860.

Notes

(1) Our aches and pains may be more wisely interpreted.
(2) This is the first article in which Dr. Quimby identifies Science with Christ. Later he used the term Christian Science.
(3) That is, without mediumship, spiritism, etc.
(4) Man's true intelligence or intuition.
(5) A cardinal proposition with Dr. Quimby.
(6) That is, the silent spiritual realization of the Divine ideal.
(7) That is through the life or reality which we attribute to it.
(8) Dr. Quimby held that death is never a fundamental or decisive change, but a relatively external or incidental experience. It is our spiritual state that is decisive. This depends on our real or external wisdom.

Chapter Fifteen - The World of the Senses

[These selections have been chosen from articles written between June, 1860, and July, 1865, and arranged, with condensations, according to topics. The omitted portions have been left out to avoid repetition. The sub-titles are usually the titles of the original articles. The first is a tentative introduction for a book.]

TO THE READER

IN introducing this work to the reader my only excuse is the existence of evils that follow the opinions of the world in regard to man's health and happiness. My practice for twenty years has put me in possession of facts that have opened my eyes to the misery of mankind, from ignorance of ourselves. My object is to correct the false ideas and strengthen the truth. I make war with what comes in contact with health and happiness, believing that God made everything good, and if there is anything wrong it is the effect of our-selves, and that man is responsible for his acts and even his thoughts. Therefore it is necessary that man should know himself so that he shall not communicate sin or error.

All my writings are the effect of impressions made on me while sitting with the sick, so that my book is of the lives and sufferings of my patients, their trials and sorrows, and my arguments are in their behalf. It may seem strange to the well that I write upon so many subjects, but when you take into consideration the great variety of persons, and the peculiar state of literature, varying from the most cultivated to that of the lowest intellect, it would not be strange if my writings did not excite the curiosity of the reader.

For instance, one is full of religious ideas and becomes almost insane, and some are entirely so. This excites me, and my thoughts run upon religion. Another will be almost insane upon spiritualism; then I have to battle that, or show the absurdity of that belief. Some are excited upon Millerism, and believe the world is coming to an end. This brings up arguments to refute their belief. Some upon witchcraft. Now their minds are continually dwelling on all these subjects and on the Bible. So to cure I have to show by the Bible that they have been made to believe a false construction. My arguments change their minds and the cure comes. This is my excuse for what I have said upon the Scriptures.

Some people are love-sick and disappointed. These are not a great many. Minds are affected in various ways. Some are ship masters. Their sickness is caused by various things. But all mankind must be reached by parables. All my illustrations are called out by the case I have to treat. Women are more spiritual than men, therefore with them my illustrations are drawn more from the Bible than from any other book. Medical science I have to use rather hard, for the sick have the most bitter feeling towards physicians and religious teachers. These two classes I have to come in contact with. The fear of these two classes makes the patient sick.

I have found this out by the effect the patient has on me. I have been so provoked when sitting by the sick, with the physician and in regard to certain classes of disease, that it was with the greatest difficulty I could keep my temper, and I had never seen the doctor or minister. But I always found that when I would get the patients clear from their opinions, they would express themselves in as strong terms as I had. I thought the fault might be with me, but I am now satisfied that I was only the scape-goat to carry off feelings they dared not lisp out, but could not tell why. Therefore I have not the slightest feeling as a man towards any person, only regarding error. That I have no sympathy with. It is a hypocrite in myself and in every one else.

You may say I have gone out of the way to attack religious denominations. If I have, the fault is in my patient. Every one knows that pious persons when sick are the most profane and talk the worst about the Bible. This is because they have the most fear.

With these remarks I will leave this part of my subject, and say a word or two in regard to words. I differ from all persons about some words. One is "mind." Mind to me is not wisdom, but spiritual matter. And I think before you get through my book you will think so too, and be convinced of the truth of what I say. So far as my education is concerned I need make no apology. If I have learning enough to explain my theory, it is all I want.

FALSE REPORTS CONCERNING MY RELIGIOUS BELIEF

In giving to the public my ideas in regard to curing the sick it will be necessary to correct some false ideas that have been circulated in regard to my religious belief. So I will say I have no belief and in regard to any person's religion or disease I know they are based on a false idea of wisdom. I take the sick as I find them and treat them according to their several diseases. As their diseases are the result of their education or belief I have to come in contact with their beliefs. Their religious beliefs are often the cause of their trouble, but the medical theory causes more than all the rest at the present day. In times of old when the priests led the masses the causes emanated from the priests, but since the right of religious freedom has been granted to all, truth has destroyed the power of the priests. Yet it has not enlightened the people, but transferred the idea of disease to the medical fraternity. . . .

All the religion I acknowledge is God or Wisdom. I will not take man's belief to guide my barque. I would rather stand at the helm, myself, but the priest and medical faculty have assumed sway, and one pretends to look after the body and the other the soul. So between both they have nearly destroyed soul and body, for you cannot find one person in ten but complains of some trouble in the form of disease. As disease leads to destruction or death, death is one of the natural results of disease. So to save persons from what may follow, a religious belief is introduced and another world is made which is to receive all men, who are to be rewarded according to their acts. This makes up the whole progress of man's life. In all this intelligence and goodness are not included. It is true we are told that to live a virtuous life is good, but you never bear that to be posted in the wisdom of the world gives a person advantage over the weak and humble believer who swallows everything the priest tells him. To be a good Christian according to their explanation of religion is to be humble and not wise at all. Now every man partakes of his belief, and in fact they are all made of belief, for everything you can think of or remember is such. Now all thins must end according to man's belief, and there has been nothing as yet that has come in collision with it. Therefore life and death are said to be the natural destiny of man. It is true that the medical faculty try to stave off death but the harder they work the surer they are to destroy the thing they are trying to save. Man's belief is the thing either to be saved or lost and to this end all their skill is directed. This was the state of the world when Jesus appeared.

MIND

In order to introduce my theory of curing disease it will be necessary to explain the use I make of a few words to which custom has given a meaning I am unable to use. For instance the word mind. All use the word applied to man's intelligence. As the word mind has never been applied to any spiritual substance or any substance at all, it strikes the reader strangely to hear it as I have to use it, still I think I can show that the author must have a different meaning in his wisdom than is commonly attributed to it. It could not be that he had an idea of any world or existence beyond this life, for mind was considered man's life and all his reasoning powers at death must end. Consequently the brain was considered the seat of the mind. Various beliefs show that this false reasoning still holds sway over mankind. The word mind as it is used and believed comprises all of man and beast that has life and instinct, which at death disappears or dies. As science progressed the weakness of the reasoning was seen, and the religious community invested the word with a new sig-nificance which the ancients never dreamed of ; for, with their limitations, it could not explain the life of man; it could not contain the word wisdom, so a new word was needed and "soul" was introduced. But if you call the soul "science" you will have a higher development than is included in mind. Let "mind," then embrace all matter of the human and brute creations, as the word "matter" embraces all inanimate substances. Then the "soul" will represent wisdom that creates from inanimate matter every manufactured article. . . . Ancient philosophers divided man into two elements, mind and matter, the body being matter and the soul mind, and one was the offspring of the other. The life of the soul was one thing and the life of the body another, but they both died together. So the word mind covered all of man's life. The intellect of the brute was termed instinct, which was included in the meaning of mind. At death all were laid in the grave together : the wise man and the fool, the rich and the poor all found their level in the grave. . . . We have evidence enough to show that what is now called the soul in ancient times had no higher meaning than mind, for we read of good souls and wicked souls. So here is an end to the soul. Such teaching is the cause of man's misery.

Every one will admit that all the qualities of "soul" which I have mentioned will apply to man's intelligence, and that "mind" according to every definition can change; also admit that Wisdom cannot change, that it is the same today and forever. Now can any one tell me what there is that is not matter that can be changed? It cannot be Wisdom. It cannot be any form that can be seen, which of course must be matter. Then what is it that is not Wisdom, God, or spirit, and not matter and yet can be changed? It is matter held in solution called mind, which the power of Wisdom can condense into a solid so dense as to become the substance called "matter." Assume this theory and then you can see how man can become sick and get well by a change of mind.

Disease is the natural result of ignorance and error governed by discords of the mind. For instance, friction produces heat, heat expansion, expansion motion, motion disturbs life, and life comes out of the motion. There are various kinds of life, vegetable, animal, etc. ; for life is what comes from the decomposition of matter. Wisdom is not life, it is from everlasting to everlasting, the same today and forever. But as life ascends from the lower to the higher kingdoms, Wisdom attaches itself to it in order to develop in man itself. . . .

I will give you the process as it comes to me by this great truth that heals all who come into it. The elements of the mineral kingdom by their chemical change bring forth life, this mingles with its mother-minerals and an offspring is produced called a vegetable. The life of minerals enters this new kingdom and a new creation springs into being. This again mingles with its parent kingdom and there comes a low form of life called the animal kingdom; one generation begets another till matter is prepared to receive some of the life from the Wisdom which rules these lower lives. Man's life comes from his peculiar development, so there is as much difference in the idea "man" as there is in the other kingdoms, for man is made of those kingdoms. He combines three parts in himself, animal, human, scientific, in different degrees in each person. Man partakes more of the animal, less of the scientific. Women have more of the scientific element, less of the animal; the latter kingdom makes them strong, the human benevolent, and the scientific spiritual and poetical.

From time immemorial the subject of mind has been a theme of ancient and modern philosophers. Now if the idea of mind did not embrace all our reason and philosophy man would not be all the time trying to investigate its nature. Mind is always associated with something else. Moses used the word wisdom in the sense of mind when he said God created the heavens and the earth, which means mind and matter.

The philosophers of our day separate matter from mind and call matter material, and mind immaterial, so that matter is not [supposed to be] under the control of mind, and as mind is immaterial it is nothing. Now can nothing produce something? This the philosophers of our day may answer. Why all these different applications of the same term? If mind is matter, what is life? To show that mind is [spiritual] matter we must illustrate by something that men will admit. But some one may ask of what consequence is it to man whether mind is substance or not? I say it is of vast im-portance to the world, for if it can be shown that mind is [spiritual] matter, it will be seen that mind is under the control of a wisdom possessed by man, so that wisdom acting upon mind changes it and destroys the error and brings man to the truth...

Every person admits that mind has a great deal to do with the body, and each one makes a difference between them. The mind is said to be the intellectual part of man, and the body the servant. In one sense this is true, but to Wisdom it is false, for all admit that the mind can be changed, and if intelligence can change it cannot be wisdom. Jesus taught that the real man is of wisdom. Wisdom cannot change, but can arrange and classify ideas each in its proper place, and show where mind falls short of wisdom. To suppose mind is wisdom is as false as to suppose power is weight.

The natural man, whose intellect is linked with the brutes, and who cannot see beyond matter, reasons this way: He is in matter, but thinks he is outside of it. He cannot see his absurd mode of reasoning, but it is shown in disease. Physical man is composed of fluids and gases, and also mind. The mind is supposed to be the offspring of his body, or brain, although in his conversation he makes a distinction between them; and being in matter his intelligence cannot see beyond it. Therefore lie only believes in a superior wisdom as a mystery. The fact that he admits it as a mysterious gift or power shows that he does not know it. To make man know himself is to convince him, that he, his wisdom, is as distinct from his belief as he is from anything that exists separate from him. Then he will give to mind an identity embracing everything having a beginning and ending. Sickness and disease are contained in it, but wisdom is no part of it.

If we see a dead person we have no idea of a wisdom that exists with all the faculties that were exhibited through the body. We try to believe but our belief is vague; we cannot describe it. Man is not developed enough to see outside of his idea "matter." He is in the idea prophesying of what may come hereafter. I have developed this wisdom, which is the real man, till I have broken through the bars of death and can see beyond the world of opinions into the light of Science. I can see what things have being, and how we take our opinions for truth.

The moon is a figure of the natural man. Its light is borrowed, or the light of the opinions of the sun. It thinks it has light of itself, but the sun's light knows that it is the reflection of the sun's light. The wise man in like manner knows that the light of the body or natural man is but the reflection of the scientific man. Our misery lies in this darkness. This is the prison that holds the natural man, till the light of Wisdom bursts his bonds, and sets the captive free. Here is where Christ went to preach to the prisoners bound by error, before the reformation of Science.

THE SCIENTIFIC MAN

I will try to define what I mean by the scientific man or man outside of matter. To do this I must assume myself in relation to mind as God stands to all creation. The natural man is only an idea made by God's wisdom, like a shadow. After this shadow goes through a certain change like any other matter it is in a state to be a medium of a higher power than itself. God sent an identity of His wisdom to take con-trol of the medium and carry out His design and bring man to a knowledge of the Father. This identity that He sends is Science or the Son of God.

To illustrate I must use a figure so you can get my meaning. For if you do not do the thing God does you cannot be the Son of God. Jesus was called the Son of God. Why was He called the Son of God? Because He did the will of His Father who sent Him. To be a Son of God you must do His will, and His will is to subject your errors to the Truth, so that you can know that you are born of God. Now, I will suppose that God, when He spoke man into existence knew that man was His own idea. A chemical change was going on for a certain time till man became of age, or men became ready to be governed by a higher principle than matter. Science is this principle put into practice.

So Science is the Son of God or Wisdom. Now Science being the Son of Wisdom, it is a part of Wisdom. Give this Science an identity with a knowledge of its Father, and then you have a Son ready to take possession of matter when matter becomes purified, or a chemical change takes place in it so that it can be governed by an independent power. . . . This Son or Science is not seen by the natural man, so the natural man thinks his life is in this belief.   Now to come to the knowledge of this Science is the new birth.

THE NATURAL MAN

All mankind have respect for wisdom or something superior to themselves that they cannot understand. Man of himself is naturally indolent, brutish, and wilfully stupid, content to live like the brute. He is pleased at any bauble or trifling thing. He has imitation and tries to copy whatever pleases him; in this he shows reverence for his superiors. As he does not posses Science he is often deceived. Thus he is made timid and willing to be led. His courage is the courage of ignorance and when he sees superior numbers be curls down like a dog when whipped by his master. Easily led and easily deceived, no confidence is to be placed on his word, for his word is always like the wag of a dog's tail, to show his submission. But when his ends are answered, his next act might be to injure the one that had saved him from trouble. He is oily in his manners if all goes well, but if needed for anything, like the dog he is ready at the whistle of his master or any one that will pat him, to bite his own master or any one else

Now because the brutes can be taught something it does not follow that they can be taught Science. They have their bounds which they cannot pass. So the natural man has his bounds which he cannot pass. But when I speak of the natural man, I speak of that wisdom that is based on an opinion. The brute is undergoing a change by the introduction of the wisdom of man. So the natural man is undergoing a change by the introduction of the Scientific Man. The brute is developed as far as the wisdom of man is capable of instructing him. So Science takes the man of opinions and instructs him in the Wisdom of God. As every man has more of the wisdom of opinions than of Science, he is ignorant of him-self, and being ignorant he can see only one character; for all the wisdom he has is public opinion. He is up today and down tomorrow, and knows not the cause of his rise or fall. His change is so gradual that he never knows he has changed but supposes that all changes go to prove that he has remained the same. These minds are often found in politics. You will hear a person say, "I was always a Democrat or Federalist, and my father and grandfather were before me." Now this is a man of one idea. He is like the old grey-headed veteran who stands on Mt. Joy and looks around on Portland and then turns to his young friend and says, "My lad, I remember when I helped cut the wood where the city now stands, eighty or ninety years ago." His young friend says "You must have changed very much." "Oh! I am older, but I am the same man I was then." In reality there is not a single idea about him that is the same. So it is with the political man. His senses are attached to the word "democrat," and as long as that word lives in the wisdom of opinions he is a Democrat; and so long as this identity lives in him he never changes, for his senses never were attached to any principle.

So the changes of principle are nothing to him, as he never had any.

Science being a stranger to both, cannot work like the demagogue appealing to one idea. For the senses of the the scientific man are attached to the Wisdom that governs both. So as progress is the order of the day, the senses of the masses become attached to new ideas and detached from old ones, and thus parties are all the time changing and minds are changing to suit the times. This gives the demagogue a chance to appeal to the masses, and as long as they can lead the masses by one popular name, they use any sort of cunning that comes up to suit their convenience.

DEATH OF THE NATURAL MAN

I am often asked where I differ from a spiritualist. In everything, but as this is an opinion I will try to make it clear. The spiritualists believe in the dead rising, and they sometimes say there is no such thing as death. Now let us see what their works show. The senses of the natural man are attached to his knowledge, and that is made of opinions, and so his senses are attached to his opinions. His opinions embrace all belief. So to destroy his belief is to destroy his life, for his life is in his belief, and a part of it.

Let us see what his belief embraces. In the first place he believes in matter, called living matter, that has life; for he says that life or matter must die or perish. Now here is the contradiction in the spiritualists' belief. They deny that the dead rise, but if the dead do not rise, what are the dead? You are pointed to a man lying motionless and to all appearance even according to a spiritualist, dead. Now is he dead, or is he not dead? The spiritualist may answer. He says the body is dead. Was it ever alive ? You must say, "yes," for I point to a man moving around and ask if that man is dead and your answer is, "no." Then he must be a living man, and according to your belief we have a living man and a dead one. Now where do they differ? Here is the mystery, their belief like all others flies back to the old superstition which they have all believed: that the dead rise, and in this fog they get lost.

I will show you where I differ from spiritualists and in fact all other sects. If you will admit that mind is spiritual matter, for the sake of listening to my ideas, I will give you my theory. I assert that according to man's belief there are certain facts admitted and established beyond a doubt, and as my wisdom is not of this world or man's belief, only in part, it follows that what I know I have no opinion about. All knowledge that is of man is based on opinions. This I call this world of matter; it embraces all that comes within the so-called senses. Man's happiness and misery is in his belief, but the wisdom of science is of God, not of man.

To separate these two kingdoms is what I am trying to do, and if I can succeed in this I have accomplished what never has been done, but what has been the aim of the philosophers since the world began. The secret of life and happiness is the aim of all mankind, and how to get at it is the mystery that has baffled the wisdom of the world. I should never under-take the task of explaining what the wise men have failed to do but for the want of some better proof to explain phenom-ena that come under my own observation. The remedies have never destroyed the cause nor can the cause be destroyed by man's reason, and Science cannot admit what cannot be proved. Until some better proof of what we see and hear and feel can be produced the world must grope in darkness and scepticism.

I will separate the two worlds of which I am now speaking and show what one has failed to do, also that the other is not acknowledged as independent of the first. The world of opinions is the old world. That of Science is the new, and a separation must take place and a battle fought between them. The world of error and opinions has held Science in bondage ever since man began to be independent of savage life. The child of Science has been nourished in the bosom of its mother in the wilderness of error till it grew up so as to assume a character, then when it has undertaken to assume its rights it has always been met with the thunder of error. But as it is so much of a friend to the happiness of man, the enemies or error could never prevent its growth, for that was in the scientific world, and that world has no matter, or it is so rarified that error cannot see through it. So the scientific man can pass through the errors and instruct the child of Science till it bursts forth and becomes a man or law. Then the natural man or error destroys its leaders and falls down and worships the scientific laws, and acknowledges them as king of this world. As Science is now acknowledged, the kings of the earth are cut off and the kingdom is divided against itself; the leaders with their armies flee into the wilderness, there to rally for another attack when any new science is started. Now the Science of Life and Happiness is the one that has met with the most opposition from the fact that it is death to all opposers. It never compromises with its enemies, nor has it any dealings with them. Its kingdom is of Truth, not of error; therefore it is not of this world of matter.

I will state its laws, how much it admits, how much it condemns and how it puts its laws in force. Its habitation is in the hearts of men, it cannot be seen by the natural man, for he is of matter. All he has is his senses, there is his residence for the time, he has no abiding city, but is a traveler or sojourner in the world. His house is not made with hands but is in the scientific world. So his whole aim is the happiness of man. The scientific man sees through matter which is only an error acknowledged as a truth, although it is to the natural man a reality. As error holds on to all territory as under its power, it keeps the scientific man in slavery or bondage. So to keep the Science of Life down, men invent all sorts of humbugs in the shape of invisible things and attribute life to them, while they pretend to be the people's guide to wisdom. It is almost impossible to tell one character from another, as both communicate through the same organs. As the scientific man has to prove his wisdom through the same matter that the natural man uses he is often misrepresented and put down by false stories of the errors of the natural man. This was where Jesus found so much trouble in His day, for the people could not tell who was speaking.

The scientific man was called by the natural man, "angel." So if an angel spoke he would listen. The natural man, being superstitious and ignorant, is easily led by the cunning errors of the world; the leaders, being crafty and superstitious, believe in every phenomenon which is produced, and they attribute it to a power from the invisible world. The locality of this world is the mystery, so all varieties of speculations are got up about it. It opens all the avenues of matter, through which to give the inhabitants "communications" But the natural man has possession of the mediums, so that the scientific man is misrepresented in nine-tenths of all he says. To be in the scientific world is to acknowledge a wisdom above the natural man, which will enter that world where wisdom sees through matter. This is the condition of those who are thrown into the clairvoyant state. To them matter is nothing but an idea that is seen or not, just as it is called out. . . . The explanation is given by these blind guides, who have eyes but cannot see, ears but cannot hear, and hearts but cannot understand Science. They are afraid of the truth lest it destroy them, for the death of error is the introduction of the Science of Life and Happiness.

As the standards of parties are established by error; it is almost imposible to introduce any new science unless it is explained on some of the theories of the natural man. Thus all phenomena are thrown into the bands of blind guides who have pronounced judgment upon everything that has appeared. Whenever anyone shows a phenomenon, the priest and doctor catch the idea out of the mouth of the author and explain it. on some theory already known to the people. The theory of health is one that has come up many times and failed because of the blindness of the wise, so that it has now almost become a terror to the one who had boldness enough to stand up and face the blind leaders of the blind. . . . This Christ whom you crucify by your theories, is the same that Jesus taught eighteen hundred years ago. It was taught by the prophets of old and has always been in the world, but has never been applied to the curing of disease, although false Christs have arisen and deceived the people, and the true Christ has been crucified by the priest and doctor to this time.

I will now try to establish this science or rock and upon it I will build the Science of Life. The starting-point is animal matter or life which set in action, leads to thought. Thoughts, like grains of sand, are held together by their own sympathy or attraction. The natural man is composed of these particles of thought combined and arranged to make a form called man. As thought is always changing, so man is always throwing off particles or thoughts and receiving others.

As man's senses are in his wisdom, and his wisdom is attached to his idea or body, his change of mind is under one of the two directions, either of this world of opinions, or of God or Science and his happiness or misery is the result of his thought. As the idea man has always been under the wisdom of this world, the scientific man has always been kept down, from the fact that no man has ever risen to that state where the scientific man could control the wisdom of the natural man. This has always caused man to be at war with himself. In this warfare if the natural man rules, disease and unhappiness are the fate of man. If Science rules, life and happiness are the reward.

Now I stand alone on this rock, fighting the errors of this world, and establishing the Science of Life by my works. What is my mode of warfare? With the axe of truth, I strike at the root of every tree of error and hew it down, so that there shall not be one error in man showing itself in the form of disease. My knowledge is my wisdom and is not matter or opinion. It decomposes the thoughts, changes the combinations and produces an idea clear from the error that makes a person unhappy or diseased. You see I have something to reason about, and this something is eternal life, which is in Science and is what Jesus tried to establish.

If I can show that man's happiness is in his belief and his misery is the effect of his belief then I shall have done what never has been done before. Establish this and man rises to a higher state of wisdom not of this world, but of that world of Science which sees that all human misery can be corrected by this principle, as well as the evil effects of error. Then the Science of Life will take place with other sciences. Then in truth can be said "Oh ! death (or error) where is thy sting. Oh! grave where is thy victory!" The sting of ignorance is death. But the wisdom of Science is life eternal.

I will show the world's reasoning and how I reason. I will take the oracles of the world, for all science of this world of opinions has oracles. These oracles of which I speak are those who pretend to instruct the people in regard to health and happiness. The first is the clergy, for they take the lead in everything pertaining to man's happiness. I will ask them what they think of Jesus, His mission if He had any, and of what advantage it was to the world. They reply that the world had gone so far astray that it was necessary to send Jesus Christ into the world to convince man of a future state of rewards and punishments, that he might repent and be saved. If this is true I ask why did Jesus devote so much time to the sick? (Oracle) To show that He came from God. (Q) What does that prove? If I cure a person does it prove that I come from God? (0) No, but do you make yourself equal with Christ? (Q) Have you any proof of any thing that you never saw and is only an opinion? (0) The Bible. (Q.) Does the Bible speak for itself or does some one explain it? (0) We must take the Bible as our guide to truth. Let us now sum up the wisdom which this oracle has delivered. All of his wisdom is founded on an opinion that there is another world and that Jesus came from that world to communicate the fact to the inhabitants of this one. The happiness of man is not increased by this theory, because this oracle cannot cure the sick. Now Jesus cured the sick and said if they understood Him they might do the same. We want a theory like that of Jesus, not of talk but of words, for a theory that cannot be put into practice is worthless.

My oracle is Jesus: He proves the goodness of wisdom. Jesus was the oracle and Christ the wisdom shown through this man for the happiness of the sick who had been deceived by the other two classes, priest and doctor. God or Wisdom has seen how these blind guides had robbed the widow and the poor of their treasures, deserted them and left them forsaken and despairing, dependent upon the charity of a wicked world.

This wisdom developed itself through the man Jesus and He fearlessly stood up and denounced these blind guides as hypocrites and devils.

THE SENSES

Are our senses mind? I answer, no. This was the problem ancient philosophers sought to solve. Most of them believed the soul, senses, and every intellectual faculty of man to be mind, therefore our senses must be mind. The translator of Lucretius says Lucretius attacks the ancient academics who held the mind to be the sole arbiter and judge of things, and establishes the senses to be the arbitrators. For, says he, "whatever can correct and confute what is false, must of neces-sity be the criterion of truth, and this is done by the senses only." This difference is true in part. Both were right. But they confused mind and senses into one, like the modern philosophers who make wisdom and knowledge, mind and senses, Jesus and Christ, ,synonymous. Now mind and senses are as distinct as light and darkness, and the same distinction holds good in wisdom and knowledge, Jesus and Christ. Christ, Wisdom and the spiritual senses are synonymous. So likewise are Jesus, knowledge and mind. Our life is in our senses: and if our wisdom is in our mind, we attach our life and senses to matter. But if our wisdom is attached to Science, our life and senses are in God, not in matter; for there is no matter in God or Wisdom; matter is the medium of Wisdom.

This difference has been overlooked by the ancients. And modern philosophers have put mind and soul in matter, thus making a distinction without a difference. Now according to modern philosophy, the soul, mind, life and senses are all liable to die; but according to this truth mind is spiritual matter, and all matter must be dissolved. Wisdom is not [physical] life. Our senses are not life. But all of these are solid and eternal; and to know them is life and life eternal. Life is in the knowledge of this wisdom, and death is in the destruction of your opinions or matter.

I will give some experiments of a man of wisdom acting through and dissolving the man of matter so the man of wisdom can escape. This process is Science. Take for example two persons, or you and myself. One wishes to communicate to the other some fact. You feel a pain, I also feel it. Now the sympathy of our minds mingling is spiritual matter. But there is no wisdom in it, for wisdom is outside of matter. If we both feel the same pain, we each call it our own; for we are devoid of that wisdom which would make us know we were affecting each other. Each one has his own identity and wants sympathy, and the ignorance of each is the vacuum that is between us. So we are drawn together by this invisible action called sympathy. Now make man wise enough to know that he can feel the pains of another, and then you get him outside of matter. The wisdom that knows this has eternal life, for life is in the knowledge of this wisdom. This the world is unacquainted with.

Now Jesus had more of this life or truth than any other person, and to teach it to another is a science. If you know it and can teach it, you are a teacher of the truth. But if you know it and cannot teach it, you are a follower of the truth. Now the knowledge of this truth is life, and the absence of it is death. There are a great many kinds of life.

The natural man begins at his birth. Animal life is not vege-table, and vegetable is not animal life. And there is another kind of life that is not understood, and that is the life that follows the knowledge of this great truth. The word "life," cannot be applied to Wisdom, for that has no beginning and life has. The word death is applied to everything that has life. All motion or action produces life, for where there is no motion there is no life. Matter in motion is called life. Life is the action of matter, and to know it is a truth, and to know how to produce it is Wisdom. This Wisdom was pos-sessed by Jesus, for He says: "My sheep hear my voice and I give unto them eternal life." "I (Christ) and my Father are one"

I shall show that Jesus was not life, but life or Christ was in Him, and He taught it. He says: "Whosoever will save his life shall lose it, and whosoever shall lose his life for my sake shall find it." The people believed their life to be in themselves. But Jesus knew their lives were in God, for if they lost their opinions and found this Truth, then they had lost their life and found it.

I will now take my own practice to explain what life is according to Jesus. I said if two persons were sitting together, and each felt a pain each would call it his own. Now this pain is life, for it contains our senses, and this life is in matter, for the pain is in our mind, and our mind, senses, and life are all the same according to the world's wisdom. I know I can take a person's feelings, and this knowledge to me is truth, and to know it is life, and this knowledge the patient does not possess. He knows he has a pain and this to him is a truth, but this life is in his belief, and so his life is liable to be lost by his losing his mind. My life is in my wisdom and my wisdom is not matter. So that to know this is a truth outside of my patient's belief, and this truth contains my life. To get his senses out of his matter into this truth is to give him eternal life. I want to give him eternal life to save him from the sufferings occasioned by his belief that he may lose his life by disease of the heart. My wisdom acting is in matter but it is no part of it, so what to him is disease is to me spiritual matter that can be changed. His ignorance keeps his senses in fear of death, and all his life subject to bondage through his belief.

I commence by describing his feelings. These he admits; but how I can tell them is to him a mystery. This I know for I see him in his error, yet he cannot see me in his wis-dom, for it is in its own prison. It wants me to explain how I can see it, and how I know how it feels. I will suppose you, the reader, to be the patient, and that you acknowledge that I tell your feelings and what you think is your disease. All this I get from you without your knowledge, therefore you do not know how I do it. So I will inform you. Ideas have life. A belief has life or matter, for it can be changed. Now all the aforesaid make up the natural man, and all this can be changed. As I am trying to convince you how I take your feelings I must use such illustrations as you understand, for my life is in my words, and if my words cannot destroy your life or matter, then I cannot give you my life or wisdom.

I will now take a rose for an illustration. You are like a rose. You throw from yourself an atmosphere or vapor. When the rose is dead all outside of it is darkness to the germ of the bud. This is the child. As the rose opens it expands and unfolds itself to the world, the same as a child's brain ex-pands and opens the folds of its understanding. As the rose comes before the world of roses it takes its stand with the rest of its kind. So it is with man. As he unfolds his knowledge, he is classed with others of his kind. As the rose throws off its peculiarities to the air, the world judges of its odor. So as man throws off his peculiar character or life, health or disease, the world is to judge of his happiness or misery by the fruits of his belief.

Take a person with consumption. The idea consumption decomposes and throws off an odor that contains all the ideas of the person affected. This is true of every idea or thought. Now I come in contact with this odor thrown from you, and being well I have found by twenty years experience that these odors affect me, and also that they contain the identity of the patient whom this odor surrounds. This called my attention to it, and I found that it was as easy to tell the feelings or thoughts of a person sick as to detect the odor of spirits from that of tobacco. I at first thought I inhaled it, but at last

99

found that my spiritual senses could be affected by it when my body was at a distance of many miles from the patient. This led to a new discovery, and I found my [real] senses were not in my body, but that my body was in my senses, and my knowledge located my senses according to my wisdom. If a man's knowledge is in matter all there is of him (to him) is contained in matter. But if his knowledge is in Wisdom, then his senses and all there is of him are outside of matter. To know this is a truth, and the effect is life in this truth, and this truth is in Wisdom. So the man who knows all this is in Wisdom with all his senses and life.

Then where do I differ from you? In this respect. My wisdom is my health, and your wisdom is your disease; for your wisdom is in your belief, and my wisdom is my life and senses, and my senses teach me that your trouble is the effect of your belief. What is light to me is darkness to you. You being in the dark stumble and are afraid of your own shadow. I with the eye of Truth see in your darkness or belief, and you seem to me blind. Or, like the rose, you cannot see the light, while I am in the light, and see through the clouds of your ignorance, see your senses and all there is of you, held in this ignorance by error, trying like the life of the rose bud to break through and come to the light. You have eyes, taste, and all your senses, but the clouds are before them, and as Jesus said, "Ye have eyes and see not, and have ears and hear not, and a heart that cannot understand." Now what is the reason? It is this. Your eyes have not seen, your ears have not heard, and your heart has not understood what happiness there is in knowing that your life, senses, and all that there is near and dear to you is no part of matter, and that matter is only a belief or casket to hold you in till Wisdom dissolves the casket, and lets you into the light of Science. Then you will hold life in the form of the rose, and live in a world of light, where the sorrows of hell and disease can never come, where you can sit and see that what man takes for reality is only the works of heathen superstition. Then you will not be afraid of disease, which leads to death.

You may ask if all I say is true what is it good for? If it is only a belief, I admit that it is of no more value to a person than any religious belief. You may ask for proof that will give some light upon the subject. I will give it, as near as a man who has eyesight can explain colors to a blind person. When I sit by a patient, if he thinks he has disease of the heart, the atmosphere surrounding him is his belief, and the fear of death is in the density of the clouds of his mind. Now knowing he is in the clouds somewhere I, as it were, try to arouse him. But it appears as though he were blind. So I shake him to arouse him out of his lethargy. At last I see him aroused and look around, but soon sink back again. By my talk I disturb the clouds, and this sometimes makes the patient very nervous, like a person coming out of a fit or awakened from a sound sleep. What I say is truth, and being solid it breaks in pieces his matter or belief, till at last he looks up to inquire what has been the trouble. My explanation rouses him and gives another change to his mind, and that is like a thunder storm. When it thunders and the lightning flashes, the patient is nervous. When the cloud of ignorance passes over and the light of truth comes, then the patient sees where his misery came from, and that it was believing a lie that made him sick. My arguments are based upon my knowledge of his feelings, and this knowledge put in practice is the Science of Health, (1) and is for the benefit of the sick and suffering.

HOW THE SENSES ARE DECEIVED

Why is it that I run a. greater risk of being misrepresented in regard to my mode of curing than practitioners of other schools? I must be allowed to offer my own explanation of this fact; because if I were understood I should not be in danger of being misrepresented and condemned by the guilty. I stand alone, a target at which all classes aim their poisonous darts, for I make war with every creed, profession, and idea that contains false reasoning. Every man's hand therefore is against me, and I am against every man's opinion.

Man's senses may be compared to a young virgin who has never been deceived by the world. Popular errors are like a young prince who stands ready to bestow his addresses upon all whom he can deceive. When he approaches the virgin he appears like an angel of light and wisdom. By soft speech and imposing address he wins the virgin maid to his belief. Having become entangled in his web or false doctrines, she is carried away from her home or state of innocence into the gulf of despair, there to live a miserable existence or become a slave to fashion. In this state a false theory holds out to her all kinds of ideas and she becomes a slave to the world. Error favors the utmost freedom in thought and conduct, and offers all the allurements of pleasure and enjoyment to the young. Each one is approached with some fascinating idea with which he is carried away and to which he becomes wedded. These are the ideas founded in man's wisdom, and manifested through man. The pure virgin ideas are also shadowed through the same medium, and each is addressed by truth or by error. Error in making a picture of Wisdom assumes an air of wisdom. Wisdom, however, like charity, is not puffed up and it is slighted by error. It is looked upon by the young as an old conservative. They say to it, "De-part for a time, while I enjoy the pleasure of error, and when I am satisfied I will call upon you." Wisdom is banished from the society of the world, and error like a raging lion goes about devouring all whom it can find.

In the shape of man it approaches the virgin mind, and in musical tones commences paying his addresses. Finally over-come by sophistry, she is won to his opinions, and is soon wedded to his ideas, and they two become one flesh. Her senses are attached to matter. What is his is hers, and she is in all respects the partner and wife of error. She is no longer a virgin but a wedded wife. The belief is the husband. When a person is converted from one belief to another she leaves her husband and marries another. This was the case with the woman whom Jesus told that she had truly said she had no husband, "for he whom thou now hast is not thy husband." She had served different religious beliefs and as each was destroyed by her wisdom, she became a widow. Then she joined herself to another and became a wife. These husbands were creeds, and the virgins were those who cared nothing for religion, and had no settled opinions about the future. The beliefs in regard to another world, were represented by men, for they were the embodiment of man's opinion, like virgin soil. When Jesus sought to explain the truth, he compared it to a wedding and all who could under-stand entered in. The ten virgins represented two classes, one having wisdom outside of the natural senses, and those who cannot believe anything outside of their senses. When the truth came they arose and trimmed their lamps, but those who had no oil or understanding could not enter. Every one who has not risen above the natural man, but is contented with being ignorant is a foolish virgin, while those who try to understand are of the other class. Every one belongs to the former till wedded to a belief.

There is still another class. Those who having professed to belong to a certain sect and having united with it after a while leave and join another. These are persons having committed adultery, for they are living with a new belief, therefore they are to be stoned and turned out of the church. This explains the case of a woman brought before Jesus as an adulterer. She had left the world's belief, and had become interested in Jesus' truth. To the Jews she had committed adultery and had been caught in advocating His truth. As she did not fully understand, she was not lawfully married, and her husband or the church had claims upon her. The Jews, therefore, thinking she deserved punishment, brought her to Jesus to see what His judgment would be.   When He had heard their story He said, "let him who is guiltless cast the first stone." They all immediately left, and He asked her, "where are thy accusers?" or thy fears that this is not the true light that lighteth every one that receiveth it! She replied "No belief has any effect on me." And He said, "Go thy way and believe in man's opinion no more."

This article was written from the impressions that came upon me while sitting by a young lady who was afraid of dying, and also was afraid of being blind. It may seem strange to those in health how our belief affects us. The fact is there is nothing of us [the natural man] but belief. It is the whole capital stock in trade of man. It is all that can be changed, and embraces everything man has made or ever will make. Wisdom is the scientific man, who can destroy the works of the natural man. Disease is made by the natural man's belief in some false idea. The error comes to the virgin mind and makes an impression. The soil is disturbed and the mind listens or waits to be taught. If it is misled, briars and thorns and troubles spring up in its path through life. These all go to make the man of belief. Wisdom destroys these false ideas, purifies the soil, and brings the mind under a higher state of cultivation. This is the work of Science. When a person has made himself a body of sin and death, truth destroys his death, and attaches his senses to a body of life.

THE SENSES AND LANGUAGE

Why is it that mankind have settled down on the fact that man has five senses, no more, no less? The wise say the spiritual man has two more, making seven. Now, what is a sense? We often say "such a thing comes within my senses." If "senses" mean what the wise say it does why is man set down above the brute?   Let us see how they compare. Man sees, hears, tastes, smells and feels, and so does the brute; neither shows any prominence of wisdom over the other. When you ask where is man's superiority you are told that man reasons and the brute does not. Ask for proof and people can show no difference only as they make their own minds. If you place them together the brute is a little the shrewder.

Now all will admit that there is a vast difference between a wise man and a brute, but the brutal man is as much below the brute as the latter is below the wise man. This wisdom that makes man above the brute is not of this brutal world, but comes from some higher source. I have so much confidence in the wisdom of the wise men of old that I have no doubt but they solved that question, and I have so little confidence in the wisdom of this world that I disbelieve every truth founded on man's opinion.

We often hear of the laws of God, but when we ask for wisdom on the subject, the wise fail to give us the information desired by the scientific man. They can give their opinion and as that contains no knowledge the scientific must look for wisdom elsewhere than to the wisdom of this brutal world of five senses. So I will leave man and brute with their five senses and search out some other way to solve the problem of the senses.

I will ask any one if seeing is matter, or is it something independent of matter? For instance, you see a shadow: is the power that sees any part of the shadow? All will say no. Then the shadow comes in contact with something. Now what is that something called sight or one of the senses? Is it matter? The natural man cannot answer that question any more than the brute. He says the eye is the sight. Jesus says the light of the body is the eye. So the natural man and Jesus differ. Settle this question and you have one of the five senses defined so that there can be no dispute between the scientific and natural or brutal man. As the natural man has failed to satisfy the scientific man let the latter try to convince the natural man of his error. The scientific man makes all sensation outside of the idea of matter, so that to him all sensation must be made on something independent of the natural idea of the senses.

All will admit that God knows all things. If you do not own it you must admit it if you are above the brute; else you, admitting that the brute knows nothing about God, put yourself on a level with the brute. So I take it for granted that this question is settled, that God knows all things. So God sees, that is one sense. All will admit that God is equal to man, at least in regard to wisdom. If we can show that man's senses can act independently of his natural body, if it can be shown that man's wisdom is not of matter but of God, we will divide him into as many senses as it is necessary for the scientific world.

What is necessary for the natural man's happiness is to eat, drink and enjoy himself in the easiest way he can. The savage is a fair specimen of the natural man and the wild beast the natural specimen of the brute creation. One has no preeminence over the other-"might is right"-each is happy when not disturbed. If never disturbed they would be like the fool without even error. But disturbance brings other senses into action, and as wisdom is developed it gives man a knowledge of himself above the natural man of five senses. Thus the wisdom of the scientific man sees the man with the five senses, a little above the brute, in error trying to free himself from his earthly matter, or ignorance, and arrive at knowledge of phenomena that keep him in a state of sin, dis-ease and death. So I will leave the man of five senses in er-ror and talk to the scientific man about the other senses.

He is not embraced in one idea. A man may be scientific in many sciences, mathematics, chemistry, astronomy, all that are acknowledged and admitted by even the natural man, though not understood. But the Science of Happiness is not acknowledged by the wisdom of the five senses. It requires more senses to put men in possession of this Science that will teach him happiness. As happiness is what follows a belief it is necessary to know whether our wisdom is of this world of opinion or of the world of Science. This world sees nothing outside of its senses. Wisdom sees nothing of the natural man's senses but ignorance, so that the wisdom of this world is opposed to the Science of Happiness.

Let us see what will be admitted by all. I believe it will not be denied that there is such a phenomenon as mesmerism; if it is denied those who do so may enjoy their own opinions and I will turn to those who admit it. This embraces a large class of the scientific world, so taking it for granted that the phenomenon can be produced, I will show how many senses a person has in a mesmerised state. I once put many persons into this state and none with one exception, had any idea of seeing through their [natural] eyes. There was one who thought he saw through his eyes but all experiments show that it is not so. In fact, a mesmerised subject is all that any person can be in the waking state; at the same time he is another person separate from his earthly identity. He can feel, fly, walk, and pass into the sea and describe things lost. He can find things that he knows not of in another state.

Now where and what was this invisible something that could pass in and out of matter? What is this clairvoyance? It is the mystery or power that has troubled the wisdom of this world to solve. Solve this problem and you give a knowledge to man that the world has always admitted but not understood. To understand the phenomenon is to go back to the First Cause and see what man was. We must go back of language to find the cause that prompted man. So let us pass back of language and we see living beings going round like beasts, not seeming to have any way of communicating with each other. Then each acted on his own responsibility, eating and drinking, as it pleased himself. Now, the desire for food prompted the mind, and as food has a sort of odor that arises from it, man, like the beast, was drawn to the odor from a desire to have this sensation gratified, so that the odor attracted the man like the beast, not by sight but by smell. Here is one sensation, but with no name. It is the same in man and beast, each eats and is satisfied. As they eat taste comes. This opens the mind to see what the thing is; this brings sight, or knowledge. So they go on until all the faculties are developed. As the faculty of smell was of more importance than sight it was the one most desired. For it not only attracted the animal to the thing smelt but also warned him of the danger of, being destroyed, so that all animals cultivate this sense for their safety. So by experience all animals learned to keep clear of each other by the peculiar faculty of smell. As they associated sight with the odor, then when the odor came in contact with their other senses they would create the thing contained in the odor. If it was an odor from some living thing that they were afraid of they would fly or run until they were free from their enemy. So little by little the wild beast settled down to a basis that gave each a faculty to counteract some other faculty in another. The lion depended on his smell and so did all animals who were inferior to their enemies, so that if the lion imitated some other animal, for instance if quick in his motions he would not be so acute in his smell, so the victim could keep out of the lion's way and still be in his sight. The atmosphere of the lion was certain death to the other animals, so that their fright threw off an odor that did not attract the lion until the object of his prey came in contact with his sight. So all things went on in this way and man was at the mercy of the wild beast, his sense of smell was as acute as that of the animal.

Now, necessity is the mother of invention, and it became necessary for man to introduce something to counteract the wild beast. Hence it was natural for man to give his fellow-man a sign of their danger, for men like all other animals would go together in herds or parties. This state must lead to language, so that language came about for the safety of the race. Now the sense of smell was the foundation of language and as language was made to apply to some sensation, it must take time to introduce it, for the odor must be so defined that a person perceiving a thing named could describe it. . . .

As language was introduced the sense of smell became more blunt till like other instincts it gave way to another standard. As imitation was developed the practice of thinking increased, so that thinking came to be as much of a sense as smelling. The action of forming thought into things or ideas became a sense, the power or sense of imitation brought up the sense of motion so that man's thought when put into an idea would seem to have life. All the above was spiritual and it could not be seen by the natural man or beast. So the spiritual man would imitate his idea in some way so that it could be seen and felt by the natural man. Thus invention in the spiritual world was shadowed forth in the natural world. As this invention was received, the spiritual senses were not relied on for the safety of man. Warfare was kept up till man could invent castles or places to defend himself against the wild beast. At last there must be laws or regulations introduced to feed those who could not fight. The ones who stayed at home would be the weaker portion of the race, including the females, the aged and children. So laws or regulations must be adopted for their support and safety and penalties attached to the disobedience of these laws. The officers of the laws would be taken from the most aspiring and cunning part of the tribes. This placed the leaders above the masses, so competition sprang up, which increased the leaders' perceptive faculties to invent all sorts of stories to keep the people quiet. As language was what they all wanted, those who could teach it would be looked upon as superior to the rest. Phenomena would then as now take place and the wise would be called on to explain; this introduced astrology and priest-craft. Then all sorts of invention would spring up to keep the people in submission when they grumbled at their leaders, not as they do now, for we are born slaves, and they were born free. Therefore it required more strict laws and punishments then than now, all sorts of ideas were started, and among others the power of creating objects that could be seen was cultivated for the benefit of the wise. This introduced spirit-ualism among civilized tribes, at first for the benefit of the leaders. So superstition became the power to worship, and as it was necessary that some one should explain the phenomena persons would be appointed, and so priests and prophets sprang up. These men must be paid and cared for and the people were taxed to support them.

At last the tribes formed themselves into nations and kingdoms and gave the power to the priest, so the priest stood at the head of 0e nation. As the priesthood was founded on superstition, it was necessary to keep the people superstitious, so all sorts of inventions were created to keep the people in ignorance, and as science was invented or discovered all the discoveries were kept a secret from the people so that any chemical or mechanical effect could be produced and the people would think it came from God. Astronomy was discovered and the priests kept it as a revelation from heaven, and all their astronomical calculations were made, not as a science for the masses, but as a direct revelation from God to bring about some great design. This kept the people in a state of nervous excitement. Whatever the prophets could make the people believe, they would create. So all they had to do was to start a storm of evil spirits, and the peoples' superstition would produce the phenomena wanted. This was proof that evil spirits did exist. Then it was not hard to make people believe evil spirits could get hold of them. At last evil spirits became a matter of fact, so much so that at the time of Saul there were some fifty ways of getting communications from God, and how many ways of getting it from the devil I know not.

MAN'S IDENTITY

We often speak of man's identity as though there were but one identity attributed to him. This is not the case. Man has as many identities as he has opinions, and the one his senses are attached to last is the one that governs him. This may seem strange but it is true. Our senses are not our identity, because they cannot change, they are principles. But our belief, thoughts and opinions can change. So when we say a person never changes it is as much as to say he is only a brute. We say that our tastes change. Does the principle change, or our belief? The fact that we are aware of the change shows the change must be in that which can change.

Then what is it that does not change? It is that Principle that never moves, the foundation of all things. It is that which says when we have found out something new, as we think, " Why did you not find it out before? " It says to us when we are investigating certain mathematical truths, "This truth has always existed, and we believed it." This something is Wisdom. It does not come or go, but is like light. You cannot keep it out of sight, in fact you acknowledge it in every act. But that which acknowledges it is not the something acknowledged. For instance, if you work out a problem aright, you acknowledge a wisdom that existed be-fore you knew it. The trouble is to get our senses attached to Wisdom so that we shall not change.

THE EFFECT OF MIND UPON MIND

It is an undisputed fact which philosophy has never explained, that persons affect each other when neither are conscious of it. According to the principle by which I cure the sick such instances can be accounted for, and it can be proved beyond a doubt that man is perfectly ignorant of the influences that act upon him, and being ignorant of the cause is constantly liable to the effect. To illustrate this I will relate a case that came under observation.

A woman brought her little son, about five years old, to be treated by me. When I sat with the child I found his symptoms were similiar to those which people have in spinal or rheumatic troubles. But the child being ignorant of names, and having no fear of disease could only describe his feelings in this way: He complained of being tired. Sometimes he said his leg was sore and sometimes his head was tired. To me his feelings were as intelligent as any odor with which I am familiar. I described his feelings to his mother, telling how he would appear at times. This she said was correct, and feeling impressed with the truth I told her she said she would sit with me and see if I were equally correct in describing her case. I found that the mother had precisely the same feelings as the child, yet she complained of disease which the child never thought of, and furthermore she had not the least idea the child had such feelings. To prove that I was right about the child, I told her to ask him if he did not feel so and so when he would lay his head down, and she found I was correct. These were the mother's symptoms: A heavy feeling over the eyes, a numbness in the hands, weakness in the back, and a pain going from the foot to the hip, all accompanied by a feeling of general prostration. To her every sensation was the effect of a sort of disease, yet every sensation she had the child had also, but he had not attached names to them. After playing his leg would pain him, and he would be restless at night; while the mother reasoned from the same feelings that she had spinal disease, trouble of the heart, and was liable to have paralysis. If she had been ignorant as the child of names, she would not have had the fear of these false ideas, and the child would have been well; for all its trouble came from its mother, and her trouble was from the invention of the medical faculty.

It may be asked, how could the child be affected by its mother? In the same way I was affected. To have the sense of smell or any other sense, requires no language. An odor can be perceived by a child as well as by a grown person. To every disease there is an odor, [mental atmosphere] and every one is affected by it when it comes within his consciousness. Every one knows that he can produce in himself heat or cold by excitement. So likewise he can produce the odor of any disease so that he is affected by it. I proved that. I could create the odor of any kind of fruit, and make a mesmerised person taste and smell it. (2)

Ignorance of this principle prevents man from investigating the operation of the human mind. Such a course would change our whole mode of reasoning. It would destroy society as it is now and place it on another basis. In the place of hypocrisy, aristocracy and democracy, the three original elements of society, science, progress and freedom would be introduced. In his ignorant state man belongs to the lowest of the aristocracy, but as he becomes scientific he subdues this element, and then the others are not needed to sustain it. His science works out patience, his patience perseverance, and perseverance wisdom, and the fruits are religion. Now the religion of today contains the elements of society and they run through all its roots and branches and poison its fruit. Science makes war upon this trinity, and the war will continue till it is crushed.

Then democracy will be subject to science, and hypocrisy will not appear in the leaders. Then will come a new heaven or dispensation, based on eternal Truth, and man will be rewarded for what he knows, and not for what he thinks he knows. The popular teachers will then publicly correct the democracy of the errors which make them sick, as well as political errors. Now political doctors in addressing the masses bind burdens on them, which they kneeling like camels receive and kiss the hands that bind them. This slavery is the will of aristocracy and consequently it is not popular to oppose it. Therefore no appeal must be made to the higher feelings but the base passions must be addressed.

Aristocracy never complains of oppression except when it cannot oppress. Its motto is "rule or ruin," and where it rules slavery is considered a divine institution. Science is mocked at in its religion and the mockery is echoed by hypocrisy, and it sits in the hearts of the rulers and delivers the law. Science like an under-current is deep and strong, and' as its tide advances it will sweep away the foundations of aristocracy. Revolutions must come, and no man can tell what will be the end of this generation. But Science will work out the problem of universal freedom to the oppressed in body and mind.

I prophesy that the time will come when men and women shall heal all manner of diseases by the words of their mouth. They will show democracy that they have been deceived by blind leaders who flattered them that they ruled, when they have no more to do with ruling the nation than the dog who is set on to the swine has to do with his master's affairs. No slave either black or white ever did or ever can rule. They both will fight for their master till they are intelligent enough to know their own rights. . . Such evils arise from man's ignorance of himself. If man knew himself his first object would be to become acquainted with sensations that affect him. He would then learn that a corrupt fountain cannot bring forth pure water, and that from aristocracy nothing but the blackest corruption can issue, which however is becoming popular because of the fountain. From the dens of iniquity comes an atmosphere as pleasant to aristocracy as tobacco to one who has been poisoned almost to paralysis by it. Tell him it hurts him; the answer is, I know it, but I can not help using it. Such abject servitude is the medium of aristocracy, for democracy would never have taken the weed had not the former set the example. All drugs when taken stupify the intellect, so that science cannot reign. Error is a tyrant and democracy is its agent to destroy the progress and happiness of man. Show a man who smokes or chews just how the habit affects him and he will part company with tobacco as quickly as a democrat will leave his leaders when he sees the corruption of their motives. A democrat is like a disease, he believes in everything popular and opposes everything unpopular, and does not regard the welfare of his government.

104

To be popular in religion, praise the institutions of the sabbath and the church. Say what you please in the street about priestcraft and fear of man: only mention that your family go to church and you will be considered sound. To be unpopular, be honest in every act; treat others with respect; mind your own affairs, and permit others to do the same. Then like an old fashioned person you will be out of society and no one will care for you. To be independent is to speak the truth on all subjects without fear or vanity; con-demn error whenever it is popular; treat others as you wish to be treated, and let your religion be shown in your acts. Such a man will be envied by aristocracy, respected by the wise, hated by hypocrites, and listened to by the thinking classes. He is at the same time popular and not popular. His style pleases the people, therefore aristocracy will be forced to admire him, in order that it may retain their power over him, for the rule is: "keep as near a kicking horse as possible."

Physicians will admit what the people believe. They will acknowledge I cure, but limit my power to a few nervous cases, and appeal to the vanity of intelligence, by saying that it is not possible that an uneducated person can really cure actual disease. . . .

IMAGINATION

This word means something or nothing. Now if it means everything it certainly means nothing, but if is applied to the power of invention or imitation it can be understood. It is wrong however to apply it to deception, for a person must first be acted upon before his imagination can produce a phe-nomenon, otherwise it would apply equally to all operators, but to apply it to one phenomenon and not to another of the same kind is not right. I tell you a lie and you believe it, immediately your inventive power or imagination commences to create that which I have said. I explain the operation of a machine to you and your inventive power immediately creates it according as you understand it. This is imagination. In the first instance the world says your imagination has deceived you and there is nothing in it, but in the latter case you are right. This is a misuse of the word and you suffer from it. This power of forming ideas called imagination is one of the highest elements in the human mind, and it is the foundation of all true discovery. Yet like all scientific facts it is abused and misrepresented.

To give you a clearer idea of the misuse of this word I will illustrate it by a

religious belief. Church members never use the word imagination in speaking of their belief and their religion. Do they mean to say that they believe without creating the image of their belief ? If so then what they call the power that understands is really the power of imagination. The fact is that religious beliefs are founded in deception and the leaders deceive the people into them. At the same time outsiders are sceptical and apply the words "imagination" and "superstition" in derision. Every person wishing to deceive the masses calls everything imagination that does not coincide with his belief. The medical faculty have assumed to themselves the power of creating by imagination every idea based on wisdom. All ideas opposed to them are said to be false, and they say that the imagination that creates these ideas is a disgrace, and belongs to ignorance and superstition.

A physician, for instance, may tell you the most absurd falsehood that his imagination can invent, but it is "true" because it has the sanction of the faculty. If you believe him you use the power which if rightly applied is one of the best of faculties for the purpose of creating a disease which you have taken for a truth. There is no dispute or controversy about that. But if some outsider should deceive you half as much and you should create an idea you would be accused of being superstitious, believing everything and imagining all sorts of humbugs.

The word imagination is so misapplied that it has lost all the value it ever had, and like religion it has a name without meaning covering numerous deceptions applied to weak-minded people. I never use the word as others do. When people think they have a disease which I know they have not, I do not ascribe it to their imagination, but to the fact that they have been deceived. A physician may tell you what is not true about yourself. If you believe it and he deceives you that is no disgrace to you, for it shows an honest heart and confidence in the physician. Then follows the creation and appearance of the thing he has told you. As far as you are concerned you are blameless, but the physician is a liar and hypocrite and has used your creative powers to deceive you for his own selfish ends. Now when their hypocrisy and deceit are exposed they cry out, "humbug, our craft is in danger: this quack works upon the imagination of the sick and makes them believe the medical faculty are not honest."

Let me call your attention to one fact; the word imagination never applies to the first cause. There is a superior power that originates, and imagination does the work and produces. Science detects the direction that is given to imagination and corrects it if false. All men have gone out of the way, and no one reasons from Science. So Wisdom classes them all, that it may save the whole by introducing the light of a new mode of reasoning that will separate error from truth. This refers to the subject of health and happiness and not to arts and sciences. The evils that affect the body and mind are included.

HOW THE OPINIONS OF PHYSICIANS OPERATE

No one knows the mischief or the misery that physicians of all kinds make by their opinions, and this never will be known till man learns that his belief makes his trouble. For instance, a person feels a slight disturbance at the pit of the stomach. Ignorant of its cause, he applies to a physician. Here comes the trouble. The physician assumes a false character. His practice makes him either a simpleton or a knave, for if honest he would know that he could not tell anything about the patient. If he were blind he could not even tell that the patient was sick, so that all his knowledge is gathered from observation and questioning. Therefore he is doctor only in name. He dare not risk his reputation by sitting down by the patient and telling his feelings as I do. There-fore he knows he is acting the part of a hypocrite. The patient is in the hands of a deceiver, whose business it is to deceive him into some belief that happens to occur to him. At this time the physician stands to the patient like a tailor ready to fit him a garment. If rich he will persuade him he has the spinal complaint, or bronchitis, or some other disease that fits the patient's fears. If very poor, and there is no chance for a speculation, he will fit an old pair of worn out lungs on to him, just enough to keep him breathing a short time. This is the way the regular faculty humbug the people. Now when the people are educated to understand that what they believe they will create, they will cease believing what the medical men say, and try to account for their feelings in some more rational way.

I know that a belief in any disease will create a chemical change (3) in the mind, and that a person will create a phenomenon corresponding to the symptoms. This creation is named disease, according to the author. The idea disease has no effect on a person who has no fear of it. The idea small pox, for instance, produces no effect on a person who has had it, or has had the varioloid, or has been vacci-nated; but on another it is not so. The doctor can produce a chemical change by his talk. It makes no difference what he says. A phenomenon will follow to which he can give a name to suit his convenience.

For instance, a person gets into an excited, heated state and a doctor is called. He gives medicine which affects the patient and he feels better. That then is what the patient needed and the doctor has the credit. If the patient grows worse the medicine makes him sick; the doctor says he has the symptoms of a fever, while in reality he himself has been the cause of nine-tenths of the trouble. Give men the knowledge of one great truth, that man is constituted of two differ-ent principles: wisdom which is seen in Science, and error which is seen in matter or in opinions. The latter is governed by no principle known to man, but is simply the action of cause and effect; but man who sees only the phenomenon puts wisdom into it, for the cause is never seen. To the natural man this is a mystery.

I will illustrate it. Take the small-pox. The first sensation upon the patient contains neither opinion, happiness nor misery. The cause was one of the natural results of motion which might be traced back through many changes containing no more harm than any breeze that reaches man at any hour, but it gives a start to the mind like the fall of a weight. This shock although containing no intelligence, disturbed the spiritual senses (the real man). I will drop this illustration here and undertake to describe the real man and separate him from what seems to be the man.

The spiritual senses are all that there is of a man. Therefore when he changes his senses,(4) it is necessary to know what he gains or loses by the change and also what he embraces. To suppose a man has but five or seven senses is as absurd as to suppose he has but a certain number of ideas. His senses are himself, what he knows and what he thinks he knows. Paul divides man into two identities: Wisdom or what could be proved by a science, and knowledge or what man believes to be true. So when a man says he thinks he knows or believes he knows it is sure that he does not know as he should. But if he can prove his knowledge by science then Science is known to him. Man's senses embrace these two characters, which are natural opponents, to both of which life has been attached. The scientific man sees and knows himself, and he also sees and knows his opponent, but the man of opinion can only see the scientific man in a mystery. As Wisdom advances in man the effect is to destroy the senses [belief] which are attached to knowledge. When knowledge overbalances a man's wisdom, his error reigns, but if wisdom is in the ascendancy his knowledge becomes subject to his wisdom. In mathematics, chemistry and all the arts and sciences that can be demonstrated knowledge submits to wisdom, but that part of man's senses attached to knowledge that is not subject to science is in the ascendancy in religion, disease, and politics. These are false sciences based on opinions. They are the same that Jesus denounced as false prophets, evil and blind guides who deceived the people. These errors embrace that part of man that believes in sickness, death, another world, and all kinds of superstition. They beget tyranny and selfishness in man, and slavery and democracy in nations. It is the mission of Science to destroy these, and Science will be developed till they are destroyed.

Therefore where man's confidence in these opinions is at an end his senses will seem to be annihilated, but in reality he will be like the young eagle which has burst its shell and soars aloft on the wings of wisdom, where he looks down upon the earth and sees the natural man crawling like a reptile waiting to devour the child of science as soon as it is born. Every development of Wisdom whether applied to creeping things or to the element of freedom, is the child of God. Concealed in the egg of slavery wisdom is kept warm by the heat of discussion, but now it has broken its shell and assumed a character and the enemies of freedom, like those of Christ stand ready to devour it as soon as it is born. But the mother of freedom will receive the child to its bosom, and will flee into the wilderness till the time arrives, when the senses of man will be so changed that slavery will be chained to the lowest grade of brutality and then in the wilderness it will die and be forgotten. The error of disease will go through a similar revolution, for it has been hatched by the church, kept concealed by the medical faculty, while their opinions are the very food that has fed the child of science whose heel shall bruise the head of the serpent disease. These two characters, science and error are separate and yet they act together and always will till Truth reigns over all the dominions of opinion. They are embraced in every man and the separation was the Science that Jesus taught. To understand the sepa-ration is eternal life in Science.

Jesus came into the world of error, not into Science for he was there with

Wisdom. All Science was with Wisdom, and when it comes to the world it comes as Jesus did. It first comes to the educated, but they having no light to dis-tinguish between truth and error, and cannot receive it. So it turns to that class which have no prejudices, and here in the wilderness it develops itself until it has attained its growth and then it comes forth. Then commences the war between the educated who are ignorant. of the truth and Science. While Science is growing in the minds of the people its opponents are eating and drinking, gloating over their spoils, till the tide of popular opinion sweeps way their foundation. They never seem to realize their danger till their house falls over their heads. This has been the case with the democratic house, while they still hold to the idea that slavery will be tolerated. The thunder of freedom is shaking the temple to its foundation, and they hide themselves in the crevice of their belief, exclaiming "I was always opposed to the extension of slavery but the constitution must, not be violated," that is, you must not break the egg by the heat of discussion and let out the bird of liberty, for if you do democracy is dead.

The medical faculty reason in the same way. "Do not destroy the medical constitution," they say, "for you will let in a swarm of quacks that will get the world in a horrid state. The regular physician will have no standing and sickness and death will triumph over the land." The ministers also exclaim, "Do not touch the Divine institution, for religion is all that keeps the world from going to destruction." Wisdom replies, "I will laugh at your fears, and I will pour out light like wrath and cut you off from the face of the earth and give the earth (or mind) to a more enlightened people, who will obey the laws of Science and teach others to do the same, and you shall be cast into everlasting misery." This is progression and it is the religion of Jesus. It is the stone of science that the builders of religion rejected. It is the star that guided the wise men to the only true God. Its body is wisdom, its blood is its life and unless you eat it and drink it you have no life in you. Happy is he who when a cloud of disease comes (for the Lord is always in clouds of error) can say I fear not, fear hath torment and perfect love casteth out fear. He will rise from the clouds and meet Christ above the opinions of man, then when Science comes you will not be harmed.

I wish to make you understand these two characters, Science and opinions. Give to each an idenity like a man and separate one from the other, and then see which you follow; for you must follow one, you cannot serve both at the same time. If you serve Science, you are in your wisdom and know it. If you serve opinion, you have no wisdom but your life is in a belief that can be destroyed. So you will live all your life subject to bondage through fear of death. But if you have passed through death or opinion to the life of Science death will have no power over you. Disease is death and the belief is the fear, therefore if death is destroyed the fear is gone. It becomes us then to search into the causes of the phenomenon called disease and find if it is not an image of our own make. The Jewish people were making all sorts of false beliefs that tormented them. So God through Moses says, "Thou shalt make no graven images" to represent any false idea which they had been taught, nor worship any superstition, for truth was jealous of error. It always condemns our error and rewards our scientific acts. Disease was conceived in priestcraft and brought forth in the iniquity of the medical faculty. The priest prophesied falsely and the doctors flourished by their lies, and the people love to have it so. Then the question arises, what can you do to prevent it? I say, repent all, and be baptized in the Science that will wash away your sins and diseases with your belief. Come out from the world of opinion, and when a doctor says you have so and so, make him prove it.

OBSTACLES IN ESTABLISHING A NEW SCIENCE

The great obstacle in establishing a new science in the under-standing of the people arises from their ignorance. Science always has had to contend with this difficulty, and no one has as yet been able to direct the mind of man towards the true mode of reasoning so that superstition should dissolve before the advancing light of science; for man has always been ignorant of himself, and his errors he has fastened upon others. There are two modes of reasoning, both true to the one that believes them, and neither anything to the person that knows the truth. To the scientific mind a superstition about anything that science has explained is nothing. But to the un-scientific mind it may be a truth. Now the science to be established is based on truth which can be applied to a false mode of reasoning and not only destroy it but bring about a more perfect and better state of society, and sweep away the lies that like the locusts of Egypt are devouring our lives and happiness. This cannot be done by any philosophy known to the world, for the present mode of reasoning is based on the errors the coming science is to destroy. If Satan cast out satan, then his kingdom is divided against itself. But if Wisdom casts out error, true Science will stand. I base my reasoning on a stone which the builders of error have rejected.

Every idea having a form visible to the world of matter, is admitted by that world as matter. The reasoning which stands on this basis is one world, and scientific knowledge is another. Science does not make peace with the world; it makes war. It seeks not to save the life of error, but to destroy it. It sets ideas at variance with each other, the father against the son. It sets the world of matter in motion, that it may like the earth be prepared to receive a higher cultivation. This has been done in a vast number of cases. But in the things that concern man's health and happiness the world is in Egyptian darkness. This subject never has been sounded. The cause of man's misery and trouble lies in our false reasoning. It always has and it always will be so till man is convinced that his happiness depends on his wisdom, and his misery on his belief. True, he may be happy for a time in believing a lie, but that is like a man finding happiness in taking opium. It stupifies him so he is not sensible of his trouble, but it really increases his misery. Mind like the earth is under the direction of a higher power, which is subject to Wisdom. The world calls it God. To one matter is nothing, to the other it is everything. To science it is an unexplained error.

To belief it is a real living substance. I am now speaking of the subject of health. I do not include any true science. But every science not based on the rock I have mentioned must crumble if that rock falls on it, and every idea that is rooted in

matter and bears the fruit of misery must be hewn down.

Theories are like trees and ideas can be grafted into them, thereby changing the whole character of the fruit. Jesus engrafted this Truth into the understanding of the people by means of parables. Every one knows that ideas can be sown in the mind like seed in the ground, and that they will grow and bear fruit. The causes of both phenomena are unknown to us, but to the world above matter they are known. To Wisdom these facts are mere ideas, but to matter they are solid truths.

As I have said, everything having a visible form is matter, but there are things into which the world has put life which bring no danger to man, because they contain no knowledge. There are others which contain misery, such as the ideas of disease.

According to the world there is such a disease as small-pox. With God or Wisdom this must be truth or it must be a lie, or belief in a lie. No one will believe that Wisdom can have small-pox. Therefore its foundation must be in this world and it must be confined to the inhabitants of this world. Wisdom teaches that error can create out of itself another error the same as a tree can bring forth another tree, and that mind can generate itself. Wisdom does not create wisdom, for it fills all space and sheds its light upon the world of matter, thus destroying the things of darkness and bringing to light things hidden.

Small-pox is like a tree whose fruits are scattered abroad infecting those who eat them. It is a superstitious idea and like all such it has a religious cast. It deceived the world so that every person was liable. Therefore the idea "kine-pox" was sent into the world that all might be saved or vaccinated. As many as received the virus or were baptized with the belief were saved. Here is introduced another world which is deliverance from small-pox. To all who have passed from their old belief into the world of vaccination there is no fear of death from small-pox, but a fear lest they have not been vaccinated with genuine virus. Now what does their salvation rest upon? It rests on no principle outside the mind. In ignorance of causes people are satisfied with some one's belief that there is virtue in this savior.. Thus their minds are quiet and the fruits are a milder disease, if the graft is put into a healthy tree (or child).

This will apply to all diseases. Every disease is the invention of man and has no identity in Wisdom, but to those who believe it it is a truth. If everything he does not understand were blotted out, what would be there left of him? Would he be better or worse, if nine-tenths of all he thinks he knows were blotted out of his mind, and he existed with what was true? I contend that he would as it were sit on the clouds and see the world beneath him tormented with ideas that form living errors whose weight is ignorance. Safe from their power, he would not return to the world's belief for any consideration. In a slight degree this is my case. I sit as it were in another world or condition, as far above belief in disease as the heavens are above the earth. Though safe myself, I grieve for my fellow man, and I am reminded of the words of Jesus when He beheld the misery of His countrymen: "O Jerusalem! How oft would I gather thee as a hen gathereth her chickens, and ye would not." I hear this truth now pleading with man, to listen to the voice of reason.

I know from my own experience with the sick that their troubles are the effect of their own belief; not that their belief is the truth, but their belief acts upon their minds, bringing them into subjection to their belief, and their troubles are a chemical change that follows.

Small-pox is a reality to all mankind. But I do not include myself, because I stand outside where I can see things real to the world and real with Wisdom. I know that I can distinguish a lie from a truth in religion, or in disease. To me disease is always a lie, but to those who believe it it is a truth, and religion the same. Until the world is shaken by investigation so that the rocks and mountains of religious error are removed and the medical Babylon destroyed, sickness and sorrow will prevail. Feeling as I do and seeing so many young people go the broad road to destruction, I can say from the bottom of my soul, "Oh priestcraft! fill up the measure of your cups of iniquity, for on your head will come sooner or later the sneers and taunts of the people." Your theory will be overthrown by the voice of Wisdom that will rouse the men of Science, who will battle your error and drive you utterly from the face of the earth. Then there will arise a new science, followed by a new mode of reasoning, which shall teach man that to be wise is to unlearn his errors. Wisdom cannot learn, .but it can destroy.

The introduction of Science is like engrafting. Every graft does not live, for some have no life except what they derive from error. When you believe a lie in the form of some disease, and the doctor comes, he does not engraft into your wisdom, but into your belief. Each must have graft of its kind.

Small-pox is a lie, and so is kine-pox. It is the offspring of the former, and the senses becoming separated from the one, cling to the other. Wisdom shows that they are both false, and that they are the inventions of superstition. Thus the world is vaccinated from one lie into another, and this is called progress. But the time must come when this false mode of reasoning shall give way to a higher wisdom by which all things are proved.

I tell you a lie which you believe and an effect follows: this does not prove that I told the truth because the effect is seen. For instance, I tell you that you have small-pox. This shocks you and you are really frightened. A phenomenon attends or follows the fright. The physicians are consulted and they pronounce the disease small-pox. To you and to the world this is proof that it is small-pox. But to me it is only proof that you believed a lie.

Now the question to settle is this, can a lie act upon a person who believes it so as to make him sick? No one will deny that statement I think. Nothing then produces something, unless a lie is something, and if it is where does it start from ? To me the lie and the effect are both nothing. So when I sit by a sick person I come in contact with what they call "something." This something frightens them, and another "something" is produced which they express by aches and pains, and other bad feelings. All these they think come from what they call disease. To me this something that they call disease is a lie which they believe, and their aches and pains are the expressions of their fears, and are like moans of a criminal sentenced to be hung or shot. Now comes the process of vaccination, or conversion, which is getting them out of one lie into another. The doctor introduces his opinion like virus which being received into the mind, a change is produced, and if his arguments are heeded, a milder disease is brought forth in the new graft, and finally the person is carried to that state of mind called "safe." The priest goes through the same process. First he affirms his belief till the people become alarmed. He then introduces his opinion as a means of safety, and when this is received the mind is quieted, and this is conversion. The world has been humbugged by these two classes till the sick are tired of life; their substance is devoured; their fields of happiness are laid waste, and every kind of enjoyment destroyed. While the people are in this state, another swarm of locusts come upon them to get what is left. These are the political demagogues, the second growth that always springs up after the others get the mind troubled and ready to be affected. These parties are the scourges that pursue society as it passes through the wilderness of error to the land of happiness and science. This journey that science has been traveling is dotted with little opinions where Wisdom has cleared up the wilderness and burned up the error. Wisdom never stops; it continues, and has now reached the wilderness of disease, and every tree that brings not forth good fruit will be hewn down by the axe of Science and burned up by the fire of Truth.

MIND AND DISEASE

I have often spoken of the word mind as something which I call matter. I use this term from the fact that man cannot conceive of wisdom except as attached to matter, although every one makes a difference between them. We always speak of mind as different from matter, one is something and the other is apparently nothing, or it is like velocity which seems to be the result of motion. There is another element called reason (like friction) which sees the effect, but being ignorant of the cause, puts weight and velocity together and calls them one. We are all taught to believe that mind is wisdom and here is the trouble, for if mind is wisdom then Wisdom cannot be relied on, for all will admit that the-mind changes. Jesus separates the two by calling one the wisdom of this world and the other the wisdom of God. If we understand what He meant by "this world" we can follow Him.

I have spoken of that element in man called reason. This is a low intellect a little above the brute which is the link between God and mind, and the same that is called by Jesus the wisdom of the world, for this world is another name for spiritual matter. Now mind is the spiritual earth which re-ceives the seed of Wisdom, and also the seeds of the wisdom of this world of reason. Disease is the fruit of the latter, and the application of the wisdom of God or Science is the clearing away the foul rubbish that springs up in the soil or mind. This rubbish is the false ideas sown in the mind by blind guides, who cry peace when there is no peace. Their wisdom is of this world that must come to an end, when the fire of Truth shall run through this world of error and burn up the stubble and the plough of Science, guided by the wisdom of God and pressed forward by the power of eternal truth, shall root out of the mind or matter every root and stubble. Then error can find no place t-a take root in the soil. Then minds like a rich cultivated vineyard shall bring forth that which shall be sweet to the taste and pleasing to the eye. Then man can see and judge of the tree for himself, whether its fruits are those of error and opinions or of Science.

DO WE KNOW ALL WE WRITE OR SAY?

It is a common remark that if Jesus should appear on earth and could hear the explanations given to the remarks which he made eighteen hundred years ago, He never would imagine that He was in any way alluded to. This may be true. Jesus was as any other man, but Christ was the Science which Jesus tried to teach. There never was and never can be a man who can express his thoughts without being governed more or less by the scientific man or Christ, and the masses will receive the idea as they receive food, and will pass judgment according to their taste. Different opinions will arise, from the fact that often the writer is as ignorant of the true meaning of his ideas as his readers are, not that he does not know what he says, but there is in each person a hidden meaning or truth that he as a man does not know. When one reads or hears anything it awakens in him some new idea which perchance the author never thought of, yet the author feels as though he had a similar idea of its meaning. It is the Christ in us making itself known through the senses, and as the senses are the only medium the world acknowledges, Wisdom uses them to destroy the darkness which prevents us from knowing ourselves.

Thus it is when we read the works of the old authors. They have been misrepresented, from the fact that the readers' minds have been so dull that there was not sufficient light to penetrate through: so the dark explanations which are given become true ones till the world becomes educated up to a higher point where it shall see that truths may have been conveyed in the writings which the author himself had no idea of. Every person is more or less clairvoyant [intuitive], and is in two states of mind at the same time, and when any one writes he is not aware that he is dictated [guided] by a Wisdom that he thought his natural senses does not know.

On this principle rogues bring their evil deeds to light. Their crimes excite the mind and expose evils to view, for by their efforts to conceal their crimes they betray them to others by looks, acts, or words. This is as it should be and the better it is understood the more it will bring about the desired effect.

Every act or thought contains the higher science. The natural man calls it reaction, but it is wisdom. If you put sufficient wisdom in an act you will see what the reaction will be. You can hardly suppose a person so ignorant as not to know that when a stone is thrown into the air, it will come down again. If you put the wisdom in the stone, the stone would not know what the reaction would be, but if you put sufficient wisdom in the act that makes the stone go up, that wisdom will know the stone will come down again with the same force that it went up. Man's body is just as ignorant as a stone, but there are two motions which act upon it, one ignorance and the other science.

In all the crimes which man commits the act embraces the intelligence, that is, the reaction which will follow sooner or later, for every act of man's must come to light. So the person who commits a crime leaves the evidence against him just as plainly as the thief who steals in open daylight. The sick expose their idea of disease, and I know by my feelings what they know by their senses. (5) The more they try to conceal the fact, the more they expose it. Now the reason of this is that disease is a disgrace, although people try to make it fashionable; but they show they do not believe it so from the fact that they try to rid themselves of it, as they would any bad habit.

Every person has acquaintances whom they would like to get rid of, yet will put up with their company rather than cause them to feel badly. So with those who use tobacco, you will hear them say, "I know it hurts me and I wish I could leave off the habit, but I cannot." Their wisdom is not equal to what it should be or they would leave their "friend," as they call it, or their enemy in disguise. Now if their wisdom could destroy a little of the milk of human kindness, which they drink for the traitor who has no respect for their happiness except to gratify their desire, they would cut off their acquaintance as they would drop from their lips a cup of poison prepared for them by the hand of a pretended friend, and their sympathy would soon cease.

Notes

(1) This was written in 1861.
(2) With his subject, Lucius, 1843.
(3) This term includes bodily changes, as well.
(4) That is, his consciousness or belief, the direction of his mind.
(5) That is, by an intuition which embraces science.

Chapter Sixteen - Disease and Healing

[Dr. Quimby is so greatly interested in calling attention to the power of human beliefs in relation to all man's troubles that he does not give much space to a description of the natural world, does not state his idea of matter very definitely, and often leaves the reader wondering how he distinguishes between matter and "spiritual matter" or the mind of opinions. He is especially interested to point out that matter can be "condensed into a solid by mind action," that it undergoes a "chemical change" as a result of mental changes. He sometimes speaks of it as an "error" or shadow, as "an idea seen or not, just as it is called out." Whatever its objective reality in the Divine purpose, matter in itself is inanimate, there is no intelligence in it. His view of matter is idealistic, therefore, and in considering his theory of disease and its cure we need to bear in mind that matter for him is plastic to thought. The ordinary or external mind which is "spiritual matter" is the intermediate term. Above this mind is the real man with his spiritual senses, his clairvoyant and intuitive powers. The final term is Wisdom, making known its truths in so far as there is responsiveness and intelligence on man's part. This is said to possess a real "identity." To find himself as an "identity" in every truth, man should know himself as the "scientific man," able through Wisdom's help to banish all errors from the world.]

THE RECEPTION OF THIS GREAT TRUTH

I BELIEVE now that the time has nearly arrived when the people will be prepared to receive a great truth that will give an impulse and set. them investigating a subject which will open to their minds new and enlarged ideas of themselves and show man what he is and how he makes himself what he is. It has been said that to know himself is the greatest study of man, but I say that for man to know his error is greater than to know himself; for every person is to himself just what he think he is, but to know his error (1) is what ought to be his greatest study. For the last twenty-five years (2) I have been trying to find out what man is and at last have come to know what he is not. To know that you exist is nothing, but to know what disturbs you is of great value to every person. The world has been developing itself, and we look on and never think it is ourselves. Through ignorance of Wisdom we have made a man of straw and given him life, intellect and a head in the image of our own creation. To this image we have given the idea "man" with certain capacities such as life and death, and have made him subject to evils such as disease. To the man of straw the words I have quoted are applied. This man of straw has been trying to find himself out and in doing this has nearly destroyed or blotted out his real existence. So in looking for man I found it was like the old lady looking for her comb and finding it in her hair. I found I was the very idea I was looking for. Then I knew myself and found that what we call man is not man but a shadow of error.

Wisdom is the true man and error the counterfeit. When Wisdom governs matter all goes well, but when error directs all goes wrong. So I shall assume the old mode of calling man as he is called and. make myself a principle outside of man, just as man makes all "laws of God," as he calls them outside of himself. So man admits he is not with God or a part of Him. Therefore he belongs to this world and expects to die and go to his God. So he lives all his life in bondage through fear of death. Now, this keeps him sick and to avoid all these fears and troubles that disturb his mind and make him sick he invents all sorts of false ideas and never thinks they are the cause of his misery. He invents all sorts of disease to torment himself. Standing outside of these ideas I know that they are the works of man; that God or wisdom has never made anything to torment mankind. Error has created its own misery.

Having had twenty-five years of practice I have seen the working of this evil on mankind, how it has grown till it is increasing and at the present time there is more misery from disease than all other evils put together, and every effort to arrest this evil only makes it worse. Within the last seven years I have sat with more than twelve thousand different persons and have taken their feelings and know what they believe their diseases were and how each person was affected, but I knew the causes. Therefore I know what I say is true that if there had never been a physician in the world there would not have been one-tenth of the suffering. It is also true that religious creeds have made a very large class of persons miserable, but religion like all creeds based on super-stition must give way to Science. So superstition in regard to religion will die out as men grow wise, for wisdom is all the religion that can stand and this is to know ourselves not as man but as a part of Wisdom. But disease is making havoc among all classes, and it seems as though there would never be an end of it unless some one should step in and check this greatest of evils.

I have been in the habit of sitting with patients separately and explaining the disease and the cure till I have come to the conclusion that I can cure persons that are sick if I am in their company, and the number only helps to hasten the cure. I have no doubt that I can go to an audience of one thousand persons and cure more persons in one lecture than can be cured by all the doctors in the state of Maine in the same time, for I know that one-half my patients I do not see as long as to explain what I should make clear in one lecture of two hours. There are a great number of sick who are not able to be cured; for man's life and happiness in this enlightened world (made so by the profession) has made dollars and cents the test, so if a man has not these he must suffer. So my object is to relieve man of some of his sufferings. I am sent for to go to different parts of the country and have always found a large class of poor sick persons not ready to be cured. I want to relieve those who are not able to be cured, and also give directions to minds so that this wisdom shall govern man. It is necessary to say that I have no religious belief. My religion is my life, and my life is the light of any wisdom that I have. So that my light is my eye, and if my eye is the eye of Truth my body is light, but if my eye or wisdom is an opinion my body is full of darkness.

CONCERNING BELIEFS

It may be necessary to explain what calls out my arguments. All that I write is intended to destroy some belief of the patient. A belief is what I call a disease, for that embraces the cause and it sets the people to reasoning until their systems are prepared like the earth to receive the idea, and when the phenomenon is brought forth the doctors call that disease. Belief in an idea that cannot be seen by the natural eye is as real as belief in the natural world. Everything that does not come within the natural senses is a belief. Disease is of this class. The phenomenon is admitted and to make man believe it involves a notion that it exists. It does not follow that he is diseased any more than it follows that a man is in the war because he believes there is one. Yet he may be liable to be caught. War like some diseases has its exempts. For instance, small-pox. A man can procure a certificate from a physician that he has had it or has been vaccinated. So the belief makes the thing to the person believing it and as the belief becomes general every person is affected more or less. Children are not exempts, they suffer if they are in the vicinity of the disease, for their parents' sins. Their diseases are the effect o f the community. These results come from the older inhabitants who embody the superstitions of the world, and they are as tenacious of their beliefs.

See how the South fights for slavery under the belief that it is a living institution. (3) The people believe the same of disease and each one will fight for his peculiar disease till truth exterminates both. One is as dangerous as the other and each has its sympathizers and traitors. Take a person sick under the law of disease which he knows will kill him if the law is put in force. People are as anxious to condemn themselves by insisting that they have a certain disease as a rebel is to swear that a Yankee is an abolitionist: each is working to have the victim condemned. Both may be summed up as the effect of man's belief.

Religious sects fight for their various beliefs which contain not a word of truth and the world has to suffer the consequences. The medical faculty, spiritualists, and every class who have wit enough to have a belief, keep up a warfare to keep their beliefs alive that they may obtain a living. But when these are cut by truth they wither and die out and from the ashes comes freedom or Science. War is always engendered by beliefs. Slavery is the only name for all evils that have affected man, of which disease is one. They all have to pass through a sea of blood before their heads can be crushed and they can be handled by reason. Religious opinions waded through blood before reason could control the mind, and then the warfare was carried on by words. Universal freedom has not yet gone through the sea of blood, but it is now in the storm and God only knows how it will come out. The belief which makes man bind his fellow man is very strong, for it appeals to religious prejudices, and these are really at the bottom of many evils. The natural man believes slavery is right and he is religious in this belief, although in everything else he is governed by party-interest. Every sick person is suffering either directly or indirectly from the effect of some belief, therefore my arguments are to show the absurdity of the beliefs whatever they are, for beliefs are catching. The child is affected by its parents' belief, which is as real an enemy to health as slavery is to freedom. Science is the true man, belief is the enemy of happiness, for every one knows that a man will die before he will give up his belief. So when a person has a belief in any particular disease, he will not give it up until it destroys the body, although he knows that fighting is his own destruction.

When I sit by the sick I find them either like a child or a person in a belief. If they have no ideas that come within their senses they are like one affected by surrounding circumstances, as a child whose parents are fighting is frightened and perhaps killed by the parents' evil acts. When I have a patient who is frightened by some feeling in the system which has not been named, the patient is like a spectator in a riot who finds himself attacked and violently abused when he has been quiet all the time. I have to reason with such persons and convince them of their error, and as they learn the truth they are safe. I take the same course with such as I should with a stranger who has been attacked by a mob. I enter the crowd, take the man by the shoulders lead him out and befriend him till he is safe.

A belief in a disease is like a belief in any other evil, but there are those who putting entire confidence in the leaders accept certain beliefs. Such are honest and are the hardest patients to cure, for they attach a religious respect to their beliefs which are their very life. They often say they would rather die than lose their belief.

A belief going to establish any religion is held on to as a child holds to its mother when afraid of strangers. I frequently have a hard battle with such where their beliefs make them sick before they will relax. They will sometimes weep and lament as though I were really going to take their life. As I have no belief to give them I try to show the absurdity of their errors. It will be seen that in all I write my reasoning is to destroy some belief that my patient has. Rheumatism or the state of mind affecting people in that way is caused by various beliefs. Their minds as I have said are deceived into bad company and they have to suffer the consequences of their acts, although their intentions may have been good.

I will state a case. A man uses tobacco freely, both chews and smokes. His wife being of a sympathetic nature enters into his error to try to reform him. This brings her into the same company that he is in. She is regarded as bad as her husband, she is beaten until blood starts out on her elbows, shoulders, and limbs, and her hands become swollen and sore so that she cannot work. Meantime her husband appears as well as ever. This is taking a disease from sympathy and it shows that such evils are catching in the world.

To such I stand in this way. I take the symptoms and know who is the devil. I expose him, and when I make the patient know him, the devil leaves, the error is cast out, the belief leaves and the patient is cured. This is a process of reasoning from cause to effect, not from effect to effect. The world reasons to make one disease in order to cure another. I destroy the disease by showing the error and showing how the error effects the patients. This was what Jesus tried to prove, so all His acts and talk went to prove the truth of what I have said. Make man responsible for his beliefs and he will be as cautious what he believes as he is in what he sees or does, for he will see that just as he measures out to another so it will be measured out to him. But does the clergy follow out this rule? Do they not dictate to their audience what to believe and what not to believe, without the least regard to their health? Now, to suppose a man can believe one thing and still have a contrary effect is not true. If you make a person believe that he is in danger of any trouble he will be affected according to his belief. So all beliefs are to be analyzed like food or drink to see what it contains and see how it acts upon the body, for the belief being in the mind it shows itself on the body. So when Jesus talked He had some object to obtain for the happiness of man. But to suppose Jesus came from heaven to destroy one error and establish another is to suppose that our beliefs alter the wisdom of God or make a man believe what he cannot understand to insure his happiness in a world that is based on belief. Now, I understand Jesus; I understand Him to condemn all beliefs and show that man is better off without a belief than with one.

What good is it to me whether I believe one thing or another if my belief does not affect my life? If my belief affects my life I get the benefit or misery of my belief, but it does not alter the wisdom of God or alter any of His plans. So if there is a world beyond this my belief cannot change it; my belief may change me. So if Jesus had no higher motive than merely introducing a belief He was like all others who wanted to establish peculiar views. But Jesus never meant to speak of what we call death. His death was the end of sin or error. To lose opinions and find His truth was life, not death. The Wisdom that taught this did not embrace the words "life" and "death."

WORKS THE FRUIT OF OUR BELIEF

What proof can be brought to show that a man is just what he thinks he is? My answer is: his works. Man is known by his works, for they are the fruit of belief and where there is no fruit there is no belief, in that case man is either perfectly ignorant or perfectly wise, and stops work because he is God and God has finished His work. Now man is not supposed to be either of the two, God or an idiot. So he must be a being between both. That makes him a man of opinions and beliefs. To show whether the works are of God or error is the great aim of man. Both cannot be of God, for one reasons from what he believes and the other from what he knows.

I will introduce a man of error who bases his knowledge on others' belief, still thinking he has an opinion of his own. The effect of his wisdom or belief is seen by its fruits. The younger son is he who listens to the wisdom of his brother and sees him contradict himself and shows him his absurdity. This is the scientific man and he is not known, for when the man of opinions is destroyed by the scientific man he is not seen at all. Take two persons talking about mesmerism; one never heard anything, the other is posted in all things pertaining to the law of mesmerism. Let A. be the wise man and B. the ignorant man. A. sits down and expounds the principles of mesmerism. He reads from those who have written on the subject, how a man sits down, takes hold of another's hand, looks him in the eye, and at length the man is affected; his eyes close and he goes to sleep. Then B. asks how this is done. Here comes the mystery or "Science" of A. Finally it enters the head of A. to go to the world of spirits. Here is a large field for operation. C. finds the dead and explains about them to A. and B. By this time they have become so wise that their light has lit up the whole world of spirits, so that everything is perfectly plain. This is as far as they can go. The whole world stops here and here ends mesmerism according to the world's belief. At last there comes a report that spirits made their appearance at Rochester, and raps and table tipping take place. Then B. asks A. how he explains these things. A. "It is by the presence of electricity." B. "I cannot believe that, I want to see something of it." So they go to a medium and everything goes to prove the belief of the medium that it is spirits. One rap means "yes" and two means "no," and these prove the spirits. B. asks A. what he thinks of that. A. says "It is a development of animal magnetism." B. says "No, I believe it must be spirits." Here is a difference of opinion. B. is as well posted as A. The medium agrees with C. B. believed A. till A. showed his ignorance, then B. embraced the opinion of the medium. So it goes on. One opinion is believed till some other opinion comes up that cannot be explained, then some one states an opinion and the multitude follow.

Like the rest of the world I began with no belief or opinion. Like a child I wanted to see. As B. did, I asked A's explanation and took it, then I went to work to prove it and did prove beyond a doubt according to my belief that it was governed by electricity. At last I ran against a stumbling block which upset all my theory and left me without anything but the bare experiments. I then went to work to prove my belief, and the experiments proved anything I believed, and I concluded that man is just what he thinks he is to himself. I have waded through the mire of ignorance, crossed the ruin of superstition, have walked on the water of my belief and at last landed on the shores of Wisdom, where I have found the other branch of truth that tells me that the water or error had dried up so that the dry land of reason is ready to receive the seed of Wisdom into the earth, or mind of man. As I have passed through the fire of superstition and been baptized in the water of error and belief, I have come up out of the water and the heavens or Wisdom are open to me and I see Wisdom in the form of a dove or sympathy saying to every one: "Behold, the truth hath prevailed to open the book of superstition; it hath broken the seal and introduced a new form of reasoning."

I have no belief in regard to religion of any kind, neither have I any belief in another world of any kind. (4) I have no belief in what is called death. In fact I am a total disbeliever in any wisdom that ever taught any religion outside of man's belief. Then you may ask what kind of a man are you without a belief ? I have a belief like all men but it does not apply to what I have been talking about. I have a belief on all subjects that are agitating the country.

I believe there was one person who had these same ideas and to that person I give all the credit of introducing this truth into the world, and that was Jesus. I have no doubt of His being the only true prophet that ever lived who had ideas entirely superior to the rest of the world. Not that He as a man was any better, but He was the embodiment of a higher Wisdom, more so than any man who has ever lived.

Perhaps you do not understand my meaning. Take the discovery of electricity. There were men who had conceived some of the ideas of Franklin,-not that Franklin was of himself the discoverer or the person who reduced it to a science, but his mind was the medium that brought the wisdom of the wise into focus, so that an experiment might be made to prove the principle. The wisdom of the world is not confined to any person, but when it begins to condense into a truth it must exhibit itself through some medium. This great truth called Christ was exhibited through the man Jesus, the same as a great truth was exhibited through the man Franklin and called "electricity." There was a belief at the time of destruction or overthrow of this great truth at the crucifixion of Jesus that it should rise again. Since then there has been a constant development of facts showing that there was some wisdom or power superior to man and the superstition of the world has kept it down, as the superstition of slavery has kept Freedom in chains.

Now, I as a man claim no preeminence or superiority over other men, but admit my superiority to the learned and wise. . . . I have none of these sins to answer for. I am free from all that false religion. But I had to contend with the devil or error for more than twenty years before I was free. Now [1864] I stand as one that has risen from the dead or error into the light of truth,-not that the dead or my error has risen with me: I have shaken off the old man or my religious garment, and put on the new man that is Christ or Science, and I fight these errors and show that they are all the makings of our own mind. As I stand outside of all religious belief, how do I stand alongside of my followers? I know that I, through this Wisdom, can go and impress a person at a dis-tance.   The world may not believe it, but to the world it is just such a belief as the belief in spirits. To me it is a fact and this is what I shall show.

THE RELATION OF THIS TRUTH TO THE SICK.

What course of argument must be used to make the masses understand this truth by which I correct the errors that make man sick? What relation has this truth to any one and how does it stand to the sick? It is the sick man's friend and those who can understand it are related to those who do not understand as a teacher who wishes to make his pupil understand the principles of mathematics. He is not to teach mathematics but to explain what the rules mean, so the pupil is not to copy a mathematical work because that gives him no wisdom in regard to the truth; the disciple is not to be above the science, nor the teacher above the truth. but the latter is to explain the science by the words of the truth. To illustrate: I stand to this Science as the teacher or expounder of it, not as the Truth itself. So when the truth says through me that all disease is in the mind you want me to explain what it means. You ask the question because you do not understand what is meant by the mind. It is this: all opinion, belief, reason, everything that can be changed. Thought is a seed or an effect of this great ocean of mind. The word mind covers all man's reasoning as the word wood covers all vegetable substances. A chair is made of wood but it is an idea made out of wood. In the same way mind is the material, and disease is manufactured out of the material, but the wisdom that forms the idea is called something else. Here you see that mind embraces every part of man but his wisdom and here is the distinction which the world makes only in a different sense. The world calls the parts mind and matter. I call them wisdom and matter. Therefore when I use "mind" I use it as matter containing no intelligence, but it is like sound connected with something to which we attach intelligence.

PARABLE

When sitting by a sick person who had a pain in the left side which I felt and described, I said, you think you have consumption. The patient acknowledged it, saying that her physician had examined her lungs and found the left one

114

very much affected. This she believed and when I told her that her disease was in her mind, it was as much as to say she imagined what was not the case. I told her she did not understand what I meant by the word mind. Then taking up a glass of water I said, suppose you should be told that this water contained a poisonous substance that works in the system and sometimes produces consumption. If you really believe it, every time you drink the idea of poison enters your mind. Presently you begin to back and cough a little. Would your fears then grow less that the water was poison? I think not. Finally you are given over by your doctor or friends and call on me. I sit down by you and tell you that you are nervous and have been deceived by your doctor and friends. You ask how? You have been told what is false, that the water you drink contains a slow poison, and now your cure hangs on the testimony in the case. If I show that there is no poison in the water then the water did not poison you. What did ? It was the doctor's opinion put in the water by your mind. As the mind can receive an impression it can be changed, This change was wrought by the doctor's opinion; so calling mind something it is easy to show that it can be changed by a wisdom superior to an opinion. This wisdom that acts upon the mind is something that never has been described by language, but it is looked upon as a superior "power." This power gives rise to all religious opinions. Man has tried to condense it into a being called God, and he worships it. My theory is based on this something that man is ignorant of, and develops from it a language as comprehensible as any language. It contains no words but speaks from impressions which cannot be mistaken if man knows himself. This language is the feelings of the sick, and to convey these feelings to the well so so that they may have some idea of the misery of the sick and its causes has been my study for twenty years. (5) I feel now that my labors have not been in vain. Arranging words to convey this truth to the well is a task very few would like to go through. But I think now that I have succeeded so that any person of ordinary talent can see that it is the key to unlock the mysteries of the spiritual world.

ANSWER TO A QUESTION

"Why do you not rub your head when sick?" Because I have nothing to rub out. Now here are the two modes of reasoning, the natural man does not see that the misery follows his acts, so the natural man is courageous at first, for he does not see his real enemy, or the natural result of his acts, which is reaction, the true wisdom that will always measure to action its own measure. The wise man sees the nature of thought before it takes effect and destroys it. When the patient asked the question he had the answer in the question, for his ignorance was what I was rubbing out, so if he had known that he would not want any rubbing.

CURES

I am often asked what I call my cures I answer, the effect of a Science because I know how I do them. If I did not know they would be a mystery to the world and myself. Science is Wisdom put into practice. To the natural man it is a power or mystery. All wisdom that has not been acknowledged by the natural man is called a "gift" or spiritual demonstration, not a science. The curing of disease has never been acknowledged to be under any wisdom superior to the medical faculty, so people have kept the world in darkness till now, and how much longer they will do so I cannot tell. If I succeed in changing the minds of men enough to investigate they will see that disease is what follows an opinion, and that wisdom that will destroy the opinion and make the cure. Then the cure will be attributed to a superior Wisdom, not a power.

I am accused of interfering with the religion of my patients. This is not the case, but if a particular passage in the Bible or some religious belief affects the patient I attack it. For instance, a person gets nervous from his belief that he has committed the unpardonable sin. His thought is then attached to the sin of his belief, and his belief is some one's opinion about a passage in the Bible that he believes applies to his case. I know this is all false, so of course I have to destroy his opinion, and this destroys the effect which is disease. His senses are attached to a disease, mine are attached to the Wisdom that shows the absurdity of the opinion. His wisdom is of man, mine is of God or Science. All disease is the punishment of our belief either directly or indirectly, and our senses are in our punishments. My senses are attached to the Wisdom that sees through the opinion, so that my love or Wisdom casteth out their disease or fear; for their fear hath torment, and perfect wisdom casteth out all opinions. . . .

I am often accused of opposing the medical faculty and the religious creeds. In answer to this I plead guilty, but you must not gather from this that I oppose goodness or virtue. I oppose all religion based on the opinions of men, and as God never gave an opinion I am not bound to believe that man's opinions are from God. The difference between man's opinions and God's wisdom is more than one would naturally suppose, but the former is taken for a truth. This makes the trouble with which the wise have to contend. If a man knew himself he would not be misled by the opinions of others, and as disease is the result of our opinions it is the duty of all to know themselves, that they may correct their own errors. Now if error is something to correct it must require more wis-dom than the knowledge which invented it. When I find a person diseased I know his trouble must have a father or beginning. If it is ignorant of its father, it is not to be sup-posed that it is not without a father or mother. So to destroy your earthly father is to destroy your opinions, and to be with your heavenly Father is to be wise; so that every one that loses his opinions and arrives at the truth is dead to the natural world, but alive to Wisdom or Christ.

When I sit down by a sick person and he or she wants to tell me what the doctor says, to me it is nonsense for I have not the least regard for their knowledge. Their opinions are what I try to destroy and if I succeed their opinions have no power to create disease. Man's profession, not his wisdom, is the standard of his popularity. I stand in direct opposition to all others in this respect and here is the conflict, whether man's opinion is to rule or his wisdom. If the medical profession is based on wisdom, then it will stand the test, and disease must have its origin outside of the profession; either this must be true or the opposite. I assert that disease is the off-spring of opinion. Ignorance produces the phenomenon or effect, as in the brute creation, but the wild animal differs from that of the domesticated animal. So it is with man; the perfect fool knows no aches or pains, where there is no fear there is no torment. Fear is error, Wisdom casts out fear, for it knows no fear. You often hear persons attempt to explain my cures by their own opinions. Thus they make themselves out wise by their own ignorance, since they deny the very power of wisdom which they acknowledge by admitting it as a mystery to them. So they admit a power outside of their knowledge and worship that of which they are completely ignorant. Now I know that this something which is a mystery to them is wisdom to me and that my wisdom sees through their opinions; and also that the explanation is the conversion from an opinion to truth or health. The two characters, wisdom and opinion, stand before each other and the people choose the one they will obey, just as they do in national affairs. . . .

Disease is the offspring of error and as long as the people worship men's opinions, just so long will they be sick. To me it is perfectly plain that if the people could see themselves they would discard all the priests' and doctors' opinions and become a law unto themselves. All I do is to put the world into possession of a wisdom that will keep them clear from these two classes of opinions. You may think I have some feeling against the character of the physicians but this is not so. Neither do I think that they who know me have anything against me as a man, but they scout the idea that I know any more about how I cure disease than any one else; they think they have the wisdom and I have the power. I stand to the medical faculty in the light of a harmless humbug perfectly ignorant of what I profess to know, and all my talk being to amuse the patients and make them believe that disease is in their imagination. If I succeed in doing this it is all well, but so far as wisdom goes, that is folly. I am aware that this is my position with the faculty and their opinions have such a strong hold on the people that most of them look upon me in the same light, and if by chance some one chooses to see that I am not the person these blind guides call me, they in time are looked upon in the same light. I acknowledge that all this is true with regard to my position in society, and how do I feel in regard to it? I know that it is all false, although my word does not prove it so, but I suppose I have the same right to give my opinion with regard to these two classes as they have to give their opinions about me and I will now give it and let the masses judge for themselves.

The principles which I am trying to establish are something new. All established theories purporting to help mankind are merely the effect of the effort which one set of demagogues make to gain the ascendency over another; the people are no better off, but worse. Disease of a person is like that of a nation, each is governed by arbitrary laws and the governing of both is alike. Disease is acknowledged to have an identity independent of man, and man makes laws to govern it, attaches penalties to their disobedience and calls these laws the "laws of God." . . .

I stand alone, as one arisen from the dead, or the old theories, having passed through all the old ideas and risen again, that I may lead you into this light that will open your eyes to the truth of Him who spake as never man spake, and who spake the truth. This truth condemns all man's opinions, it settles all creeds and priestcraft and upsets the medical profession and brings peace and good will to man. It teaches that man in order to break off from his wickedness or opinions and learn to speak the truth, must not try to deceive his fellow man by pretending to know what is merely an opinion.

Show me the doctor that really thinks his medicine has any curative qualities or any intelligence except as it is associated with his opinion and I will show you a fool, for no intelligent physician would dare risk his reputation on a homeopathic pill to cure a cough, supposing the patient took the medicine in his food and did not know it. This shows that they believe they work on the imagination of the patient. There are certain drugs that will act as an emetic or cathartic; but if the patient should take an emetic by accident, it would make him vomit. Now when the patient vomits, if a wrong direction is given, another effect might be produced; so it all goes to show that the mind must be guided by some wisdom superior to itself. If error directs, nothing certain is known of the effect. If wisdom is at the helm no medicine is wanted, for Wisdom can break opinions in pieces.

Ignorance not knowing how the mind can be affected by a direction outside of itself, identifies wisdom with error or matter, so that truth is a stranger, and it is all the time fighting against itself to get rid of an enemy of its own creation. Now teach men this simple fact, that in all action the wisdom of reaction is in the act though the act knows it not, and their happiness will be the result.

IS THERE ANY CURATIVE QUALITY IN MEDICINE?

Common opinion would answer that there is and according to my opinion there is but it is all owing to the patient's belief, and to perfect wisdom there is no curative virtue in medicine.

I will relate one case out of a hundred to show medicine proves itself according to the patient's belief or the direction of some other person. I was attending a gentleman who was sick and he thought he had consumption, but was not fully settled in his own mind, so of course he was very nervous. Under this nervousness the glands around the throat were excited and kept him hacking and raising, and also kept him heated, which heat would be thrown off in a perspiration. After I had told him the cause of his trouble, the explanation so far as he understood relieved him, he breathed more easily and was improving. One day he read in a paper an advertisement of a medicine which would cure the catarrh and prevent the discharges from the head; thinking it might cure him he bought a bottle and commenced taking it, but instead of lessening the secretion it grew worse and he ran down very rapidly.

My theory explains this fact in this way. His belief admitted that his head was diseased and in the condition of a sore and that the medicine would cure it. Under this belief the glands of the nose were excited and the medicine then proved his belief that the matter was in his head, for it was taken to make the head discharge. His belief did this by exciting the glands and the medicine was taken to throw it off, so when the matter and even blood commenced running it showed that the medicine was doing what it agreed to do. But another belief came up that I had given him, for I had exposed the absurdity of medicine and after he saw the effect he remembered what I had told him, and abandoning his medicine he returned to me again and in a few days recovered what he had lost. This is how the disease worked. His own belief produced the phenomenon; his knowledge gave the medicine the praise or blame, just as people give God the praise for their own acts while the devil has to take the blame for their troubles. I have observed the effect of medicine and have found that there is more virtue or misery in the advertisement than in the medicine.

Everyone knows how the mouth will water by a desire for something that the person wants, and low the mouth and throat will become parched by fear of detection in crime. This was known by the ancients and magicians, and from the fact that the mind could be changed by fear, so that criminals could be detected, those who understood it took advantage of it to detect a thief. The magicians made a paste that would dissolve when laid on the tongue of a person in a perfectly calm state of mind, but in case of unusual warmth or feverish thirst it would not dissolve, so when a theft was committed by the servants all the people were collected in one room and the magician was sent for. Believing in his power, their minds of course were controlled by their knowledge and if the thief were present he knew it and being sure of detection grew nervous, this would prevent the glands from acting and thus bring out his guilt. The others feeling innocent were safe, for if they were nervous it did not produce the state of mind to prevent the paste from dissolving. So the mind was the medium to detect the thief and out of his own mouth he was condemned. People put extravagant confidence in medicine supposing that it contains curative qualities. Frequently Indian doctors appear who have discovered an herb or root to cure some disease that man is afflicted with, as though God had made both the disease and the cure. The same class of people say that God has made a remedy for every disease, showing that their superstition is woven into a belief that God made all diseases and made medicines to cure them. This is the belief of mankind and it is not strange that man has gone out of the way. Now I disbelieve in diseases and remedies as understood by the world and as I once understood and believed. . . .

The opinion that God has provided a remedy for every disease gives rise to a belief that there are certain roots and herbs intended by the Creator to cure all diseases. Absurd as it seems it is the belief of ninety-nine out of a hundred, and this being the case a door is open to quackery, for new discoveries will come up every day. Dr. Herrick's pills, Ayers' sarsaparilla, and countless others are advertised as the cure-all. Then follow certificates of cures and of recommendations from some M. D., and these give the medicines a run. Next a man comes who exhibits the effect of laughing gas and also states that it will cure neuralgia and rheumatism, and the sick rush to him for a time. After he goes a learned M. D. arrives with flaring advertisements announcing free lectures on anatomy and the digestive organs. He explains the action of these organs and dwells upon the danger of getting sick by overeating and drinking, receives some fifty dollars from the poor sick and leaves. Among the throng of humbugs, where all seems dark and despairing, an announcement is whispered in the ear of the sick that God has opened a way for their recovery and sent an angel of mercy who has discovered a flower that will cure everything that can be cured. So here is introduced an imposter who will give Lobelia emetics till they cease to affect the patient, pretending that all diseases must yield to it. This has its day, and another comes up. All this goes to show that the mind of man is like an old fiddle played on by every kind of quackery relating to roots and herbs. With my wisdom I understand them all as Job said to Zophar, "What ye know the same do I also, I am not inferior unto you." I use nothing, yet I could easily use all kinds of drugs. . . .

I have seen the working of popular belief and know that diseases and remedies are the invention of man, and the very proof which is brought to establish their wisdom goes to substantiate what I say. For instance, an emetic . . . when people have eaten too much they can take a Lobelia emetic; also if they think their lungs are diseased take a Lobelia emetic, and if they have dropsy take the same. Now I will call your attention to what this belief amounts to carried out toward God. What kind of a God is it that made the earth to bring forth, trees herbs and everything that bath life? All this was before man was created, therefore did He make these medicines and the codfish with a liver to cure consumption before the disease was made? This belief would certainly suppose that God made the remedies before the disease, and if He made all the remedies these quacks say He did, He certainly is the greatest enemy to mankind. Absurd as this sounds we believe it and are affected by our beliefs and this makes man the most dependent of all God's creatures. He is merely a target to be fired at by every person's opinion. I can show by facts that every person will admit that no kind of medicine has any more effect of itself than almost any kind of food or drink that we use daily, but our ignorance places some kind of virtue in the medicines as we place wisdom in some one's opinion. The truth which places all disease in the mind can explain the operation of remedies. God is Wisdom and man is opinion, therefore man cannot live in Wisdom and be diseased. To show that there are diseases according to the belief of man is to show that they are made by circumstances which cannot be controlled except by correcting the error that brought them about, while ignorance would prescribe some medicine that God had made from the foundation of the world.

OUTLINES OF A NEW THEORY FOR CURING DISEASE

All medical practice claims that their mode of treatment is the best; yet no one has even hinted or dares to risk his reputation on the ground that disease is an invention of man and ought to be treated as an error or deception forced upon mankind by ignorance and superstition as slavery has been forced upon this country, and with all the attendant evils. My theory is that all phenomena called disease are the result of false beliefs originating in the darkness of Egyptian superstition. African slavery is a disease of ignorance and super-stition and is the cause of the present misery in this country, but it is merely the figure of white slavery which has riveted its fetters on the minds of men, while the world of mind lies crushed and humbled by the tyranny of superstitious belief. Disease is what follows a belief and a belief is like an atmosphere so universal that every one is liable to be affected by it as by chilly winds. God never made the wind to injure any person, nor has He put any intelligence into it so man should be afraid of it, but man does not "see it in this light." How often we hear this remark, "Don't expose yourself to the damp, cold air." This belief that God made the air an enemy to man is a part of the clouds that rise in the mind of every person, and when this cloud is seen and felt all persons, old and young, are affected, for the fear is the punishment of the belief, and it is no excuse that the ignorant have no belief, as they must suffer for the sins of their parents. Science is the sun that burns up the clouds or changes the beliefs of man, and a little ray of intelligence springs up and the cloud of superstition vanishes, as the true God appears. The people will bail the truth, as the peak of Teneriffe hails the rising sun long before it is seen by the horizon of the common minds.

I will bring some cases to show that phenomena that once took place can never be produced again. This fact holds good in the vegetable as well as in the mental world. Take a primeval forest, cut down the old growth and another will spring up, not like the first, but a more solid, thicker growth. So it is with error; like an old growth, error is tall and porous with a great show. Science is denser and more substantial. Error is the natural growth of man; it is a wilderness filled with all kinds of superstition and every one is liable to be caught by a native of this land. It is inhabited by every variety of creature such as consumption and liver complaint. Science is the axe in the hands of Wisdom to hew down the wilderness and destroy its inhabitants and introduce a better state of society. Like all superstition error is very religious, religion and slavery always go hand in hand; freedom and science also go together and are the same. . . . Science in religion has not made much progress except as an indirect result of some other development. Astronomy has destroyed some of the hideous features of religion and introduced a happier state of society, but it was not the design of astronomy to destroy religion. Still it is the natural result of science to destroy error and prejudice. It sometimes comes in contact with the most enlightened state of intelligence, for that is cursed with the shackles of religion of dark ages. You will see religion in its purest state under the most despotic form of government, and you will always find disease under some despotic power of religion, and those who undertake to rid the world of this evil are like demagogues in a despotism. Such is the essence of hypocrisy intended to keep the masses weak so they can be ruled. Starve the masses and you destroy their energy and make them desperate, then the more enlightened will submit to the leaders for their own safety. This keeps in power those demagogues. So it is with disease. Religion is despotism and in politics and disease the misery of the sick is the torment of their belief. Religion makes no compromise, it is rule or ruin. It sometimes takes to itself the name of reform, giving every man the liberty of speech, and then it subjects every one to its laws. Just so with the poor slave, or sick, for the sick are merely slaves of superstition, made so by the sins of our parents.

DISEASE (6)

What is disease? It is false reasoning. True scientific wisdom is health and happiness. False reasoning is sickness and death; and on these two modes of reasoning hang all of our happiness and misery. The question is, how can we know how to separate the one from the other? The truth cannot be changed; the false is always changing. The one is science, and the other is error, and our senses are attached to the one or the other. One is the natural development of matter or mind, and disease is one of the natural inventions of error. To show how disease is not what it is supposed to be, by those who use the word, I must show the absurdity of error's reasoning, for error is the father of disease.

We are all taught by this error to call disease something that is independent of man. To make it more plain and show where the two modes of reasoning act, I will suppose a case and take that of a young man who feeling a little disturbed calls on a physician. The physician sounds his lungs, examines his heart, and tells the patient he is very liable to have the heart-disease. The patient asks him how he got it, and is told that he is liable to catch disease and have it and to catch it is to admit that it exists independent of himself. Though the patient were dead it would exist the same and others would be liable to get it. At last the patient really has the heart-disease, which his physician described to him.

And has he created it himself, or has the doctor created it for him? Now I propose to show that he has made what the world calls heart-disease without any one's help. To show how a building is raised is to frame one and then take it down again, so I will take down this building heart-disease which this man has raised, and then you can see how ideas are made or raised. I will say to the patient, "You have built the disease yourself, in your sleep of ignorance." This he cannot understand. So I will tell him how he has worked in his sleep and made this very edifice, heart-disease. So I begin to tell his dream by telling bow he feels, in which he admits I am correct. Now when he was asleep, or ignorant of the feelings that disturbed him, behold a spirit in the form of a doctor sat by him. And to and behold, be called up from the dead a person with the heart-disease, as he calls it. "And he handled you, and your sleep departed from you, and your limbs became cold and clammy, and your pulse quickened. This excited your brain, and at last a figure of a person arose like unto the one you saw in your dream, and then you were afraid, and you awoke in a fright. At last the image became more terrible, till at length it overshadowed you and became a part of yourself, so that when you awoke you looked, and lo! and behold the dream had become a reality, and you had the heart-disease. Now whose dream was it, the doctor's or yours? Did you catch the doctor's or did you create it yourself, by your own reasoning in your sleep or ignorance, according to the pattern set you by the doctor?

"I say you made it yourself. Now to cure you, or take down the building, is to show you that all the feeling you had at the commencement arose from a trifling cause, and that when I can make you understand it I have performed the cure." Instead of giving medicines or going to work by guess to destroy the building, I commence by showing the patient how he framed it by his own hand. So I reason in this way: "You listened to the doctor to try and understand what caused heart-disease. He explained every variety of feeling or symptom, and you listened until you understood it. Now without knowing it you created in your mind the disease, as much as you would if an artist or mechanic had taught you how to draught a building, and you should carry in your mind the building and in your sleep create it. The only difference would be that one would please you, for it would contain wisdom, while the other would bind you, for it would contain fear and would threaten to destroy your life. Your trouble is the material with which to build the building. A chemical change in the fluids of your system takes place, governed by your belief, and you condense the changes into a phenomenon corresponding with your plan. Your ingenuity in manufacturing the disease has been the destruction of your happiness. To destroy the disease I convince you that what the doctor said was an idea gotten up by error, not knowing how to account for some little disturbance, which in itself amounted to nothing, but by the doctor's mode of reasoning about what he knew nothing, you were led astray into the darkness of heathen superstition where all kinds of evil spirits and disease dwell in the brain of man. Superstition always shows itself through the ignorance of man's reasoning, assuming as many names and forms as the father of all lies, the devil or the error of mankind."

DISEASE, LOVE, COURAGE

The question is often asked, what is disease? It could be very easily answered by a physician of the old school by simply pointing out a person coughing and saying that person has consumption. Now instead of calling that phenomenon by a name, explain how it came. This the doctor does not do, except by another phenomenon as much in the dark as the former. So you may chase him from one lie to another until you are tired and only find out at last that it is a mystery. Where do I stand as far as disease goes? I know that the bottom of these phenomena is a lie in the beginning and started by a liar till it was received as true; then the phenomenon is called disease.

Every idea is the embodiment of an opinion resolved into an idea. This idea has life or a chemical change, for it is the offspring of a man's wisdom and his senses are attached to it. For instance, you see something you would like. You attach your senses to the idea and then the value is in the idea in the shape of love or worth. If it is love, it is not in the idea but in the essence or author of the idea. I will try to make it plain. You see a person, at first sight you are affected, and you attach your senses to the idea in the form of love. You may, or may not be deceived. Passion or excitement is matter governed by error subject to love. Love is wisdom, passion is error acting upon ignorance. Science is to keep the two separate or in subjection to Wisdom. When two persons meet we think that the first impression comes from the idea or per-son, but this is not the case: the atmosphere around the idea is what is affected and this is not known to us, so we reason from a false basis, not knowing ourselves.

To give you a clearer idea of what I wish to convey, I must take myself as one person and my patient as another. When I sit down I am one person, that is, I am quiet, perfectly at ease, not afraid of any impression from my patient. My wisdom is my strength. My opponent's wisdom is in his error, for if he knew the truth he would not want me. So there are two persons in one body, or two mentalities acting through one medium, and as error is a coward it assumes a sort of courage. I do not know how to describe true courage, for wisdom needs no such word. I never knew that God showed any courage. It seems to be a sort of braggadocio element. If a dog shows courage it is based on the assumption that he is not afraid, for when overpowered his courage fails, so it shows that what is called courage in us is an element not perfectly understood. Take away the fear of danger, then man has courage. Some men see danger where others do not and so no two men reason alike, so no two men's courage is alike. I know no way of giving you a test of courage as well as to take myself.

When I first commenced my practice I thought I had courage as much as my neighbors, but as I found I was liable to be affected by another's feelings my courage failed. So I used some sort of strategem to get the advantage of my patients and being rather reckless I ran risks which the world would call courageous.

For instance, I was not afraid of an insane man if I could get his eye. To the world this looked like courage, but to me it was wisdom. I had no fear for I saw no harm. I have been trying to get wisdom in regard to the disease of mankind, for disease is like all other evils that come within our senses. When I first took the feelings of patients, it took courage to keep from taking the disease. I knew this kind of courage, it was fear lest I should be called a coward, so I would assume courage. But if I had known what I know now I should not have been in any more danger than a person would be in a boat where the water was not over three feet deep. But my courage admitted water twenty feet deep, rough at that, and myself in a leaky craft. As I began to touch bottom or get wisdom, I found that the depth of the water or the dan-ger was in my patient's mind and I believed his story without looking for myself, and the patient seemed two men to me. Thus I found out the trouble his fears were one man and his ignorance another. To make courage out of fear was to make him believe there was no danger; then his courage would come, and to destroy both was to let him know the truth.

I know that disease is the invention of man, therefore it requires no courage to say so, for there is no danger. Danger is that which calls out fear and courage is the element to face it; so just as a man loses fear he gains courage. Some men never see danger, so their courage is not courage, but a sort of artificial pride which makes them wish to be praised for what they know not, for their ignorance destroys their fear. This was the case with myself. My ignorance made me bold, for I knew no danger, but as soon as I found I was liable to be affected by the sick my fears came. Then just as I saw danger my fears increased and my courage failed; but I would feel the same reckless propensity to kill disease, so I would be more cautious and more careful till I found my enemy had the same fears that I had. At last it became a sort of warfare between myself and a patient. I found that my courage was my protection and that error was an element or odor, while ignorance and fear was what arose from that. So I came to the conclusion; that ignorance begets error, error begets fear, fear begets courage, and Wisdom destroys them all. So as man grows wise he grows strong and his wisdom makes him happy and good, for goodness is wisdom, and Wisdom is the religion of Jesus.

The [conventional] religion is the opposite of that. One is the invention of man, the other is the wisdom of God which Jesus illustrated by taking a little child. I will do the same, to show that goodness is a science and also that all religion based on man's opinions must fall. One can be proved, the other cannot. I will illustrate the two by the child. Every one will acknowledge that the child's character somewhat depends upon its bringing up. If this is admitted it shows that if the parents could see what was best for the child's happiness much of its misery might be avoided; this fact is evident to all. It is a fact like all others in science; sometimes it works well, sometimes ill, but when it works ill we see how it might be avoided, showing that if we had more knowledge we might do better. This shows that Science Wisdom reduced to practice, so as goodness is the result of our training, it is certain that to be good is a science, and as goodness is religion, that is a science. It is all summed up in this, that the world is made of ignorance, disease, religion and error, hyprocrisy and all sorts of evil; and to be a follower of Jesus and believe in the Christ is to separate yourself from the world and stand alone in your wisdom. Thus you will learn that man without wisdom is of all things the most miserable; he is liable to get into trouble by every act of his life.

WHAT DO I IMPART TO MY PATIENTS?

The question is often asked me, do you impart anything to your patients when you talk? I answer, I do, and I will try to make you understand how. To do this I must give you an illustration in language applied to something that you wish to know which gives you trouble. Suppose you are purchas-ing goods, and in your hurry you lose your wallet containing all your money. You do not miss it till you go to pay your bills, and then you find you have lost your cash. Now the shock excites your system or mind according to the amount you are disturbed. You become excited and very nervous. This is accompanied by a feverish state of mind or body, for the bodily condition is only the reflection of the state of the mind.

At last you let your trouble be known to some person and begin to look for the money. You can't find it, and borrow money to pay the person for assisting you. This adds to the trouble, and at last you take your bed and send for a physician. He feels of the pulse, says your head is affected, and orders your head shaved and a blister applied. This only aggravates the nervous excitement. So you keep on till you finally give up and dismiss all the doctors, and come to the conclusion that your money is gone and you must make the best of it. The next day you feel more reconciled, and your doctor calls a friend and finds you better and says the medicine you took has had a good effect on you. Now the question arises, who gave the medicine? Not the doctor, but wisdom took possession of you and you began to reason and send for me. I know nothing of the trouble, but have found a pocket-book, containing $10,000 and am going to advertise it. At the sight of the pocket book you start and say, "that is mine." The shock changes the mind and the cure is made. Now who imparted the cure? The $10,000 I gave you. So this is the way I cure. The person has lost something that he cannot find or has got into some trouble he cannot get rid of. He wants something to satisfy his desires, and whatever that is it is the same as the money, and the one who can impart it gives him the remedy. Suppose a person receives a shock from falling into a river, and returns home excited with a state like a cold. This produces a cough. Now, as there are many ghosts in the form of disease, he fears some of them may get hold of him. So he goes to a doctor and lays his case before him. The doctor says you are very liable to have consumption. Now of course you are troubled, and are all the time like the man who was looking for his lost money. So he inquires of every person what is good for a cough; or if they can tell where his money is. So every person gives his opinion, and there is just as much in one opinion as another. At last in despair he gives it up, and I am sent for. I first tell him what he is afraid of by telling him how he is affected. Here is something he can't get from the doctor. This makes him feel more comfortable, and then I go on to show him how he has been living on husks or opinions about an idea that never had an existence only in the superstition of the people. As he is full of these opinions I have to give him something in the form of truth that will dissolve the error and satisfy him.

EXPERIENCE OF A PATIENT WITH DR. QUIMBY

For many years I was very sick and finding no benefit resulting from the various modes of cure that I had employed, I thought of visiting Dr. Quimby. So I inquired of some friends in regard to his treatment. Some said he was a spiritualist and others that he was a mesmeriser, and others said he made war on all religious beliefs, and as I could not see what my belief had to do with my disease I gave up the idea of going to see him, but finally I was brought to the subject again through utter hopelessness and despair of recovery, so I went to see him. In my first interview I asked him if he could cure the spinal disease. He answered that he never wished a patient to tell him his feelings. "Very well" said I, "what do you want me to do?" "Nothing," said he, "but listen to what I say." I then asked him if he gave medicine. "No." "Do you employ any agent from the world of spirits?" "No" said he. "Then," said I, "it must be mesmerism." He replied "that may be your opinion but it is not the truth." "Then will you please tell me what you call your way of curing?" He said he had no name. (7) "Well," said I, "is it original with you?" He said he never knew anyone who cured as he did. "Can you give me some idea how you cure?" He said, "it would be very hard to convince a person how he felt unless I feel myself." "Yes," I said, "it would be hard for you to tell my feelings." "Well," said he, "if I tell you how you feel will you admit it?" "Certainly, but how do you cure?" He answered, "I will illustrate one thing. Do you believe the Bible?" "Certainly," I said. "When Jesus said to His disdiples 'a little while I am with you, then I go my way and you shall seek me. Where I go you cannot come,' What did He mean by the passage?" "I suppose He spoke of the crucifixion." "Then you think," said he, "that Jesus alluded to another world when He said 'If you loved me you would rejoice that I go to the Father.... In another place He says 'if I do not go away the Comforter will not come, but if I go away I will send the Comforter who will guide you to all truth.' Now I suppose you think all this refers to another world?" I said, "Yes."
"Well," said he, "now I will sit down and see if I can tell your feelings." He then sat down and took my hand and soon passed his hand on one of the vertebrae of my spine and said "You have a very sharp pain in this vertebra at this time." I said I had. Then he placed his hand on the left temple and said "you have a very bad pain here and it affects the sight of your left eye." I then told him he was right. "Now," said he, "I will explain how I cure. Will you admit that Jesus took upon Himself our infirmities?" I said yes. "Have I not taken your pain in the spine, also in the temples and eyes?" "Yes," I said. "I will now explain those passages which I have mentioned. My theory is that disease is the invention of man, a burden bound on the people, laid on their shoulders, grievous to be borne; that man has been deceived and led away and is unable to get back to health and happiness; that Jesus' mission was to break the bands that bound the sick and restore them to health and happiness. In order to do this He had to find them, for they had wandered away like sheep without a shepherd. So He took their aches and pains to show them He was with them and knew how they felt and said, 'Come unto Me all you who are heavy laden and I will give you rest.'" I said, "You seem to talk a great deal about the Bible. I came here to be cured and not to have my religion destroyed." He answered, "Have I said anything about religion?" "No, but I cannot see why you quote the Bible." "I will tell you" said he, "you admit I took your feelings?" "Yes." "Well, I want to give you to understand that when I take your feelings I am with you, not myself as a man but this great truth which I call Christ or God." "What do you mean by that? That you are equal with Christ?" "What do you mean by Christ?" he

asked. "I mean Jesus." "Then Jesus and Christ are one?" "Yes." "Then" said he, "how is Jesus God?" "God manifest in the flesh," I replied. "He asked "What do you mean by God manifest in the flesh?" "That God took upon Himself flesh and blood to convince man of His power and save man from an endless eternity of misery." "Can God exist outside of matter?" he asked. I answered "Yes." "Is there anything of man that exists when God is out of him?" "Yes," said I, "flesh and blood." "Then flesh and blood is something of itself?" "Yes." "What do you call that, the natural man?" "Yes," "This Jesus would be the natural man of flesh and blood and Christ the God manifested in the man Jesus?" I said, "Yes, I think so." "Well," said be, "that is just what I want to prove to you, that the Christ is the God in us all. Do you deny that you have a particle of God in you?" "No. I believe it" I said. "Then we do not disagree in this. I want to make you understand that this Christ or God in us is the same that is in Jesus, only in a greater degree in Him-,like this: You teach music?" "Yes," I said. "Do your pupils know as much about the science of music as you do?" "No, if they did I could not teach them." "Then you have the science more than they?" "Yes." "They have some?" "Yes." "What they know is science? Is it not equal to the same amount in you?" "Yes," I said. "Then if one of your pupils should say I understand the science of music, it is to be understood that he is equal to you?" "No." "Well, so it is with me" said he; "when I say that by this great truth I cast out error, or in other words correct your opinion and free you from that curse of all evils, disease, I do not mean to say that P. P. Quimby is equal to the man Jesus or equal to His wisdom or Christ, but merely admit that I recognize the great principle in man, of God as a distinct Being.

"While I am explaining this Christ I will give you the trinity that I believe in, that is P. P. Quimby's trinity, not that P. P. Q. is the trinity but that P. P. Q. believes it. He believes in one living and true wisdom called God, in Jesus (flesh and blood) a medium of this truth, and in the Holy Ghost or explanation of God to man. Here is my trinity and the Holy Ghost is the Science that will lead you into all truth: it will break the band of error and triumph over the opinion of the world. 'This Holy Ghost is what is with your Christ that your fleshly man knows not of; this is the Christ in you that has been cast into prison since you were first sick; it is the Christ that Jesus speaks of that preached to the prisoners long before the flood. This same Christ was crucified at the death of Jesus and laid in the tomb of Joseph's new doctrines, not with the body of Jesus. The Jews crucified Christ by their false religion and the masses crucified the man Jesus, so Christ in the tomb of every true disciple had the Christ lying in his breast crucified by the world of opinions. This Christ is the one that Jesus Christ spake of, not of the flesh and blood that the people saw by their natural eyes. So all the truth that came through the man Jesus was Christ and it was the garment of Jesus. So Jesus was clothed with the gospel or wisdom of God. When the error mur-dered the man, they stole the body of Christ and parted His garments or wisdom among them, while the people believed that the flesh and blood that was laid in the tomb was the one that they heard, when it was nothing but the medium of the one whom they never saw, only in a mystery. This same Christ rose again and is still in the world of matter recon-ciling the world of error to the science of God.

"I will now commence anew to preach Christ to you to cure you of your errors or disease and bring you into this living Truth that will set you free from the evils of man's opinions that binds burdens upon you in the form of a disease. So when I say I am with you I mean this Christ or truth, not P. P. Quimby as a man. I have acknowledged it as my leader and master. So when I speak of it I speak of it as a wisdom superior to P. P. Q's, and you have the same Christ in you confined by the errors of this world. So I will now sit down by you again and listen to your groans, for I feel the pain of the bands that bind you across the chest. Now this that feels is not P. P. Quimby, but the Christ and that which complains is not Mrs. P. but the Christ in Mrs. P. struggling to roll the stone from the sepulchre of her tomb, to rise from the dead or error, into the living God or Wisdom. You see that, I, that is, this Wisdom, makes a sick man two,-a man beside himself and the servant above his master. When the master is acknowledged the servant is not known, no more than an error is known when the truth comes. I will show my meaning by an illustration: If you believe your lungs are diseased, the servant or belief is the master, and Wisdom the true master becomes the servant; but when the Lord of the vineyard comes, then the wicked servant is cast out and another is put in his place that will render to his Lord his dues. So when I, this truth, shall convince the error of its wrong, it cannot stand the fire of Truth, so it will submit to Wisdom, then truth will resume its sway and health and happiness will be the result. Your disease is the result of your belief and to change your belief is to convince you of an error that binds you and the pains and depleted state of mind are the natural results of your punishment. Truth never binds or separates one truth from another and all belief that has a tendency to separate us is error and makes unhappiness. Error always tries to separate one from another.

"I will illustrate: Suppose you are my child and you become sick as you are now; according to the religious belief we must separate and perhaps at some future time we shall meet again in that world whence no traveller ever returned. The chances according to your own and your friends' belief are that you are bound for that world of spirits. Suppose I believe as you and the rest of the religious world, what must be my feelings when I see you hastening to that world whence no traveller returns; how must you feel, knowing that you are about to be snatched from the bosom of your friends to enter that dark and dismal grave, with only the hope of a resurrection from the dead and that based on a belief? Is not that enough to rock the very foundation of your building and make the walls of your belief tremble even to the foundation? To me this is a horrid belief.

"Now this is your true state, standing trembling between hope and fear, holding back through fear and clinging to your friends, while the nearest and dearest of them are trying to drive you off through their blind faith. Suppose you are a parent and your only son should be pressed into the army and your neighbors who have sons should come round and console you by saying he would be better off for going even if he should die fighting for his country, would you feel happy to part with him? Must not the separation be almost enough to break your heart? Then your husband is called upon and now your cup is filled to overflowing. Can all this happen without a sunken eye, a pale and hollow cheek, with hectic flush, a purple lip, and nervous cough? In all this the chances are not one out of fifty that they will not both re-turn to cheer you up in your last moments when your life is almost run out. In all this your spirits mingle as though you were only separated like other friends, but when they die, according to our belief, the thread that binds us is severed by the knife that cuts our life and our souls launch into the world of our belief. Which is worse? To go through either is bad enough, but I believe the religious belief is worse. The religious belief prepares the mind for the medical belief, one is based on old superstitions; this gets the mind worked up like mortar, then the potter or doctor moulds the mind into disease. I have no sympathy with either. Science knows no such beliefs; Science never separates, it is from everlasting to everlasting, it has no beginning nor end.

"I will now return to you again as my child to convince you that although your eyes are sunken and your cheek hectic your pains and trouble are all in your false ideas of yourself. We are all a part and parcel of each other, that is, in our wisdom or that life eternal which cannot be severed, but our beliefs may hold it in bondage. Now as you sit and listen, suppose you grow quiet and pass into that happy state of mind where you meet your husband and son, talk with them about the war and learn from them that they find it rather a hard life, but they will not return till the rebellion is crushed. On the whole you are satisfied that they are better off so far as their situation is concerned than you thought for. Would you not feel relieved? I know you would. While you are in this state suppose you believed you were dying and your friends were weeping around you for the last time and you could not speak. Which do you think would have the most reviving effect on you when you awoke? You need not answer. Now, my belief is this: Wisdom never separates you. from me but makes us a part of each other in Wisdom; for what I feel I know and what I do not know I cannot feel. To believe my child is separate and apart from me is a horrid belief to us both, but to know that God cannot be divided is to know that we cannot be separated from our Heavenly Father. The error is only held together by opinions that can deceive, but Science is eternal life. This is in all mankind and is progress, it knows no death or separation. To know this is more than the religious world ever had. This was the doctrine of Jesus; Christ is the child of this wisdom and this is what I am trying to get into your mind like the little leaven that leaveneth the whole lump. If this is infidel doctrine, then P. P. Quimby is an infidel; but I would rather part with everything on earth than part with this Truth which is my shepherd that leadeth me through the dark valley of the shadow of death, and lodges me where no belief or opinion can give me one drop of water to cool my tongue when tormented by religious belief."

THE SILENT METHOD

[It is noticeable that Quimby does not spend time analyzing the process of healing, does not write about concentration, meditation or "the silence." Possessing exceptional powers of concentration, he immediately turned to the patient to make his intuitive diagnosis, then gave his thought to the realization of the Divine ideal of health and happiness. The nearest he comes to a description of the process is in the following illustration, drawn from his experience as a daguerreotypist in his early years.]
A patient comes to see Dr. Q. He renders himself absent to everything but the impression of the patient's feelings. These are quickly daguerreotyped on him. They contain no intelligence, but shadow forth a reflection of themselves which he looks at: this contains the disease as it appears to the patient. Being confident that it is the shadow of a false idea, he is not afraid of it, but laughs at it. Then his feelings in regard to the disease, which are health and strength, are daguerreotyped on the receptive-plate of the patient, which also throws forth a shadow. The patient, seeing this shadow of the disease in a new light, gains confidence. This change of feeling is daguerreotyped on the doctor again, and this [new impression] also throws forth a shadow, and he sees the change and continues to treat it in the same way. So the patient's feelings sympathize with his, the shadow grows dim, and finally the light takes its place, and there is nothing left of the disease. [This description refers to the successive intuitions concerning the whole individual, the error to be banished, the fears to be overcome, the haunting mental pictures to be blotted out; and the picturing of the Divine image of health, made concrete by Quimby's great power of focussing the attention, as well as his insight into the causes on which he based the explanation following the silent treatment. The "receptive-plate" of the patient includes part of what we now call the subconscious. When actual changes were wrought the patient began to feel the benefit. Then the process of re-education could be begun. Quimby judged by the ideal or "scientific" man, in contrast with which the patient's own idea of himself as a sick person was a mere shadow.]

TREATMENT OF A CHILD

To show the effect of the will upon the mind of a child, I will state the case of one about two years old who was brought to me to be treated for lameness. The mother held the child in her lap and informed me that it was lame in its knee. This was the information I received from its mother; but when I sat by the child I experienced a queer feeling in the hip and groin, but no bad feelings in the knee. I told the mother that the lameness was in the hip, and that I would show her how the child walked, and how it would walk were it lame in the knee. I then imitated the walk of the child, and also showed how it would walk were the lameness in the knee. After I explained the difference to her the mother admitted I was right.

I then informed her that to cure the child's lameness I must cure her (the mother) of the disease which was in her senses [mind] while the phenomenon was exhibited in the child. She said the doctor told her the disease was in the knee, and ordered it splintered. To splinter up the knee and keep it from bending would be to encourage the evil in the hip, and make a cripple of the child. I was obliged to explain away the doctor's opinion. When I suceeded in doing that, it changed the mother's mind so much that when she put the child down she could see that her will guided its motion. This was so apparent to her that she could in some measure counteract the wrong motion of the child. With my own wisdom attached to the child's will I soon changed the mind so that the child walked much better.

THE HEALING PRINCIPLE

It is an undisputed fact that Dr. Quimby cures disease, and that without any medicine or outward applications. How does he do it? is the question that agitates and interests the people. If he has any new way different from the mysterious and superstitious mode acknowledged by others who have appeared to cure disease by personal virtue alone, what is it? Where does he get his power?

He denies that he has any power or gift superior to other men. He contends that he operates intelligently under the direction of a Principle which is always his guide while with the sick. He follows this Principle in practice and theory, and under it he learns facts of real life that he could never get in any other way. He has found the way by which all errors can be corrected....

It might be called the Principle of Goodness. It is the highest intelligence that operates in the affairs of man, always producing harmony, and making man feel that he has more to learn and is a progressive being.... It has been his aim to develop this principle in relation to human misery and make life a science. The cause of all misery is in ignorance of ourselves, and in proportion as he develops this higher, happier portion of mankind, which he calls Science, he sees through the miseries and the ills, and just in proportion as he sees through them he can correct them.... With a knowledge that all trouble is a false alarm ... he proceeds to undermine the foundations, and the structure gives way. However well established are the facts of any disease, he believes the basis all wrong, dependent on the opinions of men for an existence.... To destroy the belief identified with a. patient's feelings, changes the mind, and that is the cure....

The mind is something and embraces a much larger compass of our being than we are taught to consider it. It includes all opinions and [conventional] religion, and everything about us which can change; not that part which is seen by the natural eye, but that which acts upon the natural man. It embraces all excitement and agitation, and all the variations of humanity.... It is not matter that comes to our bodily senses. It is another kind which is just as sensible to him as that which he touches with his hands. Around every one is an atmosphere of intelligence which contains our whole identity, and he has become so sen-sitive to that atmosphere that its existence is a fact, and with that he operates. [If this seems to imply a sixth sense, the answer is that Dr. Quimby has not] found any one faculty that would answer to a "sense," but he has refined and spiritualized those faculties which mankind exercise toward each other till he has arrived at the true way of communicating with and influencing minds. For instance, his sympathy for his patients is pure from any feeling like blame or contempt, or discouragement, and is a transparency to reflect their feelings just as they come to him, with light from a higher source, to account for and explain them to the patient, and his explanation illumines the patient's mind.

How does he know he has got hold of a true method? How does be know he is not mistaken? There are many reasons which confirm his method as a science. One is that he constantly improves it. He finds he can cure more quickly, and harder cases. Then as he explains his method to others and they understand it confirms him.... Admitting that there is a First Cause or God, it is not so hard to demonstrate that Dr. Quimby knows more about His wisdom in regard to health .. . and unto Him he gives all the glory. He knows that while treating disease he is purely under the influence of the highest truth.... He knows that his peculiar belief is not an invention of his own, for it is contrary to what as a natural man he has been taught: it rests on the facts of his own experience with the sick. . .

HEALTH AND DISEASE

Disease is that part of the mind that can be compared to a wilderness. It is full of erroneous opinions and false ideas of all kinds, and it opens a field for speculators to explore. . . . When I sit by a sick person he tells me the story of his travels, and his experience of the evils that beset him in this wilderness. The scientific character is like the prodigal son, it desires to enter this land of mystery to see what it can gain. . . . As health is the thing most desired, to find out how to keep it and when lost how to restore it, is the object of our journey into this territory.

The question may be asked, What is health? I know of no better answer than this: it is perfect wisdom, and just as a man is wise is his health; but as no man is perfectly wise no man has perfect health. Ignorance is disease, although not accompanied by pain. Pain is not disease itself, but is what follows disease. According to my theory, disease is a belief, and where there is no fear there can be no pain; for pain is not the act but the reaction of something which creates pain. But, says some one, I never thought of pain till it came. But if it came something must have started it. Therefore it must be an effect, whether it came from some place or from ourselves. I take the ground that it is generated in ourselves, and that it must have a cause. Every one knows that in his natural state a person is sensitive to what is called pain, and if his sensitiveness is destroyed he shows no signs of pain. But to suppose his senses are destroyed because he feels no pain is not correct: his senses [or consciousness] may be detached from his body and attached to another idea, so that he is not sensitive to any effect upon the body which in his natural state would give him pain. This shows that pain is in the mind, like all trouble, though the cause may be in the belief or body.

For instance, suppose a tumor appears on the body, the person feeling no sensation or trouble from it. He consults a physician who, after examining it, asks the man if he has shooting pains and hot flashes. The man says, "No, why do you ask the question?" The doctor replies that it looks like a cancer, and then explains the nature and symptoms of the disease. In the course of an hour the man feels shooting pains. Now where is the pain, in the tumor, or in the belief in a cancer? I answer, in the belief. . . . Error gives direction to the mind, and a cancer is formed just as far as the belief is received by the patient. Every thought is a part of a person's identity, and if it contains a belief he must suffer the penalty of his acts; for to believe is to act.

LEARNING TO HEAL

How can a person learn to cure the sick? As a pupil in mathematics learns to work out a problem. Every word is supposed to have a meaning. Now words are like nuts, some are full, some partially full, some are empty, the food or wisdom is in the word, and if the word contains no wisdom, then it is like husks or froth, it fails to satisfy the desire of the person who seeks the substance. Natural food is to satisfy the natural man and spiritual food or wisdom is to satisfy the inner or scientific man. The child before it begins to know is fed by natural food, while its spiritual food is opinions expressed in words. Therefore as I said, words contain more or less truth; all are not full and some are empty; but when a person speaks a word that contains the real substance and applies it to the thing spoken of, that is what is called the bread of life and he neither hungers nor thirsts for wisdom in regard to that. The sick have been deceived by false words and have fed on food that contains no wisdom. Hungry and thirsty they apply to strangers for food; they ask for health or the bread of life and the natural man taking bread as a natural substance, brings bread to them, but their state of mind does not hunger for natural food, therefore to them it is a stone.

There is a bread, which if a man eat, he is filled, and this bread is Christ or Science. It is the body of Christ. Jesus says, "whoso eateth my flesh and drinketh my blood hath eternal life." "For my flesh is meat indeed and my blood is drink." The Jews of His days were like the scholars of the present day. Bread is bread, and blood is blood, and they say, "how can this man give us his flesh to eat?" They do not understand that Wisdom is a body and opinion a shadow. The natural man's belief is his body, and to eat and drink the world's wisdom is to eat condemnation or disease.

Now I will illustrate a cure. I sit down by a sick person and you also sit down, I feel her trouble and the state of her mind, and find her faint and weary for the want of wisdom. I tell her what she calls this feeling that troubles her, and knowing her trouble my words contain food that you know not of. My words are words of wisdom and they strengthen her, while if you should speak the same words and the sound should fall on the natural ear precisely as mine, they would be only empty sounds and the sick would derive no nourishment from them.

I will describe this food that you may taste it and be wiser for your meal. In order to prove that food satisfies a person's hunger, I must find a person who is hungry, and in order to prove that my words satisfy the sick, I must take one who hungers and thirsts for the bread of life or health. Being weak and faint from exhaustion she applied to a physician for food to satisfy her desire, for she was famished for the want of wisdom in regard to her trouble. Instead of giving her wisdom which would have satisfied her, he in his ignorance gave her these words full of poison. "Your trouble is a cancer in the breast." As she received these words she became more faint and exhausted till she became sick at her stomach. She ate of this poisonous food till seeds of misery began to agitate the matter, the idea began to form and a bunch appeared in the breast. As she attached the name cancer to the bunch the name and the bunch became one body. The physician's words contained the poison, the poison pro-duced the bunch, their ignorance associated the name with the bunch and called it cancer.

I was called to see the lady and being perfectly ignorant of her trouble, I felt the faint and hungry feeling and as I felt the effect of the doctor's food or opinions on her, I said, The food you eat does not nourish you, it gives you a pain in the breast. This I said in reference to the way she reasoned in regard to her trouble.

"How do you know?" said she. I then told her that she thought her trouble was a cancer and she admitted that it was so. I then told her she had no cancer except what she made herself. I will admit the swelling, said I, but it is of your own make. You received the seed from the doctor, and he prepared the mind or matter for its growth, but the fruit is the work of the medical faculty.

Let us see how much the idea cancer exists in truth. The name exists before the bunch, then the bunch before it ap-peared must have been in the mind, for it was not in sight when the word was first applied to it, or when you were first told that you had one.

You know that you can be affected by another mind. Now I wish to show you that every phenomenon that takes form in the human body is first conceived in the mind. Some sensation is felt which we cannot account for, we then conjure up some idea which we create into a belief, and soon it is condensed into a. form and a name given to it. Then every phenomenon taking the name of disease, is a pattern of some false idea started without the least foundation in truth. Now, this bunch I call a phenomenon, for I cannot call it a cancer, because if I do I admit a thing outside of the mind. The senses are the man independent of flesh, that is one thing, the word cancer is another. Now, I want to find the matter that the word is applied to. To say a thing exists and to prove its existence are two different things. If any doctor will tell where that cancer was before it was in sight, I will ask him how he knows. Let him say it was in the blood, that the state of the blood indicates the presence of cancerous humor.

Now, do you deny that I told your feelings? "Certainly not." Then have I a cancerous humor? "By no means." Then there is no wisdom in that argument. Again, he never knew you had an ill-feeling till you told him. Then where did he get his knowledge? Not from you for you never thought of a cancer. It must have been from what you said about your pain. Suppose I had said that I felt these same pains and you had kept your peace, then according to his theory I must have a cancerous humor. Now, I know that I have no humor nor had I an idea or pain till I sat by you, therefore his story of a cancer is a lie made out of whole cloth, without the least shadow of truth. It is like the stories of Sinbad the Sailor, or some witch fables that have no existence in truth. Then you will ask, what is this bunch? It is a bunch of solid matter, not a ghost or any invisible thing, but it was made by yourself, and no one else.

I will tell you how you made it. You remember I spoke of your having a heat. This heat contained no good or ill, but it was a mere decomposition of your body brought about by some little excitement. It troubled you, then your superstitious fear of disease began to haunt you in your sleep, creating an action in the part of your breast where the error had made a stand. You commenced then to foster the idea till at last you have excited the muscles to such an extent that the bunch has appeared. If now I have proved the cure I have affected it and the bunch will disappear.

Do you wish to know why? "Yes." Can the effect re-main when the cause is removed? "I presume not." How do you feel ? "I feel easy." How do you feel in regard to your trouble, and in regard to what I have said? "I think you are right, and it looks more reasonable than the doctor's story." Then your senses have left his opinion and have come to my wisdom. This is the new birth, you have risen from the dead and you are free from the doctor's ideas. This truth has destroyed death, and brought life and health through Science. Now, I say unto you, Take up your bed or this Truth and go your way, and when the night of error comes spread out the garment of Wisdom that enfolded Jesus, and wrap yourself in its folds or Truth, till the sun of Life shall shine upon your body, and you rise free from the evils of the old belief. (8)

STRENGTH

What is strength? This question sounds as though it might be easily answered, but on consideration it is not so easy. Words are so misused that it is impossible to get at the original meaning, feeling or state when the word was introduced. If you choose to apply the word strength to machinery, then I have no fault to find with the definition, but if it is applied to man also the definition is wrong; for man's strength is in his will, and that is independent of the thing you call "strong." If you say, "that is a strong lever," then it does not include the force that is applied to it. If the person who first used the word applied it to his wisdom as a powerful intellect, then it will only apply where there is intellect, the quality of which is taken into account. This confusion of meaning makes a great deal of trouble, for we put intelligence into everything that has resistance instead of in the intelligence having the strength. A man's legs are a combined lever, and if you mean that they have strength you might as well say that a lever has strength, for one is as much alive as the other and neither of itself can do anything.

The word strength does not convey the author's feelings when he made the expression. He either meant to apply it to wisdom or to matter. If the author meant to give a name to the phenomenon called will, then it makes a vast difference in reasoning about strength. For instance, a person is "weak" in the back or limbs. Now the medical faculty prescribe strengthening linaments, as though there were intelligence in the medicine and it imparted strength to the weak part.

126

This absurd idea is carried out through all our lives, and it deprives man of the true wisdom that might make him happy and intelligent.

My theory disproves the assertion, for I have seen that the word strength is a mere word with no more meaning than to lead man astray.

The corner stone of the medical science is based on this word strength. This or that thing is said to give a person strength. In the case of a fever the whole invention of the medical faculty is brought to play to discover some medicine that will give strength. The chemist is employed to discover the chemical properties which such and such things contain, and numberless articles are said to contain strengthening virtue. The food is strengthening, the air is strengthening and you can find no end to the strengthening things given to the sick, and all the while they are growing weaker.

Every one knows that a horse is stronger than a man, it cannot be the food, for a man fed on grass would die accord-ing to our belief, while the animal will live, and so he will live on the same food as man and still grow no stronger. Man puts the construction on the word to suit himself. If the power applied to man's will is called strength; the thing that will is applied to is not called strong. You may ask what this has to do with the curing of disease. I will tell you, for it is the very thing to correct. There is such a term as resistance and this is opposed to strength. For instance, you wish to raise a stone, the wish that wants to raise a stone is one thing, and the stone is another. If wisdom chooses to apply its strength through the arms its motive or will is applied according to the idea of resistance. If a horse is attached to a dead weight it applies its will or strength and if it fails it makes another effort to overcome the resistance. Strength is intelligence; it embraces all man's wisdom, and if his wisdom is of God or Science his strength is not in himself, and to be wise is to be strong.

I will illustrate my idea of strength as I apply it to the sick. When I use the word I couple it with skill. These two are governed either by natural wisdom or scientific wis-dom. I will state a case of my own experience. I treated a man who had lost the use of his lower limbs, he could not move them when he was sitting in his chair. The doctor called it spinal affection. When he attempted to rise he had not strength enough in his spine to keep his body erect, he would give out at the pit of the stomach, and this took all the power from his legs. This was the doctor's theory and the man believed it and applied his will or strength according to his wisdom. His hope was cut off. He believed the spine was diseased and so did all his friends and physicians. According to my theory his body was like the weight to be moved, his will or strength was applied to his body just as it would be to a lever which you believed would break if you applied too much power to it; his reason directed the power, and being deceived he could do nothing. To cure him, or make his legs strong and his spine well, was to first convince him that there never was any strength in the idea body, that strength came from some other source.

Every one knows that, the will being put into action, an effect is produced called strength. For instance, a person by the power of his will can hold another. What is the grasp? Strength, or is it the will applied to the hand? No one supposes that the hand would catch hold and grasp unless directed by another power. This power is the will governed by the wisdom and the effect is called strength. Strength is the name of the act, so will without an act or motive is no will or strength and availeth nothing. So to sit till his legs grew strong would be as absurd as to make a. steam engine and after it was ready to work sit and wait till the wood made its own fire, its steam, and let its steam on to the piston head. For a man that has lost his strength to sit still and wait for it to come is just as absurd as to prepare a clay bin and then wait for it to make a vessel. Such an idea of strength is so absurd that it takes away a man's reasoning faculties. Let man know that this darkness is the want of right direction to his ambition, then his strength is in putting his will into action, both are the result of his wisdom. Destroy a man's prospects and happiness, and you destroy his strength. So as you rouse his ambition and will, his strength comes. The course taken by the medical faculty in their mode of reasoning destroys man's natural powers and makes him. a mere tool in the hands of a quack. Every man who reasons that strength can be made by food, air, or rubbing, or any linament, is a fool, although he may be honest.

I have tried the experiment and know. I do not guess at it when I say that there is not one particle of virtue in any sort of medicine that people take to give them strength. Neither is there any kind of strength in one kind of food more than another, but it may be all summed up in this, the gratification of man's desires embraces all there is of him, and these vary according to circumstances. All men have a desire for happiness, and this desire creates an appetite, and the desire wants to be gratified. This brings up this feeling [activity] called will, and then it is forced on by wisdom to accomplish a desire. The wants of the animal are limited, therefore it is lively and happy, for it acts according to its will. It is often said that the beasts are sick. Granted, but man takes their freedom from them as well as from the human species. Let both be wild and you see a bold race.

Look at the uncultivated savage and you will not see him creeping around as though he had done some mean, dirty act, like the civilized man. Of all mean looking things a human being completely under the medical faculty is the lowest, he is as much a slave as the negro at the South, and in fact more so. Look at a sick woman suffering from some opinion that the doctors have made her believe, see the mind completely under the doctor, she is not allowed to eat or drink or even walk or think except as the family physician gives direction. The sick have given their souls to the priests and their bodies to the physicians. They then tell about the good doctor, how much he has done for them, showing that he has deprived them of all noble manly feelings, left them sick, feeble in mind and body, while the doctor struts around like a slave-driver, and the sick curl under the lash of their tongue, as the negroes under the lash of their masters. This may seem strange, but it is God's truth, that the sick are a mere tool in the hands of the medical faculty, to be treated just as they please. It never will be any better till the sick rise in their wisdom and declare their independence. You may say I am making war for my own gain, but I think I can convince any one who is out from under these slave drivers, that I could make ten dollars where I now make one. My object is to raise my fellow man to his original state. I am a white abolitionist. The blacks it is true are slaves, but their slavery is a blessing compared with that of the sick. I have seen many a white slave that would change places with the black. The only difference is that white slavery is sanctioned by public opinion. But make the slave know that he is one, and you will see a difference in the result. It is hard for me to keep myself in bounds when I think of the groans of the sick, knowing that it is all the effect of a superstitious ignorance. Does not the South quote the Bible to prove that slavery is of Divine origin? Do not the priests and doctors quote the old heathen superstition to bolster up a weak and feeble edifice just ready to crumble and crush the leaders? Is not Science raising her voice and crying aloud to the people saying how long shall it be till the old heathen idolatry shall come to an end and man shall learn wisdom and be his own master and not a slave? (9)

MIND AND DISEASE

Men create ideas which are matter. These ideas have a real existence in the spiritual world, and their power is according to the nature that is attributed to them, and the fear that men have of them. Fear of an idea thus created, on the part of its creator, condenses its matter so that it might be seen even by the natural eye, a creation composed of the loathsome characteristics conceived of by the person's own belief, an offspring of an excited and degraded mind. Such an idea is disease, the child of the devil. This disease was first one simple, uncompounded idea. But when that finally was pushed into an identity, when men were once afraid of it, then it grew rapidly, like a poisonous weed, and derived its sustenance from the very life-blood to which it owed its existence. All its horrible characteristics it draws from the mind of men, who, could they only understand what they are doing, would plant a good seed in their soil or mind, which could bear no fruit fit for disease to live on, and thus it would starve to death. . . . As mind is matter, its form can be annihilated.

The basis of Dr. Quimby's theory is that there is no intelligence, no power or action in matter of itself, that the spiritual world to which our eyes are closed by ignorance or unbelief is the real world, that in it lie all the causes for every effect visible in the natural world, and that if this spiritual life can be revealed to us, in other words if we can understand ourselves, we shall then have our happiness or misery in our own hands; and of course much of the suffering of the world will be done away with.

He does not deny that cures, as many and great as you please to claim, have taken place under the old belief, but that they were brought about by the inherent efficacy of the medicine itself he does deny.

He admits the possibility of a derangement of the bodily organs, but it is in regard to the cause of this effect that he differs from all others. Doctors consider the cause of disease to lie in the body, while he does not. The doctors have set up a standard of right and wrong with regard to health, and have made the people accept and believe it, and now disease comes from the belief in this.

When our belief embraces disease, we must be liable to it. Consumption will be in the world as long as people are under their present rulers. But when they come to understand that matter is nothing of itself except it be used by mind, and everything that is embraced in this, then consumption will no longer be in existence.

It is hard to talk about it before the science is admitted. . . . It is nothing more than or less than the Christian religion rendered intelligible by being revealed as a Science.

Happiness is not dependent on externals, but lies within us, and is the consciousness of keeping our loftier impulses free from contamination, and revealing in our acts a strength which arises from uncorrupted motives.

Disease is the effect of a wrong direction given to the mind. Unhappiness is its handmaid.

By "spiritual matter" Dr. Quimby does not mean the matter which is visible to the natural eye, but a matter which can be changed into any form which a person chooses. This mind or matter surrounds every person, and contains an expression of character. You know how often in sitting down by a person we have different impressions. For instance, we say such a person is disagreeable, another is gentle, a third selfish; and these impressions we have without being able to account for them in any way to ourselves or others. We should have had the same if we had been blind. Now that which we perceive without the aid of the natural senses is the mind or spiritual matter, or atmosphere or vapor, or whatever you choose to call it, that surrounds every one and is an index of character. This is what we come in contacts with in our intercourse with men, and through this medium we influence others and are influenced ourselves. It contains opinions, thoughts, and everything in us which can be changed.

What we know we have no opinion about. That is eternal and never can be changed. What we do not know, if we have ever been excited on the subject, we have some opinion or belief about, and that opinion or belief may be the cause of unhappiness.

In order that a disease shall be created, a shock must first be produced. You cannot move anything unless you first start it. There must be a shock, be it ever so slight, a little excitement, fright, pleasure, anything which would produce a disturbance in the system. When thus disturbed, the natural heat of the body always either increases or diminishes. Suppose you turn red. A stranger meets you and says you look flushed. That would not be likely to take down your color but would increase it. After two or three remarks of that kind you would begin to feel uncomfortable, your head would feel hot, and the heat might be so great that you would have pain, and presently you would be informed that you look feverish. That would keep up the excitement, and when you went out of doors you would be likely to cough from the irritation caused by, the upward tendency of the heat. That would frighten you a little, though you might not own it or know it. But the disturbance would keep up till some kind friend should inform you that you had taken cold, for your face was flushed and you coughed. That, mind you, is an opinion, for a person may flush and cough from excitement without any cold at all. Now you only need a little help from mistaken friends and a finishing touch from a doctor to put you into a lung, brain, or any other kind of fever they please. That, to use a very simple case, is the way a disease is made. The countless opinions we are brought up with, and believe as much as we do in our existence, of course affect us, and we have a body according to our belief. The belief comes first, then the system changes accordingly.

Even before the child is born, it is affected by the mother, and receives its mental and physical constitution from her. After it has taken up existence on its own account, it is still affected by her, whether she speaks or not. The greater number of influences which act upon us do not come through the natural senses, and are all the more dangerous of course because unknown.

One object of Dr. Quimby's theory is to bring our spiritual existence to our senses, or rather to prove that our senses are not located in the body as we think they are. Thus we shall be able to protect ourselves.

By thoughts we are all affected, and even by the settled opinions of people, whether they trouble themselves to apply them to our case or not.

Dr. Quimby never accuses any one of imagining that they are sick. He admits every sensation that a person may claim. Indeed he takes their feelings himself, so he has positive proof that they exist independently of what the patient says. You tell me I "look sick." I say I do not feel sick, in fact I don't know what you mean by the word, so you have to invent some story to tell me or explain by some intelligent sign. I lay my hand on my left side, you ask me what I feel. Now if I had never heard of sickness or disease, I should not know what to say, neither would I be frightened, so it would pass off without anything of any account. But you tell me that people. often die with just such a feeling as I have. This starts me, although I have no idea what you mean, my feelings not containing danger or trouble, but your opinions trouble me exceedingly. I begin now to twist and turn, not knowing what to do. This convinces you that I have disease of the heart and you try to explain to me what I have and how it affects a person. By mesmerizing me into your belief you disturb my mind and create the very idea you have invented, and at last I die just as you foretold. All this is disease and you made it. If I had never seen you nor any one wiser than myself I should not have died.

Notes

(1) That is, his bondage to opinion, his mistaken view of his body, and its supposed tendencies to disease.
(2) This was written in 1865,
(3) This was written, Dec. 1862.
(4) Quimby sincerely believed in the real spiritual world of the living, in contrast with "the other world" of the dead.
(5) Written, 1861.
(6) Published in part in "The Philosophy of P. P. Quimby," 1895.
(7) This is the kind of statement a critic distorted into the notion that Dr. Quimby did not know how he cured.
(8) 1864
(9) Nov., 1861.

Chapter Seventeen – God and Man

WHAT is disease? This question involves much speculative reasoning. Some suppose that disease is independent of man; some think it is a punishment from God for the wrongs of our first parents; others that it comes from disobeying the laws of God. Now let us analyze the above and see if there is any truth in these statements. If there were not a living creature on earth then there could not be any disease. Otherwise disease must have had an existence before man was created, and, if so, God created it for some purpose. According to man's reasoning disease is his enemy and if God created an enemy to destroy man, God cannot be man's friend as is thought. Thus the idea that a benevolent God had anything to do with disease is a superstition; then the question comes up again, where does it come from? I answer, it does not come, it is created, not by God, but by man.

We have not a true idea of God. God is not a man any more than man is a Principle. When we speak of God we are taught to believe in a Person, so we attach our ideas to a Person called God and then talk about His laws and the violation of them is said to be our trouble. How often we hear these words: "If a man would obey all the laws of God he would never be sick." But the acknowledgment of the error is the cause of nine-tenths of our sickness. When God's law is [deemed] so severe that man is liable to be put into prison for committing an act or even thinking a thought not in accord with the law, it is no wonder people murmur and complain. The Christian's God is a tyrant of the worst kind.

God is the name of a man's belief and our senses are attached to our opinions about our belief or God. The God of the savages is their belief; the God of the Mohammedans is their belief, and so on to the Christian's God. The Christian's God like themselves is like a house divided against itself. The God of the North and the God of the South are as much at war as the Christian worshippers; each prays to God for help and each condemns the other. Thus it is plain that gods of this kind are a farce and all our worship of such is from a superstitious fear of a tyrant whose name we dare not take in vain. The time will come when the true God will be worshipped in spirit and truth, for God is a Spirit and not a man. Wisdom is the sower and God the vineyard, and as man is made in the image of God his [inner] mind is spirit and receives the seed of Wisdom.

Wisdom has no laws, it is the true light. The law of man is the invention of evil thoughts. In proportion as Wisdom is in us the law is dead. So to be wise is to be dead to the law, for law is man's belief and Wisdom is of God or Science. Now if we could understand the true idea of causes and effects, we could learn where the true cause of disease originated.

Man has invented a God according to his belief so that God is the embodiment of man's belief. As man's belief changes so his God changes, but the true God never changes. So the wisdom of man condensed into a being called God is set up for the ignorant to worship, and as all men have been made to acknowledge what they have no proof of the idea of a personal God is received, so that no one questions the identity of such a being. This God was made up for the wisdom of the heathen world and we have revered and worshipped it not from love, but from fear. Its only opponent is Science, so as Science enters this God gives way, but not without a struggle. The true God is not acknowledged by this man's God, but it is in the hearts of the people working like leaven till it leavens the whole lump. It is called by the children of this world of opinions infidelity. So to be an infidel is to question the God of man's opinions. Jesus saw through all this hypocrisy, that the God of the heathen was not the God of peace, but of war, and this same God is worshipped now as then. He is called on now [1861] more than he has been since the American revolution. He is the most convenient God I know of. He listens to the North and the South and leads their men on to battle and from the prayers of his followers is as much interested in the victory as the winning party. All this sort of cant is kept up with a certain solemnity of form as though there were real truth in it. But the time will come when all this must give way to a higher worship, for it is a vain worship that shows itself in every church in Christendom. They worship they know not what. This false idea is the foundation on which the Christian world stands and the waters that flow from this fountain are corrupt, for where the foundation is corrupt the stream is also. When the angel of truth disturbs the waters they throw forth every kind of corruption, this poisons the minds of the multitudes and makes them sick. The true wisdom like Science explains away this earthly God and brings man into a more happy state where opinions give way to facts.

1.   In the preceding article I asked the question, what is disease? And in that I gave the cause. Now I will describe how it is brought about and the cure. I said that God was the embodiment of man's belief or opinions. These opinions have been forced on man like burdens, till the people have had to yield to their weight and make the best of it. Yet they murmur and complain but dare not raise their voice in support of the God of wisdom. Opinions of themselves have no element of adhesion, therefore their life depends on coercion. So laws are established and penalties attached and if the people grumble, laws and penalties are applied, sanctioned by God, and you are told of the laws of God, while this same God is only the embodiment of their opinions reduced to a law. Disease is the result of disobeying these laws, so man is made to believe a lie that he may be condemned to disease. For instance, we are often told that if we go out and expose ourselves to God's cold or law we shall be sick. Here man makes God the author of his own act that he sometimes cannot help and then punishes him for disobeying it. If he exposes himself he dare not find fault with the punishment, so he lives all his life subject to a tyrant that will take advantage of his ignorance to torment him. This belief makes him a servant to sin and to man's opinion. So his life is in the hands of priests and doctors to be handled to suit their convenience. Thus man is a mere lump of clay in the hands of blind guides and whatever they say to the people they believe. Their beliefs disturb their minds and the doctors sow the seed of disease which they nurse till it grows to a belief, then comes the misery.

Now the God I worship has no fellowship with man's opinions, so to cure the disease is to break in pieces his opinions. This places man on his own wisdom, independent of man's God or opinions. Then he sees the one living and true God who rewards every one according to his acts, not his beliefs. To believe in this God is to know ourselves and that is the religion of Christ. It is Christ in us, not opinions that we are in. Just as we know this truth we are of and a part of God; then we become joint heirs of God and will be guided by the wisdom of the Father of all Truth. This purifies and cleanses our minds from all opinions and leads us into the world of Science where opinions never come. There one man shall not lead us by his opinions, but if one says "here is the truth," let him prove it. This raises man to a higher self-respect, and if man does not respect himself he cannot complain if others do not respect him.

All nations have a God according to their belief. A belief contains no wisdom but is a shadow of something that cannot be seen, worshipped by man who knows not what it is. This something is what the world of opinions reasons about. The Jews prophesied about it, looking for its coming as for a man of great power who would free them from the Roman yoke. Heathen nations had a vague idea of this something. They incorporated it into their beliefs as a monarch or king. So it has always been in the world or in man's belief, but man knows it not. Even to the wise it is a stranger. It has no place in their hearts or in the religious world except as an unexplained mystery. It comes to man's senses but man knows it not. It stands knocking at the door but it is not recognized as having an identity; so it is mocked at, spit upon, hated and despised by all men. Yet it is always the same, calm and unmoved, sympathizing with its friends, who are bound down by the opinions of this world's belief.

Now, what is it? It is an invisible Wisdom which never can be seen by the eye of opinion, any more than truth can be seen by error, for when the truth comes the opinion or matter is seen to be the shadow of this Light or Substance that I call something. Again, what is it? If I should tell you what it is you would ask for proof, so I will give the proof of it from your own opinion. Still what is it? It is what never has been acknowledged to have an identity. Then what is it that has been admitted but cannot be seen and yet is not acknowledged to have an identity? Can the reader answer? "Yes, it is God." I ask, Is God without an identity? You say no. Then it is not God. What then is it? I will try and tell you and bring the opinions of the world to prove my answer. It is the key that unlocks the innermost secrets of the heart in the prison of man's belief, and it leads the prisoner who has been bound a captive to health. Opinions are like a shadow, the substance is God. True wisdom is attached to the substance; false wisdom to the shadow. Language is attached to the shadow, which is attached to the substance; language is not in harmony with wisdom; and the discord lies in opinion. If the senses are attached to opinion, when the opinion is lost man loses his opinion but not his senses or life, for his life is his wisdom or self-existence. . . .

This something is a knowledge of this wisdom which puts man in possession of a truth that he can explain to another. It does not come to the man of opinions. This shows that every man has two selves, one acknowledged by the natural man, the other by the spiritual man. Here is the proof. The sick will admit that I can tell them how they feel better than they themselves can do. This shows that I know more than they do and also that this wisdom by which I tell these things is not known by the natural man.

To give the proof I must make the reader detach his senses from a God of man's belief and attach them to this invisible Wisdom which fills all space, and whose attributes are all light, all wisdom, all goodness and love, which is free from all selfishness and hypocrisy, which makes or breaks no laws, but lets man work out his own salvation; which has no laws, and restrictions and sanctions men's acts according to their belief, and holds them responsible for their belief, right or wrong, without respect to persons. For the natural man is only a shadow of man's wisdom, and if the shadow is from this world of opinions it will be destroyed when the light of the Wisdom comes. But the life will be saved, and when the senses shall be attached to this Wisdom, then shall be brought to pass that saying, "Oh! death! where is thy sting! Oh, grave! where is thy victory!" Death is robbed of its victim, the grave gives up its idea of death. Then life rises to that happy state where death, hell, and disease and the torments of existence find no place, from whence no traveler ever returns but where man knows himself. This wisdom teaches him that when our senses are attached to opinions of any kind we become the subject of that opinion and suffer according to the penalty attached to it, unless forgiven or the debt paid by the truth.

This is the new truth spoken of by Jesus; to know this is to have eternal life and the life is the wisdom that can enter the dark prisons of man's mind and find his life imprisoned by the opinions of this world and there hear his groans, feel his sorrows and break the prison walls of his belief and set him free. When a person professes this Wisdom and attaches his life to it, his life is to him a blessing, for it is of use to man. Then he is happiest when relieving those who have fallen into trouble or into the hands of thieves, who have been robbed of their substance and imprisoned in a creed, there to languish from the wounds of the priests and doctors till the angel of Wisdom or the tide of progress, forced along by popular opin-ions, shall beat against the walls of this superstition and break down the medical opinions, lay priestcraft low and overflow the superstitious world with Science and good order. Then all men will be judged by what they know and all can prove themselves by this standard.

2.   Every science has its standard, based on actual knowl-edge, not on opinion. I say nothing about such, for they prove their wisdom by their works. But it is of false standards with no evidence of truth except the misery they produce that I shall speak. The two most dangerous to the happiness of man are those of medical science and the priests. These two classes are the foundation of more misery than all other evils, for they have such a strong hold on the minds of the people by their deception and cant. They claim all the virtue and wisdom of the nation, and have so deceived the people that their claims are acknowledged in war and peace. Let us analyze the beliefs of these guides. Take the medical man, what is his science except that of killing human beings?

Is the world wiser by their opinions? Do not the very medical men themselves recommend to the people not to read medical books? Does the mathematician warn the people to keep clear of mathematical books? Is not the world wiser, better and more enlightened by them? Is the world made wiser or better by quack medicine or opinions of the faculty? Are not their opinions like the locusts of Egypt in everything you eat and drink? Science and progress have had to fight both theories ever since the world began to think and act.

It is a common saying that the religious and Christian souls are the foundation of God's moral government, but let us see if it is not the reverse. Take the North and South of this American Republic as specimens of mankind. According to religious statistics, the South is more religious than the North, for all religion is confined to sectarian creeds. For instance, how long is it since the Unitarians were admitted as Christians? Even now the Universalists are scarcely ad-mitted within the pale of Christianity. The religion of which I speak and with which Science and revelation has had to contend includes more of the liberal classes. Show me where the people are called the most intelligent. It is in New England. This mixing up of religion and science is like establishing honor among thieves. Religion and politics always went together, but Science, progress and good order never had anything to do with either.

Religion was what crucified Christ. Pilate's wisdom found no fault with Him, but the religion of the priests said "crucify him." Paul had this idea of religion when he said to the Athenians, "I perceive you are altogether too religious or superstitious." Then he goes on to show them how their religion led them to worship this something of which I am talking, so he said, "This something that you so ignorantly worship, I declare unto you." Here you see that Paul was not a religious man, but was converted from a man of religious and superstitious opinions to a man of science and progress and he showed that this, something was not far off, though the religious world did not know it. And the world will never know it till wisdom separates religion and politics from the scientific world. All Science is spiritual and is not known by the priests and demagogues or doctors. The theories of these three classes are not based on wisdom but on opinions. Wisdom is the solid or substance. Matter or mind is the shadow of the spirit of real wisdom. Now put man in possession of this wisdom so that he can make an application of it for the benefit of the suffering community, then this wisdom will soon separate the chaff from the wheat.

3.   All the parables were intended to illustrate the two prin-ciples, truth and error. Truth is the wisdom of God; error is the god of opinions, and the two have no dealing with each other. Each has his disciples, the God of opinion and the God of science or love; but their acts are so different that their characters can be easily explained. I will give you the religious or political god. He is represented as watching the movements of the armies and dictating to the heads of the nation. No one approaches him except the ordained priest. He takes particular care of the president and the heads of departments, in fact he is ruler and dictator of all things. But he must be approached with as much reverence as a king. The South have another god, not so great, according to the account of Jeff Davis; he seems to be of a lower intellect for he sanctions this low guerilla warfare and a kind of cruelty which is only practised by the Indians. These are the gods of the religious world.

Now where is the God in whose wisdom I believe? He is in the hearts of the people. He is not a man, neither has He form, He is neither male nor female. I will give you an il-lustration of His wisdom. If you see a man in trouble you are or you are not bound to help him. If you have admitted it right to help a man in distress then He will put you in mind of your agreement. If you neglect your duty, punishment must follow, for that action and reaction are equal is a truth which never varies. This embraces the law and the gospel, and on this hangs all man's happiness and misery. If man is governed by this truth, it develops his higher wisdom and enables him to prove all things by a standard based not on opinions but on truth. All man's happiness or misery is in keeping or breaking this agreement. Now if a man is in trouble, although you may bind yourself to help him to the best of your ability, if you do not know it you cannot be punished. . . . This higher law is not known as having any responsibilities, but it is the most perfect of all laws. It is very little understood, and not at all intelligently. To understand it intelligently is to make it your rule of action with the sick, or those in trouble, for the well are not bound by it.

I will show how a well person is not bound by this higher wisdom. Suppose a person is sick or in great distress. A well person sees the sick one but cannot feel his aches and pains. Then he is not bound to relieve him. In order that a person in trouble may be bound so that he is responsible for his acts, he must be born again as it is said of Christ so that he can feel another's feelings. Then he knows what the world of opinions is ignorant of. Here he stands in relation to the sick as one man stands to another of the natural world who is in trouble. I will take myself as one risen from these dead ideas or opinions into that higher kingdom of wisdom where my acts have as much restriction over my life as they have over the well.

I will here say a word or two which the well must take as an opinion but which the sick will admit as a truth. The sick are imprisoned for their belief; the imprisonment is what they suffer. When I come in contact with them they affect me not in the way one man of opinion affects another. Their language is different. The well speak in my own tongue, but the sick cannot do that for the language of the well cannot describe the feeling of the sick. Thus they are prisoners in their own land, among strangers and not understood.

4.   I will illustrate the manner in which the sick express themselves. Ideas or thoughts are matter or opinions. These opinions are in the world of matter and our senses or life are attached to our belief or opinion. As opinions are something believed and admitted they become matter according to the wisdom of the world. Thus the priests invent creeds with penalties attached to their disobedience and the doctors invent diseases with other penalties. The teachers of the young are instructed to establish the sayings of the priests and doctors in the children's minds. Now everyone knows if he will stop and think that if a child when it is first born is given to the savages it will grow up one and with all the peculiarities of one, or nearly so; this proves that the life of the child is attached to the belief of the savage and the child has become subject to its teachers. In the same way religion or belief in another world is binding on the child and the penalties of the doctors' belief are also binding. Suppose you bring the same child into our country at the age of a man, will anyone say or believe that he is bound in his conscience to obey the laws of our priests and doctors? I think not. This then shows that the child's mind or wisdom can be moulded into a savage and if this can be done it will not require a great stretch of imagination to make a disease. Just admit this child's mind as matter. According to common belief every form of matter can make a shadow according to its identity or description. For instance, consumption is a belief, this belief is matter and throws off a shadow. As life is in the senses and the senses are in the mind or matter, they are all associated together; here is where the mistake lies.

I will make an illustration to show where the mind affects the senses or life and yet you will see they are different. Suppose you are ignorant of the effect of a charcoal fire. You sit down in a room, the heat affects the mind or matter; all this contains no intelligence. At last the life is disturbed, just as the cold would be and would wish to rid itself of the sensation of heat. The senses being attached to life become disturbed. Opinions enter which are like more coal and increase the heat or excitement. Reason which is another ele-ment of fire fans the flames till life and the senses are so affected that they will not remain. This is disease. Suppose I come in; the instant the heat affects my mind my wisdom communicates to my senses [consciousness] the cause and the remedy. My senses become composed, my wisdom directs my senses, and they act on the body; the door is opened, the trouble is explained, the patient is saved from his torment, his mind or opinion is destroyed, but his life is saved and his trouble is at an end. Opinions are the elements used to torment life or the senses. They contain no wisdom above the brute, but are matter and can be destroyed. All the opinions of the priests are condensed into a solid according to their belief, and although they cannot be seen by the natural eye, the eye of opinion can see them and lead the senses that are attached to the opinion to the locality where the beliefs are. For instance, the priests tell their hearers that there is another world separate from this. They give such a glowing account of it that their opinions like fuel set fire to the audience and a chemical change takes place; their minds are disturbed like mortar and their senses are affected by the opinions of the priests and an expedition is fitted out to go to this world, which is actually created by the priests' opinions. The minds are so disturbed that the life, losing its relish for this world, is persuaded to embark for the world of the priests' opinions, to which their thoughts are attached. Their senses are held between two opinions, not knowing what to do; this is called by the doctors "disease of the mind." They, not knowing the cause of the trouble take the story of the patient, who also being ignorant, is ready to be deceived by the ignorance of the doctor. So the doctor, like the priest, gets up a false idea of disease and engrafts into the patient's belief a new idea of some disease which affects the body. Then he reasons till it takes root in the mind and comes forth in the image of its father. The life or senses are then attached and the thing is brought to the doctor to receive a name. So after he examines it he gives it the name of cancer. The patient now wants to know what is to be done. The doctor gives the punishment of such a disease; this troubles the life or senses so that life wants to leave the opinions of the doctor or cancer and escape to the priests' world where they are told that diseases never come. Here they are halting between two opinions; this last stand is called a real disease of the body. Now these two blind guides quarrel with each other. The doctor accuses the priest of frightening the patient and the priest accuses the doctor of the same. Between the two a war is made and the whole world is affected by their opinions. Parties spring up, reason is brought to inflame the minds and the weakest portion of the people are disturbed till the whole world of man's mind is overrun with false theories.

5.   In the darkness of this superstition, when all are either sleeping or ignorant of the danger that awaits them and the sentinels on the watch tower of those minds that see the craft of these two classes are warning the multitude of the danger, when the enemies of Science and progress are mustering the thoughts of the scientific world and casting every one into prison for their belief, I enter this land of darkness with the light of liberty, search out the dungeons where the lives of sick are bound, enter them and set the prisoners free. These prisons, like the prisons of this world, can be detected by the atmosphere or description. I have said all diseases were opinions condensed into an idea of matter that can be seen by the eye of Wisdom. In like manner all ideas of the priests can be seen, each throws off its shadow or spiritual matter, and each has its particular odor, so that it can be detected as easily by the eye of Wisdom as an apple or an orange can be detected by the eye of opinion. . . .

To be in a state to become a teacher of this unknown God is what never has been acknowledged by the opinions of man's wisdom. Thousands of persons have undertaken to pene-trate this land of mystery and have returned with the idea that they have made the discovery and thus have deceived many people, broken up families, led the weak and timid, stimulated the strong, till the people, like the children of Israel, have left their happy land or state of mind to follow these blind guides, and the v have wandered so far from health or home that they have lost their way and fallen among strangers or doctors, who pretending to be their friends have robbed them of their happiness and left them like the prodigal son sick and disheartened in this land of superstition. Like Moses, I enter this land and lead them out, and as I pass through the sea of blood or beliefs of those blind guides I feed them with the bread of wisdom and smite the rock of truth and the water or wisdom gushes out and cools the parched tongues. I go before them in this wilderness, holding up the (priests,) serpent or creed, and all that listen to my explanation are healed from the bite of these creeds. The people murmur and complain, some call me humbug and quack; others want to return to their old ideas of religion, but I stand up and entreat them, stimulating them to press forward and not to give up till I have restored them once more to the happy land of health whence they have been decoyed away. So I am hated by some, laughed at by others, spit upon by the doctors, and sneered at by the priest, but received into the arms of the sick who know me.

6.   Perhaps by this time it would be well to sum up all this journey, describing how I entered this land and how I passed through it. I will do so in a few words. After I found that mind was spiritual matter I found that ideas were matter, condensed into a solid called disease, and that this, like a book contained all the wisdom of its author. Seeing the book (for sight with Wisdom embraces all senses; hearing, tasting, etc.) I open it and see through it. To the patient it is a sealed book but to Wisdom there is nothing hid which cannot be revealed or seen, nor so far off that it cannot be reached. So I read the contents of the book to the patient and show that it is false, then as the truth changes his mind light takes the place of darkness, till he sees through the error of disease. The light of Wisdom dissipates the matter, or disease, the patient once more finds himself freed of opinions and happiness is restored. What I have said is produced on me by the patient, by lighting up the mind and making the patient clairvoyant, so that he sees through the priests' and doctors' opinion. This dissipates the opinion, for it is nothing but a shadow taken for a substance and the misery comes from mistaking the opinion for a truth; here is the trouble that arises from opinions. Now let men cease from giving opinions or let the people understand that there is no wisdom in one, then you shut the mouths of these barking dogs, howling night and day, which keep the people in constant excitement.

How often you hear this expression used, "such a person murders the King's English" This I admit may be the case, if language is applied to the things of this natural world, but if it is to be applied to the spiritual world, or to ideas that cannot be seen by the natural man, then I beg leave to differ from the knowledge of this world, for I know that in such a case the world cannot judge of the correctness of language. In the first place a healthy person is not a judge of a sick person's feelings. Therefore, if anyone gives a name to a feeling which a sick person has he names a sensation that he knows nothing of except as described by the sick. In this there is no standard of right or wrong that the people can agree upon. So every one sets up his own standard of right and wrong, and if a person is ever so sensitive to another's feelings, he must use such terms as the world admits, or he is ignorant of the King's English. So the invisible things must be judged by the visible. Here is a great mistake, for if the learned had to prove to the unlearned everything they said, it would be as hard as for those who are sensitive to feelings of the sick to prove them to the learned. Who is to say what God is? Webster, Worcester, or any author, unless he can give some evidence that comes within a person's feeling or senses? Here is where the trouble commences, with the idea of God. What is God? This is the question, and let man come forward and show who and what God is.

The word God is the name of something material or im-material. If He is material

then God can be seen by the material eyes, and if He is immaterial, the natural man cannot see Him. So that if His name sprang from the natural man, he gives a name of something that he knows nothing of. Therefore one man's opinion is as good as another's, till some one can give the substance or impression that caused the word to be applied. Now suppose that man calls Wisdom the First Cause, and that from this Wisdom there issues forth an es-sence that fills all space, like the odor of a rose. This essence, like the odor, contains the character or wisdom of its father, or author, and man's wisdom wants a name given to it, so man calls this essence God. Then you have wisdom manifest in God or the essence, then this essence would be called the Son of Wisdom. Then Wisdom said, "let us create matter or mind or man in our image," or in the likeness of this essence or God. So they formed man out of the odor called matter or dust, that rises from the grosser matter, and breathed into him the living essence, or God, and the matter took the form of man.

ON WISDOM

Perfect wisdom embraces every idea in existence, and therefore every idea that comes to light through the senses existed before to Wisdom. Every person who was or ever will be existed as much before he ever came to our senses as afterwards, the same as any mathematical truth. Alan's intelligence is a truth that existed before he took form or was seen by the natural eye. Man's body is only a machine and its senses are its medium to wisdom. The real man is never seen by the natural senses, but the real man makes him-self known through Science to his natural senses, as a person who knows a fact can teach it to another. Wisdom or knowledge he teaches through Science, and he uses his senses to explain this Science, for his senses are all the medium the natural man knows. The real man is God, or the First Cause. Every idea that man embraces comes through his natural senses, but this real man is not seen, but is truth or Wisdom. The natural man may be compared to a checker board, and Science and opinion the players. Public opinion or common sense stands looking on and represents spectators. The Wisdom that is superior is that which sees and knows the principle of the game. Now opinion makes a move, and the natural man or common sense says it cannot be bettered. But Science sees the working of opinion, and makes him move in such a way as to compel his opponent to destroy himself, for he knows that opinion knows nothing as he should know it. Every move of opinion suggests his opponent's move. So if one knows his game and the other does not, the ignorant one is beaten every time. But if both are ignorant they think they play a very scientific game. Now there are certain games or arguments which men play called theories, that have no foundation or basis, and there is no way to test them, because one is not the least above his neighbor and neither can prove anything.

THE CHRISTIANS GOD

I will now sum up by introducing the Gods of the two foregoing theories and as one of them is only man's opinion, I will introduce a priest, a doctor, and the law as the God-head, for the three are equal in power. Religion is the father, medicine is the son, and law is the Holy Ghost, or explanation. All these make up the Godhead of our superstitious belief. These two first give the people their beliefs, which are sanctioned by an appearance of divine wisdom, and according to their belief acknowledged by the wisdom of the father of all. Strange as this may seem, it is the foundation of all the misery that man suffers. Although we are taught to love and re-spect this man's God, as the giver of everything we receive, yet if one half of what we attribute to Him were true, He would be of all tyrants the worst. If we should look upon a parent as we are taught to look upon God, we should hate our very parents. Let us see what kind of God He is and how He compares with a parent. In the first place, He is represented as knowing all our acts and having a watchful care over us like a good father. Now if any parent could have half the power that they say God has over His children, His children would curse Him to his face and look upon Him as a tyrant. Now all this talk about a God who reasons and makes bargains accompanied by rewards and punishments is so much like the natural man's wisdom that no one can help seeing that our Christian God is the embodiment of man's belief when man was far behind the present generation. (1) No attribute of their God shows any wisdom, but a sweeping idea of everything when His wisdom or acts are spoken of; it is like a military officer, or some grand monarch, or king. He is king of kings, the great High Priest. Once it was the height of honor to be a military officer, for that was the greatest of all professions; therefore God must be a military character, for the Bible says He had war in heaven. The devil was the first secessionist we find and he was driven out of heaven. You never hear God compared to a statesman or any learned man. It is true that when He came to earth some eighteen hundred years ago in the person of Jesus, He was not represented as a military character but was far superior to the wise. He was called a very simple man, uneducated, full of sympathy, so He must have come down since the writers of the Old Testament. How natural it is for man to court the company of the great, especially the military. Aristocracy would not have anything to do with Jesus because he had none of the military turn of mind. Their superstition could not account for His cures, so they had no claim on Him. The wise of this world who base their theory on opinions steal all they can from their neighbors, and when Jesus was crucified they stole His ideas and engrafted them into their aristocratic creeds. This kept them aloof from the masses and God was not permitted to associate with the people but could only communicate through the priest what information they got from heaven.

We all really believe more of this than we are willing to acknowledge and it keeps the people in bondage under the priests. The burden of false ideas makes men nervous and superstitious. This gets their systems in a condition for another swarm of hungry dogs called doctors who invent diseases, make the people admit their opinions, and after their opinions are admitted then they are ready to bring about any disease that can be introduced to them. As people cannot see how disease is made, this false theory has always led the people and always will till the true idea is explained how disease is made. According to my theory, all errors can be explained on scientific truths, so that man can be his own doctor and priest and he shall not say to his neighbor, "Know you the Lord?" but all shall know Him from the least to the greatest. This theory will explain all the phenomenon. If you read the first article in Vol. I you will see that according to that theory mind can be changed and any kind of an idea produced. So apply this truth to the mind, and you can cure or correct the error and establish the truth. (2)

MAN

What truth did Jesus come to bring to the world? One simple fact that man is a progressive being, that his happiness and misery are of his own make, that his belief is his wisdom and if founded on an opinion it is liable to make him unhappy. To separate the truth from the error is a Science the knowledge of which teaches how to correct an error or disease, and in this knowledge is eternal life. Jesus never intended to teach the people a belief in another world, His words and acts showed them that their beliefs were false, and that they were the cause of their misery, but this they could not understand, and being in their belief, their belief became part of their identity. As they were taught to believe in spirits their misery was attributed to them, and as error begets error the people were tormented by their own beliefs. It never entered into the minds of these blind leaders that as a man sows so shall he reap; that action and reaction are equal.

Knowledge of science was not general, and the possibility that the belief of man had anything to do with his health was not dreamed of. All that was believed was something that could not be seen, so the prophets prophesied of some one coming from heaven. Now if heaven had not been something that people believed in away and apart from this earth it would not have been in the prophecies. So this heaven was an established fact and all their controversies were in regard to it. They introduced all sorts of mediums who purported to come from and have communication with that place. There was the dwelling of God and all religious theories were based upon the belief that there was another world where God dwelt and where He ordered all things according to His own will.

Absurd as this is, a man is made of this composition, for man is only a mass of ideas combined together by a wisdom superior to the matter of which the ideas are formed.

Science is not recognized in this belief for it belongs to that class of minds which have never risen to a state where they can discern that man perceives anything independently of his natural senses. To this class of minds whatever is not established is a mystery. If a lead ball is thrown into the water it sinks to the bottom, that is a fact; if a wooden ball is also thrown into the water it floats, and then comes the mystery. A medium from the other world is required to explain the phenomenon; argument is of no force, the explanation must come from God, and thus it is with every mysterious phenomenon: supernatural power only can explain it. Thus man is kept constantly excited to understand every little thing that happens. He never has thought that heaven and hell were part of his belief and consequently part of himself, but he believes that these two places are independent of himself and he is liable to go to one or the other after he is dead. So he lives in hell all his life trying to get to heaven, but he never gets there for it is always at a distance, and he is looking for a saviour to save him from hell.

How often we hear very good people say that they are weary of this wicked world and long to be with Christ, showing that they are not with Him now but hope to be. Their faith contains a belief, not a substance. The faith that is of man is merely a belief in something not obtained, for when the substance is obtained their faith or belief is lost in the substance, and they have what they hope for. Jesus' faith was the substance of our belief and that substance was Christ. The Christ or faith is intended to be applied to man, and Jesus put this in practice for our happiness. The question arises, has the Christ an identity? I answer it has; it is all that ever had an unchangeable identity, it is Wisdom itself. But the Christian's faith is an opinion about this Wisdom. I have said that the faith of Jesus had an identity and to this His senses were attached. Then Jesus could say to His faith, "Father forgive them, for they know not what they do." What did this Christ strive to do? It strove to enter the heart of man and teach him to break away from his errors and learn the truth. Jesus taught Christ and put it in practice by His words. Do the Christians the same? No, they preach about it. So their faith is not of works but a belief. The world is no wiser or better for it. To prove your faith in music is to play a tune on an instrument by your faith or science, not to talk about music, telling how beautiful it is. The Science of Health which Jesus taught was practised by His faith or wisdom, and His instrument was man. He took man after he had been beaten, bruised and deceived by the priests and doctors, and applied His Science or Christ to put man in tune so that he could sing psalms to the one loving and true Science, and appreciate Jesus; for "He hath opened the seventh seal," that which can correct the errors of man who shall be saved from disease and misery.

How does Jesus stand by the side of His pretended followers? He talked and taught His Christ to the people, priests and doctors talk about it. Here is a vast difference. Jesus put intelligence in the Christ or Science; the Christians put no intelligence in Christ or Science, but apply all the intelligence to Jesus, calling the Christ a "power." This difference has always been kept up; the natural man cannot see intelligence in anything he cannot understand, therefore Christ or the intelligence of Jesus is to him a mystery, and he wants to know whence it came. This ignorance on the part of the priests and the people originated all this speculation about Jesus. The Christ or higher intelligence to them was shrouded in darkness, for they could not see why He, merely a man, should be more than a man.

Every one knows that a clairvoyant state is different from the natural state. Let me illustrate what all will admit. Persons in a clairvoyant state can talk, using the same organs as when awake, they also have every faculty which they possess in the waking state, independent of the natural body, and space and time may or may not be annihilated. They act independently of any one, independently of the natural body or identity of flesh and blood. Now where is the identity when the natural man is acting, for both cannot be acting at the same time? Every one will perceive that if a man could retain his reason and natural senses, and at the same time be conscious of the other state he would be a man beside himself, thus making two living intelligences in one identity acting through one [organism]. Thus the clairvoyant man could correct the errors of the man of the flesh and blood and keep him in subjection to his wisdom.

This Wisdom or Christ was the mystery to mankind, this was the Christ that should reign till all error should be subject to it. Disease being the offspring of error, it deceives the people, making them nervous, sick, and liable to death. But it is the design of Wisdom that matter should be the servant of this clairvoyant man or Science, therefore when Jesus received this Wisdom He received God and man. When the man spoke it was like any one else, but when the Christ spoke it spoke not as man for that is of God or Wisdom from above. Jesus taught the people to distinguish by their works the true Christ from the false. It must have proved its source by works, for He says, "Not every man who says, I am Christ, is so himself, but he who doeth the will of the Father (Wisdom) that sent me."

Let us see if a test can be found such as Jesus laid down. When He called his disciples together He gave them power over all unclean spirits and sent them forth to heal the sick. Here is the test of the Christ-power or Wisdom. How did he apply it when he cured disease? Of course if He was in this state all the time all things were present to Him so that not a sparrow could fall to the ground unnoticed by Him, not Jesus, for although Christ was made known through Jesus, it was only made known according to the necessity of the time when He, Jesus, lived.I will take one of His miracles to show that Jesus and Christ acted together. When the centurion came to Jesus to tell Him that his servant was sick, Jesus was not aware of the fact, but immediately became subject to His clairvoyant [or intuitive] state, saw the servant and administered unto him. Then He said to the centurion, "Go, thy way, and according to thy faith be it unto thee." " So the centurion left and the servant was healed in the selfsame hour.

This is as plain to me as any cure I ever performed. This was not a "power" but a higher wisdom that the world knows not of. I will now introduce myself showing that I cure the same way. Every one knows that there is a difference in clairvoyance: subjects differ in the direction of their minds. I do not practise clairvoyance except with the sick and I will show others how to be clairvoyant like myself. . . . To make a good clairvoyant one must, beginning on earth, rid himself of all beliefs and every theory of man, and as he sees the absurdity of his own opinions he becomes lighted up in another atmosphere [on a higher plane] where he feels the discords of this world. He then becomes sensitive to the errors and opinons of man. They affect him and his spiritual senses act independently of his natural will or senses; then he is two persons.

This is my state as far as regards the sick. When I sit by the sick and take a patient by the band I feel a sensation; this affects me and the sensation is produced by something coming within my senses as a man of flesh and blood. This excites the spiritual or scientific man, and the senses being freed from matter or opinions see the natural man or opinion that causes the trouble. As I retain two identities (3) I see the error and explain it to the natural senses. These are set at rest and harmony is restored. I cannot find language to explain this so
that you will understand it. . . .

LOVE

What is the element that receives all sensation? Love for ourselves. This is the groundwork or foundation of all our acts. It is the mortar or dough in which all sensation is made. Of itself it contains no knowledge, it is perfect harmony; its elements or language is its perfection. It embraces all the senses; it is not Wisdom but the power Wisdom uses to bring all things into harmony with itself. To this world of ignorance it is not known but admitted and the matter or ideas of this world is put into this element. Like the ocean it can hold all sorts of ideas, be disturbed to its lowest depths and then calmed by Wisdom so that not a ripple on the surface can be seen. But in the depth of this ocean of love lie all sorts of evil spirits that are gnawing the life of the soul and are identified with it; this is the disease in the mind.

When the storm of ignorance and superstition was raging and all the ships or minds were tossing to and fro, even Jesus' disciples were in danger of being swamped by the errors of the age: when their bark or belief was just going down into hea-then idolatry and their enemies disturbed their water or belief, in the darkness of the night of error, when there was no eye to see nor heart to feel, no arm to reach out nor voice to be heard, Christ or Truth was seen walking upon their waters or belief, saying to the waves "Be still!" And the wind and waves obeyed Him and there was a great calm.

This was the state of their minds in the days of Jesus, the people's belief was the disease and to embrace their error was taking their disease. Their misery was what followed their belief, and their happiness was the unlearning of their errors. The ships were their theories, the water was their mind, and their ideas were the danger. Their wisdom was of this world of matter, but the wisdom of God could say to their wisdom, "Be thou still," and their ideas or mind and matter would obey. The introduction of Jesus' ideas was a new heaven or wisdom and a new earth or belief. The new heaven under the wisdom of God or Science could create a new belief wherein could be peace and happiness that the old heaven or wisdom knew nothing of where there should be peace and joy in the Holy Ghost or explanation of this new world, where no error, selfishness, or jealousy dwells, so that all ignorance and superstition shall be cast out into outer darkness, never to return.

Now, as Jesus was walking by the seaside, seeing the leaders' ideas, He saw two men, Andrew and Peter, fishing in the old Mosaic laws or sea, and said to them, "Follow me and I will make you teachers of this truth to men." So they abandoned their nets or old belief and followed Him. They went on and saw others mending their creeds or nets, for their nets like the priesthood were worn out and were like a garment ready to drop to pieces. So they left their father (or old belief) in their ships (or error) and followed Jesus. He travelled all through the land curing all sorts of diseases, preaching the kingdom of Science, and His fame went everywhere. Great multitudes followed Him and He went up into a higher state or Science and opened His mouth to them in truth or parables.

The laws of Moses laid a tax on the people for paying the priests to forgive their sins, and the doctors exacted a fee for forgiving or curing the sins that affected the body. So all persons who were not of their belief were strangers and needed teaching to have their eyes opened to the truth. Their ideas or opinions were like fish in a great sea, so they asked tribute money or an answer to all questions to pay for teaching strangers. When Jesus came into Capernaum, those who received tribute money, or gave information in regard to the truth, asked Peter if his Master paid tribute money or sought information concerning their religion, and Peter said, "Yes." Then as he went into. the house Jesus said to Peter, Who pays tribute money, the children or the believers (sceptics or strangers)? He answered, "Strangers." Then He said, "Lest they be offended let us ask a question for them to answer. Go to the priest (or sea) and cast in a hook, or put a question, catch an idea or fish, and open it and in it you will find an answer, or a piece of money. Go and give it for you and me." Now this sea, or belief, was the ocean which contained all the wisdom of the world, for the preachers, or spouters, fished in it, and the ships were the little societies or churches where the people congregated to catch spiritual food. When Peter and Andrew left their father or belief, their nets or society or ships and followed Him, then they left all for His sake. When the young man came to Jesus and asked Him what he should do to inherit eternal life or His (Jesus') wisdom, He said, " keep the commandments." The young man replied, "this have I done from my youth upwards, what lack I?" Then Jesus said, "if you wish to be perfect, go and give your religious ideas away and follow the Science or Me." As he could not understand, he went away sorrowful, for he had much wisdom of this world. When His disciples heard this they thought it a hard saying, so they said to Him, "we have forsaken our old ships and nets and even our father and mother for your sake, what shall we have?" Jesus said, "if they could understand His truth so that they could teach the people, they would sit on twelve thrones judging or teaching the twelve tribes of Israel." This they could not understand so when called upon to stand up and defend the Science they all forsook Him and there never has been a person since Jesus who has ever thrown a particle of light on His Science. As soon as Jesus was crucified the disciples were driven away or killed. So all the writings fell into the hands of men who knew nothing of Jesus' Science, they took the records and put such a construction on them as they pleased, and all we have is the opinions of men who lived hundreds of years after the crucifixion of Jesus.

They could not cure any persons, so of course the teachings of Jesus must be explained in some other way which did not require proof. So right in the face and eyes of Jesus' teaching where He gave His disciples power or wisdom and told what would follow-that they should cure all diseases as He did and perform greater works than His-the priest had to get over this by saying that the days of miracles are past. The people have crucified Christ in every way error could invent by believing in these fake-guides. Now, Jesus stood alone in the world of flesh and blood, weeping over their sins or errors that bound them down and well might He say as He did, "Oh! Jerusalem thou that stoneth the wisdom of God and hateth those that teach it to you, how oft would I gather you together in love for each other as a hen gathers her chickens under her wings of sympathy, and run the risk of her life for her young." To them this was all nothing, they could not see any sympathy outside of dollars and cents, or feel another's woes. So He said to them, "You have eyes but see not, ears but cannot hear the voice of misery, and no heart to feel another's woes." Now they did not want to understand, for it would make them break off from their sins, turn to the truth and become honest and good. Jesus' love for the sake of the world's happiness He laid down for the sins or belief of man, and, was received into the bosom of this love or sympathy, which was pure, not a selfish idea independent of all, but a love for the sake of all.

Jesus, as a man of flesh and blood as we all are, purified His own life, received this eternal life in the name of Christ and took all of our opinions that would have killed Him if He had been ignorant of the truth, and rose again pure and clear from all priestcraft. He then denounced the priests and doctors as enemies to the happiness of man. Now to be a follower of Christ is to do things that He did, but to be a believer in Christ only embraces what you know nothing of only as a belief. There is a vast difference between a belief and knowledge: knowledge is wisdom, and contains no belief, a belief is error, or the wisdom of this world, and the only way to detect them is by their works or fruits.

I will give you the key of heaven or Science, as far as correcting the errors in regard to your health is concerned so you cannot be deceived by the errors of the world. I will give you a sign so you can tell the difference between my theory as a teacher of Christ or Science and my opinion as a man, so you need not be deceived by false teachers who will come and say to you, " I understand this Science and can treat disease as Dr. Quimby does." Then if you understand me you will answer, "by your fruits I shall know you." Then if he tells you how you feel, locates a disease and offers any opinion in regard to your health, giving you a glimpse of a long train of suffering which you are liable to have, to such you can say, "your fruits show you to be ignorant." My theory teaches me to look upon you as an intelligent creature. I take upon myself all your feeling and see all your troubles. These feelings are my knowledge of your troubles as they are yours, but to me they contain the true answer and when my explanations satisfy you, then your difficulty is gone and you are happy. Jesus knew that the misery of mankind arose from their ignorance of immortality, and Christ revealed to the people that man was spiritual and his unhappiness lay in wrong belief. Their belief amounted to this, that the natural world is all there is, and as man required something higher to satisfy him the spiritual world was admitted and made to contain all sorts of witches and frightful things to keep the people in submission. So this spiritual world as it is called, has never been investigated as a science and all revelations from and allusions to it are steeped in mystery and superstition. Thus the most of our identity is in this mystic land, we know only our bodies and further than that we are in the dark. Christ is that revelation or Science of the spiritual world which is the knowledge and cure of all the ills flesh is heir to.

The people are divided into two classes, followers of Christ and followers of

Jesus. To illustrate the difference between Jesus and Christ I will take myself. There are many persons who believe in my "power" of healing, as they call it, but they know nothing of the truth of it. So they make me as a man responsible for my acts or my belief in all things. Thus my private character as a man is brought into my belief, just as though I could not be a teacher of truth unless my character as a man were in harmony with the errors of the world. Now, I stand before the people judged according to my outward acts, by one class and by my Science by another; so if I should put on the cloak of hypocrisy, attend church and be very strict in all things pertaining to the wisdom of the world, I should be received by the wisdom of this world, but the scientific would look upon me as a hypocrite. Jesus' private character as a man had just as much to do with Christ as P. P. Quimby has to do with his cures. Jesus as a man knew nothing of Christ, neither does P. P. Quimby as a man know anything of this Wisdom or Truth, but when he feels it he speaks not as P. P. Q. but as the patient's troubles reveal it to him. This Science of P. P. Q. takes the sins or troubles and the answer is accompanied by the feelings. Thus P. P. Q. is the medium of the Truth to correct the errors of the world, just as Jesus was the medium of God or Science to convince man of his errors and lead him to Christ, health, or Truth. (4)

I will take myself as a figure. Suppose music had never been reduced to a science and I had discovered that it could be taught to others, and I undertook to teach it, and I called the Science, Christ. Then it would be P. P. Quimby's Christ or theory. Suppose you should try to learn it so as to teach it. Would my Christ or theory have anything to do with my character as a man? All will say, no. If I am a very good man, that has nothing to do with my science, only to make it more admired, or it might make persons give more heed to what I say. Now suppose I am as bad a man as I can be, does that prevent me from teaching my Christ or Science? Now suppose the wisdom of the world sits in judgment on me, they all admit that I play very well, but that I do not know any more about it than they do. So they say he has a power which is of God, but he knows nothing of it himself. So they put all the power on me as a man and call my music P. P. Q's music. Now suppose I am a very good man and a pattern of society, kind in my manners and the possessor of every quality which is necessary to a very good man of this world. Here are two classes who profess to be believers in me, one the scientific and the other the aristocratic or ignorant, but as they cannot agree it is left for me to decide. So I decide in this way. All you who believe in me as a scientific musician of Christ, and under-stand the Science, shall teach as I do; and all you who do not understand but believe that I, the man, P. P. Quimby, have a power that you acknowledge, shall be called followers of me; so you undertake to follow me by acting as I do and try to imitate my character. Of course we should prefer a person who is amiable and pleasant, if he is a teacher of any science, but it is not absolutely necessary that he should be a good or a bad man. So far as Jesus stands I do not pretend to be or not to be a disciple of Jesus, for I let my life and acts as a man speak for themselves. I do not pin my belief on Jesus' character, nor do I care anything about it any more than He did Himself. Like all men who are willing to be judged by their acts, He let His character speak for itself. It was the Christ that Jesus was proud of, and so all men ought to be proud of any science that would make the world wiser and better. I profess to be a disciple of Christ, not of Jesus or the man. I let my man speak for himself, but I believe in Christ, which I put in practice on all those who live in this world of misery without this Science. So all my prayers are offered to Christ, not Jesus. The world prays to Jesus, but Jesus prayed to God to forgive or teach them, for they knew not what they prayed to. Now this Christ is in this element of love or sympathy that contains no error, but is an element of pure love that will wash away all error that chances to get into it. It knows no evil, it sees no wrong in itself, it is perfect harmony and attraction. It contains our higher senses. So it is as it were our life, and all that is good and harmonious. It seeks the wisdom of this world of error, as a person seeks gold to purify the gold from the dross. Its happiness is the developing of God's love or Science, it analyzes all misery and trouble to liberate the soul that is bound in this world of error. (5) -July, 1860.

Notes

(1) Many of Quimby's patients were ardent Calvinists, hence their God was out of date.

(2) Repetitions of ideas contained in other articles have not been crossed out from the selections in this chapter, because it seemed desirable to show how concrete was Dr. Quimby's thought of God. He plainly did not mean to teach pantheism or identify his own individuality with God as a mere "part" of Him. But he did wish to attribute to this "invisible Wisdom" whatever power he possessed as healer, as instrument of the Christ within. Quimby did not spend time in mere affirmations about his "oneness" with God. He aimed to establish the Divine presence by ministering to the sick so as to overcome all separateness.

(3) That is, consciousness on two planes or levels.

(4) These statements show plainly why Quimby did not claim his Christian Science as a special "revelation," and why he took no credit to himself as expounder of the spiritual meaning of the Bible. The Science or Christ is not dependent on persons, books, or organizations. It is demonstrable by its works or "fruits."

(5) Dr. Quimby's idea of Jesus was midway between the humanism of those who deemed Him "mere man" and the theological teachings of those who called Jesus "our Lord" or "the Lord." No merely humanistic conception could account for "the Christ" or Divine wisdom disclosed as universal, the source of all true Science.

Chapter Eighteen - Religious Questions

DEFENCE AGAINST AN ACCUSATION OF MAKING MYSELF EQUAL TO CHRIST

I am often accused of making myself equal with Christ. When I ask what Christ is I am told that Jesus Christ is one and the same. If I ask if Jesus the man was God, the answer is, "no, but God manifest in the flesh." Then can flesh and blood be God? "No." Then what was that being of flesh and blood crucified eighteen hundred years ago? "Jesus Christ." Is Christ God? "Yes." Is God flesh and blood? "No" Will you give some idea of what that being was called Jesus Christ? "Why, that God took upon Himself flesh and blood." Then what took upon itself flesh and blood? "God." Is God a substance? "No." Then can that which is not matter take matter upon itself? "You ask too many questions." Well, if you cannot answer my questions, must I believe what you say without any proof? "No, but we have the Bible and that says Christ is God." Well suppose it does and you are asked to explain Christ, and I receive this answer, "God manifest in the flesh." When I ask to have this explained I get no correct answer. Some think words are all that is necessary, so they quibble about the name "Christ," said to mean "anointed." Well, anointed is the name of something and this is what I want explained. To call it Christ or Messiah, the Prince of Peace or God, is only hopping from one name to another. I want to know what made Jesus different from other men. His birth I care nothing about, nor is it of consequence why He was called Jesus Christ. If different from other men how was the world benefited by that difference ?

Jesus was a man of flesh and blood like any one else. The difference between Him and other men was called Christ. Now what did the difference consist in? "In His life." What had His life to do with the healing of the sick? Has your life anything to do with healing a palsied limb? "No." Then your good life cannot cure diseases? Did Jesus' life cure? "Yes." Then you must not claim to be a disciple of Jesus, for if you claim to be a good man and we see no proof of your goodness on others, your goodness is of this world and not of Christ. You say He had a "power," now what do you mean by a power? We call steam a power and electricity a power but no one ever associates wisdom with it. Do you mean that Jesus' power was like the above, or was it what He said and did? "It was in what He said and did." Well, what did He do? Did He not cure the sick? "Yes." Well, how did He do it? Was it His power? "Yes, it came from God." Did you not say that Jesus was God? "Yes." Then how could God come from one place when you and I believe that God fills all space? "Well, there is a mystery in the Godhead or trinity that man cannot find out or understand." Was not the Bible written for our understanding? "Yes, but mystery cannot be found out, so we have no right to penetrate the ways of God, for there is enough in the Bible to learn and make us happy without searching into the mysteries of another world." If the Bible was not for man's belief what was it for? If we are to take it for the Word of God, who is to explain it? "It explains itself." Do you understand it? "In a measure." What do I understand by your answer? Can you give me any more light in regard to what Christ is than you have? "No." Then I am as ignorant as I was when I began. "Give me your opinion of Jesus Christ." Well, if you will listen I will tell you what I know of Christ and what I believe of the man Jesus...

RELIGION IN DISEASE

The question is often asked why I talk about religion and quote Scripture while I cure the sick. My answer is that sickness being what follows a belief the belief contains the evil which I must correct. As I do this a chemical change takes place. Disease is an error the only remedy for which is the truth. The fear of what will come after death is the begin-ning of man's troubles, for he tries to get evidence that he will be happy, and the fear that he will never arrive at happiness makes him miserable.

We are taught to believe that if we pray we shall receive an answer to our prayer. A superstitious person believing this is ready to believe that he may be punished, for some one may pray that God may remove him. Each army prays that God will direct the weapons that will slay their enemies. In biblical times did not God answer the prayer of those who wished to destroy their enemies and did they not die? The facts prove that what we believe may follow. We really believe in disease, hence it is the result of our belief. People never seem to have thought that they are responsible for their belief. To analyze their beliefs is to know themselves, which is the greatest study of man. All theories for the happiness of man contain more misery than happiness, either directly or indirectly. To destroy the beliefs of man is to leave him where God left him: to work out happiness by His own wisdom. One half of the diseases arise from a false belief in the Bible. It may seem strange that the belief in the Bible affects us, yet every belief affects us more or less, directly or indirectly.

I will relate a case where the religious belief affected the patient and caused the disease. The lady was aged. She was so lame and bound down that she could hardly rise from her chair, and could take only a step by the aid of her crutches, feeling so heavy that she dare not step. In this condition she had lived some years, and all the happiness she had was in reading and thinking on the Bible. She was a Calvinist Baptist and by her belief she bad imprisoned her senses [consciousness] in a creed so small and contracted that she could not stand upright or move ahead. Here in this tomb of Calvin her senses were laid, wrapt in her creed. Yet in this tomb was Christ or Science, trying to burst the bars and break through the bands and rise from the dead. She labored to be free from the bands and no one came to her relief. When she would ask for an explanation of some passage the answer would be a stone, and then she would hunger for the bread of life. At last in her misery she called upon me and I found her as I have stated. I knew not what caused her trouble. She thought it was from a fall. After explaining how she felt, I told her her trouble was caused by a series of excitements from studying upon what she could not reconcile. She thought upon religious subjects and not seeing the Scriptures clearly her mind became cloudy and stagnated. This showcd itself on the body by her heavy and sluggish feeling which would terminate in paralysis. She said she could not understand how her belief could make her so numb. I said to her, you will admit I have described your feelings. "Certainly," she replied. Then, said I, what do you suppose Jesus meant by these words, "a little while I am with you, then I go my way," and "you shall seek for me and where I go ye cannot come." Do you believe that Jesus went to heaven? "Yes," she replied. Now let me tell you what I think He meant by these words. I had told her before that in order to cure her I must make a change in the fluids and produce a healthy circulation, for she by her belief had produced stagnation. You have admitted that I have told you your feelings. Then I was with you as Christ was with His disciples in sympathy. And when I go my way I go into health and am not in sympathy with your feelings. Therefore where I go you cannot come, for you are in Calvin's belief, and I am in health. This explanation produced an instantaneous sensation, and a change came over her mind. This mortal put on immortality or health, and she exclaimed in joy, "This is a true answer to my thoughts." I continued explaining Scripture and a complete change took place. She walked without her crutches. Her case is so singular an example of my practice, that I will give the substance of my reasoning. It seemed as though all her feelings were in her belief, and if I wished to give her an idea of them I would make a comparison from the Bible. She was as it were dead in sin or error, and to bring her to life or truth was to raise her from the dead. I quoted the resurrection of Christ and applied it to her own Christ or health, and produced a powerful effect on her. I commenced in this way :

Your belief is the sepulchre in which your wisdom is confined. The world is your enemy. Your opinions and ideas are your garments, and the truth is the Holy Ghost or angel which will roll away the stone and heal your grief. The God in you will burst the bands of your creed and you will rise from the dead or your belief into the truth. You will then walk into the sitting room, and the friends will start as though you were a spirit, and you will say, "Hath a spirit flesh and bones as ye see me have? Give me a chair." Then the friends will inquire where the Christ is. The truth will say, "She has risen from her old religious body of sin and death and gone to meet her friends in heaven." Then will come false ideas, and as they cannot see the truth, the body being changed to them will seem to be gone, and they will report it stolen. You will leave the body of belief and take that of Science and rise into health. This is the resurrection of the dead.

This with the explanation produced such an effect on the lady that she could rise from her chair as quickly as any person of her age.

The natural world is full of figures that may illustrate man's belief. The silk worm spins out his life and wrapping himself in his labor dies. The infidel and brutal man reason that they do the same. The caterpillar is a good illustration of the natural man groping in the dark, guided by a superior wisdom that prompts his acts. When his days are numbered, wrapt in the mantle of this earth he lies down to sleep the sleep of death; but the Wisdom that brings forth the butterfly, also develops its science. In order that truth may come forth, error must be destroyed, and Science groping in dark-ness bursts into light and rises from the dead as the butterfly, not the caterpillar.

All men have sinned or embraced beliefs, so all must die to their belief. Disease is a belief ; health is in Wisdom. So as man dies to his belief he lives in Wisdom. My theory is to destroy death or belief and bring life and Wisdom into the world, therefore I come to the sick, not to save their beliefs or life in disease, but to destroy it. And he that loseth his belief for Wisdom will find his health or life.

I will now give what I believe to be the ideas of Jesus on the resurrection. I address my words to the sick, for I cannot make illustrations for the well; they are not affected [in the same way] by their belief. According to the Scriptures sin is a transgression of the law. What law? It must be of God, for it says, "the soul that sinneth shall surely die." So sin is death, and the law to which man is liable whose penalty is death is God's law. Therefore God is supposed to make laws to punish man for his thought, for every idle word is to be accounted for. This law heads countless evils and it is the part of Wisdom to correct it. But to believe that God is the author of our evils is as absurd as to believe that He made the remedies and laws before He made man. How often do you hear this remark: "There is a remedy for every disease." When we ask what it is, we are referred to some root or herb. But no hint is ever given that disease can be cured by the power of Truth.

Did Jesus employ such remedies? On the contrary had not the sick whom He cured tried them? He said: "my words are life eternal, and by my words I cure all manner of diseases." If the palsied limb was the thing to be cured, why did He say to the man: "Stretch forth thy hand, and immediately it was made whole?" Why did He not apply remedies to the arm? The fact was Jesus knew that the arm was not the cause but the effect, and he addressed Himself to the intelligence, and applied His wisdom to the cause. "He spake as never man spake," for He spoke to the cause. But when man speaks he gives an opinion. All the acts of Jesus were based on Truth, while man acts from an opinion and chooses darkness rather than light. The light of truth will showman his error. He shrinks from investigating his belief since he knows it cannot stand the test of Science. It is folly to apply an inanimate something to cure an inanimate disease, for neither contains any intelligence. If a man's face is dirty and he is satisfied, there is no disease; but if it troubles him, the trouble is in him not in the dirt. To cure him would be to tell him to wash. If the person believes he is cured, the water proves that what was told him was true.

The war between my patients and myself is here: they make disease the dirt. I make the dirt the cause. They put intelligence in the dirt. I put intelligence in the person. To cure him I must convince him that the dirt is nothing that need trouble him, and that water will remove it. By knowing the truth they are able to remove the cause. The doctors put the trouble in the dirt as though the trouble and the dirt were one and the same. They never address the intelligence, but the opinions, while the cause being unintelligent, like the dirt, affects the intelligence and is reflected on the body.

JESUS' HEALING AND HIS MISSION

Why should there be such a controversy in regard to the way in which Jesus cured disease, also what was the real object of His mission in this world? These questions naturally arise in the minds of men and bring up doubts. By some it is believed that Jesus came to save man from being lost in another world and it is thought that He intended to reform the world. All admit He had a gift superior to other men but what it was has never been ascertained. The same controversy was going on in the days of Jesus and in fact it has always been a mystery to the natural man. Phenomena are taking place everywhere proving this power or gift and all admit it, but as yet it has not been reduced to a science so that it can be taught and learned. Its opponents speak as though it were governed by natural laws, but when asked to put these laws into practice they get off by saying, "Why it is nothing but mesmerism." When asked to explain mesmerism they say it is "psychology." Ask what psychology is, the answer is mesmerism. So the world is as wise as before. Mesmer tried to explain this power on the ground of electricity. Those who believe it is governed by some law attribute it to galvanism. The religious classes vary. The spiritualists ascribe it to the spirits of the dead; Christians to the power of God when speaking of Jesus, but when they speak of this power in man they attribute it to natural causes. Some say it is the power of the devil. When Herod the king was told Jesus was performing cures he said it was John the Baptist, that is, John's spirit came and took possession of Jesus and cured disease. When the Pharisees asked Jesus where it came from, Jesus said if they would tell Him where John's power came from then He would tell them how He performed his cures. This they could not do. So it has never been explained.   Settle this point and you establish a basis for investigation. As it stands it puts Jesus on a level with all the spiritualists of His day. If it is a gift or power, why should He be called God or anything else above His followers? And if He knew how He wrought miracles it is knowledge and not a gift, and to call it a gift or power is depriving Jesus of any knowledge superior to His followers. When it is admitted as a Science that Jesus taught for the happiness of man, man will try to learn it. Then the inquiry will be made, how can it be proved a Science? I answer, never till the people admit that matter and mind are under direction of Intelligence superior to matter. Then man will take a higher standard and be governed by Science, not mind. When matter becomes subject to Science and is the medium or power to be put in motion, this medium or matter can be changed into any form or state and be destroyed but not lost. The identity of a thing can be put out of this world, as it is called, and only remains as a thing that once was but now is not.

I will give an illustration: Suppose a person believes he has a tumor in his left side. His error believes in the idea of tumors independent of his mind; he then admits an error to begin with. His mind gives direction to matter and the idea is formed; this seems to be proof that there is such a thing as a tumor. No one will deny that one is a phenomenon brought about by false knowledge, and that true knowledge or Science can destroy that tumor or idea and establish a knowledge of the truth that will prevent the person from being deceived into that error again . . Our bodies [in relation to mind] are nothing but an idea of matter that is either under the control of error or false knowledge, or under the control of Science or true knowledge. If Truth or Science reigns, all goes well; if error reigns the wage is death, for all acts of error lead to death; death is an idea or matter, (1) and all the acts of Science destroy death and lead to life and happiness.

RELIGION

What does Jesus mean by the kingdom of heaven? We all know the common opinion was that heaven was a place. Some suppose it to be a state of mind. Had Jesus either of these ideas? I say He did not, and will show what His ideas were. God is represented as all wisdom and love. Now love is not wisdom, but a desire for wisdom, and a desire to get wisdom for the sake of happiness that follows is the highest love. This is heaven and to be deprived of this love is to be out of heaven. The sick are strangers to this heaven. It is true they have a sort of love but it is governed by the light or wisdom of man. This leads to death. The sick being strangers, are deceived into a false belief that lulls them to sleep. To cure them it is necessary to arouse them from their lethargy and show them their errors.

I will now give the true conversion of a sick man of this world converted to the religion of Christ or cured intelligently, and also one converted from one disease or error to another. I call all error disease that leads to death. The remedy is religion or a knowledge of the Truth that will save us from the evils that flow from our sins. To illustrate the different forms of religion is to show the different modes of restoring the lost child of disease to health and happiness. To show how Jesus differed from all others is to show each religion separately and how the belief affects mankind.

All will admit that Jesus opposed the religion by which medical men and priests used to save the people from sins or evils called diseases. For to be diseased was an evil and the sick were dealt with accordingly, and the false idea that the sins or diseases of the parents are visited upon the children is handed down to this generation. (2) To save them from their sins was to cure them of their disease. . . .

Now what was the idea the world had of heaven? People never had such an idea as Christians have now. They never seriously believed in any other world. But their suffering was their evil and to be cured was their heaven or happiness. For this object they employed every means in their power according to their belief. The people were taught that there were certain rivers and pools the angels would disturb and all who visited them were healed. Certain diseases were held so sinful that the victims were kept aloof from the people till the priest cured them. So their religion was all for their health or happiness. It is true there was a small class who believed that at the end of the world the dead would rise. Jesus called the people to Him and said, "Beware of the doctrines of the Scribes and Pharisees, for their doctrines bind burdens on you." It made them superstitious; made them believe in ghosts, spirits, and all sorts of juggling. This kept the people under the rule 'of the priests who invented all sorts of craft to deceive, pretending to take away sins so that God would not torment them with evil spirits and disease. Jesus knew it all in their belief, and if He could introduce a higher principle or better mode of reasoning that could take away their sins or errors so that they would be more enlightened, He would be doing them a great favor, and would estab-lish universal truth that would work out a more excellent law.

To do this it was necessary to bring proof of His superior wisdom. He was talking about this great truth called God that governs every true and scientific mind. He made two worlds, one the natural or superstitious man that all were in: the other the scientific man, which He called a resurrection from the dead. Not that the dead rose, for if you cannot get a man out of his error there is no resurrection. As Paul says (1 Cor. XV, 12), if Christ (or this Science) be preached that it rose from the dead (or error) how say some among you that there is no higher truth than man's opinion? As Science is spiritual it must be explained by literal things. So Jesus used parables to explain how this truth grows in the minds, and he takes for example a little child, before its mind is filled with errors of the priest as a figure of heaven. Not that the mind contains any wisdom, but like the soil of the earth it is pure from foul seeds or error, ready to receive the true seed of wisdom. He says, "Of such is the kingdom of heaven:" this truth could live and grow in the child. Not that heaven or kingdom was happiness, but happiness was in the one who entered into it. But as the kingdom grew, false ideas would creep in; for it is not to be supposed that Jesus ever intended to make His kingdom perfect till every enemy or error should be destroyed. So he likens it unto a great many things, to a sower in a field, and an enemy sowing in the same field. Here you have good seed and bad seed, truth and error, good and evil. But the good was good, and the bad was bad, and they never mingled.

I will take a person as he would come to Jesus, and show how He preached the kingdom of heaven. Take the little child. Jesus asked how long this child had been in this way, (Mark IX, 21). When told, He said, "Do you believe all things possible with God?" They said, "Yes." So then He cured the child, not by a "power," but by His wisdom, for He knew what He was about. So their faith in Him kept the child from having any more fits. All His cures went to prove His theory of the Christ, which He preached and illustrated by parables, and proved by showing Himself to the multitude after they believed Him dead. The identity of it was a body, and the doctrine of it was its blood. So He says, "if you eat not my flesh and drink not my blood, you have no life in you."

I will give an illustration. Suppose a person comes to me to learn navigation. I say, "You must be born again, for your ideas of navigation are all false." He says, How can I learn or be born again when I am so old? I answer, "You must be born in the science of navigation." This he cannot understand, but still he wishes to learn. So I begin to explain. As he begins to learn, this is called the love that is spoken of with which God so loved the world. Now, love for wisdom prompts him to learn, and as he learns his happiness is full. This is entering into heaven. This is the heaven God has prepared for every one who will try to learn, and if every one will search for God or Wisdom God will not cast him off.

I will apply this to disease. I take upon myself your infirmities that I may lead you to health, for health to you is heaven. The love for health prompts you to come. My love for you prompts me to lead you to health. This I do by teaching you the errors of your belief and showing you where you have been deceivd. The truth like love leads you to see your error, and the happiness of your recovery is heaven. People believe that religion is one thing and health another. This is a false idea, and if you look at it you will see that to be happy is the chief end of man. Happiness is what we think we have obtained. Take the religion of our day: that is a poor illustration of happiness, for the misery it occasions is twice the happiness. We are taught our belief is one thing, and our health another. But it is not so. Man's belief is his heaven or his hell. You may not be aware of the effect of your belief.

Disease is one of the evils that follow our belief. For instance, take a young lady: begin to tell her that her happiness depends upon her having religion. She has no idea of what you mean. So to convince her you give an account of what religion is and show that she must get it or be eternally lost. This makes her nervous. So you tell her to come to Christ. This to her is blind. You say Christ is standing with His arms extended to embrace her. Now to fall into the arms of a stranger is more than she can do. She weeps, not knowing what to do. This you tell her is the conversion of her soul. At last she is made to believe she is not worthy to be a Christian. Then comes the soothing words of the priest and his words soothe her aching head and she quiets down. Then you tell her this is a change of heart. Now she is in a state to get religion.

What has been brought to pass? The young lady has been deceived into a belief that has cost her all the happiness she had. It will be said her religion had nothing to do with her health, but this cannot be the case; for every person is responsible to God or Wisdom for his belief, and he must take the consequences of his belief.

Now, as I said, religion is a belief and disease or happiness is what follows. So as all men have sinned or got a belief, the sentence of death has been passed upon them, for all have come short of the truth. So this truth came into the world of opinions to open the eyes of the blind, or appeal to a higher intelligence to lead them to the Truth that would cure them of their sins or errors. Now a religion or theory was to explain to the masses to keep them out of their trouble. We suppose that Jesus wanted to convey the idea that man was in danger of being destroyed after death, but if he would believe in Jesus be should be saved. So our belief depends upon our beliefs. Now what was Jesus' idea?

Jesus had no words or ceremonies but a love for a higher development of the human soul. This was Jesus' religion and He put it in practice by His acts upon the sick. Not by giving an opinion of what He knew nothing, but by showing that their sickness was the effect of their belief.

How often have you heard persons say they are not nervous and they never change their mind. That is as much as to say they have no wisdom, for wisdom changes the mind. Make a person believe a thing. The belief being matter or mind it is an obstacle to wisdom. This obstacle must be removed be-fore the truth can shine. If there is not wisdom enough to remove the obstruction we say such a man has a strong mind. It is true he has a strong error to be overcome, but his mind embraces just as much intelligence as a stumbling block in the way of a train of cars. The dissensions among the passengers represent the contrast between the strongminded and the intellectual man. One sees no way to remove the obstacle and concludes that it cannot be overcome, and settles down in the strength of his own mind, while wisdom investigates the chances and sets himself to work to remove the burden. As the intellectual man works, his mind changes, while the strong man sits and contends that he knows, and when he makes up his mind nothing can change it. The other is fickle and therefore has no mind or stability. This is the case with disease. The belief is the burden to be overcome. In any disease the strong mind means a man deficient in mechanical wisdom who can't see whether the world develops him, or he develops the world. The strong-minded man is a man whom the world develops, his foundation is on what has been handed down from one generation to another.

THE EFFECT OF RELIGION ON HEALTH

I will give my opinion of the inconsistency of our religious beliefs and their effect upon health. I was visiting a patient whose state differed very much from what is called rheumatism and general disability of the nervous system. (3) The doctors had tried their best to relieve her but to no effect; their efforts only made her worse, and at last she sent for me. I found her very nervous, complaining of aches and pains all over. When I told her that it was her mind that was disturbed she replied, "Oh, no, my mind is at rest. I know I am in the hands of a merciful God who will deal with me according to His will. I have full faith in Him." Do you suppose He knows your troubles? I asked. "Yes, He knows all things." Suppose Jesus were here as He was eighteen hundred years ago do you think He could cure you? "Oh, yes. I know He knows all my suffering." Then why does He not cure you? "Because it is His will that I should go through all this suffering to fit me for the kingdom of heaven." Now suppose your daughter should be taken sick away from home in a strange land among strangers and suppose some kind friend should call on her and say, "You seem very low spirited" and she should reply, "Oh, no I know that it is all right." "Suppose your mother were here, would you not get well?" "Yes, she knows all my sufferings, but she knows it is all right to make me better prepared to enjoy her company when I get home." "Do you believe that if she had a mind to cure you she could do so ?" "Certainly." "Can you say you love your mother when you admit your life is in her hands and she permits you to suffer so much?" "Oh, she is my mother, and I feel that she knows what is for the best. It gives me comfort to know that I am in the hands of a merciful being." [Despite this reasoning the patient fails to admit a point, and so Dr. Quimby, once more addressing her, says:] Would you like to have me cure you? "Yes, if you can, but not if I must give up my belief in my religion. I should rather go down to the grave with my religion than be cured and lose my belief. If you can cure me of my lameness and not talk to me about my religion I should like to get well, but if you cannot cure me without that I do not know as I will be cured, for I don't think my religion has anything to do with my disease." Do you not think your belief has something to do with your happiness? "Oh, yes, but it has nothing to do with my disease." What is your disease? "Why it is rheumatism, the doctors say, and a general prostration of the nervous system" What is that? "Neuralgia, I suppose." What is that? "I do not know." Suppose I should try to explain how you came to be in this condition, would you listen? "Yes, if you do not talk religion." I have no religion to talk. "I know you have not." Have you? "I hope I have." Well, I do not want it if it makes me as sick and unhappy as you. "All the comfort I take while lying here all these long nights is to think that I am in the hands of a merciful God who will do all things right." Would you like to get well? "If it is the will of God, I should be very glad to get well." Do you think I can cure you? "I do not know, but I hope you can; if you can't I shall give up all hopes of ever being well." Then you think your health depends on my science? "Yes." If I should cure you would you give me credit? "Oh, yes." But would it be right to upset the will of God who is keeping you in this misery for His own pleasure? "Oh, if God sees fit to have it I believe it is all right. I know I feel badly and I should like to feel better, but if it is the will of God that I must suffer I will submit for I know it is for the best. God suffered in the flesh to teach us to be better prepared for heaven."

Then you think if you should die you would go to heaven ? "I hope so, for I cannot suffer these pains always." Where is heaven? Do you believe it is a place? "Oh, no." Then what is it? "It is a state of mind." Then you are not very near it, I should judge by your own mind. "Well, I do not know as that has anything to do with my pains." What is pain? "I don't know what it is, but I know how it feels." How do you know it? "I know it through my senses." Are your senses affected by your mind? "I suppose so." Then if your mind is disturbed and you put a false construction on the disturbance, won't it produce an unpleasant effect upon the senses? "I suppose so." Suppose this unpleasant effect should be pain, is it not the effect produced on the mind? "I don't know what that has to do with my lameness. I want to get well." Who wants to get well? "I." That is, you, Mrs. H-? "Yes." Is not that all there is of you that has any mind or knowledge? "Yes." You do not expect this flesh and blood to go to heaven? "No." Why not? "Because the Bible says flesh and blood cannot inherit the kingdom of heaven." I thought you just said heaven was a state of mind. "So I did." Well, do you mean that flesh and blood are in the mind? "Oh, you make me so nervous, you will kill me." Why? "Because I don't like to hear you talk so. My mind is all made up and I do not want to be disturbed in this way." Do you mean your flesh and blood are disturbed? "Oh you disturb my mind and body." Then your mind is one thing and your body another. You believe in the soul? "Yes." You believe it goes to heaven when you die? "Yes." I thought you said heaven was a state of mind. "Oh, yes, but we must die." What dies? "This flesh and blood." Well, has it life? "Yes." Has it feeling? "You would think so if you suffered as much as I" Then this that suffers is the flesh and blood? "Yes" Then it is conscious of all these bad feelings? "Yes." Are the feelings its consciousness or has it another consciousness independent of itself? "No." Then at death you mean that all of these aches and pains leave you and you will be happy? "Yes."

Then these aches and pains are the body's identity and belong to the flesh and blood? "Yes." Are you happy when you feel so badly? "No." Then you are not in heaven? "I don't expect to be happy until I get to heaven." Can you get there and have these pains? "No." Then when the pains leave you it will be heaven on earth? "Yes, if that ever takes place."

Now, let us see where you stand. You have admitted enough to show that your mind is in a confused state like a person in trouble. You have not one particle of true knowledge. Your supposed knowledge is the effect of an impression on the senses, due to the opinion of some one who explained some one's ideas according to his own view of truth. This opinion taken for truth makes you nervous and brings about all your suffering. You are afraid of your enemies and you pray to the God whom you admit keeps you in misery. You are taught to believe that God is watching all your actions, that He has laid down certain laws and regulations for you to follow and if you disobey you will be punished. This keeps you in bondage and all your life subject to disease. But to suppose God selects you to be punished above your companions is to believe God is partial. This you cannot believe.

Now look at those who worship God; they have a false idea of the God they worship. God is not in any kind of worship that man has established. God is not an identity as man is, if He were He would be in matter. The ignorance of man cannot see intelligence out of matter, so all prayers are in matter, and all that people are afraid of contains matter. This false idea keeps man in the dark. You never see a man praying to the fire that warms him, nor does he pray to the elements. How is it with steam? Is not the person who knows the most about steam the best one to control it, and does not every one have more confidence in such a person than in one who is ignorant of it? So it is with the elements. Man differs in one respect from living matter: he has undertaken to control the elements so as to make them subservient to his will. We often hear persons talking about the laws of nature, as though they were the laws of God and they say if we did not disobey them all would go right. Now, here is the mistake. The laws of nature are very simple of themselves and they never trouble man if he does not trouble them. The beasts conform to these laws, for when they are thirsty they find the laws that quench their thirst, if left to themselves, and when hungry the same intelligence dictates the remedy. But man in his eagerness to be lord over the brutes and elements has developed faculties called senses. These are under a superior wisdom which can control the elements and use them for the benefit of the human race. Now, it is not to be expected that every person who happens to think of flying can make a flying machine that will be successful. Nor is it certain that any invention to control the elements will always work so that accidents as they are called will not take place and lives lost and much trouble made before Science is established. So it is with life. Life is a science that is little understood. The brutes have no desire to investigate science. Man is the only one who has undertaken it. Let us see how far he has progressed. It is a fact that man's life is shortened by his own belief, for his belief is his practice and the length of his life is in his theory. Every one has his theory in regard to the lengthening of life, but all admit it must end, that it is set in motion and may run down sometime. Some think life is a perpetual machine that never was set in motion and can never stop. To solve this life and save it from being lost is the great problem. Theories for the benefit of man are invented to save his life. He is given the knowledge of every danger he is liable to pass through and is warned against them. These call out the science and skill of the world, to put man in possession of a science to save his life as though his life were something independent of himself. This makes competition. . . .

Our lives are like a journey through a wilderness. We first take the priests' opinion, that is, to trust in God. When we ask an explanation of God we are answered that He knows all things and not a hair of our head falls to the ground without God knows it; if we look to Him, He will deliver us from all danger, and He takes better care of us than a parent does of his child. This is a brief sketch of God's goodness. Now suppose we should not do quite as well as we expect, then what follows? God has made a devil, a something worse that stands ready to catch us if we don't go according to His will or laws. These things are not defined, but like the laws of the United States, every president can construe them according to his belief. The laws of God made by man are arbitrary, though not acknowledged as such. Jesus said "Call no man master but one and that is God" Here you see you have made a God that is full of inconsistencies and cannot stand the test of common reason. Now look at the true scientific answer to all our beliefs and it shows us that they contain no knowledge of God or life, for God is life eternal and this life was in His Son, Jesus, which was Christ or Science. Now to suppose you lose your life is to be cut off from God, for God is not the God of the dead but of the living, for all live to Him. Now destroy man's belief and introduce God's truth, then we are set free from this world of error and introduced into the world of light or Science, where there is no death but the living God. This Science will lead us to that happy state where there is no sickness, sorrow, or grief, where all tears are wiped away from our eyes, and there we shall be in the presence of this great Truth that will watch us and hold us in the hollow of its hand and will be to us a light that will open our eyes. We shall not then be deceived by blind guides who say peace, peace, when there is no peace. Then we shall call no one master or leader, for there is but One that leads us and that is God. He puts no restriction upon us, for our lives are in His hands or Science. . . . If you can see God in your knowledge you will admit that everything you do intelligently you do under the direction of a power or intelligence superior to yourself. So when you do anything ignorantly and the effect is bad, giving you trouble, you try to correct your errors, thereby showing that you admit a power superior to yourself. This power is called Christ or God and if you have not this power or Christ you are not of Him. To know God is to know ourselves, and to know ourselves is to know the difference between Science and error. Error is of man and truth is of God, and as truth is not in the cause of disease it is not in the effect. Therefore to say we are happy when in disease is to admit we have no disease, for disease is the error and the effect. Now as opinions contain either truth or error (not known) we are affected by the effect when it comes to the light of Science and then the happiness or misery follows. This is called by the doctors disease and they treat the effect, denying the cause or letting it go as of no account. Here is the difference. I put the disease in the direction of mind and then I know what will be the effect.

Our happiness is the result of correcting our impressions when first made. Our error is the ignorance of these impressions. The opinions of the world and ignorance of ourselves are the causes of our trouble. Suppose you were afraid of some person and you dare not stir lest he should kill you, do you think you would be any worse off to know that he was your friend and he felt unhappy to know that you had such an opinion of him? So it is in every act of our lives, knowledge of ourselves never harmed man. Disease is not in knowledge but in ignorance. For instance, the fear of any trouble is the disease.

Go with me back to the time of the persecution of the church and the Salem witchcraft. All the people believed in evil spirits and witches and considered it wrong to have anything to do with them. Here you see was the disease in the people's belief, and their belief was put in practice for the safety of mankind. Therefore every invention of their belief was called out to get rid of an evil that was tormenting man. Here you see the belief was one thing and the evil another, and so it is in everything. The wisdom of this world sees the mind one thing and disease another, and reasons by saying the pain came before I had any thought about it, and I had no mind about it. . . . So it is with rheumatic pains, the state of mind or disease is admitted to have an existence as much as evil spirits and we are affected by our belief. If anything disturbs our happiness we fly to some one for protection and in our trouble create a form of something in the mind to locate it in some place in the body. We suffer ourselves to be tormented to get rid of the enemy or disease, as those who believed themselves bewitched would suffer being whipped to drive out the devils. I could name hundreds of cases where persons have called in physicians and between them both they, have made an enemy, the patient suffering himself to be poulticed and blistered almost to death to get rid of the bronchitis or spinal disease or white swelling or some other devil supposed to exist independent of the mind. The doctors who use these means show about as much knowledge as the people in Connecticut did who beat the beer barrel if it worked on Sunday. It is the relic of heathen superstition that wisdom will some time eradicate from the mind by explaining it on scientific principles. Till then the knife, the lance and calomel and such things that are only introduced by a show of truth not much in advance of nailing a horse shoe over the door, or sleeping with the Bible under you to keep off the witches, must govern the people. Jesus knew that all the foregoing belief was founded in ignorance, therefore He was not afraid of these beliefs and said these words: "Greater love hath no man than to lay down his life for his friends."

CONTROVERSY ABOUT THE DEAD

The religious world has always been in a controversy in regard to the dead. Before Jesus taught a resurrection from the dead, the Pharisees believed the dead rose at the end of the world. Others believed spirits came back and entered the living, but there was no idea that was satisfactory to the thinking classes. The Sadducees disbelieved in everything but admitted one living God. This was the state of man's belief at the time Jesus appeared before the people. He spake as never man spake for He spoke the Truth and gave the lie to all the opinions of mankind. I will take the liberty of putting my own construction on Jesus' truth and leave it to the common sense of the people to decide which is consistent with Science. You see that at the time Jesus spoke the idea [the persistence] of an identity after death was never taught, and to teach that was to the Jews blasphemy. So Jesus admitted their various beliefs, but attached a spiritual meaning to them. Jesus spoke to the people in parables, for His object was to rid the world of superstition. His words were called out in answer to some question asked by the rulers of the people, and His answer was in accordance with the question, but in it was shown the absurdity of the belief; so they could not catch Him.

The greatest evil to overcome was the resurrection of the dead. This was a difficult question to solve, for Jesus never believed in the natural body rising and to deny the resurrection of man was as absurd as to deny the resurrection of the body, so to deny one and prove the other was to admit a resurrection and teach it. But as the people called sin "death" and truth "life," it was easy to adopt these meanings. He could then show that the resurrection from the dead was a resurrection from an error to a truth. But this must be explained by a parable. Here is what Jesus intended to convey: that this power that the people could not account for and which they ascribed to evil spirits or the dead was a Science of ourselves, which embraces all we are and our senses. It is life itself, and a knowledge of it is to put it into practice so the world can be benefited. Ignorance of it embraces all phenomena. This makes man superstitious, for he is ignorant of himself, man thinks his belief is all there is of him, and so it is till he is brought into a higher state which shows that he has two minds. One mind embraces matter and is in it. The other is Science and is out of mat-ter, and uses matter as a medium to convince the natural man of a higher knowledge of himself. It was Jesus' mission to convince the natural man of this truth; so when He spoke of Jesus He spoke of the earthly man, but when He spoke of Christ He spoke of the heavenly man or Science. This the people could not understand, so when He said He should rise from the earthly man, (Jesus) He spoke of this Christ, and the people had no idea what He meant to convey to them. So when they saw Him taken and tried they all forsook Him and stood afar off and some denied Him. This showed that they expected that Jesus would be crucified. This embraced Jesus Christ and all of His preaching and when He was crucified that ended the life of Jesus Christ to them.

Now, to rise from the dead was what He had promised His followers and they believed that Jesus intended to prove that His body, or Jesus, which was flesh and blood, should rise. Here was where they misunderstood Him. Jesus never intended to convey any such idea. If the people had understood what Jesus meant they would have put a different construction on everything. If they had known the facts they never would have troubled themselves about the man Jesus, but would have let that body remain in the tomb and when Christ showed Himself to His disciples and others they could have seen the flesh and blood in the tomb. Then He, that is Christ, had established the saying, although you destroy this flesh and blood you do not destroy the knowledge of it, and this same knowledge can make to itself another body and show it to the people, to convince them of eternal existence, not after death, but after a progress of our knowledge. Now, I want to be as liberal as I can to the friends of Jesus, but I must say that in their zeal to establish what Jesus told they made a great mistake. For I do believe they did steal or take away the body of Jesus to establish their belief that it rose again. This upset what Jesus intended to prove, that is, that although they should destroy this flesh and blood, Christ would show Himself to prove that man can live and have all his faculties and knowledge after the world calls him dead. But as it stands it shows nothing, for no one expects the body to rise. Like all religious fanatics, in their zeal to carry out an idea they left the whole affair in a worse state than before. This gave rise to all sorts of controversies, and as Christ had made Himself manifest to the people they of course believed that Jesus' body rose, Others saw the absurdity of the idea that flesh and blood rose, so it was not long before the believers were fighting, just as in our days.

147

Paul said to them, "I understand there is a dissension among you as touching the resurrection of the dead. Now, "if Christ be preached (not Jesus but this truth or Science) that he rose from the dead (or from Jesus) how say some among you, there is no resurrection (or Science) and all is of no force?" You see the people confounded the two ideas, that is, the people called Jesus Christ one and when Jesus Christ rose He was one because they had no idea of two identities. Those that differ from them had to contend against the deception of these fanatics who stole the body of Jesus, for those who believed the body rose were more enthusiastic in their belief than those who believed in the science. You see how all those persons that can work them-selves up to believe that the time is coming when our bodies will rise again are about as far behind the times as those old persons who believe the time will come when the factories will be abolished and the girls will return to the spinning wheel and loom, when steam will be abolished. If they can get any comfort out of that kind of food I for one will not disturb their repose. I have commenced climbing Jacob's ladder, whose top round I have never heard of it is said to reach to heaven so that the angels could descend on it. The Christian ladder has from one to seventy or eighty rounds, so when man climbs half his life it takes the other half to get back to where he started. That makes him once a man and twice a child. So I suppose he commences a child and climbs to a man and then steps over and returns back to a child. This is proof that the natural man is a mere bubble.

THE RESURRECTION

What is the true meaning of another world? It is supposed that man lives in this world and goes to God or a spirit-world. This is the general belief and if this is true, why should it be so strange that some persons should believe their friends return to earth and appear to the people? This was the belief of a large class of mankind in the days of Jesus. All this is called truth, it is founded on an opinion that there is another world and the Bible is quoted in proof of it. To me this is error based on ignorance of Science. Science would never have led man to that belief.
It is said men had wandered away from God and become so wicked that they were in danger of eternal punishment. What does this mean? Man is here on the earth as he always was, so it did not mean that he got off the globe. To wander away from God is to suppose that He had some locality, and to be in His presence is to return to His place of residence. This place must be somewhere where God resided because the belief was that Christ came to lead man back to God. If God is in another world and Jesus came from that place down to the earth to lead man there, or to open a way whereby man could get there himself, then it is to be supposed man had been in heaven in the presence of God but had wandered away and could not get back. All this looks very silly when we think of asking men to believe it, but we embrace it without giving it the least thought.
Man is made up of thought and ideas. There is nothing about man unchangeable but his science, for Science embraces a principle [and the spirit] and principles are not matter or ideas but a knowledge of them. Life is an evidence of Science, so is feeling, taste, etc. All the senses are admitted by Science to exist independently of matter, and the senses are all there is of man that cannot be changed. (4) They may be obstructed by error but not destroyed. To separate these two is to explain the true meaning of life and death.
All the people believed in death. Jesus did not; therefore His arguments were to prove that death was a false idea. So if we believe in death we are in our belief, if we know it as an error we are in life. Jesus had to prove that what we call death was only a separation of His Truth from the people's belief. But the crucifixion of Jesus was death according to their belief. Jesus never intended to allude to the natural body. So when He speaks of a resurrection it is from the dead; not that the dead rise, for that would go to show that He was still a believer in matter, and if He believed in matter [in that way] He must have believed it dies and then rises again. But if He believed it is nothing but a medium for the senses to use and control, then all that He meant was that His senses should rise from the dead or the error of the people who believed that the senses are a part of the idea called body. To prove His truth was to show Himself to the disciples, after they had seen Him as they supposed dead, alive again. To them this was a resurrection of the dead, or the same idea. But if Jesus' same idea or body rose it would have been a resurrection of the dead, not Christ's or Jesus' ideas. Jesus' teachings were to show that Christ was a truth o f God, a higher knowledge that separated Science from ignorance, and this Christ was in Jesus.
When the people saw their idea of form destroyed their hope was cut off. But when in the clouds of their ignorance they saw this same Christ or Truth take form again they were afraid, and as it became dense enough to be identified it was recognized as Jesus' body. But it was not the body or idea that they had believed in some days before. This is where the trouble was. The people's mind was changing but not scientifically, and they were left in a more nervous state than before. For now they thought Jesus' body rose and if Jesus' body rose it went to show that His ideas were not changed from the common belief. It amounted to nothing at all, for no man has ever risen since, and there was no proof of Jesus' soul being separated from His body.
So man has to get up a belief in opposition to the Bible's belief, he must believe Jesus went to heaven with a body of flesh and blood. So the common explanation of the resurrection leaves it worse than before. But to take the man Jesus as a man of flesh and blood like all other men and give Him the knowledge that matter is under the control of a higher power

that can act independently of matter, and that He, Jesus, could be in two places at the same time and be outside of the body called Jesus-then it would not be hard to believe that this knowledge called Christ which Jesus had should say, though you destroy the idea of Jesus, Christ will rise or make Himself known to the people. For this Christ or Truth had the power to assume any form it pleased. But as the people knew it only as it came within their senses as the natural man, they could not believe till it took the form of Jesus as a man. This form the people called Jesus; therefore the report went out that Jesus rose from the dead, and it has always been believed by those who call themselves disciples of Jesus. Now, here is my belief: I believe in Christ or the Truth. Christ knew that they knew not what they did; therefore the Christ said, "Father forgive them, for they know not what they do." This same Christ was not in the idea that the people had, but just as far as this power was made known, it could make itself manifest. Now to believe that the idea, or Jesus, or flesh and blood, rose is to believe that the dead rise. This Jesus denied when he said that what rises from the dead never marries or is given in marriage. As touching the dead that they rise, He says: "God is not the God of the dead but of the living, for all live unto Him."

ANOTHER WORLD

Did St. Paul teach another world as it is taught by Christians? I answer "no," and shall prove that Paul preached this very Science I am trying to preach and that he put it into practice as far as he was able; but he taught it more than he put it into practice from the fact that it was necessary that the theory should be acknowledged. The world believed in religion and religion taught another world. This was Paul's belief before he was converted to this Science, but this Science taught him that the wisdom or religion of this world was foolishness with the wisdom of God. Paul admitted Jesus as his teacher and Christ as God or Science. Therefore when he spoke of Christ he meant something more than the natural man or Jesus. When Paul tried to make the Corinthians understand the difference he said that he came not to teach the wisdom of this world, so that their faith should stand on the wisdom of God. But he spake of the wisdom of God in a hidden mystery that was with God before the world or man was formed, which none of the princes of this world knew, for if they had known this Science they would not have crucified the man who taught it. Even to this day it is not admitted by the Christian churches except as a mystery. Still they stand as they always have, looking for it to come, when it is in their mouth and they know it not, but eat and drink with the wisdom of this world as they did in the old world till the floods came and swept them all away. So it will be. The world will all oppose it, it will be crucified by the church, hated by the doctors, despised by the proud, laughed at by fools and received by the foolish of this world. . . . So to teach Science is to put it in practice so that the world shall be put in possession of a truth that shall be acknowledged above the natural man. If you will read all Paul's writings you will see that this Science was what he was trying to make the people understand, for if they could understand it it would change their motives of action. I have been twenty years trying to learn and teach it and I am at times nearly worn out, but when I think of Moses teaching it for forty years and then only seeing for other generations what he could never enjoy it makes me almost sink to the earth. Even Jesus as a man thought it would become a science in his generation, but he was not sure for he says, "no man knoweth, not the angels in heaven (or the men wise in God's wisdom) but God alone." He knew that it would be established on earth as in heaven. So eighteen hundred years have passed and the same angel is sounding with a loud trumpet saying, "how long shall it be till the wisdom of the world shall become reduced to Science so that it can be taught for the healing of the nations, and man shall cease from teaching lies and learn to speak the truth?" Then an opinion will be looked upon as an opinion and Science will judge of the correctness of it. Then all kinds of opinions will be weighed in the balance and the wisdom of this world will come to naught. Then will arise a new heaven and a new earth to free man from disease or error, for this old world or belief shall be burned up with the fire of Science and the new heaven shall arise wherein shall not be found these old superstitions of bigotry and disease, but there will be no more death or sighing from an ache or pain which arises from the superstitions of the old world. . . . Eternal life was taught to man by Jesus and called Christ instead of Science, and to know this Christ is to know eternal progress. This science teaches man how to break off from all error or bad habits that lead to disease, for as disease is in his belief to be good is to be wise. But health does not always show itself in science, for the fool in his heart says there is no science of God, therefore the fool is happy in his knowledge. So are a great many persons happy, according to Paul's idea, who are wise in their own conceit and puffed up by the flattery of the world. They come up like the flower of the field and flourish as a politician in some other way for a time. But the dew or wisdom of Science passes over them and they wither for the want of something to sustain them; and seeing themselves behind the times as scientific men and all their wisdom taken from them and turned out with the ox to eat this world's food or grass, they then see themselves as a man sees himself in a glass and then turns round, walks off and forgets what manner of man he was. Then his place that once knew him shall know him no more, for his wisdom is numbered with the dead ideas that never had any life except of the wisdom of this world. So here ends the life of the small and the great, the earthly prince and the ignorant beggar find their level in the grave of their belief.

WHAT IS RELIGION?

This question is more easily asked than answered, for when you ask to have it defined it vanishes as a thing and only remains as a belief. All persons have a right to a belief, so all persons can have religion if they have any desire to get up a belief. I have tried to find if there is any such thing defined in the dictionary, and I find the definition of religion to be a system of faith and worship or pious practice. Then pious means religious or godly, and so you get right back where you started from, as you do in thou-sands of errors founded on error. For instance, ask a physician what causes pains on the shoulders or side. The answer is, rheumatism. What is that? Neuralgia. What is that? Nervous affection. So he will go on from one thing to another till you get him angry and drive him back where he started. Is it so in science ? No. The chemist tells the truth, and if you do not believe he shows you the fact so you have no doubt. In all the above theories there are phenomena which cannot be accounted for by the natural man, for he reasons in matter and he never can understand the things of the Spirit; for all these are governed or created in the heavens or spiritual world, and this spiritual world, is Science. . . . When Science comes wisdom takes the place of religion, and this world of opinions gives way to the scientific world. Then is established Christ's kingdom or religion in this world as it is in heaven.

THE OTHER WORLD

I will take the man Jesus as I find Him and see if I can gather from what He has said and done what His ideas of another world were. No one doubts that He was a very good man, independent of what He taught, but so far as this world's goods went He had no where to lay His head; so His goodness must spring from another source than dollars and cents, as He had none of these. His food or wisdom was not of man, it was above the common opinion of the world. As far this world's goodness went He did not make much account of it, for when they were boasting about the Christian goodness, He asked, "If you love and help them that love you what reward have ye? Do not sinners the same?" His goodness was not in anything that man, could do as man, for when called to pay His tribute money He sent Peter to catch a fish and get the money out of it. Here He showed some wisdom to know that the very fish that would bite the hook contained the money. Perhaps the opinions of the wise may explain whether Jesus caused the fish to come round and bite or how it was. I shall not try to explain now but leave it to those who believe it a literal truth.

Now I think I can give an explanation of Jesus' belief. At the time of the birth of Jesus the people were superstitious and ready to catch at any marvelous thing they could not explain. Jesus had been studying into the laws of the mind till He came to the conclusion that the priests were a set of blind guides, talking about what they knew nothing of, except as an opinion, and that they were deceiving the people by pretending to have power from another world. Jesus knew all their theories and pretences were based on ignorance of opinion, but He could see there must be something in all the phenomena. Hearing of John's preaching He went to hear him, and then saw how the truth might be reduced to a Science. Here was His temptation; if He used this wisdom for money-making business He could not meet with the same results, it must make Him selfish. So He concluded He would risk all the sneers and opposition of the religious world and stand up and defend a Science that struck at the roots of all religious superstition and public opinion and tested all things by one living and true principle. The Old Testament being their Bible, He had to explain its meaning and show that the writers taught this great truth, so He had to speak in parables. His wisdom being based on 'Science that He could prove, He commenced to put it in practice toward disease. . . . All the world's wisdom was based on an opinion, and to meet it was to spiritualize every idea. They believed in a literal heaven; to this He gave a spiritual meaning, saying His heaven was not of this world of opinions but of Science, and He would bring it down to man's understanding. This they could not understand, for their belief located His kingdom in space and attached their senses to it as a place. But the priests had condensed these phenomena into an identity called God, had given Him power over everything they could not understand, and robbed Him of wisdom that explained their ignorance. They created a God after their own wisdom and set Him in the heaven of their own belief. Thus the priests have placed misconstruction on every passage in the Bible which condemns superstition and taken all the wisdom to themselves; while the very Science that the Bible contains is their worst enemy. This has made the man spoken of in Revelation, which seemed to be written by an insane man. If any one will look at it it will be seen it is a book of the progress of Science over the opinions of the priest. It will be seen how John labored to show the people that the priests' ideas bound them and kept them in bondage. But his writings fell into the hands of the priests who put their own construction upon them and turned the minds of the people, who might be taught to see through their wisdom. So the book of Revelation, like all the others of the New Testament, has been stolen by the priests, turned and twisted and misconstrued to prove that men were writing to establish the truth of the priests' opinions.

Now I know by the cures I make that disease was made by the false construction of priests and I shall show that not one of the writers of the New Testament ever had an idea of priestcraft; but the priests knowing that the people fell in with their views stole the ideas and persecuted the authors, just as they do at this day. The priests claim to be the teachers of morals and good order.

Jesus had to establish a kingdom as the priests had done; theirs was based on opinions, His on Science, so everything that they believed was only an opinion, which His Science could tear to pieces. So He begins by saying "Seek first the kingdom of heaven;" That is, seek wisdom, then all their craft could be explained. Then He says, the kingdom of heaven has come unto you and ye will not receive it, that is, the Science is here but you will not try to understand. In the Old Testament David called this Science wisdom and exhorted his son to seek it first of all. Jesus called it the kingdom of heaven and calls on all men to seek it. If this wisdom and the kingdom of heaven were not the same, then Jesus and David had different ideas of wisdom. Does the priest call on the people to get understanding? No, that is what be fears. The priests want them to have religion, that is, to believe in the creeds which cramp the intellect and bind burdens upon them so that they can lead them. They fear investigation, for it is death to their craft. . . .

DEFENCE AGAINST AN ACCUSATION OF PUTTING DOWN RELIGION

I am often accused of putting down religion and when I ask what is religion I am told the same old story that every one knows, to be good and to worship God. Now all this sort of cant may do if it is not analyzed, but if you undertake to analyze it it vanishes like dew before the morning sun. Religion is what it was before Christ and I think I know what that was. The religion that Christ opposed consisted in forms and ceremonies. Now why did Jesus oppose it if belief had nothing to do with health and happiness? He said they that are well need no physician. So if a person were well it made no difference to Jesus what he believed, but he came to those that had been deceived. Well, how did he cure them? By changing their minds, for if he could not change their minds he could not cure them. This was the way with the young man who was rich who came to Jesus to know what he should do to be saved. Now if the young man was really in danger of being doomed to "eternal punishment," as we are taught, then all that was wanted was to believe; so if his belief changed him I ask if it changed his identity or mind? We are taught that man cannot do anything of himself to save himself, but was this the case with this young man? No, for Jesus told him what to do, to keep the commandments and these were not Jesus' but Moses' commandments. The young man said. "This have I done from my youth upward." So according to the young man's story he was a very good man and Jesus found no fault with him but said, if you will be perfect go sell all you have and follow me. Now here was a young man who had done everything to be saved and Jesus would not save him unless he would give all that he had to the poor and follow Him. As absurd as this looks you cannot find any one who will comply with it, but people get over it by saying we must give up all sinful acts. Well, be as honest to that young man who went away sorrowful, for he could not understand. This is a fair specimen of the parables. Jesus never hinted that He or the young man had the slightest idea of another world, but it shows on the face of it that a man like Jesus could not be so little or narrow minded as to send a person to endless misery because he would not give all his riches to the poor.

Now I will give my construction, and if I do not make Jesus more of a man than the other I will never explain the Bible again. The Jews thought they were the chosen people of God and were the best and knew the most. So riches were wisdom and they were rich in the laws of Moses. This young man came to Jesus to ask Him what be should do to obtain this belief that Jesus taught. Jesus said, "Keep the commandments." This he had done. Well, go and give away your ideas and try to learn mine. This he could not do for he could not see into it. So he went away sorrowful. Jesus' own disciples were in the same way for they said, "we have forsaken all, what lack we more?" He then goes on to tell what they must do, but they did it not for they all forsook Him. Now if it requires such a sacrifice to go to heaven, he never found one that went, for they asked Him if these things are so how a man can be saved. . . .

My religion, like Jesus', is in my acts, not in my belief. The sick are in their belief and not in their acts, for if it were in their acts they would be better; for to be wise is to be good and to be good is to show your goodness by your acts. So if a man is sick he is not good and if he is not good he is not happy, and if he is not good his evil must be something else than good. His goodness is Science or Christ, his badness must be an opinion or religion. Now to be born again is to separate the true religion from the dross, and I know of no better rule than Jesus laid down when He said, "by their fruits ye shall know them." I am willing to be judged by my works, and if they bear me out I do not know as the wisdom of this world of opinions has any right to pass judgment on me....

When I sit by a person, if I find no opinion I find no disease, but if I find a disease I find an opinion, so that the misery that is in the opinion or belief is the disease. I have to make war with the disease or opinion and as there are a great many that make their disease out of the world's religion it is my duty to change the belief to make the cure, and it is astonishing to see persons cling to their opinions as though they contained the substance, when if they knew the substance of their belief they would laugh at their folly. Now to me it is as plain as twice two makes four. I can sum up the religion of Jesus in one simple parable and that is the parable of the child when the people were disputing about the kingdom of heaven. Jesus took up a little child from their midst and said, "of such is the kingdom of heaven" Every one knows it is harder to unlearn an error than to learn a truth, so Jesus, knowing that a child was free from both, took him as a parable. So the Christian world must get rid or give away all errors and become as a little child to receive the Holy Ghost or Science. This was the new birth; therefore to enter into Science or the kingdom of heaven was not a very easy thing. So if any one says he is born of God or Science let him show it for many shall come saying, "I am Christ," and shall deceive many, but by their fruits ye shall know them. So you see that Jesus' religion had nothing to do with the opinions of the world. (5)

Notes

(1) This is explained below, Chap. 19.
(2) Quimby did not believe in the heredity of disease save so far as one generation adopts the beliefs (not the diseases) of another.
(3) This is a typical instance of Quimby's method of re-education.
(4) Dr. Quimby's term "senses" is here widely inclusive.
*(5)   It is important to note that Quimby's Christian Science was founded on two principles: **(1)** the idea of "the Christ within," or the Divine wisdom which Jesus taught, which is the guide to the spiritual interpretation of the Bible; and **(2)** the idea that all causation is mental and spiritual: the body contains no intelligence or power of its own; hence "every phenomenon that takes form in the body was first conceived in the mind." The latter proposition Quimby demonstrates in his reasonings concerning such a disease as cancer, and in what he writes about strength. See above, Chap. 16.*

Chapter Nineteen - Science, Life, Death

[By the term Science Dr. Quimby meant that wisdom which, superior to all opinions or wisdom of the world, and all knowledge founded on externals, mere facts or speculation, is Divine in origin; is beyond all doubt, and capable of verification by all. It is Divine, not in the sense of a "revelation" given on authority, but because it is "Wisdom reduced to self-evident propositions," "reduced to practice for the benefit of man," therefore the basis of sciences such as chemistry or mathematics in which unchangeable principles are implied. Science is aggressive, it is the Truth which shall set men free, the Christ which Jesus came to declare. It is discoverable in the Bible, if we have spiritual eyes to see the meaning beneath the symbols. It is within the reach of all who, led by intuition and, aware of man's true nature, distinguish between shadows and realities, the mind which is always changing and the spirit which never changes. Man then may learn to identify his true self with Science as the "scientific man," the man with spiritual senses and an immortal identity. Dr. Quimby did not undertake to found a new religion on this "great truth" or Science, but believed that spiritual science is altogether superior to religion as ordinarily understood. His writings as a whole show what he means by the term. The first selection is from an article written in July, 1860, in which he defines his meaning, in part:]

SCIENCE

THE word science is frequently used, but so loosely defined that its true meaning cannot be understood. Ask a man what science is, he answers, "It is knowledge, a collection of general principles." This leaves the question just where we find it. So every one sets up his standard of a collection of general principles.

Let us see if the word can be explained so that every one may know what science is. Science embraces something spiritual or a revelation from a higher state of being. Science is the name of that wisdom that accounts for all phenomena that the natural man or beast cannot understand.

To illustrate. You throw a ball into the air, every child will soon learn that the ball will return. This is not science. But to know understandingly that it will return with just as much energy as it received, is science. Science is in the act, although the person knows it not, and God is in the world and the world knows Him not. This principle Jesus tried to teach to man. The acts of man were sometimes according to this law, but the actors knew it not. So they being ignorant of Science were a science unto themselves. As they did not know the motive, they could not teach it to others.

Paul, speaking of this Science, says some have not even heard of it, and how shall they believe in what they have not heard of as a science; how shall they hear without a preacher, and how shall they preach a science unless they be sent? So he says, How beautiful are the feet of those who preach the gospel of peace (or the words of that person who can teach Science). He uses the word "charity" for the same wisdom, and goes on to tell that although we give all our money to the poor, and suffer our bodies to be burned, and do not understand Science or charity, it is of no use. To understand wisdom or charity so as to put it into practice, so that it becomes a science, is not an easy task. Well might the disciples say this is a hard saying, and how can a man believe or understand? Therefore, if they cannot understand, must the wisdom of God be of no effect? Wisdom says, "No! Let God (Science) be true, but every man a liar."

This Science was in the minds of the people, but the priests and doctors led the people and explained it according to their own notions, so when Jesus came to establish this truth as a science, to them it was a stumbling-block. The wisdom of this world never had put science into goodness, but thought goodness was a dispensation. This wisdom or charity was known by some to have an identity, but was never admtted as anything independent of the natural man. So goodness was considered by the priests as a sort of subjection to the rulers. A good person was like a good dog, ready to obey his master; then his master would pat him and call him a good dog, although he had just torn another dog in pieces, or had done something else to please his master.

This was the way with the Christian church: to be good was to persecute all who would not bow the knee to the leaders. All who had the boldness to speak their opinions were heretics or infidels. The priests patted the heads of their dogs and set them on the swine or those who opposed them, so that to steal from or rob one of these sceptics was a virtue rather than a wrong.

I have seen this effect in my own practice. There are people who are honest according to their religion who will come and tell me a lie, as I call it, to deceive me into a belief that they mean just what they say. I have just the same confidence in their honesty that I have in a bull dog who looks as innocent as a lamb when you have something that he wants, and when he gets it will bite you as soon as your back is turned. This all arises from smothering the Science or charity, or revelation from God. And this is done by the priest. The priests make their goodness a matter of self-interest, and charge people a fee to pardon their sins, which the honest part of the community would look upon as a wrong. The priest flatters them with the idea that they are doing just right. So they worship the priest as the masses worship the leaders, and every person knows that a leading demagogue will uphold any crime his party is guilty of, and applaud the actor for his honesty or goodness.

Charity has no friend with any of these leaders. It finds no foothold. Therefore, like the dove of the ark, after trying to find a place to rest it returns to its house and is gone to the world. This was the case in the days of Jesus. He came to establish this Science or charity. This word Science not being used to explain this truth, it was called by Jesus "Christ," and by Paul it was called "charity." By the wise who admitted it, it was called a power or gift, but it was never admitted to have an identity with the teaching to which the senses were attached. This was Jesus' religion, so that He talked His religion, instead of talking about it. To talk wisdom is Wisdom, whereas to talk about wisdom is to talk an unknown God. Jesus tells just where the people stood in regard to this truth. There were none who understood it, but many who acted according to their principles. These he called persons who being ignorant of the law were a law to themselves, because they did right and did not know why they wanted to do it. He describes their minds as half wise and half foolish. But the wise were ignorant of the cause of their own wisdom, so that in trying to make people understand this truth, which he called the greatest of sciences or the kingdom of God, he spoke in parables.

He commences by a parable of the foundation of this Science, or the ground in which it is sown, and then shows the growth by parables. So when he was asked for an explanation of this Science or power, or kingdom, he took a little child in his arms and said, "Of such is the foundation or kingdom of heaven." Now, every one knows that a child is a blank as far as virtue or vice is concerned, and with it "might is right." The growth of this child's wisdom depends entirely upon the direction given to its mind. Then He asks, "What shall I compare its little wisdom to? I will compare it to a grain of mustard-seed that a man sowed in his garden"

So God sowed in this little child's mind wisdom, and this wisdom if properly developed would teach him that his body, like the earth, is the casket or loom for this wisdom to develop itself in. As it developed itself, it would leave its mother earth and derive its life from a higher and more perfect mother that had no matter, but which lifts one above all the fog or atmosphere of earth, and the decomposition of matter or ideas that contain all sorts of evil. The growth of this wisdom was likely to be destroyed, for Herod sought to kill it. But its mother hid it in the ignorance or bushes, in the sea of superstition, till it could grow in the hearts of the people. So when its branches began to put forth, and the fowls or theories began to build nests or attack it, then came the devil and made war against it. Then the priests and doctors joined in and stirred up the multitude to search out where the true wisdom was, that they might take counsel together how they should destroy it.

When Jesus appeared at the common age of man, ready to defend Himself, John sent to Him to know if He was this Science or Christ, or must we look for another. As Jesus began to preach this truth or Science it struck at the root of all the old superstitions. This was the very thing the people had looked for. The prophets had prophesied that the time would come when man should act from a higher motive than dollars and cents, when goodness would be a virtue and would be appreciated: the priests had looked upon all virtue as passion, and had treated it as such. Thus sympathy or love was misrepresented by these blind guides, so that people ac-knowledged and thought that they were born dishonest, and all kinds of vice and passion were elements of our nature. When Jesus began to separate vice from virtue the war began. This separation was His religion.

Vice and passions were the inventions of man. I will not say brutish, for that is a stain on God or goodness. For the brutes act as they were intended to, and to compare them to man who debases himself below the brute is a stain on the whole character of the horse, for instance. I have seen a thing driving a horse who looked more out of place than he would if he were in the thills and the horse had the reins. This sort of intellect, which is made up of the lowest passions of man, is as much beneath the brute as the hawk is beneath the dove. These two characters make up man. One is ignorance, superstition and all kinds of passion, to gratify the lusts of a low, contemptible mind which cannot see honesty in anything except as a restraint upon the appetites; so he looks upon all restraints as burdens and oppressions. This is the wisdom of this world. This wisdom has always been in the ascendency. It has been the enemy of truth or Science. So when any new development of truth comes up, this brutal intellect catches the seed or idea and puts a low construction on its acts. This causes the war of error, to see which shall get the mastery. Science comes as a natural result of the quarrel. For the truth never makes war for anything. All the fighting is done by ignorance and superstition.

Now, as I have already said, the beasts were made perfect as they were intended to be; no change is visible in each succeeding generation. The combination of the natural brute is perfect. But it does not contain science or wisdom. Man, being what is called the noblest work of God, has a higher development, and shows that there is something outside of matter which can control matter. This something is what the world has always been looking for. It is not in the beasts, for it is not life, and that the beasts have; nor is it reason, for the beasts have that; nor is it passion, nor is it love, for all of these the beasts have. Then what is it that makes man above the beast? Science or a revelation from a spiritual world, higher than the natural world. And this wisdom or Science is progression. For it is in the beastly man, although in such it has never been developed.

Wisdom or Science makes the distinction in man by this figure: man is of the earth earthly, yet in him was this Science in the form of a rib, or this higher power, and the Science called it woman. And this woman or wisdom is to lead man or ignorance to truth and happiness. Now, neither the man nor the woman had any science, and man like the beast was willing to live under restriction, as all other animals did; for God placed all other animals under the law of might. But it was not so with the rib. The rib saw farther ahead than the beast; it had more sagacity, and like the serpent, said to itself, here is a tree or knowledge of good and evil, or judge of right and wrong, and if you eat it or investigate you shall be like the father of it, more than the brute. Here you see the true character of wisdom. It shrinks not from investigating, although it is unpopular and has the whole world to contend with. It fights its way regardless of danger. So it ate or investigated whatever it saw.

Now I will suppose the tree. Theories are something called trees. The tree that bears not good fruit, and is to be hewn down, is anything man wants to investigate. . . . You must go back to Adam and Eve, or to a little child, as Jesus said when He undertook to explain the same idea. So of course it had no reference to man and woman as we see them, but to the development of knowledge above the brute. So He takes man and woman as figures of truth and error, and shows that the mind of woman is better calculated to receive seed or investigate. Women have more endurance and more patience to investigate any new science than man. And their wisdom is not of this world, but of that higher power called Science. When they give their idea to man, he then eats or understands, and then goes to work to form the idea that has been given to him by the woman. It has always been the case that all spiritual wisdom has been received through the female. The oracle of Delphi was a woman. As men's minds are more brutal and less scientific or spiritual, they never believe till they can see with the natural man's eyes. Science to them is a shadow. Now as [the natural] man is of matter and his thoughts are a part of himself, he lives on his ideas and forms all his plans in matter and carries them out in matter; thus the natural man knows nothing about matter. The spiritual man or the woman is out of matter, and sees all the changes of matter. These two characters are in every man, and to distinguish them is what is taught by this Science. Science suffers long before it becomes a fact. It envieth not other science. It vaunteth not itself, is not puffed up; doth not behave unseemly; is not easily provoked; thinketh no evil; rejoiceth not in iniquity, but rejoices in the truth. Science never faileth, but prophecies do. The knowledge of this world fails, but Science never fails.

CHRISTIAN SCIENCE

[In most of his articles Dr. Quimby used the expressions "Christ or Truth," "Christ or Science," and so the term Science came to stand for "the Science of the Christ," or "Science of Health and Happiness." In an article on "Aristocracy and Democracy," written, February, 1863, he uses the term "Christian Science" for the first time. The paragraph in which the term occurs is as follows:]
The leaders of the medical schools, through the hypocrisy of their profession, deceive the people into submission to their opinions, while democracy forges the fetters which are to bind them to disease. Science, which would destroy this bondage, is looked upon as blasphemy when it dares oppose the faculty, and religion has no place in medical science. So in the church the religion of Jesus' Science is never heard; for it would drive aristocracy out of the pulpit, and scatter seeds of freedom among the people. Nevertheless, the religion of Christ is shown in the progress of Christian Science, while the religion of society decays as the liberal principles are developed. Man's religion labors to keep Science down in all churches North and South, by suppressing free discussion, for aristocracy will not have anything tending to freedom.
[In lengthy articles devoted to biblical interpretation, Dr. Quimby endeavored to show that there is a spiritual Science in the Bible underneath the letter of the Word, and in all these studies he contrasts the two forces at work within man, for example, Cain and Abel, Law and Gospel, Saul and Paul. He believed that the Bible was never intended as a religious book in the common acceptance of the term, it "has nothing to do with theology," but contains a "scientific" explanation of cause and effect, showing how man must act and think for his happiness. Thus the account of creation pertains to

man's spiritual development, not to the production of a literal earth. Dr. Quimby also expounded many passages in the New Testament so as to free his patients from a literal view and show that Jesus' sayings implied "the Christ within" or true healing principle. Thus he set the example followed by all his adherents who have found a key to the Scriptures in spiritual interpretation.

[It will be noticed that statements appear from time to time in the foregoing selections from which it would be easy to make the inferences on which "Christian Science" ordinarily so-called was based. For example, in "Questions and Answers" we read, "There is no wisdom in matter," and that the truth or understanding on which Quimby bases his teaching "is God, . . . for in that there is no matter; and so to understand is Wisdom, not matter." Matter is said to be merely "an idea" or "shadow." Combine these statements with the proposition that "matter contains no life or intelligence" and that life or intelligence is to be attributed to God only, and it is only a step to infer that "all is mind, there is no matter"-that is, no matter in God. Matter comes into view when it is a question of opinions or errors which take shape according to our allegiance to them, our bondage to the mind of opinions-called by Mrs. Eddy "mortal mind." Dr. Quimby did not deny the existence of matter as an expression of mind. But he did say that there is "no matter in God." Hence it is legitimate to say in that connection "all is mind, there is no matter."

[Again, we find Quimby saying, "The Science of Health which I teach was practised by Jesus. . . . His Science or Christ put man in tune." "This knowledge which I put in practice is the Science of Health." He also refers to the "Principle that never moves, the foundation of all things." God to Quimby was this "Principle" which Jesus taught as "the Christ." Here we have the origin of the term "Science and Health," and the other terms on which the later "Christian Science" was founded. This Science was to Quimby the clue to the spiritual interpretation of Scripture. He also speaks of it as "revelation."

[It is noticeable that in "Questions and Answers" there is no clear idea of the human self, and that other points ob-scure in that manuscript are obscure in "Christian Science," also. On the whole "Questions and Answers" is very obscure. Nor is there to be found anywhere in the earlier writings a clear idea concerning the nature and origin of evil. Hence it would have been easy to make the inference: "all is good, there is no evil," since Quimby attributes all evil to human opinion or error, and finds no reality in an ultimate sense in human opinions and errors. Later, he is more explicit, and plainly says that goodness is to be attributed to God only, goodness is due to Science, and should be taught to young and old as a Science. It is therefore right to infer that evil is due to our ignorance, to opinion. Had we been taught Science from the beginning, we would have grown up without diseases, without evil; and we would never have mistaken appearances or shadows for reality.

[Dr. Quimby never uses the language of denial. He never explicitly says, "there is no matter," or "there is no evil." This is a legitimate back-handed way of declaring what to him was the greatest truth: there is no reality save that which exists in God or Science. His realization of this truth was so strong that he did not need denials. Furthermore, as the foregoing selections make plain, he believed it necessary to explain as well as cure or heal; and to explain was to show precisely in what way shadows had been misinterpreted as substances. His realization for Mrs. Patterson-Eddy gave her the impetus which started her on the way we find her following as indicated by her letters, 1862-64, while she is gradually gaining strength and learning to apply the new "Science." Her later statements, like those of Rev. Mr. Evans and the other followers of Quimby, are conditioned by her understanding of what Quimby meant. Whether her inferences were right. or not, or whether Evans in his "Mental Cure" and "The Divine Law of Cure" was a clearer reasoner, must be left for the reader to determine.]

LIFE

When we speak of life we speak of it as though it were a thing. But there are as many kinds of life as there are birds or fishes or anything which grows, and the life of a plant is not the same as that of a tree; neither is the life of man the same as that of a beast. All life is the result of the chemical action of some idea, so that life is matter, and it lives on life or matter; therefore the material man is made up of life and death. This life is continually changing, so that we live on life which we receive from others. Ideas are [spiritual] matter and of course they contain life.

We eat or receive life in the wrong sense. For instance, the Jews when they ate pork thought they ate life, for their belief was that it would produce a disease: although the pork was dead it would rise again in the form of scrofula. So to avoid having that life in them they would not eat pork.

Now, as absurd as this idea is, it is the basis of our knowledge about disease. How often are we reminded not to eat such and such things. We all admit that animal food has life in it. So we eat it as life; for when we say that it is so far decayed that it is not good we look on it as poison. So also we receive life into our stomach as though it really added to our life or strength. How often we talk about fat making us warmer. All these ideas are the result of error and their fruits are disease.

Does the dog eat meat as though it had life? No, he eats it as "dead" and expects no bad effects from it. So it is with all living beings but man. Man has reasoned himself into a belief that all he eats and drinks contains life, and this life or food is his enemy or friend according to his belief. Thus he is kept continually on the watch what kind of food he receives.

Although the life or food that he receives contains the idea of death, yet his belief is that he lives, and he is affected by his belief.

Now when I eat or drink, the life that was in the substance eaten is dead to me, and has no life in it. So I am not afraid in eating pork of any bad effects. Neither am I afraid if I listen and take a person's feelings arising from scrofula or any other disease that I shall have the disease, for the life of the disease is in the person who believes it.

What is the weapon that destroys this life or disease? Science. This is eternal, and that destroys all other life. This is to the animal life, death. So Science to the natural man is nothing that contains life. But this Science is a Principle. This is the only living and eternal life. This Science is what rose from the dead or natural life.

Man in his natural state was no more liable to disease than the beast. But as soon as he began to reason he became diseased, for his disease was in his reason. Therefore his reason was his life, and this made him afraid of his reason. This the doctors called nervousness, and to prevent this nervous life they introduced disease in certain things we eat or drink.

Let man rid himself of these blind guides and follow the command of God, and take no thought of what he shall eat or drink as having anything to do with his health and he will then be much better off. Seek first Science at the appearance of every phenomenon, and pay no attention to your food any more than the rest of God's creatures do. If man were as wise in regard to what goes into his stomach as the beast he would be much better off. Let the health alone. Seek to enlighten man in Science, and as Science is developed man will become wise and happy. This life is in his wisdom and his wisdom is a science. To put his science into practice for his own happiness is to correct some error that he has embraced. To prove the science to others is to take something that man is troubled about in the form of a disease which creates unhappiness, ,and correct the opinion so that health is established.

I have shown that there is no matter independent of mind or life. It is proved by geologists that matter is going through a process of change which is called life. Then life is in the atmosphere or space. And if life is in a state invisible to matter it may fill all space. In this space there must be diversity of matter or life, namely, the life of minerals, the life of vegetables, and the life of animals; and all these are in the atmosphere like the mist that went up from the earth at creation. Thus matter or life is in an invisible state to the visible matter, but governed by the same God. This makes the material earth or natural world. God made matter and condensed it into certain forms and elements that were necessary for man. And to be a combination of these it was necessary that there should be a chemical union of all matter dissolved into space before man could be formed. For man's body is made of the dust of this living matter.

As man contains all the elements of this material world or life, he is a minature world in himself. This matter or life under the wisdom of God forms the identity of what is called the natural man, so that man, spoken into being, was made up of all the elements of the material world. . . . The natural man commences his life in a higher state of matter. The field or garden in which he is placed is with all the creation of animal forms, and he is liable to all the evils which his life is capable of knowing. . . . It is not strange that phenomena should appear while man is so ignorant of what he is composed of which can be traced to the animal kingdom. All phenomena are the effect of what man receives from this animal life . . . and as his life is in his belief he reasons his life out of existence. Being a progressive process, his life has to contend with all the grosser life or matter of the animal. But as he is the rib or purest part of animal life, he contains the elements of knowledge, and this the lower life does not contain. . . .

MAN AND WOMAN

Man, like the earth, is throwing off a vapor, and that contains his knowledge. Out of this vapor comes a more perfect identity of living matter, more rarified than the former, and consequently in danger of being devoured by it. The latter life is less gross, therefore more spiritual, so that what it loses in physical strength it receives from a higher power approaching God or Science. This Science is the wisdom of God that controls the higher intellect. As the earth is composed of different kinds of soil, so man varies from the lowest grade of animal intelligence to that higher state of consciousness which can receive Science. . . . The spiritual rib that rises from man is more perfect matter or soil, called woman. . . . I do not mean that. woman means every female. Nor do I pretend to say that man means everything of the animal. But that the mind of the female contains more of that superior substance required to receive the higher development of God's wisdom. For this element is pure love that has been purified by the change life has gone through... Phenomena have always occurred in the form of Science, as though man had once been advanced far beyond his present condition. . . . The male creation feeds on the lower order of life. It makes the higher order a sort of pet for a while, the natural man sports and plays with the female. While the purer part of his nature is sympathizing with its own love in a higher soil or life, the animal life is prowling around to devour the little pleasure that is striving to grow in this barren soil. This keeps science down, for it is not known to the natural man. But put this science into the life or soul of the female, and then she is safe from the animal life, and it puts her in possession of a Science that the natural man knows nothing of. It separates her from matter and brings her into that spiritual state that rises from all animal life with a knowledge of its character. Like a chemist she then stands among all kinds of matter, which are under her control, and which she has the power of changing. Then she becomes a teacher of that Science which puts man in possession of a wisdom that can subject all animal life to his own control, and separate the wisdom of this world from the wisdom of God. Then woman becomes a teacher of the young, and man stands to woman as a servant to his Lord, ready to investigate all phenomena by Science. The woman is the one who gives all the impressions to the child. . . . But man from some cause, probably from having more physical strength, and looking upon all things as inferior to his own wisdom, is not content to subject all the brute creation to his will, but must subject the very creature that his best life or nature adores, and in this way woman is deprived of carrying out the science that God intended. By this physical force woman is kept down, and does not take the place in the world which God intended. But I maintain that wherever in the world matter or life becomes pure enough for science to reign over ignorance, then Science will become the master and ignorance the servant. . . Mind is only another state called life that is purifying itself to receive a higher life that will never end; that is Science. . . . Man lives on such active life as his appetite craves, and as he separates the animal from the spiritual, his appetite or passions change till he is completely carried away by the spiritual life. . . .

Science teaches man that although he is not of this world he is a teacher in it, and being a teacher he is a soldier in the hands of Science. To fight the life of error like a soldier and contend for the truth or Science requires more courage than it does to fight for your own bread. . . . As the soil of California is rich enough to produce gold, so the soul or life of the female is rich enough to produce the wisdom of Cod. It does not follow that the life of woman is the only soil capable of producing Science, but it contains more spiritual wisdom than is found in man. This is as should be, and if it could be admitted by man, so that woman could have her place in the life of man, the world would in a short time be rid of the scourges, the medical faculty and priests that now infest the land. Women are religious from Science naturally, and had not man instructed them the world would have been free now from super-stition and evils that follow our belief. Woman is not so superstitious as man. . . . Her sympathy is inexhaustible. While men would get out of patience and would leave the sick, woman will cling to them as much as to say, "Death, you shall not have this life."

Now, where is woman placed? Just where man puts her to satisfy himself. She has nothing to do with her situation, but she must be content with what man chooses to assign her. In wisdom he of course is to be the great center of attraction, and although he has no light, only as it is thrown from the sun or higher power of his wisdom, woman thinks his light is derived' from a power superior to himself. . . . But a female coming forward in public to advocate man's ideas is as much below the male as a male who personifies a brute for the gratification of an audience is below the brute itself. . . . Where is woman's true position? As a teacher of the Science of Health and Happiness. This is what man does not want to do. It is too much like labor to toil over little children, and sit by the sick and take their sufferings upon oneself. Men will not do this. But they are very willing to bind burdens upon their neighbors, which they will not lift one finger to remove: by teaching false doctrines, whose effect on the people they do not know, which keep the people in bondage and all their lives subject to death. . .

Man is the life of all life before him. He becomes a sort of living matter, subject to all the laws of life or matter. . . . At last he becomes more refined, and becomes the medium of the life of Science or everlasting life, where there is no death, but where all things are tried by Science. . . .

LIGHT

Every man is a part of God, just so far as he is wisdom. So I will tell what I know, not what I believe. I worship no God except my own and I will tell you what He teaches me. In the first place He puts no restrictions on me, in fact He is in me, and just as I know myself I know Him; so that God and I are one, just as my children and I are one. To please myself I please God, and to injure myself is to injure my God. So all I have to do is to please myself. As God and I are one so you and I are one, and to please myself is to please you, and to injure myself is to injure you, so just as I measure out to you I measure out to myself. As you and I are one, you and your neighbor are one, and to love your neighbor as yourself is more than all the prayers made by all the priests in the world. I know that if I do by another as I would be done by in like circumstances I feel right, so I judge no man. I do not judge of myself, for my knowledge of this Wisdom is as plain to me as my senses.

To the world this is a belief, but to me it is wisdom that the religious world knows not of. It they did they would never crucify me as they do in their ignorance. So my religion is my wisdom which 'is not of this world, but of that Wisdom that will break in pieces the wisdom of men. Man's wisdom is the superstition of heathen idolatry; all Science is at variance with it. I stand alone, not believing in anything independent of Science; so you can put me down as having no sympathy with any belief or religion concerning another world, or in anything belonging to the Christian death. Neither have I any belief in the resurrection of the body. My death is this, ignorance; life is Wisdom, death is darkness or matter. All men have wandered from light and believed in darkness. To destroy matter you introduce light or life.

I will illustrate. Suppose you are sitting in the dark, call that this world. Now as the light springs up where is the darkness? The light is the resurrection of this body or darkness. What becomes of it when the light rises? So it is with man. Man is an idea of matter or darkness, and as his mind becomes lit up or clairvoyant the darkness of the idea of matter is gone, and he is in light that the wisdom of this world or darkness has not. So light came into darkness and the darkness comprehended it not.

When I sit down by a patient I come out of this matter or darkness and stand by the patient's senses, which are attached to some idea of the wisdom of this world which troubles him. I retain my former man and senses. I also have another identity independent of matter, and as I (knowing what is the cause of his misery) stand by the matter or belief of my patient and destroy his belief or the effect it has on his senses, then as the darkness or belief is lit up by the wisdom of Science, his darkness disappears and he rejoices in the light. The light leads him back to his health, from whence he had been decoyed by the blind guides spoken of in scripture. Here you have what I believe and what I disbelieve-the two are my law and gospel. By the law no one can be saved, but by the gospel of Truth, Science will have all saved, -not from the Christian world, but from this world of superstition and ignorance, saved for the greater truth that was prepared from the beginning of the world for all those who search and try to find it. You cannot go into the clouds to call it down, nor into the sea to call it up, but it is in you, in your very thoughts. It is not of this world, but of a higher state, that can penetrate this earthly matter as light through darkness. As the senses are the body of truth they travel through the light, as a man with a lamp travels through the dark. So it is not every one who has a lamp with oil, nor is every one wise who says he is so. But he is wise who can come up to the one in the dark, and lead him through this wilderness of disease into the light of reason and health. Like the good man who had the hundred sheep and one wandered away in the dark, he left the ninety and nine that were in the light and went and found the lost one and restored him to the fold. Now let those who pretend to be shepherds of the sheep, or of poor sick persons starving to death like the prodigal son for spiritual food, eating the husks of science, not the priest's food, go and guide them along to the father of health where they can eat and be glad and have music and dancing. This was Christ's truth; He was the good shepherd, the people were His sheep, and all who looked at Him and listened to the true wisdom, were saved from the errors of the priests and doctors. As Moses lifted up the serpent of the old Egyptian theology or creed, and explained them, and all those who looked on his explanation were healed of their errors that made disease, so Christ was lifted up, and all who understood were healed from the doctrine of the Scribes and Pharisees. So in our day [November, 1860] I hold up the serpent of creeds and doctors' theories, and show the absurdity of their beliefs and all who understand are healed of their diseases.

DEATH

What is death? Man from ignorance has associated truth with error till error has got to be as true as life itself. Life cannot be seen except as it is made manifest in some idea. This idea is called matter, and it has become so identified with life that life cannot exist without it. This is the way man reasons: To destroy life is to destroy the idea that contains it. Therefore when we see our idea without life we say our life is dead. This would be true if death were life. But this is not so, according to the words of Jesus. He says, "I am the way, the truth, and the life." He came to destroy death, and him who had the power of death, that is, the devil. Now if the devil has the power of death, death cannot mean what the people think it does. If death means what we are taught to believe it does, then Jesus knew not what He said. It either means an idea can be changed or it means the destruction of life, and in the latter case what Jesus said amounts to nothing.

I am certain that I know what Jesus meant to convey to the people, for I have seen death myself and the eternal life He spoke of, and can testify that I have passed from death unto life, as He taught the disciples. And knowing this life that is in Christ I teach it to you, not by opinions but by words of wisdom that will destroy death and put you in possession of that true life that will make death only an idea, like all other ideas man must be rid of to be happy.

At the time Jesus taught this eternal world the world was in darkness in regard to one thing, that was life independent of a belief. But as the lamp of Science was lit up it dispelled the shadow of opinions and embraced life. Matter is with Science nothing but a shadow. As its belief is changed death is destroyed and life takes its place. . . .

We have all been made to believe that we were flesh and blood. . . . I believed as all the world did that this body would die, and that I might be raised and reunited with my friends in another world, either happy or miserable. Now, all this is under the law, but by the law no flesh can be saved. In the darkness of this error the light sprang up and I rose from the dead or unbelief to the light of Science, and am now out of my old belief.

I will illustrate. You were once ignorant of mathematics. If some one had given you a mathematical book it would have been darkness to you. But the principle or spiritual wisdom. was in the book. As you began to understand you would have life, and the life would be in your understanding. You would still have a body of flesh and blood in your belief. Losing your ignorance, you would rise from the dead into the scientific world, where those in the law or ignorance would not see you; for the dead know nothing of mathematics.

Instead of being in the book, therefore, you are out of it, and to prove this you say to those who are struggling with the world that you will show yourself by your resurrection. So you do a mathematical problem without the book, and then show people that they are to be judged by their own books, and if they are not found in the book of Science they are dead in their own sins or ignorance. You have a body of flesh and blood in both worlds.

So it is with all other error. Death is ignorance, and unless you are made to destroy it by your own belief [effort] you cannot get rid of it. The world has made an end of life, but Jesus was the end of the world's life; so the world's life to Him was death and His life was the destruction of their belief. So I believe in flesh and blood but not in death, for I have passed from that belief into a life that is eternal. I have flesh and blood, as you all see; I shall never be without it [never without a body]. But you from belief may destroy my life to yourself, while to me it is the same today and forever. Here you have the belief of one who has seen the idea death swallowed up in Science, therefore to me the change is not a thing of belief but a truth.

You may ask me if I do not believe in what is called death. I answer, yes, if I did not I should not try to destroy it in others. To know that my friends are separated from me on account of their unbelief makes me more earnest that they should believe the truth. If your father or mother were carried out of your sight and you thought they were dead, if they knew it would they not weep for your unbelief ? They know they are alive with flesh and blood. But your belief makes a wall so dense that you cannot penetrate your own belief.

I will now say a few words in regard to the state called death. As this error is so well established that it is folly to deny it, I must explain my grounds for denying what every one believes. Let us see what man loses by the change called death. If you make a man admit that his happiness is in this state of error or opinions, then to get out of it would be death. But convince every person that he might sit down and fall into a state in which he might go where he pleased, and enjoy the society of those he did in his waking state, and be responsible for his acts the same as though awake, and if his ability and genius and good character earn for him the sympathy of some friend that would like to have him accompany him to a foreign country, and he should go and enjoy all the privileges of a guest, then wake up, don't you suppose he would like to take another trip ?

Now destroy all ideas of death and that would destroy disease. Then man would labor for wisdom, and when he grew rich he would say to himself, "I am rich enough, so I will now lie down and rest and enjoy my friends, and listen to the world's talk." So he gives up his cares and lies down, and rides around and enjoys himself. One is a figure of the other; but one is real, and the other is a shadow. The man who is rich in this world's goods to the exclusion of some scientific capital cannot travel in the world of Science with his money. To have money and no wisdom is to be like the rich man in the Bible spoken of by Jesus. He had been at work and got rich, and his crops were so large that he said to himself: "I will tear down my old house and barn, and build me a more expensive establishment; or I will dress up and go into more educated society, among the literary world and enjoy myself." But Science says to him, "This night shalt thou be satisfied that all thy riches will not make thee a man of Science." So you must lose all that foolish pride that impels the rules of the world, for where Science comes riches take to themselves wings and fly away into the wilderness of darkness. When these two characters lie down together, they are received into society according to their worth or talent. For money is not wisdom. So the rich man of this world may be the beggar of the scientific, while this beggar or man of small means with scientific riches will be as far removed from his neighbor as Dives from Lazarus. One must die to become the other. See the man that is made of money and knows nothing but his money when he is past making it. He is feverish and all he thinks of is his money. This is his happiness and some one is all the time getting it away; so he is in trouble, while the man of science is investigating all the improvements of the age and becoming acquainted with scientific secrets. Now they both lie down to enjoy their riches. The miser is all the time nervous and frightened about his money, while the scientific man is travelling on the interest of his capital; and if an expedition is fitted out for some great discovery, where his science is wanted, he receives an invitation and goes and enjoys himself; while the miser is prowling around to buy some secondhand lock to put on his door to keep out robbers. These two characters may go on for hundreds of years, for time is nothing in eternity. So we see every day figures of change. How many persons are there in this city who get up in the morning and pass the day without gaining enough wisdom to last them till nine o'clock? But you will see them up in the morning before day looking around to find some hole to creep into to get a drop of water or a substance to moisten their tongue, for they are tormented by an appetite for this world's goods. So their life is one continual state of excitement, always opposing everything that enlightens men's minds and elevates character. Such a man is dead to the world of Science, whether he is on top of the ground or underneath, while the man of Science is alive whether on the earth or in it. They both lie down in their own sepulchre. If one is made of opinions, he must take it. If the other is science, he will be in it. So while one is progressing, the other is looking on. They are both rewarded for their acts.

What is the true definition of death ? Death is the name of an idea; an idea is matter, so that the destruction of an idea is death. Every opinion has its center, and its center is the idea. Now if a person believes in anything that is founded on an opinion the idea is in the opinion, and the senses being also in the opinion are attached to the idea. This imprisons the senses in the opinion. Now the idea is of itself nothing but an opinion condensed into a solid and called matter and every word goes to make the idea. So to make an idea men reason about something they have no proof of only as an opinion. So they build their building and in the center is the idea, and if they succeed in establishing their opinion they imprison their opponent and the misery is what flows from the idea.

I will illustrate. Take the word "consumption" This word is of itself nothing to the person who never heard of it. To make it is to create the opinion or building and then reduce it to an idea. So matter in the form of words is so arranged as to make the idea in the opinion. While the opinion is forming in the mind a chemical change is going on, and the matter is held in solution till it is condensed into a form according to the pattern given by the direction of mind, and after the opinion is fairly established in the mind and the person in the idea which is in the center, the senses are attached to the idea and become part of it. Now to separate the senses from the idea is death to the idea, but life to the senses. This separation called death is only death to the one idea.

Man is always dying and living in progression, for error or opinion must always be in the mind and mind must always exist till time is no more. Man is made of science and ignorance, or life and death. Man, seen by the senses is the center of our belief, and the senses are attached to the idea called man, so the idea "man" varies as much as one star differs from another. . . .

The animal is content to be just as he is, and seeks no wisdom above his kind; he lives the animal and when his identity is destroyed he is forgotten by his race, but this is only my opinion. But the animal that is dead to the living is as much alive in the higher state of matter or mind as the man who loses his idea. Each retains his own identity, but man is progressive and the beast is the same forever. The beast has but one rotation of life and death, but man lives all his life subject to death. So although he destroys one idea called death, he is liable to die again and again to the end of time unless his wisdom destroys death by the Science of Life. The last enemy is death, so the scientific man or idea shall reign till all error is destroyed. All identities called man are not the same. There is the well identity of man, the lame, the sick, the deaf, the dumb, and so on. All men are liable to have a combination of all these identities. For instance, a well man or child is an identity. Now it changes to a sick identity, so the well identity is destroyed, and the child's senses are attached to the identity of a disease. The Science of Life is to know how to keep man from getting into death or error. This is my theory; to put man in possession of a Science that will destroy the ideas of the sick and teach man one living progression [development] of his own identity, with life free from error and disease. Now as man passes through these combinations, they differ one from another. So it will be in the resurrection (of the dead), to life, freed from false ideas and in truth. Suppose a man could be so wise as to know every sensation that affects his senses. He could never change, so he would be always the same. Now take another who believes in all the opinions of man, and he is dying and living all the time, dying to error and living to truth, till he dies the death 'of all his opinions or beliefs. Therefore to be free from death is to be alive in Truth, for sin or error is death and Science is eternal life, and this life is in Christ.

I said that every opinion had a center, and this center was an idea. I will try to make this more plain, for it is the center or foundation on which all error rests. Destroy this and disease is out of the mind, for this central idea is the fortress error erects to keep the subject in submission. As wisdom is its enemy, it keeps up a constant cannonading to frighten wisdom into subjection. This idea is built by public opinion, got up by demagogues or doctors and priests, its father or founder was a liar, its foundation is ignorance and superstition; its reign is tyranny and slavery to wisdom, its victims are ignorance. This kingdom of darkness is the error of man, every man's mind is subject to this prince of darkness, its power is in its popularity; its laws are arbitrary and binding on all; it knows no mercy; its chief end is the destruction of man's happiness. For that purpose it holds out large rewards, as it did to Jesus, to those who will enter its service. Its honesty is hypocrisy, and in fact its whole aim is slavery and power. What classes does it embrace? It embraces every opinion of man. Ignorance is the foundation, destruction to freedom or Science is its chief end, so its leaders invent all sorts of falsehoods and bind them on the people, or matter, which is liable to be changed or moulded into their belief. Every inducement is held out to persuade the senses to become interested in their idea or opinion. Now an opinion is like a city or town that has its center or laws. So as man's senses are traveling, like the man going down to Jericho, who fell among thieves, he listens to these false leaders and hears of some idea like a place. It is described to him by some doctor or priest in an earnest manner; this excites the mind, curiosity is aroused, the senses leave their home or father's house like the prodigal son, and wander away into this place or state; here he is accused of being a stranger and is cast into the belief. The belief is a prison, the idea is the laws, and if he chances to hear of diphtheria, he believes it is as much a place as Boston; so if he chances to go near the place and happens to feel a soreness in the throat, he is accused, and if he acknowledges that he has it, his acknowledgment becomes a belief, this places him in the prison and the sentence being passed, punishment commences. The prison or belief em-braces all persons who have transgressed the laws of diphtheria. So every opinion is a. prison or place, to hold the per-son that believes it, and man's senses may have as many in-dictments against him as he has opinions. So Science or Christ enters the cities or towns, and pleads the case of the senses that are impriseoned, and if he gets the case, the prisoner is set at liberty, or the senses detached from the idea, and the error in the mind explained. Then the prisoner or senses rises from the place of torment into the kingdom of health. Its boundaries are opinions, its subjects are superstitions, and its laws are for the destruction of science. To destroy this kingdom is to introduce Science, is that the warfare is endless, for neither party will yield, no compromise is en-tered into by Science, but as the kingdom is divided against itself it cannot stand. Now as these two parties are in one man, it may be necessary to define their tactics and show how the senses may keep clear of both. One party assumes an idea and uses all their cunning to make it admitted by the senses, so when that is established, then commences the argument. The opposite side being more ignorant, but more honest, admits the idea but tries to destroy it. Here is an illus-tration; the children of the kingdom assert that sin is of divine origin, so the opposite acknowledge it and then try to reason it out of existence. They say that Adam's sin was the cause of all sin. Admitting it, then they try to show how inconsistent it is. They say sin is death; when admitted it becomes a law, so they go on assuming anything, and the other side admit, then argue about it, so that the kingdom of Science is not known in all their reason. Science has battled down the walls of error and established liberty or truth in much of their kingdom. It has hewn down the trees of superstition and established the science of mathematics. It has struck at the Science of Health, this is an unbroken wilderness never entered by man. Ever since the days of Moses there have been adventurers, but none has as yet planted the standard of life with such an inscription, "the Science of Life is in the wilderness." Jesus tried to do it but was crucified, Paul and all of his disciples also tried, but no one has ever yet been able to penetrate this dark wilderness and raise the standard and sustain it. . . .

As I explained but one side of the question I will now give the other which is life. I showed that death is opposed to life. I did not use that term, but you will see that is what I mean. Now death is life to the natural man as much as error is. Truth and error have their kingdom, and our senses are in one or the other according to our acts. I gave an explanation of the natural man or error which is matter and showed that all our misery is in our ignorance of the other kingdom called life or Science. This Kingdom is that spoken of in the Scriptures, which was hewn out and came down to earth or the natural man, and became embedded in the hearts of the people. This was the stone or Science that the builders of error rejected which has been the head or foundation of the new Science of Life, and on whomsoever it shall fall, it will grind him to powder. This child was the one without father or mother. It had no beginning of days nor ending of years, but it is from everlasting to everlasting. It was the rock that followed Moses in the wilderness of superstition. It is progress, it knows no evil. It is a consuming fire, that will rage till it burns up every selfish idea. It is never found boasting of its wisdom; it is not puffed up, it sits and sees itself swell in the hearts of the people, but they see it not. Their minds are now seeing the light that is going before them; they are afraid, so that even the kingdom of darkness is in rebellion against itself. The leaders begin to tremble, for they see that the angel of Science has sounded his trumpet, the earth or matter is moved out of its place, the stars or parties are falling, and the powers of the kingdom are shaken.

The spears of superstition have been beaten into plough-shares, Science has ploughed up all the stubble and burnt up the rubbish, the fields of life are bringing forth flowers of happiness, the streams of blood have turned into living waters. The birds of wisdom are sounding their notes of peace, and all the people rejoice. The old beliefs are passed away, and a new belief or heaven is established in the hearts of men where all beliefs shall be tested by Science and the wicked or error shall be destroyed. Wisdom aims at opinions, its march is progress. It knows no fear, its qualities are love. It neither turns to the right nor to the left. It is death to error, when error undertakes to retard its progress, it seeks not its own kingdom or happiness but works on earth or in man for his happiness. Its aim is to establish wisdom in man, and as it is a Science, its identity is eternal life or progress. For this cause it leaves father and mother or error and ignorance, goes into the kingdom of darkness, and seeks out the sick ideas which are prisons, wherein are the children of Science who have been deceived by blind guides. It enters the prison or belief, unknown to the keeper; for wisdom can not be seen by error, and error or matter is no obstacle to wisdom. It pleads in the prison with the captive, reasons and teaches the Science of Happiness, and protects the prisoner from its enemies in the wilderness of darkness.

THOUGHTS

If these principles are true, there is no good in dying, for that does not change us at all. We are just what we were before. If we have any ideas which make us unhappy we still have them. Our influences are changed, it is true, for our friends believe us to be dead and away from all communication with them. So we stand a chance to be changed. But that we get rid of all sickness and sorrow when we shuffle off this mortal coil is a mistaken idea.

If mind is spiritual matter, and all effects in the natural world have their cause in the spiritual world, it is evident that heat and cold, food, in short all those things which are addressed to the outward senses, as we call them, must first gain access to us through other means than are apparent.

The first mistake is in locating the senses in the body, when they really exist entirely independent of it. But "according as a man thinketh, so is he," and if we believe that taste is in the tongue, hearing in the ear, sight in the eye, and feeling in the nerves of the surface, etc., we must be affected according to our belief.

Our spiritual senses are often more acute and sensitive than the natural ones.

Is experience wisdom? Certainly not. Experience is the construction which we put upon any event which occurs in our life. For instance, the death of a friend : one person may draw one experience from it, and another, another. When Science proves that there is no such thing as death, all the various experiences which are the result of belief in the idea are annihilated.

Jesus, when he appeared after the crucifixion, had con-densed His spiritual self so that it could be seen by the natural eyes, and He did it scientificallv.

I use words merely for convenience which I say are wrong. For example, "death." The time will come when such words will be obsolete. They will not be used when there is knowledge.

If we become acquainted with each other spiritually, where is the need of the natural senses, and how can we ever be separated ?

Our next world is here where we are and always must be. This teaches us to do to others as we would have others do to us, because we are all a part of each other. When we injure one part the whole feels it.

Destroy the man of opinions and Christ lives in the flesh.

Man is just as large as he is wise in Science.

Man is a complete image of the God he ought to worship.

This which I put in practice I call Christ acting through the man Quimby.

As Science is of light, it makes no shadow, but like the rising sun burns up the darkness or error.

God, not being matter, has no matter only as an idea. So matter to God or Science is a medium of communication with the natural man in his own language or semblance.

Every man is a part of God just so far as he is Wisdom. To cure an error intelligently is to know how to produce it. The idea that matter and mind make the man prevents man from understanding himself.

Jesus had no religious opinions; His works were in His life, and His life was His Christ or theory. His natural man had become subject to His scientific man or Wisdom.

Death is the name of something error wants to destroy, and this something is life. So the warfare is between life and death. Life cannot be destroyed but death can. Man is the battlefield of these two, life and death.

There never was a man who could translate the original language of God, for He never spoke at all. So we must listen to the sound of God's voice, not in the language of any person, for God speaks in that still small voice of sympathy which says to the poor sick, "Be of good cheer, your sins or errors will be explained, and. your soul set at liberty."

If God spoke [to Moses] it must have been in the common language of the day. So man must have invented language before God could communicate with him. This God keeps up with the times, and every now and then man finds out that God was mistaken about certain passages in the Bible.

The beast has five senses, and a great many human beings have not half so many.

We are affected according to the fear we associate with our senses.

Death and disease are matter, and when the senses are attached to the body we become subject to the laws of matter.

Here is the theory of my religion: My God is wisdom, and all wisdom is of God; where there is no wisdom there is no God. God is not matter, and matter is only an idea that fills no space in Wisdom, and as Wisdom fills all space, all ideas are in Wisdom. To make creation larger than the Creator is absurd to me. The Christian God is in everything; my God is in nothing, but everything is in Him. Attach all sight, smell, and all the senses to Wisdom, then they fill all space; everything to which we attach wisdom, and all inanimate substances are in this Wisdom.

There is no such thing as reality with God except Himself. He is all Wisdom and nothing else. All other things having form are things of His creation. His life is attached to all that we call life.

God is the embodiment of light or clairvoyance, and to His light all is a mere nothing. When He spoke man into existence His wisdom breathed into the shadow and it received life. So the shadowed life is in God, for in this light it moves and has its being, and it becomes the son of God.

As Jesus became clairvoyant He became the son of God, and a part of God. He said, Although you destroy this temple (or thought) I, that is, this clairvoyant self, can speak into existence another like the one you believe you have destroyed. Jesus attached His senses as a man to this light or Wisdom, and the rest of the world attached theirs to the thought of darkness or the natural man.

Every man is a representative of the natural and spiritual worlds as taught in the religion of Jesus and illustrated in His life and death. The natural world spoken of by Jesus is man's belief, and the knowledge of the truth is the spiritual world; and as opinions and error die truth and science rise from the dead.

Like other men, Jesus bore the image of opinions, but He also bore the image of God or Science.

When Jesus cured the sick He saved them from the other world into which the priests were forcing them.

Christ is that unseen principle in man of which man is conscious, but which he has never considered as intelligence. It is God in us, and when man comes to recognize it as intelligence transcending belief and learns its principles, then death will be swallowed up in Wisdom.

A river has its bed into which little streams flow to supply it. So man has an intellect which is sustained by various streams from the fountain of Wisdom. The banks take the name of the river as a man's name is affixed to his bodily form, but both man and river existed before they were named. . . . Man's wisdom exists and when it is discovered it is named, and the name is of man. The water of the river is like the mind, both are continually changing . . . and the mind seeks the heights of Wisdom that it may draw others to it. Suppose every particle of water to have an identity of intelligence; its continual motion does not destroy its iden-tity; it is water alike in the stream, the lake, the river and the sea; and when it is taken into the earth and replenished it is water still. So man's intellect has its identity whether in one condition or another, and the body is to the intellect what the banks of the river are to the water: an identity to signify that water can be condensed into a form.

Wisdom outside of matter is not recognized, but when it is reduced so that its effects can be seen it is acknowledged, though not separated from matter. The banks are generally admitted to be the river, and when there is no water in the bed we say it is dead. Now the water is as much alive as ever, and it retains its identity, but man's name is de-stroyed. In the same way God in man is not recognized except in the body, and when man sees the wisdom depart, to him the man is dead.

Intellect, like water, is always flowing and cutting new channels, and each new channel is like the birth of a child it receives a name but retains that of its father.

Man in his wisdom gives life to his own name, and when his idea is destroyed the life seems to be dead. Man puts wisdom in the water and not in the principle, so when matter is destroyed the principle appears to be dead. But man's wisdom is not of God. God's wisdom is not in matter but outside of it and through it, as the identity of water is distinct from a particular valley. It may be said that this is what all men believe, but actions show that our wisdom is placed in the natural man or matter. Man has no idea of wisdom identified with anything but his own belief. But if God or Wisdom is the First Cause everything that is seen is only a representation of Wisdom developed into form. Therefore all identities of man and beast exist with the Father. . . . When a form is seen the world says it is in existence, but it existed before Wisdom brought it to man to name. Thus everything exists with God and man names it. But Wisdom has already given it a name which man does not recognize, and by that name it will always exist and recognize itself.

My body sits and writes, and all that can be seen is myself and it is my opinion. But the Wisdom that knows what I say as a man is not an opinion. . . . There cannot be an identity without intelligence, therefore man's identity is not in what we see, but in the Wisdom which cannot be seen, and only shows itself through some medium of expression. . . . Look beyond the body for the created being which is prior to intelligence.

We speak of an intelligent, scientific or patriotic man as if all intelligence, science or patriotism died with him. What are all these when he dies? Do they emanate from his material organism, and die with it? In short, are wisdom and progress the developments of matter?

Man lives and acts in an element different from matter, the universal nature of man can be traced to a different principle than that which would have him, a transitory being. What element is that which is not matter yet in which man lives and acts? It is impossible to describe it in one word or in a few words, but it may be illustrated by facts that are known by all. A child knows its mother, not by looks or voice, but by something not included within these two senses: it is that something that makes her different in her relation to the child from any other woman. Suppose it be called love, or a desire for the child's happiness identified with her own. According as she directs the child in the pure intelligence of that love or yields her feelings to knowledge derived from a source which does not contain that love, so shall the fruits be. This love contains an intelligence which if followed in spirit and truth might destroy every obstacle in the way of the child's happiness, and develop it into a self-governing responsible being. Then why is it not so? Because from our religious and social education no woman can carry out the high principle of her affection. She is taught by established morality to put restrictions on the child that would make her miserable in the child's place.

All feelings and thoughts have an origin and can be referred to their causes as certainly as actions can be proved the result of a certain state of mind. The spiritual man has a knowledge of these causes and knows what every sensation is good for, where it springs from, what its effect would be if not corrected before it condenses into a belief.

It seems strange to the well why I do not cure every one who comes to me as easily as I do some. The reasons are plain to me and I can explain them to the sick, but to the well it is a mystery from the fact that they are under an influence that is adverse to the sick. The well have no sympathy with the sick, and every dollar they pay comes as hard as though they had contributed to some charitable object which they took no interest in but from fear of being called mean they would subscribe a small sum. When a sick person is brought to me the real person is not known in the controversy, but the error or person that brings him. So I have to address myself to that character called by the world our natural man, but the victim is not known and has nothing to say. Every case is a variation of these feelings, and I know the difficulty I have to contend with, while the well do not understand.

I divide man into two characters. One governs by selfish-ness and the other by sympathy, and man's senses are attached to one or the other of these elements. . . . Every combination that leads to disease is like the little streams that run into the ocean of death. As all men live and move in their belief, their belief is like a house or barque either in the ocean of death or the rivers that enter into it. Men find it hard to stem the current when the tide of public opinion is running so fast that they are in danger of being driven on the rocks. The pilots who are waiting to, get a call are found to be under the pay of the master of the seas, the devil. So the streams and rivers are filled up with false lights to deceive the mariners while sailing on a voyage of discovery. This may seem strange to the well, but I can make it plain to the sick. Fashion and pride cover a multitude of sins. I do not like to blame the well, but we are so constituted as to look upon disease as an evil and the sick as afflicted that we cannot help being affected by these opinions. . . . The Chris-tian has no sympathy with his neighbor's children if they do not walk up to the mark, while his own children are provided with a seat in heaven because he is a pious man...

People do not stand in relation to each other as they should, owing in a great measure to our religion.

Money, it is said, is the root of all evil, but this is not the case: pride and selfishness and love of power are the evils; this creates the desire for money.

Spiritual wisdom is always shadowed forth by some earthly or literal figure. Thus the Bible is spiritual truth illustrated by literal things, but religious people follow the shadow or literal explanation and know nothing of the true meaning. When God said "Let us create man in our own image," it means Wisdom created man in the image of Truth. When He formed man or matter, that was the medium for this image to have and control, like all other living things that He made out of matter.

What is there that all will admit as existing independently of matter? Take the senses of man and see if there is any matter in them. All will admit that God is not matter. No one will say that sight is matter, for God sees all things, His sight penetrates the darkest places, and not a thing can be hidden from His sight. So it is with all the [spiritual] senses of man, and there is no matter in them. A knowledge of these senses condensed into an idea, spoken into existence called man and the senses attached to it- this is man in the image of his Maker.

Sympathy annihilates space. Discord makes it. Man is in one and Christ in the other. To be with Christ is to be in harmony with his wisdom, and this Wisdom will keep us from the evils of man's opinion. When our senses are attached to Truth we are heirs of Christ, and when attached to error we are heirs of this world. The Christ is to separate the error from the truth, for truth is harmony and error discord.

Man reasons in this was about the body: a child commences to grow, and man calls the growth of the child "life." When the child has reached a certain maturity the body begins to decompose and die, like the tree; then the dust returns to the dust and the life of the body departs. No such ideas as these come from Wisdom, for Wisdom puts life in the spiritual senses: if we attach these to Wisdom, our life is in Wisdom, and as that never dies our life never dies.

Happiness is contentment, not life or death. Misery is discord, not Wisdom but error. If then you attach your life to an error, like distributing life to the body, then your life is unhappy according to the loss or disturbance.

If our happiness is from Wisdom it becomes a part of ourselves, but if it is from a belief it is adopted and we may lose it. We often hear people say that their religion makes them happy. But if religion is anything outside of ourselves it contains neither happiness nor misery. Can any person define what he gets except that it is a belief? A belief that will make one person happy will make another miserable.

Look at any religious society and you will find that the individuals cannot agree in belief. So those who cannot agree are slaves to those whose authority they admit as their rulers.

The poor soldier who fights for the leaders sinks under the burden bound upon him. To keep up his courage the officers hold out the idea that he is fighting for a great and good cause, and a crown of glory in heaven awaits those who die upon the battlefield. This is all the happiness the privates get. So they fight to keep society from ruin while their reward is the satisfaction of fighting the devil and supporting the officers.

Reverse the tables, making the priest the soldier, and tax him to pay the former soldier for his instructions, then it would be shown how well their principle of action, which they preach to others, applies to themselves.

The minds of individuals mingle like atmospheres, and every person's identity exists in this atmosphere. The odor ascends and contains all the passions and feelings of the natural man.

Jesus contended that He understood what He said and did, but that the prejudices of the people were so strongly in favor of His having a "power" that they could not understand when He tried to teach them that His acts and words proceeded from a Wisdom superior to their belief, and that it could be taught. To question their belief was to make Himself equal with God. In the same way when I say that I know how I cure, people say I blaspheme and make myself equal with Christ. They do not know how I cure and dislike to admit that any one else does. Consequently they strive to make my explanation as objectionable as possible.

According to my experience, mind in solution is a thing in common, which all admit contains life. Each person has his senses in this life or mind, as a globule of water in the ocean. So if a sensation is made on the water each particle is affected, and each person may locate the trouble in himself. For instance, when the idea "consumption" is called up man's senses see the image in this mind. Fear comes and the reflection is thrown on the idea-body... . When sitting by a patient I feel the sensation in my mind, and immediately a figure or spirit is made which is reflected as an impression on my body. Now, if I were not aware of the cause I might think I was the author or originator of this horrid belief. But knowing that it is only the reflection from my patient's mind, the idea dies. The wisdom that puts me in possession of this truth is Christ, the Wisdom above my patient. By this wisdom I explain the fears away and destroy the torments, and this process is a science. Is it a sin to know this and teach it for the happiness of mankind, and do I make myself equal with Christ? If I do then I will submit to the odium willingly.

Ideas are as separate as seeds. An apple seed will not produce a pear, neither will the seed or idea of consumption produce liver complaint.

To know that you exist is a truth, but to prove that you always will exist is a science.

The matter which is seen is the condensation of the matter not seen, and the unseen matter is mind, and in that are all our beliefs, opinions, emotions, etc. When the mind is disturbed by some opinion, or unknown fear, it must take a form before it can affect the body. So when the mind is disturbed the disturbance is shown in the body.

The Christ or Truth can walk on the water of opinions and know that it is no part of itself.

I fitted out my barque some twenty years ago and started without chart or compass, trusting to the wisdom of my experience, determined to be guided by the inhabitants of the land where I journeyed, and make my way to the passage that led to the other world, or to a new world on this globe. . . .

Sometimes I was nearly exhausted and on the point of returning, when a light would spring up, or a solitary bird would sing its beautiful notes from the clear sky, while from this light came a mild breath of pure air that would revive my very soul. In this warmth it seemed as though I heard a voice say, "Come up hither."

The earth is round . . . and man is ambitious to explain the outside and also the inside of it. So exploring parties are fitted out to discover hidden truths. But there is a different class of minds who believe there is another world called the spiritual or scientific world which is as much a world as the natural world and which contains the latter. So the people are all inside the spiritual world together. . . . The scientific contains strata of scientific wisdom whence all science springs.

When this came to light that all I had been doing was to burn up my error by progressing in wisdom, and as the light of science sprang up in my mind I could see men walking on their belief as I was walking on my science, I asked, How can I make the natural man understand this? The answer came, The natural man is not of the world of Science, but the child of Science is in the world of error striving to escape and this is disease.

Then came an illustration of all I saw: Man as we see him is a representation of the earth; his internal structure is the attraction for the natural man to explore, the surface of his body is where he looks to see how he is affected by outward sensations, his wisdom sits in the upper chamber, called his brain, and in the majesty of his knowledge he gives his opinion and all lesser lights bow their heads in subjection to his will. This kingdom being all over the world, it rules its subjects. So when the son of Science encounters it, a decree goes forth to put every one to death.

Science is light and the wisdom of this world is in darkness, hence it does not see the light. Therefore Wisdom governs the natural man, although to him it is unknown. It suggests to the natural man, and he being vain and dishonest assumes to be the author of his own wisdom. . . . Like all demagogues, error pretends to be kind to the poor, especially when its life depends on holding wisdom in slavery.

. . . So the error in the sick brings the patient to me. The Science which is confined in bondage knows the language of Wisdom and secretly tells me its misery, but the natural man or error knows it not. When I tell error how the sick feel, to him it is a mystery; for error is matter and has no feeling, while sympathy is the language of the sick. While I sit by the sick I feel their pain, which is the grief of their wisdom; this is outside of their opinions or body, and my wisdom being outside of my opinions, I, in my wisdom, see their belief, but their errors do not see me, therefore to them I am a mystery.

Suppose a patient sits by my side who has the idea of heart disease. If he believes it, to him it is a reality, his belief contains the substance or identity of a man with heart disease. From this substance goes an atmosphere, and in it is the person. His body is to his mind a sort of mirror which reflects the shadow of the idea: by the doctors this is called disease. I see the original idea and also the shadow, and to cure the disease I destroy the matter by explaining the error, and the shadow on the body disappears.

Language is used in two senses. The natural man uses it to express whatever can be demonstrated. This embraces what is called truth by the learned. But the feelings of the sick and wretched cannot be described by one who cannot feel them, and the sick are at the mercy of those who cannot understand their feelings, and who attempt to relieve them of something they have no sympathy with. Now the Bible is written to convey to such the cause of their trouble, and the New Testament applies more particularly to the sick. The language which Jesus used was not used to describe any-thing that could be seen, or understood by the wisest men of the day. For if what He wished to explain could be seen then language could have described it.

Sympathy is not matter but is what is troubled by matter. A patient has feelings which cannot be felt by another in his natural state, and which cannot be described by the natural man. But the latter without any knowledge of himself names a feeling and undertakes to account for it.

To understand how I cure is to see yourself outside of the natural man or your opinions, with all your senses and reason; then instead of the essence being in matter [you will see that] matter is in the essence. It is often said that God is in everything. This makes God less than the thing He is in. Now make God the essence with all the senses attached to it, then you have an eternal and everlasting Essence without matter or [visible] form, a point without magnitude but eternal. Call this eternal Wisdom the Father of all that is out of matter, see this Wisdom by its will speak the idea matter into existence, and every shape and form that ever was or will be, and everything that man calls life. All these things are in the knowledge of this Wisdom, not the Wisdom in the things that are spoken.

It is the same with man. His wisdom is the living man. To put his wisdom into his body or natural man is to make an opinion greater than a scientific truth. Disease is an opinion. To put man's wisdom into it is to make the disease larger than the real man.

It is a common remark that after we shake off this mortal coil the spirit will be set free. This is to acknowledge that the body is larger than the spirit or wisdom. No wonder with such a belief men pray to be delivered from the body of sin and death.

Thanks to this wisdom I, my wisdom, can see myself out-side this earthly belief and afloat in the ocean of space, where opinions are like stones and pebbles that men throw at each other, while to me they have no weight at all. All these are in me, that is, in my wisdom, and not wisdom in them. I stand in my wisdom to the sick who are in their opinions trying to get me out, and the harder they try the deeper they go into the mire. So Wisdom pleads their case, and if I get their case then opinion is destroyed and health resumes its sway. If you understand this you can cure.

All that is seen by the natural man is mind reduced to a state called matter.

Man's happiness is in knowing that he is no part of what can be seen by the eye of opinion.

This world is the shadow of Wisdom's amusements.

EDITOR'S SUMMARY

It is noticeable that Dr. Quimby holds very steadily to a few great ideas, those that yield a vision of the spiritual life in contrast with worldly matters. Thus we find him contrasting Science with opinion, the spiritual with the natural man, and the spiritual senses with bodily sensibility. He dwells without limit upon the superstitions to which the race has been subjected by priests and the bondages which are traceable to medical opinion. With endless repetition he classifies disease as an "error of mind" or "invention of man," showing how sensations or pains of minor import have been misinterpreted so as to generate such maladies as cancer and consumption. He is always tracing a patient's trouble to the particular beliefs, religious, social, medical, which have been accepted in place of realities. Thus his main interest seems to be to disclose the power of adverse suggestion, fear, error, ill-founded belief. His thought therefore seems to lack scope. He seldom takes his readers into the larger world of social problems. He draws few illustrations from history. Even when describing the inner life he passes by such subjects as poise, composure, serenity, spontaneity, and interior self-control; he does not analyze faith, inward guidance or receptivity.

Yet amidst this apparent narrowness he emphasizes certain characteristics which he believes to be universally verifiable, and it is for the reader to see their scope. Having learned, for example, the power of words or names, when associated with painful sensations and supported by medical authority, he passes to a study of the nature and origin of language; and in lengthy articles which we have not had space for he contrasts truth and error so as to show the difference between language as a human invention and that tongue which the spirit speaks, "the language of sympathy" understood by those who know the meaning of the "still, small voice." Having seen that the sick are slaves to those who pretend to heal them, he turns to African slavery and discourses at length on the Civil War, then in full progress, taking Lincoln and Jefferson Davis as types of men prominent in the struggle. So too he writes at length concerning aristocracy and de-mocracy, and discovers in all human society the same typical forces which he finds in the inner life. Again, his knowl-edge of the inner life leads-him to write on government, the standard of law, the origin f political parties, and the nature of patriotism. History is to him an enlargement of the conflict taking place within. Society becomes intelligible when we understand the forces operating upon man.

There are but few references to nature as the subject of study of the special sciences, although chemistry and mechanics sometimes figure by way of illustration. Physical substances are usually referred to from the point of view of the effects which people produce upon themselves through ad-verse suggestion, as in the case of medicines and poisons, or food associated with trouble-making opinion. But this is for the sake of acquainting man with the fact, never adequately recognized till Quimby's time, that because of the dominance of beliefs man is often more influenced by suggestion than by the actual qualities of foods, drugs and poisons. Quimby aims to show that through acceptance of prevalent beliefs man often lives in realms of shadows, subject to his own fancies, literally creating what he believes in. Before we can see things as they are, as God meant them to be, we must learn what it is we think we see. The natural world is beset by appearances. The natural man knows nothing as he ought to know. What we need is a wholly different point of view. Then, in possession of true Science, we should be able to found the special sciences on Divine wisdom. Matter is a term which Quimby uses in so many ways that some of his statements are scarcely intelligible. Matter is what appears before us in the physical world, without intelligence, inanimate; it can be condensed into a solid by mind-action, undergoes changes as the result of mental changes and responses in "the fluids" of the system ; it is the natural man's mind, the stuff which ideas are made of, "an idea used like language to convey some wisdom to another," "the shadow of our wisdom," in which are all our beliefs, opinions, emotions; and so as "spiritual matter" or substance it is "an idea seen or not, just as it is called out," and is compared to a belief or casket. "Matter which is seen is the condensation of the matter not seen, and the unseen matter is mind." "God, not being matter, has matter only as an idea." "God is not matter, and matter is only an idea that fills no space in Wisdom."

What is meant by this apparent confusion is that we should disengage our thought from matter altogether at times, in order to look upon life with the spiritual eye. If by the term "mind" you mean a vague, airy something without influence on the body, then Quimby shows that it is indeed substantial, that thoughts are things which take shape or condense and come forth in bodily manifestation. If by the word "spirit" you mean anything as indefinite as spiritists believe in, he points out that spirit too is substantial, is alive, not "dead." But when you realize what he means by "substance" your thought has travelled far from material things to the thought of God, in whom is no matter at all, who manifests Himself through matter as a mere vehicle or language. "There is no such thing as reality with God except Himself. He is all Wisdom and nothing else." "All will admit that God is not matter, for God sees all things. His sight penetrates the darkest places, and not a thing can be hidden from His sight." You must see the true Sub-stance or "invisible Wisdom that can never be seen by the eye of opinion" before you can look forth upon the panorama of the world, beholding forms taking shape, coming and going at the behest of spiritual powers.

The mind is the medium in which ideas are sown. Ideas, as distinct from one another as different kinds of seeds, grow like seeds, take to themselves character, and become known by their fruits. When the mind is disturbed, the disturbance is shown in the body as a result of sub-conscious processes and "chemical changes." Mind in relation to body is "spiritual matter" because it can be changed, is excited through fears, is always in process even when we sleep, is not intelligence but subject to it, and because it receives thought-seeds as the earth receives plant-seeds.

Sensation contains no intelligence in itself, but is a mere disturbance of the spiritual matter called "agitation," ready to respond to any direction given it by our suggestion. So pain is "in the mind," not in the hip, for example, not in any organ. It contains no intelligence, but might be wisely interpreted. Disease is due to the misconstruing of sensation or pain, it is due to a wrong direction of mind. Hence it is not an evil but an "error." It is not inflicted on us by God God created man to be well, happy, free. The reflection or shadow' on the body is what the doctors call disease. Our senses or life become imprisoned in the false direction of mind, as a result of "false reasoning." Dr. Quimby says that he sees both the reflection on the body, the symptoms diag-nosed, and the original which casts the shadow, that is, the inward disturbance which might have been wisely interpreted. To cure disease is to **(1)** see its mental causes, **(2)** understand the false directions of mind or reasonings, **(3)** see the truth concerning health as a Divine ideal, **(4)** realize the great truth that the spirit is not sick; hence **(5)** to separate the true or "scientific" man from the man of opinion or error. This means undoing the "false reasoning" and learning what would have been the right interpretation of the first sensation or pain.

The senses give us a "knowledge of sensation, with or with-out Science." They have their spiritual counterparts, the true or "real" senses, not in and of matter. These are "light," "life," and are "in light," in contrast with the wis-dom of this world (in darkness). The true senses constitute the real man or, spirit, the child of God. They are larger than the natural man or body. Hence they are not "in" the body. They include our higher consciousness, clairvoyance or intuition, with the inner impressions coming to us independently of the brain. Thus we have discernment of objects at a distance, we behold spiritual events, conditions, states; we detect "odors" or mental atmospheres at a distance. Through these senses we have immediate access to Divine wisdom and love. They include the feminine side of our nature, the receptivity or higher love. In brief, they yield Science or "the Christ within." Through this priceless possession man is able to make Divine wisdom manifest in spiritual healing.

Science or Truth is fundamental knowledge of this our real nature, with its inner states and possibilities. It is light in contrast with the wisdom of the world. It is harmony in contrast with disease or discord. It corrects all errors, holds no doubts, proves all things, explains causes and effects. It is Divine wisdom "reduced to self-evident propositions." It is the basis of all special branches of knowledge- when those other sciences are rightly founded. It is Christ, the wisdom of Jesus. It is in all, accessible to all. We all become parts of it in so far as we discern real truth. In fact, Quimby often says the real man "is" Science. In contrast with it, the body is only a "tenement for man to occupy when he pleases."

Jesus was the man who brought the true light or Christ to light. Christ was His religion, the God in Him. It is the sympathy "which annihilates space." It separates Truth from error, Wisdom from opinion. "Christ is that unseen principle in man of which he is conscious, but which be has never considered as intelligence." It is in reality the basis of all true intelligence. It is Wisdom reduced to practice so that it is made tangible or visible in the concrete things of life. More than that, it is the real man in us all, the spiritual self or ego. To be a disciple of Jesus is not only to realize the Christ within as an individual possession, but to put this wisdom into practice in daily life. The New Testament, rightly understood, is the great book o f life. We might read the Bible, as indeed we might read the human heart, if we began with the Christ, if we had overcome bond-age to the wisdom of the world. To overcome this servitude is to become spiritually free.

God is an eternal and everlasting Essence without matter or visible form. 'This eternal Wisdom spoke the idea "matter" into existence and everything else that man calls life. The original language was not then the invention of man but was God, sympathy, going forth into expression in the human heart and the world. Man invented language to some extent, but because he had lost the original and was not content to live by Divine guidance: he invented language to "explain his own wisdom." But language might be used to undeceive. Even now the language of sympathy is the language of the sick. What we need is intuition to read that language, according to Divine guidance. Quimby is a great believer in the guidance of the moment, the inward light which shows where a patient stands, what the needs are, what wisdom is needed to clear away the errors. He emphasizes guidance as wisdom, rather than "power." He claims no special "power" and maintains that any one can learn to read the original language.

This language discloses man's true identity or inner con-sciousness. Man, to be sure, has as many identities as he has directions of mind. But these are transitory. We "attach our senses" to that which we take to be real for the time being, we are imprisoned in certain directions of mind through our "false constructions" or errors. The great point is to observe the central contrast within the self, between **(1)** the mind of opinions, man's natural mind, subject to suggestion, changeable like plastic substance, amenable to falsities, "the mind of the flesh;" and, **(2)** the mind of the scientific man, accessible to Divine truth, possessing an intelli-gence which does not change, "the Christ within." There is need of the most clear-cut distinction between the two. Divine truth can accomplish great results in us, far more than the mere "power of thought." A fundamental change can be wrought by making this incisive distinction, through intuition or "clairvoyance," by direct openness to Divine wisdom. Then error or darkness will be dispelled.

Again, there is a great contrast between the natural and spiritual worlds. For the moment, in some of Quimby's critiques on religion, the "other world" seems to have dis-appeared, and there is apparently nothing left but a collection of beliefs. But this is because Quimby is chiefly concerned with man's religious belief in a supposed other world as a place of punishment or mere beatitude; because he is convinced that Jesus did not refer to the same sort of "world" which the Jews believed in. Man must first see that his theological heaven or hell is an artifical region created for him by his religious creed, peopled by his own fancies or made vivid by his own fears. The two worlds thus far are in man's mind and nowhere else. Jesus came to destroy both the world of opinion and the "other world" of theology, that He might reveal the Christ within. But once aware that our "other world" is non-existent, we are ready for the profound truth that all phenomena appearing in the natural world are manifestations of the spiritual world, or world of causes. To attain this vision is no small accomplishment, for it means total victory over all conventional ideas of death, with all its terrors, its supposed decisiveness for salvation and everything else which theology has invented.

The Bible, strange as it may seem, "has nothing to do with theology." It is a scientific explanation of cause and effect, showing how man must act and think for his happiness. It is a study of contrasted elements, such as Adam and Eve, Cain and Abel, Moses and Aaron, Saul and Paul, Law and Gospel, tares and wheat. It was never intended as a religious book according to the opinion of the world. As a book it "contains no intelligence of itself," but Intelligence is in it. That is to say, it contains what Swedenborg called "the Word." Had Quimby been acquainted with Swedenborg's "Arcana Coelestia," he would have found a completely worked out science of spiritual correspondences which he would have been inclined to accept at once in principle, although his teachings concerning Jesus are not those of Swedenborg concerning the Lord. His writings contain long articles based on his endeavors to interpret the Scriptures spiritually to his patients. Further than that his exegesis did not go. But he went far enough to set the example followed by Christian Scientists and New-Thought devotees to the present time. He had at least the ideal of a spiritual Science which should be its own evidence, which any one might verify by seeking out the Word.

Religion in the true sense was to Quimby a Science which can be applied for the happiness and health of man here and now. To be religious is to be "more than the natural man." It yields that wisdom which can say to the sick and palsied man, Stretch forth thine hand, and I will apply the Christ or Science and restore it. Naturally enough Quimby is not interested in the question of sin, and he hardly ever uses the word "evil." For him it is all a question of ignorance or error. There is neither ignorance nor error in Science, hence no sin or evil. The problem of evil differs in no way from that of disease. Therefore Quimby says nothing about repentance and regeneration. Man already is good in reality. He is Science. He becomes "a part of God" by accepting Divine wisdom as his guide. Quimby does not mean this in the sense of pantheistic submergence of individuality, but in the sense of intimate relationship with that "invisible Wisdom which never can be seen by the eye of opinion."

If, however, Quimby's spiritual exegesis might have been fulfilled in Swedenborg's science of correspondences, we find nothing in his writings pertaining to the realms of evil spirits and angels, and nothing that tells us what for him was the content of the spiritual world. He is not at all interested in psychical experiences except so far as they imply belief in the spiritism of the day, and he opposes this because be finds it fundamentally misleading. He does not raise the question whether there is anything real behind the phenomena, for his interest is to direct attention to the world of Science or "the Christ within." He is clairvoyant in high degree, but not as "mediums" are, not through self-surrender, but through openness to Divine guidance and intuition.

In one of his critiques of spiritualism, for example, Quimby puts to the typical spiritist the direct questions: "When I speak is it I or my spirit? If it is I, do I think also, and if I think when do I cease thinking? If I lose my organs of speech, etc. belonging to the body, where am I? Am I any-thing? If I am a spirit, when was I not one? How came I to be flesh and blood and then a spirit? I am either a spirit all the time or I am not, and if I am one what is the change called death, and what dies?" He goes on to say that if the spirit is not "dead" it cannot. give an account of what is supposed to have happened, and if it does not "die" there is apparently no way to account for communications purporting to come from the "dead."

He protests, therefore, against the whole notion that the spirit is the mere thing a seance would make it out to be. Our real existence or selfhood does not change. True mem-ory persists, for it is eternal, while memory attached to this existence "belongs to the idea, matter." Our real life is composed of light and wisdom, while matter is employed to work out our problems. We are spirits now even while in the flesh. In the spirit we do our real thinking, real living. Hence our real "future life" will have continuity with this life according to the persistence of our most interior identity.

To realize what the spirit is now we should lift our thoughts into spiritual light, bringing together the various items of inner experience to make vivid our conception of the self with all its real or spiritual senses. We do not need to "die" to apprehend these apart from matter, for there never was any matter in them. They are from God or Wisdom. They are what give us visions of objects at a distance, disclosing the inner states of the sick, acquainting us with interior thoughts, revealing "odors" or atmospheres, in short, the whole sphere of the
inner life.

A mesmeriser or spiritist medium has, in Quimby's description, but one identity; while he, Quimby, when clairvoyant has two. To have but one is to yield one's selfhood to a mysterious power or "spirit" without awareness of what is taking place. But if one has learned, as Quimby knew from long experience, that the real identity, self or spirit possesses these inner powers as a completely equipped being of intelligence, made in the Divine image and likeness, endowed with Divine wisdom as guidance, then one also has a secondary consciousness or identity which is aware of what is going on in the natural world and in man's natural mind.

So acute was Quimby's own intuition that in two of his descriptive articles he tells what he saw as if beholding reality itself, when sitting by patients who thought they were dying, and who visualized death by peopling the supposed future world according to their own belief. So vivid was his experience in one instance that he refers to evil spirits almost as if he were afraid of them, though speaking of them as mere creations in the world of opinion. That is, he saw the alleged future life with the eyes of his patient, knew that it was an alleged world simply, and that tho patient's real world was still an unknown quantity to the patient himself. So he was in the habit of entering the thought-world of all his patients, to see how the situation appeared to the patient. He was able to do this with remarkable sympathy. But thereupon he would make the sharpest sort of distinction between this world of seeming reality and the true spiritual world of the Divine wisdom. A spiritist's world may be as full of error as a theologian's future state. Each world sends off its "atmosphere" which the intuitive can discern. We are not free until we make the same discrimination, noting the difference between the world we have been taught to create through error or belief and the world we might know through the inner disclosures of Wisdom.

The spirits most of us believe in are the shadows of our own imagination as surely as the ghosts supposed to haunt graveyards at night. Man should know that he lives in the world of his beliefs. "The whole error on which spiritualism is based is a belief in a world separate and apart from the living." We should learn that "belief separates, Wisdom unites." We should begin by learning„ therefore, what the true basis of union is even here and now while we live with the flesh, when we communicate with the living. For the real world of the living is the same for all, whereas the world of mere belief is purely relative. Not until we have begun to grow in first-hand acquaintance with spiritual truth, not until we enter the world of Science do we know the one true spiritual world which exists for all. We might go on gener-ating phenomena to the end of time, each in his particular world of Protestantism or Catholicism, Mormonism, rein-carnationism and the like, and never arrive anywhere. The only way to arrive is to put a stop to the whole procedure, right about face and ask ourselves what we actually know, what the facts are, what that truth is which can be demonstrated like mathematics.

Dr. Quimby's great conviction is that there is a spiritual Science, superior even to the most exact of the natural sciences, which is the basis of all true knowledge and the source of all true wisdom. He is willing to be misunderstood, charged with putting down religion, making himself equal to Christ, classified as a mere mesmerist or in any other way if only he can make it clear that there is a straight pathway to this Science. So he frequently speaks of himself as a lawyer pleading the case of the sick in "the court of Science." In some of his longest articles he introduces the patient first, questioning her to show how little the patient really knows, then he summons the typical doctor, afterwards a typical minister, till the whole case is perfectly clear so far as the wisdom of the world is concerned. He speaks with entire fearlessness when exposing hypocrisy and sordidness. He proves that the sufferer has been victimized. Then when error has not a vestige of reality to stand upon he bespeaks "the Christ within" as manifesting real justice, true health and freedom.

It is impressively significant that Quimby never judges a case by affirming abstract perfection. The patient would not be free if he did not understand his own case, its causes and illusions. The doctor's verdict or the minister's diagnosis in terms of sin is as real to the victim as a spiritist's world to a believer in spiritism or the political world to a demagogue. We are all victims of some sort of demagogue, and must know this for a fact. Why then should we deny what we must understand in order to overcome our servitude? The patient realizes that he is entering an entirely new world when he finds his great healer so sympathetic that the healer puts himself absolutely in the patient's place, taking upon himself the burdens which doctors and priests have created. This wins the patient's confidence. Then he is astonished to find that the whole burden dissipates when the power of Quimby's Science is brought upon it.

This is the picture Quimby would have us bear away with our study of his writings. God or Wisdom is so very real that external forms are mere semblances put on to objectify His truth. We are not to think of the universe as the home of matter, as that in which God dwells; instead all things are in God as intimately as ideas are in the mind, all things are meant for good, all things are guided by Wisdom. This Wisdom is in us, we live in this Wisdom, and when we identify ourselves with His image and likeness the new birth will begin, we shall begin in very truth to live and think from Him. This Life within us will accomplish the work, as shadows disappear before the morning sun. This Wisdom will create the same true world in us all.

Appendices

List of Articles By Dr. P. P. Quimby

1859.

OCT.: What is Disease? Mind is Spiritual Matter; How Does the Mind Produce Disease? Nov.: Mind is not Intelligence; Is Disease a Belief? Dec.: What is Disease? Love, I; Love, II; My Belief; Truth and Error; Two Sciences; Obstacles in Establishing a New Science; A Communication (William).

1860.

Jan.: Am I a Spiritualist? Clairvoyance; Your Position in Regard to the World; What is My Theory? How Dr. Quimby Cures; Christ and Truth; Difference between My Belief and Others; True and False Christs; What Lives After Death? Your True Position Towards Truth and Error; My Religion. Feb.: Happiness. March: Letter to Mrs. W. of Wayne; To a Patient Recently Helped; Prayer, I; Prayer, II; How I Hold my Patients; Illustration of How I Cure the Sick; Do Persons Really Believe in What They Think They Do? Jesus and Christ? Wrong Use of Words (Weight). April: Harmony, I; Harmony, II; Differences of Opinion About the Dead; Resurrection; Jesus, The Real Object of His Mission; Another World. May: Controversy About the Dead; Life (Senses); Matter and Life; Breathing, I; Breathing, II; Science; Effect or Religious Opinions on Health; Religion and Science. June: Consumption (Breathing); Odors; What is Religion? July: Love; Science; One Character of God; Taking a Disease (Consumption, Breathing). Aug.: My Use of the Word Mind; The Senses; Science in the Bible; The Parables of Jesus; Why are Females more Sickly than Males? What the Parables Taught; Did St. Paul Teach Another World? What is the Relation of God to Man? Matter is Life; Answer to an Article in the New York Ledger; Revelation; Parable. Sept.: Right and Wrong; Letter to a Young Physician; Letter Regarding a Patient. Oct.: God; Letter to a Gentleman; Letter to a Clergyman; Advertisements (Hair Restorative) : Disease (Insanity) ; Language (Murdering the King's English). Nov.: Mrs. C.; Character; The Natural Man, I; The Natural Man, II; Symptoms of a Patient, I; Symptoms of a Patient, II. Dec.: Substance and Shadow (The Senses).

1861

Jan.: The Senses; Doctor and Patient (Dialogue). Feb.: Mind. March: Death, I; Death, II; Spiritualism; Where do I Differ from a Spiritualist and Others? Dr. Quimby as Reformer: How he Cures; How Dr. Quimby Cures; Spiritualism (Death of the Natural Man); Difference from Spiritualists (Continued) ; A Prophecy Concerning the Nation, I.
April: Man and Society; How Disease is Made; Letter to a Patient; Government; A Prophecy Concerning the Nation, II. May: Letter to a Patient; The Standard of Law; What I call my Cures. June: Opposing Doctors and Priests; What is Disease: (Disease, Love, Courage). July: Mind and Matter. Aug.: What is Disease? How Brought About and Cured? The Christian's God; Language (Parable) ; What is God? (Six Parts) ; Is There Another World Beyond This? Origin of Political Parties; Patriotism, I; Patriotism, II; Popular Definition of the Word Mind; Cancer; Proverbs; Vaccination; True Wisdom. Sept.: What is a Clairvoyant Person? Conflicting Elements in Man (To the Sick) ; Identity of God or Wisdom (Ignorance of Man in Regard to the True God) ; Man; Life; Exposition of I Corinthians, VIII, 1-3; To the Old Whigs. Oct.: Life and Death; Belief of Man; To those Seeking the Truth; About a Patient (Exposition of Dr. Quimby's Method) ; Introduction (Dr. Quimby vs. Spiritualism) ; Introduction (How Dr. Quimby Treats Disease). Nov.: Truth Based on Wisdom (Re-ligion Analyzed) ; Strength. Dec.: The First Symptoms of Disease: Sickness an Effect of Belief in Disease; Popular Belief of Curing Disease; Where do I differ from Others in Curing? About a Patient.

1862.

Jan.: Disease Traced to the Early Ages; How does Dr. Quimby Stand Toward his Patients? Where do I Differ from a Spirit-ualist? The Natural Man; Death. Feb.: What is a Belief The Subject of Mind; Disease (Caspar Hauser). Questions and Answers [Chap. XIII]. March: Prayer for the Sick; Two Brothers; Mind: Not Wisdom; My Position as a Man and as a Doctor; Why do I not Cure All Alike? Christian Explanation of the Bible. April: Religion for the Well and for the Sick; Foundations of Religious Beliefs; True and False Science; Clairvoyance (A Detective in Disease) ; Do I Know How I Cure? Sight, Substance and Shadow; Does Imagination Cure Disease? Music; The Two Trinities. May: The Two Worlds; Bad Belief Worse than None; What is Spiritualism? What is a Spirit? June: Proof that a Person can be in Two places at the

Same Time and be Aware of the Fact; Unconscious Effect of Persons on Each Other. July: What is Human Life? Aug.: The Phenomena of Spiritualism; What is Man? Sept.: Spiritual Communication between the Living and the Dead; Are We Governed by our Belief? Curing Children and Fools through the Mind; Conversation with Patients; Communications from the Dead (Physical Demonstrations) ; Outlines of My Theory; The White Man and the Negro Race; Science: Error; Opinions: Wisdom; Spiritualism and Mesmerism (To the Editor) ; Difference on Philosophy of Mind. Oct.: Experience of a Patient with Dr. Quimby; Works: the Fruit of our Belief; Is there any Curative Quality in Medicine? The Religion of Jesus: A Belief or a Truth? The Relation of this Truth to the Sick; Introduction (Words) ; Concerning the Dying; Life: Its Application. Nov.: Happiness and Misery; Mind; Resurrection; My Ignorance of the English Language; Difficulty in Introducing My Ideas to the World. Dec.: Language: Its Application; Do Words Contain Wisdom? Man Outside of His Body; The Language of Truth; What has my Writing and Talking to do with Curing? What calls out my Arguments?

1863.

Jan. May: The Body of Jesus and The Body of Christ: The Kingdom of Heaven; My Conversion to Health; The Issue of the Rebellion; The Poor vs. the Rich; Assassination of Lincoln; The Explanation, I; The Explanation, II; Defence Against an Accusation of Putting down Religion; What is Death? Disease and Sickness; Man a Progressive Organization (Elements of Progress) ; My Mode of Treating Disease; Mind; Nothing, Something; Words; The Definition of Words, Introduction, Marriage; Misery; President Lincoln's Death; Aristocracy and Democracy; (Christian Science) ; Lecturers (Their Atmosphere) ; Dialogue on Immortality; New England; Revolutions and Rebellions; Concerning the Use of Medicine; Nations and Individuals; On the Draft; The Scientific Man; Introduction (Mesmerism and Spiritualism) ; Supplement to an Article (Two Patients) ; To the Reader; Disease: An Example; The Honeymoon; Spirits: Substance and Shadow; Illustrations of Immortality, (A View). Sept.: Every Person a Book. Nov.: Defence Against an Accusation of Making Myself Equal with Christ. Dec.: Circulation of the Blood; Illustration of the Above; Method of Treatment for a Child.

1864.

February-June: Ignorance: The Obstacle in Establishing a New Science; The Power of Mind; Imagination, I; Imagination, II; Had Jesus a Belief ? Objects and Shadows; Spiritualism and Mesmerism; Difference between My Belief and that of Others; Copperheads Caught in Their Own Trap; Truth: Error; Senses; Words, Truth: Its Application; Unconscious Effect of Persons on Each Other (The Effect of Mind on Mind) ; The Power of Lies; Man's Identities; Truth (How Determined) ; Disease; Its Causes; The Cause of Man's Troubles; Disease: An Example; Language, I; Language, II; Language, III; Curing Without Medicine; The Higher Intelligence; The Effect of Disbelief in Another World; My Experience in Mesmerism; Is Man's Strength in his Legs? July-Sept.: Understanding My Theory is the Cure of Disease: Death: A Scene; Disease: White Swelling; Does Man Separate Body and Soul in Reasoning? Conservatism; Death; How Can a Person Learn to Cure the Sick? Illustrations of What I Claim to have Discovered; Disease and Sickness Its Causes; Mind: Not Wisdom; Misery (We Never See That which We Are Afraid Of) ; Had Jesus a Belief? Nothing Produces Nothing; Man's Senses; Cures Made outside of the Medical Faculty.

1865.

Experiments in Detaching the Soul from the Body; The Immortality of the Soul; Happiness; Concerning Happiness; Why do I Talk about Religion? Ignorance and Wisdom; How the Senses are Deceived (The Senses Compared to a Virgin) ; Why I am Misrepresented; My System of Reasoning; Preaching; The Reception of this Great Truth; What I Impart to My Patients; False Reports Concerning My Religious Belief; Spiritualism; The Two Principles Acting in Man; Introduction (The Science of Happiness) ; Right and Wrong; The Evidence of Sight (Dr. Quimby's last article, July 15, 1865).

The Quimby-Eddy Controversy

AFTER Dr. Quimby's death, Mrs. Eddy continued to teach the new ideas and methods, as one of his followers until the period of her more public work. She lived in Stoughton, Mass., 1868-70, where she left a manuscript known as "Extracts from P. P. Quimby's Writings," on which she based her teachings. (A part of the Ms., with a facsimile showing emendations in Mrs. Eddy's hand, was published in the New York Times, July 10, 1904, with a "deadly parallel" showing Quimby's teachings and those of Mrs. Eddy in "Science and Health") In 1872, while teaching in Lynn, Mass., Mrs. Eddy claimed this Ms. as her own, and in this and other writings she gradually changed the terminology so that it bore less resemblance to Quimby's. After publishing "Science and Health," in 1875, she put forward progressive claims as discoverer and founder. In her "Metaphysical College," in Boston, Mrs. Eddy began in 1882 to have trouble with her students, who criticized her teaching and disputed her claims.

One of these students, Mr. E. J. Arens, learned from Mr. J. A. Dresser, October, 1882, that the methods and ideas claimed as hers by right of "revelation" were derived from Dr. Quimby. Arens gave full credit to Quimby and claimed the right to publish the new ideas without giving credit to Christian Science, but was sued by Mrs. Eddy for plagiarism. The suit was won, Sept. 24, 1883, by Mrs. Eddy, because Arens could not persuade George Quimby to let him take the Quimby Mss. into court. Meanwhile, the controversy in the press was begun, Feb., 1883, by "A. 0.," in a letter to the editor of the Boston Post, entitled "The Founder of the Mental Method of Treating Disease," in which the facts, acquired from Mr. Dresser, were accurately stated.

1883. Feb. 19. "E. G.," ostensibly a sometime patient of Dr. Quimby's but in reality a publicist for Mrs. Eddy, writes a letter to the Post, representing Quimby as a mere "mesmerist" and trickster.

1883. Feb. 23. Mr. Dresser refutes these statements and puts Quimby's work in its true light.

1883.   March 7. Mrs. Eddy writes to the Post over her own signature, trying to meet Mr. Dresser's reply by introducing irrelevant subjects.

1884.   The scene of the controversy is changed to Hartford, Conn; in the Hartford Times Mr. Dresser recounts the true history of Quimby's discovery and practice.

1885.   Mrs. Eddy collects her "facts" in "Historical Sketch of Metaphysical Healing," Boston, pub. by the author; tries to show that Quimby was a mere mesmerist: alleges that she left Mss. with him in 1862.

1887.   By request, Mr. Dresser gives lecture in Boston entitled "The True History of Mental Science," quotes from a Ms. by Quimby, explains the ideas and methods to show that they involve neither mesmerism nor manipulation, reads Mrs. Eddy's articles, verses and letter showing her loyalty to Quimby during his life-time. This lecture, published in pamphlet form by the author, Boston, 1887, becomes basis of true history everywhere; revised, with additions, by H. W. Dresser, Boston, 1899.

1887.   June. Having no answer to the "True History," Mrs. Eddy makes a general denial and adds further fuel to the controversial fires in "Mind-Healing History," in the Christian Science Journal.

1888.   March. George Quimby writes about his father's life and work, in New England Magazine, showing how Dr. Quimby changed from mesmerism and discovered mental healing.

1888.   Mr. A. J. Swarts visits Boston, Portland and Belfast, learns the facts at first hand from Mr. Dresser and Mr. George Quimby, and publishes his findings in various issues of the Mental Science Magazine, Chicago.

1895. In "The Philosophy of P. P. Quimby," Boston, Geo. H. Ellis, Mrs. Annetta G. Dresser, Dr. Quimby's patient 1862, newspaper excerpts concerning Quimby's work and brief quotations from the Mss. are published.

1899. Mr. Septimus J. Hanna, publicist, summarizes Mrs. Eddy's side of the case in "Christian Science History," Boston, Christian Science Pub. Co.

1899. May. H. W. Dresser publishes in The Arena, the facts about Mrs. Eddy's indebtedness to Dr. Quimby, also portions of Mrs. Eddy's letters; Mrs. Woodbury, former student under Mrs. Eddy, puts the latter's statements in Portland papers, 1862, in deadly parallel with those in Mrs. Eddy's article in the Christian Science Journal, June, 1887.

1902. Another publicist, Alfred Farlow, issues "Christian Science: Historical Facts," in which the usual claims are made without any examination of the true history.

1907. Miss Georgine Milmine, after painstaking research, publishes in McClure's Magazine accurate life of Mrs. Eddy, which appears in book form as "The Life of Mary Baker G. Eddy," New York, Doubleday Page and Co., 1909. Miss Milmine carefully traces history of Quimby's Ms., "Questions and Answers," showing how it has been modified by Mrs. Eddy in her "Science of Man," and "Science and Health."

1907. Miss Sybil Wilbur, writer, undertakes to prepare an off-setting "Life" without inquiring into the truth of the "facts" put at her disposal. The result is seen in Human Life, Boston, April, 1907, which contains a sensational report of an interview with George Quimby, trying to discredit him and doubting the authenticity of the Quimby Mss. These statements somewhat modified in "Life of Mary Baker Eddy," New York, The Concord Pub. Co., 1908.

1907. The controversy is taken up by various clergymen, including Lyman P. Powell, "Christian Science, the Faith and its Founder," New York, Putman's Sons, 1907, and James H. Snowden, "The Truth about Christian Science," Philadelphia, The Westminister Press, 1920, in which the facts are impartially stated.

1921. The publication of "The Quimby Manuscripts" and a review in the Springfield Republican called forth a letter from Clifford P. Smith, which appeared in the Springfield Republican of September, 29, 1921.

After the publication of portions of the Quimby Ms., with facsimiles and the deadly parallel, in the New York Times, July 10, 1904, conclusively establishing the original source, Miss Milmine, who had thoroughly investigated the subject, wrote to George Quimby, Oct. 27, 1905, as follows:

"It is quite true that she (Mrs. Eddy) did use your father's Ms. entitled 'Questions and Answers' to teach from in the beginning. In fact, she used nothing else for many years, and hired a student to make copies of it for the use of each pupil. I have photographs of one of these copies, and have seen several of them belonging to early pupils who have kept them and who showed them to me. With the change of a word here and there, it is exactly your father's Ms. This manuscript of your father's was used largely to form a chapter called 'Recapitulation' in 'Science and Health' in later years; but with each new edition it was revised until the present chapter of that title is a long way off from the original. Nevertheless this is the only chapter in her book from which her students are taught in classes, today. The course in C. S. consists of a series of talks on this one chapter, which is elucidated and explained to the class. So everybody who is learning C. S. healing today is learning the essential truth almost directly from your father's old manuscript, as in the beginning. The rest of C. S. and all the objectionable part is simply 'frills' added by Mrs. Eddy. Of course she has used your father's ideas and many of his phrases all through the book.... The Ms. you sent [printed above, Chap. XIII.] is almost word for word, as you have seen, like the one she used to teach from."

Even Miss Wilbur, in her "interview" with Mrs. Crosby, of Waterville, as reported in Human Life, March, 1907, puts in as fact that "Mrs. Patterson spent most of her time reducing to writing the remembered sayings of Quimby," while living with Mrs. Crosby.

Turning once more to one who knew the whole history of the production of the Quimby Mss. from within. In a letter dated Belfast, Me., Nov. 11th, 1901, to one of his many inquiring correspondents, George Quimby says: "As far as the book, 'Science and Health,' is concerned, Mrs. Eddy had no access to father's Mss. [Save 'Questions and Answers'] when she wrote it, but that she did have a very full knowledge of his ideas and beliefs is also true. The religion which she teaches certainly is hers, for which I cannot be too thankful; for I should be loath to go down to my grave feeling that my father was in any way connected with 'Christian Science.' That she got her inspiration and idea from father is beyond question. In other words, had there been no Dr. Quimby there would have been no Mrs. Eddy. Father claimed to believe, and taught and practiced his belief, that disease was a mental condition and was an invention of man ... while he held strong views, and acknowledged God as first cause-and no one ever believed in God and Jesus more than he -he differed entirely as to the Bible, and interpreted it in a way entirely orginal with himself. In curing the sick [conventional] religion played no part. There were no prayers, there was no asking assistance from God or any other divinity. He cured by his wisdom.... Don't confuse his method of healing with Mrs. Eddy's Christian Science, so far as her religious teachings go. Disease as a mental condition caused by error or beliefs, and capable of being cured mentally without medicine or appliances or applications-these ideas are embodied in Mrs. Eddy's book- she certainly heard father teach years before she wrote her book. While under his care, off and on for several years, she became deeply interested in his theory of disease and its cure. She heard many of his essays read; wrote many herself which she submitted to him for inspection and correction. But she never left any of hers with him, and never had any of his, to more than look at. (1) She had the opportunity to copy some, and possibly did. After she left his care, she delivered some lectures on his method of healing.... Up to the time of his death, no one could have been more loyal to father than she. She gave him full credit for curing her and teaching her the very ideas she later had revealed to her from Heaven.

"Now a word about that great court decision. One E. J. Arens, of Boston, made a statement which he could not prove, that Mrs. Eddy got her ideas from father, and that his writings and Mss. would prove it. He went into court and could not prove what he said, and now Mrs. Eddy and her adherents claim that because he could not prove that there were such Mss., that there are none! I would not allow him to use the Mss. in court, and consequently he could not prove what he said." (2)

Writing to another man, George Quimby said in part:

"The basis of the whole misunderstanding has been that everything that has emanated from the Eddy side has been taken for God's truth, and everything that has been stated in opposition to her has been pronounced and believed to be lies. By assuming all she has said as true, on the start, it doesn't leave much for the other side.

"To begin with, you must understand that I was with my father during the term he was in Portland, and had had an intimate personal acquaintance extending over two or more years with Mrs. Eddy (then Mrs. Patterson). I am not stating hearsay, but personal knowledge. As I was father's clerk, bookkeeper and sec'y, and as it was the wish of his life that I take his place and carry on his work, I ought to know what he believed and claimed, and how he treated the sick, and what he wanted me to learn. I have a package of Mrs. Eddy's letters to my father, covering a period from 1862 to 1864...

In all her letters she gives him full credit for discovering and reducing mental healing to a science. . . . This Mrs. Patterson knew, and this she learned from him, not as a student receiving a regular course as she taught in her college, but by sitting in his room, talking with him, reading his Mss., copying some of them, writing some herself and reading them to him for his criticism. In that sense she and many others of his patients were his pupils, in the same way that the disciples were pupils of Jesus. I have heard him talk hours and hours, week in and week out, when she was present, listening and asking questions. After these talks he would put on paper in the shape of an essay or conversation what subject his talk had covered. These writings we would then copy into blank books. . . Five or six were written before Mrs. Patterson came to Portland.

"Now, I have had since the article appeared in The Times several letters from Mr. Wentworth, who claims to have the document from which The Times gave extracts. I wrote him and asked him to give me the 'Questions and Answers' of which there purported to be fifteen, and also the beginning of the 'Answers.' He did so. I have in my possession the original of these questions and answers.

"Mrs. Eddy did live in Stoughton. She did board with those people. And it does not seem possible nor probable to me that they would absolutely lie about this matter-I mean as to where they obtained the paper. If they did not get it from Mrs. Eddy, where did it come from?. They never saw father, and father wrote the original article, and I have it before me now, and it is dated Portland, Feb. 1862. .

"If he was a mesmerist or spiritualist, what did he write that for? And why did he say in his Circular to the Sick, which he issued from 1860 to 1865, 'I give no medicine and make no outward applications. I tell the patient his feelings, and my explanation is the cure'? Why did he do this? Because that was his method and no one knew it better than Mrs. Eddy.

"In your statement of Mrs. Eddy's offer to print father's writings, if any such existed, and because her offer was not accepted it proved there were no such writings, you did not give her whole offer which was, 'provided' she first be allowed to examine them and see if they were not some she left with him! Just think of it! my letting her, or any one else, have Mss. I knew were father's because I saw him write them, and copied many of them myself, to see if she didn't write them and leave them with him."

Notes

(1) *That is, Vol. I, loaned her by Mr. Dresser, as already stated.*

(2) *[Mr. Quimby did not loan his father's manuscripts to Mr. Arens because be was not in a position financially to engage in a suit. Moreover, he was naturally and rightly asked why he should take part in a suit to establish what was true? Dr. Quimby had taught that truth could take care of itself, when the time came. His son believed that his father's rights would be established when the time should come to publish the Mss. Finally, Mr. Arens had made unwarranted statements to the effect that Dr. Quimby was not only the originator of mental healing and the terminology of Christian Science, but was actually the author of the book, "Science and Health." To put the matter in the right light it would have been necessary to show, as we have shown in this volume, that there was a large collection of manuscripts, original and revised, containing the whole theory of mental healing and Christian Science; and that what Mrs. Eddy used was the essential terminology, the methods, and the reasonings which establish the principle that "all causation is mental" in the origination and cure of disease.]*

Photographic Reproductions of Manuscripts

I

II

only ~~that~~ ~~intelligence~~ ~~bones~~
~~motion~~ ~~and~~ ~~knowledge~~, ~~it~~ was not "all p.
sure. ~~Error~~ As health is the enjoyment of all our
faculties, any ~~false idea~~ ~~foreign~~ ~~substance~~ ~~lodges~~ the wheels and ~~its~~
~~&~~ retards the motion, So ~~can~~ ~~things~~ the mind of
retards the motion This was the state of this man
body. Now to put ~~this~~ ~~man~~ him in full possession of
his ~~faculties~~ powers is to remove ~~the~~ burden & give a right
direction to his mind ~~being~~ ~~again~~ ~~this~~ ~~burden~~ This burden was the effect of error
having ~~the~~ control over of the mind or matter These
errors are made of mind ~~or~~ ~~matter~~ ~~first~~ formed.
to an opinion. Then comes reason, then ~~comes~~ disease
or death accompanied by all the misery the *idea
contains. —————————— *11* —————————— Oct 1859

8

have   IV
I told you that mind is not intelligence.
Intelligence contains no thought, no opinion nor
reason. Mind contains them all. Disease is
the offspring of the mind, not of intelligence
~~All the~~ ~~storm~~ ~~is~~ the result of a chemical change
to bring about or develope some scientific law
that will put man in possession of a knowledge
of himself, so that he will avoid the evils that
~~man~~ is subject to.

Thoughts are like electric sparks. Knowledg
classifies & arranges them into a language
nearer to itself. so as to use them for a medium
to communicate an idea. This is the
state of all men. Under this state of mind
all the laws of science have been developed.
Every day brings to light some new idea, not
yet developed. but bursting forth to the nat
ural world. During this process the mind
undergoes some very powerful changes, which
affect the body even to the destruction of
the same. But this destruction contains no
wisdom It is only the destruction of the idea

15

Nov. 1859   √ VI

Is disease a belief? I answer it is, for an
is to himself just what he thinks he is. & he is in he
belief sick. If I believe I am sick, I am sick, for
my feelings are my sickness & my sickness is my be
lief & my belief is my mind. therefore all disease is
in the mind or belief. Now as our belief or disease
is made up of ideas which are matter: it is necessa
to know what belief we are in, for, to cure the disease
is to correct the error, & as disease is what follows

the error, destroy the cause & the effect ceases.
' Now the question arises, how can this be done? By
a knowledge of the law of harmony. To illustrate
this law of harmony. I must take some law that
you will admit. I will take the law of mathematics
' You hear of a mathematical problem. you wish
to solve it; the answer is in the problem, the
error is in it, also, the happiness & misery are also in
it. Your error is the cause of your sickness or
trouble. Now to cure your sickness or trouble is to correct the
error. If you knew your real condition the real state of things, you would act
on a person who knows no more than you do; you knew your own case

There are two beliefs. In the one is true
life which is health, knowledge & happiness.
In the other is death which is disease &
' True life is health, knowledge & happiness, all in
his belief. Death is disease, error, misery & pain; all
in this belief. Each of the above is called our knowledge
, to believe in the one, is to disbelieve in the other, for our
life is in our belief. Death is the destruction of the
one & the life of the other, or the disbelief of the one,
& the belief of the other. Christ came to destroy
death or belief & bring "life & immortality to light" &
this life or belief was in Christ. They that lost their

life or belief for his sake (or belief;) should find it.
"Upon this life ^rock or belief I build my faith; & the gates
of (death) cannot ~~change~~ me. Now your life is in your
belief & you are known by the fruits ^thereof. My life is in my
belief — Now as I impart my belief to you, it is your
life or health & as you recieve my life or belief, you
die to your own & my life in you grows to a belief &
this belief is your health or happiness.

Nov. 1859

Original manuscript — Written by
P. P. Quimby himself.
The spelling is also original.
Geo. A. Q.

Belfast May th 22 856

Mr Andrew   Dear Sir

Sir in answer to your Derpatch would
say it will be Out of my power to Can to your place till som
time Next week if that will answer pleas say so by return of
mail on as soon as may be

Yours &c P. P. Quimby

Belfast Nov 4 56

Madame yours of the second inst was received
and I now sit down to answer your enquirery in regard to your
Lameneap, It seames to me that the shin on the Lemd is

A New theory on the Cure of Diseases

A Gentleman of Belfast by the Name of P. P. Quimby has who has been
for the Last sixteen years been ingaged in the investagation
of the seance of Mesmerism so far as it relates to the Cure of dies
to say if it Could be reduced to a seance and after Carfful
investagation has Can to this result that the Cure of Diseases
as much a seance as ~~Correcting~~ Correcting the Error of any other seance
his Ground is that all the Knowledge of dieeas is in the Mind
he Calls ~~know~~ Our feling, the dieeas; the Mind Changes the
flewids therfor to Corret the Mind you Corret the flewids
he believes Mind is ~~matter~~ Sperital matter and by Changing the

Combination of this matter it is shone in the from of dieeas
he shoes the difference between his theory and all Others he
he places all other theorys on the one platform diffiring only in
the Mediums he sais all theorys admit of dieeas indipendant of the
Mind they also admit dieeas as a thing which Can be acted upon
by sin eday or malane he places all the indily knonledg from a
spirit world in the same Category Each and all of the aprair
theorys have ther peulier mediums threw which they act
upon the mind of ther patient Each and all acting upon the

send for Quemby to sit down and tell her how he feels
and at the same time tolling her the trubble is on her mind
this must oxjurn proof for it stroker at the root of all
the Others theary he then shoes that a profer understanding
of themselve will Change the Mind and bring a bout the
very thing desiard he beleave that Every word or idea spoken
Cantains somthing and this somthing Chainges the mind
of the pasient he seas the spireial form of the pasient
whomes he Convurses with and ums it back to it self
this he refeals till the pasient is restord to helth his Idea
of dieeas is Even that Chainges the mind truth restors
the mind and Chainge the fleweds

now you often hear this text Preached from by the Clergy
Acts 16 - 22 & 23 vrs. how Paul stood in the mids of Mars Hill
and did sue men of Athens I perceive in all things you are to
be superstitious." for as I past by & behold your devotion. I found
an altar with this inscription. To the unknown God whom there
fore ye ignorantly worship him declare I unto you," the people
were very religious & Paul new it but when Paul was religious
he was a Very religious Man & persecuted all that disbelieve
in his religious but when he saw the truth or Christ the truth
let up. his wisdom is that he knew all his religious was of man
& so he Condemned it as superstition & & religious worship is the
invention of man there is not one particul of the wisdom of
Christ in it, it is only the superstition of the old Church.

that Jesus afored. Jesus had got rid of his religion before
he undertook to teach the Christ or truth. now here is the
difference one teaches what he believes about som thing he
nows nothing a tout & if they succeed in Convincing others of there
belief, this is religion. now to Convince them they convey
them of all sorts of Errors and please all sorts of ministers on
them & that that then prove of som horrible som thing got
them narves & this is religion & the feeling is the trouls
So religion is to make men more miserable then they were
before this is always the Case it may be that at times that
religion seames to make som ons Better but it is not the
Case Jesus says no som one take this shall we do evil that
good may Com he says no but the truth by truth & every man

List of Photographic Reproductions of Manuscripts

I. Facsimile of Mrs. Eddy's Sonnet to Dr. Quimby.

II-IX. These eight pages contain facsimiles of four pages from one of the copy-books into which the articles constituting "Volume I" were copied after the Misses Ware had consulted Dr. Quimby concerning revisions and changes. The articles from which these facsimiles are taken are printed in full. (See Chapter 14.) The dates show the time when the articles were first written and copied. The changes made in the text in the handwriting of Miss Emma Ware, were made at a later time, probably in 1865, with a view to revising these articles for publication in a volume of Dr. Quimby's writings. Similar emendations for the sake of clearness were made in several volumes of the copy-books prior to Dr. Quimby's death. These changes indicate the kind of revision approved of by Dr. Quimby.

X. Facsimile of George Quimby's note on a wrapper covering a package of original manuscripts by P. P. Quimby, preserved in the Bank in Belfast, Maine. Mr. Quimby calls attention to the fact that not even the spelling has been changed in these writings.

XI. This page contains a facsimile of a letter and the beginning of another, written during the period when Dr. Quimby was developing his ideas and methods of healing in Belfast. This facsimile is included with the others to show Quimby's handwriting, his signature, and the dates.

XII-XIV. These three pages reproduce the original notes of one of the earliest articles, written prior to those included in the list of the Quimby Manuscripts. The date is 1856. Here Dr. Quimby, writing impersonally about his "new theory," states his opinion that it "could be reduced to a science as correcting the error of any other science." He declares that "all knowledge of disease is in the mind," that is, in the "feeling," not in the body. Using the general term "fluids" to cover not only the bodily fluids but the nervous activities, he speaks of the mind as "spiritual matter" using this term interchangeably as if it stood for mind or the matter which is nearest mind. The disease is due to a "combination of this matter," and the cure is accomplished by establishing a different combination. In the last of these three pages Quimby says that "truth restores the mind and changes the fluids."

These pages are without revisions save by the author himself. No corrections have been made in the spelling. Dr Quimby's statements show that even in this crude early formulation of his theory he already possessed the elements of his "Science."

XV-XVI. Facsimiles of first notes for other articles, characteristic of many of the originals of later writings.

Printed in Poland
by Amazon Fulfillment
Poland Sp. z o.o., Wrocław